CRITICAL PERSPECTIVES

The purpose of the works in this series is to provide the teacher and student with the most important critical and historic commentary on major authors, themes, and national literatures of the non-western world.

In a period when vast realignments of power and long overdue reassessments of the cultures of the third world are occurring, the documents and polemics reflecting and often speeding these changes should be readily available.

Senior Editors of the Series: Donald Herdeck, Georgetown University, Washington, D. C. and Bernth Lindfors, University of Texas, Austin.

Subjects of the first works in the Series:
1. Amos Tutuola (B. Lindfors, ed.)
2. V. S. Naipaul (R. D. Hamner, ed.)
3. Nigerian Literatures (B. Lindfors, ed.)
4. Chinua Achebe (C. L. Innes and B. Lindfors, eds.)
5. Wole Soyinka (J. Gibbs, ed.)
6. Lusophone Literature from Africa (D. Burness, ed.)
7. Aimé Césaire (T. Hale, ed.)
8. Léon Gontran Damas (K. Q. Warner, ed.)
9. Modern Arabic Literature (I. Boullata, ed.)

Future Volumes:
10. Wilson Harris (K. Ramchand)
11. Modern Persian Literature (T. Ricks)
12. Algerian Literature (A. Lippert)
13. (James) Ngugi wa Thiong'o (G. D. Killam)
14. Jean Rhys (H. Tiffin)
15. Saint-John Perse (D. Racine)
16. Goan Literature: Five Centuries, with anthological selection (P. Nazareth)
17. Cuba South: Caribbean Writing (D. Herdeck)
18. West African Writing (J. Peters)
19. Thomas Mofolo
20. Christopher Okigbo
21. Sembène Ousmane
22. Modern Turkish Literature
23. South African Writing by South Africans
24. Derek Walcott
25. Naguib Mahfouz
26. Contemporary Arabic Women Writers
27. Contemporary African Women Writers
28. Contemporary Anglo-Indian Women Writers
29. Twentieth Century Latin-American Women Writers
30. Caribbean Fiction Dealing with the U. S. Presence

CRITICAL PERSPECTIVES
ON
WOLE SOYINKA

EDITED BY
JAMES GIBBS

Three Continents Press, Inc.
Washington, D. C.

AN ORIGINAL BY THREE CONTINENTS PRESS, INC.

First Edition

© 1980 Three Continents Press,

ISBN: 0-914478-49-4

ISBN: 0-914478-50-8 (pbk)

LC No: 79-89931

Cover Design by Tom Gladden

Three Continents Press, Inc.
1346 Connecticut Avenue, N. W.
Washington, D. C. 20036
USA

ACKNOWLEDGMENTS

Bernth Lindfors, "The Early Writings of Wole Soyinka," *Journal of African Studies,* 2, 1 (1975), 64-86.

Abiola Irele, "Tradition and the Yoruba Writer: D. O. Fagunwa, Amos Tutuola and Wole Soyinka," *Odu,* N.S. 11 (1975), 75-100.

Nick Wilkinson, "Demoke's Choice in Soyinka's *A Dance of the Forests,*" *Journal of Commonwealth Literature,* 10, 3 (1976), 22-27.

K. E. Senanu, "Thoughts on Creating the Popular Theatre," *Legon Observer,* 2, 20 (1967), 25-26; 2, 21 (1967), 22,23.

Richard Priebe, "Soyinka's Brother Jero: Prophet, Politician and Trickster," *Pan-African Journal,* 4 (1971), 431-39.

Boyd M. Berry, *"Kongi's Harvest* (A Review)," *Ibadan,* 23 (1966), 53-55.

D. S. Izevbaye, "Language and Meaning in Soyinka's *The Road,*" *African Literature Today,* 8 (1976), 52-65.

Ronald Bryden, "The Asphalt God," *New Statesman,* 24 September 1965, 460.

Penelope Gilliatt, "A Nigerian Original," *The Observer,* 19 September 1965, 25.

Albert Hunt, "Amateurs in Horror," *New Society* (London, the weekly review of the Social Sciences), 9 August 1975, 342-43.

K. E. Senanu, "The Exigencies of Adaptation: The Case of Soyinka's *Bacchae,*" a paper presented at the First Ibadan African Literature Conference, July 1976.

D. S. Izevbaye, "Mediation in Soyinka: The Case of the King's Horseman," a paper presented at the First Ibadan African Literature Conference, July 1976.

Gerald Moore, "Soyinka's New Play," *West Africa,* 10 January 1977, 60-61.

Mario Relich, "Soyinka's 'Beggars' Opera'," *West Africa,* 30 January 1978, 188-89.

Annemarie Heywood, "The Fox's Dance: The Staging of Wole Soyinka's Plays," *African Literature Today,* 8 (1976), 42-51.

Andrew Gurr, "Third-World Drama: Soyinka and Tragedy," *Journal of Commonwealth Literature,* 10, 3 (1976), 45-52.

Ann B. Davis, "Dramatic Theory of Wole Soyinka," *Ba Shiru,* 7, 1 (1976) 1-12.

Roderick Wilson, "Complexity and Confusion in Soyinka's Shorter Poems," *Journal of Commonwealth Literature,* 8 (1973), 69-80.

M. J. Salt, "Mr. Wilson's Interpretation of a Soyinka Poem," *Journal of Commonwealth Literature,* 9, 3 (1975), 76-78.

D. I. Nwoga, "Poetry as Revelation: Wole Soyinka," *Conch,* 6, (1974), 60-79.

C. Tighe, "In Detentio Preventione in Aeternum: Soyinka's *A Shuttle in the Crypt,*" *Journal of Commonwealth Literature,* 10, 3 (1976), 9-22.

Omolara Ogundipe-Leslie, "Comment on *Ogun Abibiman*," *Opon Ifa* (Ibadan), June 1976, Supp. i-iv.

Stanley Macebuh, "Poetics and the Mythic Imagination," *Transition/ Chi'Indaba*, 50/1 (December 1975), 79-84.

Robin Graham, "Wole Soyinka: Romanticism, Obscurity and Dylan Thomas." Previously unpublished. Author retains copyright.

Mark Kinkead-Weekes, *"The Interpreters:* A Form of Criticism." Previously unpublished. Author retains copyright.

Peter Enahoro, *"The Man Died," Africa,* 17 (January 1973), 42-43.

A. R. Crewe, *"The Man Died," Africa,* 20 (April 1973), 64 and 66.

D. S. Izevbaye, "Soyinka's Black Orpheus," *Neo-African Literature and Culture,* ed. Bernth Lindfors and Ulla Schild. Wiesbadan: Heymann, 1976. 147-58.

Table of Contents

Acknowledgments   *v*
Introduction   *3*

Introductory Essays

The Early Writings of Wole Soyinka—Bernth Lindfors   19

Tradition and the Yoruba Writer: D. O. Fagunwa, Amos Tutuola   45
and Wole Soyinka—Abiola Irele

Plays

Demoke's Choice in Soyinka's *A Dance of the Forests*—   69
Nick Wilkinson

Thoughts on Creating the Popular Theatre—K. E. Senanu   74

Soyinka's Brother Jero: Prophet, Politician and Trickster—   79
Richard Priebe

Kongi's Harvest (A Review)—Boyd M. Berry   87

Language and Meaning in Soyinka's *The Road*—D. S. Izevbaye   90

The Asphalt God—Ronald Bryden   104

A Nigerian Original—Penelope Gilliat   106

The Exigencies of Adaptation: The Case of Soyinka's *Bacchae*—   108
K. E. Senanu

Amateurs in Horror—Albert Hunt   113

Mediation in Soyinka: The Case of the King's Horseman—   116
D. S. Izevbaye

Soyinka's New Play—Gerald Moore   126

Soyinka's "Beggars Opera"—Mario Relich   128

The Fox's Dance: The Staging of Soyinka's Plays—   130
Annemarie Heywood

Third-World Drama: Soyinka and Tragedy—Andrew Gurr   139

Dramatic Theory of Wole Soyinka—Ann B. Davis   147

Poetry

Complexity and Confusion in Soyinka's Shorter Poems—   158
Roderick Wilson

Mr. Wilson's Interpretation of a Soyinka Poem—M. J. Salt   170

Poetry as Revelation: Wole Soyinka—D. I. Nwoga   173

In Detentio Preventione in Aeternum: Soyinka's *A Shuttle in the*   186
Crypt—C. Tighe

A Comment on *Ogun Abibiman*—Omolara Ogundipe-Leslie   198

Poetics and the Mythic Imagination—Stanley Macebuh   200
Wole Soyinka: Obscurity, Romanticism and Dylan Thomas—   213
    Robin Graham

Prose

The Interpreters: A Form of Criticism—Mark Kinkead-Weekes   219
The Man Died—Peter Enahoro   239
The Man Died—A. R. Crewe   241
Soyinka's *Black Orpheus*—D. S. Izevbaye   243

Bibliography   *253*
Notes on Contributors   *273*
Photographs

    Wole Soyinka   *17*
    Production Photo of Rush Theatre Cast, Chicago,   *127*
        November 1979, Death and the King's Horseman

INTRODUCTION

Wole Soyinka has spoken for himself in an autobiographical statement which appears in *World Authors 1950 - 1970*, edited by John Wakeman and published by H.W. Wilson Company. I recommend it as a preface to this volume of critical essays, since it provides a clear self-portrait of the writer. The statement also provides a useful preface to this Introduction, a row of pegs on which comments on Soyinka's life and work can be hung.

I shall concentrate on the pegs in the first paragraph of the statement and introduce Soyinka from five points of view: as a Yoruba; as an academic; as a man-of-the-theatre; as a political activist, and as a writer. These five categories do not aspire to cover even cursorily the whole man—since his patron god is Ogun I would expect Soyinka to have seven parts. Nor do I presume to fragment the individual. Soyinka reacted to the tendency to categorize and compartmentalize in an exchange at Washington, Seattle, an exchange which catches the easy humor of the man:

Participant: You seem to wear three caps: the poet, playwright, and novelist. Is there any conflict between the three? And which do you prefer?

Soyinka: Yes, well there were more than three caps. One which you omitted to mention is that first and foremost I wear the cap of a human being. And, therefore, the other three caps are really very minor: you know, rain covers, sun shields, and things like that.[1]

My categories do not seek to eliminate the human being, or control the "fluid operation of the creative mind,"[2] but rather to provide a context in which the man can be seen at work, to describe briefly his "rain covers, sun shields, and things like that." I hope that at the end the reader will feel the current of a life which is not pursuing different courses separated by islands and delta flats, but a strong river, full of eddies and subtle flows. But all one stream, one river, one flow.

Soyinka as a Yoruba:

Oluwole Akinwande Soyinka was, born on July 13th, 1934 in Ijebu Isara. His parents, Ayo and Eniola, came from adjoining kingdoms, Ijebu and Egba,[3] and his father was a school supervisor. One aspect of his mother is glimpsed briefly in a discussion about Amope:

> ... My own mother, for instance, was a terror. Not by nature, but she was a trader, and I know that even she, who was a rather gentle person, when she got fed up and wanted to collect her debts from her customers - it is no joke - suddenly she was transformed.[4]

Soyinka was brought up, educated and worked - until the age of twenty - in what was then called the Western Region of Nigeria and in Lagos. He is a Yoruba and, although he has travelled widely, he has returned to Yorubaland to work. His present post at Ife, a spiritual center of the Yoruba, is conveniently symbolic. It is his actual and spiritual home.

Much of his work is linked to Yoruba culture and Yoruba concepts. Some of the most obvious examples of the use of Yoruba material and the presence of Yoruba influence, and examples which show his *abiding* concern with the Yoruba world-view, include: "Abiku" and "Alagemo," written in England and read in London in 1959; "Egbe's Sworn Enemy," a "folk-tale" and a comment, written in 1960; "Salutations to the Gut," an essay which salutes the Yoruba as a "race of lyrical gastronomes," published in 1962; *Kongi's Harvest,* which includes songs in Yoruba, uses Yoruba ritual and variations on Yoruba verse forms, produced in 1965; *The Interpreters* and "Idanre," which are deeply informed by Yoruba myths, or Soyinka's versions of them, (both works were published in 1965, though *The Interpreters* was probably more or less complete in 1962);[5] "The Fourth Stage - Through the Mysteries of Ogun to the Origin of Yoruba Tragedy," an exercise in cultural analysis, written during 1967;[6] *The Forest of a Thousand Daemons,* a translation of a Yoruba novel by Chief D.O. Fagunwa (although it was published in 1968, Soyinka had been at work on this translation since, at least, 1964, and he must have finished it before he was detained in August 1967);[7] *Death and the King's Horseman,* a play partly based on an historical event, the interruption of a ritual suicide which took place in Oyo in 1946, and written at Cambridge during 1973/1974; *Myth, Literature and the African World,* largely a series of lectures delivered at Cambridge which explores and makes use of a variety of Yoruba concepts, as well as a multitude of "European" ideas.[8]

This list illustrates what no one would challenge, that Soyinka has drawn on his Yoruba background. The question invited by most of these works is: how authentic and how idiosyncratic is his approach? It should be pointed out straightaway that this is a false antithesis; it implies a dogmatic tradition which does not exist. Soyinka treats mythology as the work of individuals which has been adopted by the community, but which nevertheless remains susceptible to manipulation by individuals.[9] In Soyinka's situation it is a case of bending or reinterpreting within an "aesthetic matrix." He admits as much. In talking to a *Flamingo* interviewer about *A Dance of the Forests,* he said:

> ... when I use myth it is necessary for me to bend it to my own requirements. I don't believe in carbon-copies in any art form. You have to select what you want from traditional sources and distort it if necessary.[10]

More recently, and in the midst of a debate, he wrote:

> ... I cannot claim a transparency of communication even from the sculpture, music and poetry of my own people, the Yoruba, but the aesthetic matrix is the fount of my own creative inspiration; it influences my critical responses to other cultures and validates selective eclecticism as the right of every productive being, scientist or artist.[11]

The degree to which "the aesthetic matrix" is recognizably Yoruba must be decided by Yoruba scholars and the debate has been opened. For the outsider, the non-Yoruba, an introduction to the Yoruba world-view and to Yoruba verse forms is valuable, perhaps through the work of E. Bolaji Idowu and S.A. Babalola.[12] Tutuola also prepares us, through his television-handed ghostess and the Complete Gentleman whose beauty prevents bombs from exploding,[13] for a country in which Sango, the God of Lightning, stands outside the headquarters of the electricity supply company, in which Kola fits his interpreter friends into his painting of the Yoruba pantheon and in which Ogun becomes Soyinka's patron god. The reference to "selective eclecticism" explains the echoes and quotations from Gerard Manley Hopkins, Wilfred Owen, Shakespeare, Brecht, James Joyce, J.M. Synge, etc., etc., in "Yoruba" work.[14]

Soyinka as an academic:
   Soyinka went to primary school in Abeokuta and to secondary school in Ibadan. After some months working in Lagos he went to University College Ibadan, an institution affiliated to the University of London. He then did an English Honours degree at Leeds, a well-staffed and exciting British University. He had a privileged education in highly reputed institutions, and he distinguished himself in the course of his studies.
   Soyinka has since held a number of University appointments and, I suppose, has supported himself and his family largely by his work as lecturer.[15] He has, however, been a rather maverick academic, and one might with some justification amend Chekhov and describe the University as his wife and the theatre as his mistress. His *curriculum vitae* must look something like this:

	Primary Schooling in Abeokuta.
	Secondary Schooling at Government College, Ibadan.
1952-54:	University College, Ibadan.
1954-57:	University of Leeds; graduated with an Upper Second in English Honours; began work for an M.A. which he did not complete.
1960-62:	Rockefeller Research Fellow; attached to the English Department at the University of Ibadan; area of interest: African drama.
1962-63:	Lecturer, Department of English, University of Ife.
1965-67:	Senior Lecturer, Department of English, University of Lagos.
1967-	Head of the Department of Theatre Arts, University of Ibadan; note: detained from August 1967 to October 1969.
1973-74:	Overseas Fellow, Churchill College, Cambridge. Visiting Professor, Department of English, University of Sheffield.
1976-?	Visiting Professor, Institute of African Studies, University of Ghana, Legon.
1976-	Professor, University of Ife. He is variously credited with the Professorship of Comparative Literature and the Professorship of Literature and Dramatic Arts.[16]

Soyinka was awarded an Honorary Ph.D. by the University of Leeds in May 1973. He has delivered papers at a variety of literary and academic gatherings, and these, together with reviews and critical essays, are listed in the bibliography. What is not recorded is the influence he has had and the pre-eminence his contributions have been accorded. In 1960 he published an article on "The Future of African Writing" in which he put forward a point of view on Negritude which became more or less "the Nigerian view."[17] He opened the African-Scandinavian Writers' Conference (1967) with a seminal statement on "The Writer in a Modern

African State." The paper dominated discussion at the conference and has become a point of constant reference in a widening debate. Ten years later he made a considerable impact at the Second World Black and African Festival of Arts and Culture (FESTAC) with an appeal for commitment to Swahili as the continental language and for the recognition of the rights of writers in Africa.

His intellectual concerns are many. He has written articles about novels, poetry, films, plays, and travel. His quotations are drawn from philosophers, political scientists, historians, as well as literary and dramatic sources. He is familiar with black traditions in the United States, South America, and the Caribbean, as well as with European and African culture.

His most comprehensive academic and critical statement, one which posits an aesthetic as well as touching on many related literary and social issues, is *Myth, Literature and the African World,* his Cambridge lectures published with "The Fourth Stage" as an appendix. This contains critical bones he has been chewing over since the early sixties, romanticism in William Conton's *The African* and Negritude for example, as well as preoccupations of more recent origin, such as the claims of leftist ideologies.

In an account of his early work for the BBC he indicates that he was once, very early on, accuses of "talking down to his audience" on the subject of African literature.[18] He has never made the same mistake again and he certainly does not make it in the lectures or in "The Fourth Stage," which reveal a distinguished, amusing and demanding lecturer and writer. He ranges freely and with authority over several disciplines and literatures, addressing himself to a community whose vocabulary, reading and intellect he assumes to be large, broad and quick. As a result of his assumptions he leaves me bewildered at times. Indeed G. Wilson Knight, in whose honor the "The Fourth Stage" was written, said that he hoped Soyinka would clarify the ideas put forward in it.[19] In fact, as Soyinka indicates in the Introduction to *Myth, Literature and the African World,* he has tried "to reduce what a student... of (his) complained of as 'elliptical' obstacles to its comprehension."[20] I think that even Wilson Knight would have appreciated something more extensive than the minor additions which were made.

The complexity of Soyinka's prose style in these lectures is, I suppose, partly because his tragic vision takes him to the frontiers of language through contrasts and juxtapositions. The origin of Yoruba tragedy is, Soyinka maintains, to be found in "the abyss," "the chthonic realm," "the primordial marsh," the chaos which Ogun had to cross in his "tragic dare" to unite gods and men. Ogun's deed is, in Soyinka's view, duplicated by the Ogun worshipper who expresses his self-assertion not in words at all but in music - a feat which is, I suspect, easier in Yoruba, because of the close links between that language and music, than in English. Soyinka's creative writing characteristically uses counterpoint of image, mood and tone rather than, say, narrative development. This is related to the development Soyinka has observed in traditional ritual,[21] but it makes for a literary, and to a lesser degree an academic, style which is hard for pedestrian wits to follow.

The overall pattern is of an unconventional academic career. His decision not to complete his M.A. revealed his commitment to his "mistress," the theatre. His resignation from his first post at Ife for "political reasons" showed that both his wife and his mistress were - and they still are - the handmaidens of his sense of political responsibility. This sense of responsibility also affected his teaching at

Lagos and his decision to spend 1972-1974 outside Nigeria. It is an encouraging sign of the vision of the University of Ife that it can attract, appropriately recognize, and provide scope for Soyinka, whether in the Department of Comparative Literature or in the Department of Literature and Dramatic Arts.

Soyinka as a man-of-the-theatre:
Soyinka left Leeds and spent about eighteen months in London, during which time he was attached to the Royal Court Theatre as a play reader. It is as a man-of-the-theatre, actor, company creator, director and, of course, playwright, that Soyinka has expended most energy and achieved most importance. Once again a list, illustrative rather than comprehensive, helps to suggest Soyinka's involvement in the theatre and, through references to major productions of his work in three continents, hints at his impact on the world stage:

September	1958:	Soyinka produced *The Swamp Dwellers* for the Annual University of London Drama Festival.
February	1959:	*The Swamp Dwellers* and *The Lion and the Jewel* produced at Ibadan.
November	1959:	Wrote, produced and acted in "An Evening without Decor" at the Royal Court. The program included excerpts from *A Dance of the African Forest* and *The Invention*.[22]
March	1960:	*The Trials of Brother Jero* produced at Ibadan.
May	1960:	Acted Yang Sun in *The Good Woman of Setzuan* at Ibadan.
October	1960:	Completed, directed and acted in *A Dance of the Forests* at Ibadan, with his newly-formed company, 1960 Masks.
	1961:	Directed *The Trials of Brother Jero* and *Dear Parent and Ogre* (R. Sarif Easmon). Acted Dauda Touray in the latter.
	1963:	Directed *Song of a Goat* (J.P. Clark).
March	1964:	Largely responsible for writing and directing *The (New) Republican* with Orisun Theatre, a newly formed group of young, "professional" actors.
April	1964:	Directed *The Raft* (J.P. Clark).
August	1964:	Arranged, with Folk Opera and other groups, the "Orisun Repertory Theatre Season" in Lagos and Ibadan.
December	1964:	Founded, with others, the Drama Association of Nigeria.
April	1965:	Wrote and directed, with Orisun Theatre, *Before the Blackout*.
August	1965:	Directed *Kongi's Harvest* with a company from Lagos and Ibadan, premiered in Lagos. (See Boyd M. Berry's review in this collection.)
September	1965:	Recorded *The Detainee* for the BBC in London.

September   1965:   Advised on Stage 60's production of *The Road*, at the
                    Theatre Royal, Stratford East.

April   1966:   Revived *Kongi's Harvest* for the Dakar Festival.

June   1966:   *The Trials of Brother Jero* produced at the Hampstead
                    Theatre Club, London.

December   1966:   *The Lion and the Jewel* produced at the Royal Court. With
                    the June production of *Jero* this play earned Soyinka the
                    John Whiting Award, which he shared with Tom
                    Stoppard.

September   1967:   *The Lion and the Jewel* produced by G.A. Wilson and
                    A.M. Opoku, Accra. Revived August 1968. (See K.E.
                    Senanu's review in this collection.)

November   1967:   *The Trials of Brother Jero* and *The Strong Breed* produced
                    at the Greenwich Mews Theatre, New York.

April   1968:   *Kongi's Harvest* produced by the Negro Ensemble Compa-
                    ny, New York.

February   1969:   *The Road* produced by David Rubadiri with Theatre
                    Limited, Kampala.

November   1969:   Directed *Kongi's Harvest* at Ife and Ibadan.

            1970:   Involved in the ill-fated Calpenny Films production of
                    Kongi's Harvest; acted Kongi.

            1970:   Literary Editor of Orisun (Acting) Editions which pub-
                    lished a number of scripts, including, in 1970, *Eshu
                    Elegbara* by Wale Ogunyemi.

April   1970:   G.A. Wilson produced *Kongi's Harvest* in post-Nkrumah
                    Accra. (Soyinka did not give permission for this produc-
                    tion and disassociated himself from it.)

August   1970:   Completed and directed *Madmen and Specialists*, with
                    Ibadan University Theatre Arts Company, in New Haven,
                    Conn. Toured to Harlem.

            1970:   Directed *The Jar* (Pirandello), *Eshu Elegbara* (Wale Ogun-
                    yemi) and *The Fanatic* (Ben Caldwell) in Ibadan.

March   1971:   Revived and revised *Madmen and Specialists* in Ibadan.

April   1971:   Acted Patrice Lumumba in John Littlewood's French
                    production of *Murderous Angels* by Conor Cruise O'Brien,
                    in Paris.

July   1972:   Produced extracts from *A Dance of the Forests* in Paris.

August   1973:   *The Bacchae of Euripides* produced by the National
                    Theatre, London, who had commissioned it.

September   1976:   *A Dance of the Forests* produced by Nairobi High School.

October   1976:   *The Lion and the Jewel* produced, in French, as part of
                    President Senghor's birthday celebrations, Dakar.

December   1976:   Produced *Death and the King's Horseman* at Ife.

Soyinka's interest in the theatre began at school, where he wrote sketches for "concerts." After he left school and before he went to University College, Ibadan he began writing "pun-demented radio comedies." At Leeds he concentrated on the drama content of his course, perhaps because "plays took less time to read than novels," and began writing "seriously."[23] One of his plays, *The Lion and the Jewel* I think, brought him to the attention of the Royal Court. There he saw drama as a social force in action and came into contact with a generation of stimulating British playwrights and producers.[24]

When he returned to Nigeria in 1960, he organized and promoted, wrote and directed, with great enthusiasm and to considerable effect - and not only in the straight theatre. Bernth Lindfors's article, "Wole Soyinka Talking Through his Hat," indicates the range and frequency of Soyinka's contacts with radio during the opening years of the sixties, and he was doing research, and, I suspect, writing *The Interpreters* as well. At this time Soyinka seems to have seen his career in terms of the theatre, rather than of the university. In 1962 he answered Lewis Nkosi's question about his "current plans" by saying:

> It is simply this, that the sooner we can get a professional theatre going the better. I would like to be able to work full-time in the theatre. I find I'm as much interested in producing and in acting as I am in writing and with a professional theatre I find I can live a very fulfilled existence.[25]

Soyinka's ideas about the need for and form of a national theatre have changed over the years.[26] His recent interest seems to be less in the establishment of Orisun Theatre as a full-time acting group, than in using universities as bases for "professional" theatre companies. The company which he took to New Haven and the company which performed *Death and the King's Horseman* appear to be the results of this deliberate policy or, of accommodation to reality, or, of a recognition that the only hope of an independent, non-political theatre lies under the protection of "the University idea."

Soyinka's range as a writer for the stage is very broad. He is a satirist ("The satires give me the greatest pleasure"); a comic playwright ("I just can't describe to you how absolutely delighted I was to find that I had written *The Trials of Brother Jero* which in production and in reading I find people enjoy tremendously.");[27] a melodramatist (see Gerald Moore on *The Swamp Dwellers*); an "absurdist" (in parts of *The Road* and *Madmen and Specialists*); a tragic author (in the Author's Note to *Death and the King's Horseman* he advises the producer to "elicit the play's threnodic essence"). In fact each play has been a new departure in terms of convention and treatment, and each genre has been given a new expression in his hands. His most recent play, *Death and the King's Horseman*, wins through to a new clarity of action and contrast, and a new subtlety of language.

Soyinka's standing in the theatre is hard to estimate. As the list of productions shows, he emerged on the London scene before his work was produced in Nigeria and since then he has grown on both the international and the national "stage." In Nigeria he is pre-eminent among a company of enterprising writers, directors and folk-opera and comic theatre actor-managers. He is part, the most distinguished part, of a vigorous national theatre movement. In the rest of Anglophone Africa he looms larger, and the more embryonic the local theatre movement, the more impressive his achievements appear. He is an imposing, though at times amusing, Nigerian whose works are set for examinations and whose "articulate hero of Christ's crusade" is a familiar and entertaining figure on school stages. Substantial amateur and university groups tend to regard Soyinka as "*the* African dramatist" and to see his more serious plays as "*the* challenge." In Francophone Africa his plays seem, at last, to have broken the language barrier (perhaps, since his work in Paris?) thanks to translations by P. Laburthe-Tolra, J. Chute and others. Fifteen years separate *Brother Jero* in Ibadan from *Frère Jero* in Abidjan! And seventeen years separate *The Lion and the Jewel* (Ibadan) from *Le lion et la perle* (Dakar)! Meanwhile *The Swamp Dwellers* has been translated into Japanese!

In England, where he produced his first important play, he is still unusual enough to attract experimental university groups, popular enough to have *Brother Jero* toured (at one point two touring groups were presenting *Jero* in Northern Ireland at the same time!) and established enough to have had major productins, though no unqualified successes, in London. It should be pointed out that, not surprisingly, it has been the committed and the art theatres, rather than Shaftesbury Avenue and the commercial play-houses, which have welcomed him. It is a pity that the sensitivity which prompted the commissioning of *The Bacchae of Euripides* for the National Theatre did not extend to the production.[28]

In the United States the pattern is somewhat similar. There have been numerous campus productions, significant off-Broadway offerings and enlightened sponsorship. In this case the sponsor was The Eugene O'Neill Center, which carried Soyinka and the University of Ibadan Theatre Arts Company to New Haven, provided them with an opportunity to prepare *Madmen and Specialists* and enabled them to take it to New York. I hope that this pattern of encouragement will be repeated—it seems to be the only way of getting adequate productions of Soyinka's work outside Nigeria.

Soyinka's *impact* on the theatre is also hard to estimate. He has influenced a number of African playwrights. Ola Rotimi, for example, has acknowledged the affect of Soyinka's use of cultural elements on his own writing.[29] He has made stages throughout Africa a meeting point of enjoyment and thought. And he has, as the two experiences described below indicate, been recognized as a threat by reactionary forces. During performances of the satirical revues, *The (New) Republican* and *Before the Blackout,* the actors guarded the stage doors against hired thugs. In the spleen of Africa where I am writing this, under the sway of "Babuzu, Lion of Malladi" and under the eye of his (His?) Censorship Board, *A Dance of the Forests, The Lion and the Jewel, Camwood on the Leaves, The Jero Plays, The Detainee* and *Kongi's Harvest* have been banned from the stage. Indeed the Chariman of the Censorship Board has said that he will ban everything by Soyinka which is submitted to him.[30]

Soyinka as a political activist

In his autobiographical statement Soyinka records that he left Ife for "political reasons" and that in 1967 he was held in Kaduna prison as a political detainee. The reason Soyinka gives for his political involvement is related to his insistence on his integrity as a human being and to the following statement from the *World Authors* entry: "I have one abiding religion - human liberty." To this can be added his special sense of responsibility. In an interview in 1973 he said:

I have a special responsibility, because I can smell the reactionary sperm years before the rape of the nation takes place.[31]

The most comprehensive account of his religious observance and his exercise of his "special responsibility" can be found in *The Man Died*. There Soyinka's faith is spelt out in slogan ("The Man dies in all who keep silent in the face of tyranny"), in outrage and indictment, in accounts of actions and in descriptions of events he was powerless to affect. *The Man Died* is unique among his writings for the directness of the challenges it throws down, but in other works there are fairly specific political concerns. Again a list, and once again an illustrative rather than an exhaustive one, helps. In this case it indicates the variety of issues that have drawn him into print, before the microphone, on to the stage or into the political arena:

1959:   Colonial repression in Africa, *Eleven Men Dead* at Hola, a Royal Court production which Soyinka contributed to and acted in, based on reports about British detention camps in Kenya. Sharpeville: *A Dance of the African Forest*. Racial prejudices: "Telephone Conversation," "Castration Blues."

1960:   Independence and the burden of national consciousness: *A Dance of the Forests*. (Note: I do not, of course, regard the political point as the only element in this and in most of the other works listed.)

1962:   The effect of the emergency on Western Nigeria: "Emergency Sketches," press lampoons on Dr. Majekodumni *et al.*

1963:   Misguided sense of national priorities: controversy over the Dick Tiger Title Fight.

1964/65: Corruption, political intriguing, manipulation of the mass media, etc., etc.: *The (new) Republican* and *Before the Blackout*.

1965:   Personality cults and dictatorship in Africa, political rhetoric and jargon as impediments to understanding: *Kongi's Harvest*. Local politics and social tensions: *The Road*.

1965:   Ballot rigging: "The Tape Fiasco."[32]

1966:   The great importance of Nkrumah to Africa: "Of Power and Change."

1967-71: The causes and conduct of The Nigerian Civil War: *The Man Died*. Soyinka's analysis covers the massacres, repression of trades unionists, the alliance between a corrupt generation of politicians and the army - "The Mafia," etc. The civil war provides the background to *Season of Anomy, Madmen and Specialist, A Shuttle in the Crypt*, and in those works he develops issues and insights afforded by the war.

1971:   Student rights: evidence before the Kazeem Enquiry.

1975:   The quality of life in Guinea-Bissau: *Transition*, 48. The Monstrosity of Amin's rule: *Transition*, 49.

1976:   Machell's decision to put Moçambique on a war footing: *Ogun Abibimañ*. Lowering of standards "to accommodate the dwarfish

> intellect of assembly-line diplomats," etc. etc.: resignation from the
> International Secretariat of FESTAC.

These diverse causes have been brought together by Soyinka's concern for justice (on release from detention in 1969 he parodied the Federal war cry with: "To keep Nigeria one, justice must be done"); his desire for an egalitarian society (he has spoken on "the need to redistribute Nigeria's wealth equally"), human liberty and human rights (he has described the United Nations declaration on Human Rights as "a work of collective genius").[33]

In most of his political ventures Soyinka has acted alone. It is part of his creed that individual effort can effect change. In the Seattle lecture on "Drama and the Revolutionary Ideal," he said:

> It is the individual, working as a part of a social milieu - and this may be a fluctuating milieu - who raises the consciousness of the community of which he is a part.[34]

In a subsequent discussion he clarified his position in such a way as to relate it to his writing:

> I believe implicitly that any work of art which opens out the horizons of the human mind, the human intellect, is by its very nature a force for change, a medium for change.[35]

This implicit faith translates into the lonely heroism of Eman and Daodu. They both "prefer the clarity of action"[36] but alongside the clarity which their confrontation produces, there is also confusion. Some of Soyinka's own actions have been tinged with the same qualitites, have led to similar confusions. Don Quixote, too, sought "the clarity of action."

Soyinka's kind of individualism is, naturally enough, the despair of the ideologically committed. He is familiar with the claims and the writings of major political thinkers, and he has quoted Mao ("I think Mao's thoughts are African")[37] and Fanon ("I think a favourite phrase of mine from Fanon might sum it up, brutality of thought,"[38] with approval. But he has rejected ideological alignment. In an interview with John Agetua he said:

> I would rather not be bracketed with those pseudo-stalinists-leninists and maoists who are totally unproductive and merely protect themselves behind a whole barrage of terminologies which bear no relation to the immediate needs of society.[38]

In the Preface to the Cambridge lectures he combined this rejection, significantly based partly on the misuse of language ("terminologies"), with the argument that the "new black ideologues" are latter-day evangelists of alien creeds:

> There is nothing to choose ultimately between the colonial mentality of an Ajayi Crowther, West Africa's first black bishop, who grovelled before his white missionary superiors in a plea for patience and understanding of his "backward, heathen, brutish" brothers, and the new black ideologues who are embarrassed by statements of self-apprehension by the new "ideologically backward" African. Both suffer from externally induced fantasies of redemptive transformation in the image of alien masters.[40]

Characteristically Soyinka takes his bitterest ideological critics and those who see a regrettable lack of a firm coherent groundwork of social and political thought in his whole vision,[41] more seriously than they take themselves. He has been at considerable pains to establish the appropriateness and "African-ness" of his humanism.

The weapons Soyinka has used to fight for "human liberty" have been the weapons to hand. Over the last decade and half these have included lampoons in the press, satirical dramatic sketches, full-length plays, British publishers and *Transition/Ch'Indaba*. In the early sixties he was concerned, largely, with Nigerian issues, and he used locally available means to reach a local audience. Since then his increasing international prestige has brought him access to international publications and press agencies. His Ife appointment was reported even in the Malawi press.[42] FESTAC and his position as Secretary General of the Union of Writers of the African People/Union of African Writers have raised him to an unprecedented height of what Lakunle would call "international conspicuosity." During FESTAC, as mentioned above, he spoke about the need for governments to adopt Swahili as *the* African language and to respect human rights, particularly the human rights of writers. He also called a press conference and, as Secretary General of the 'African Writers' Union:

> urged African Governments to end the rampant torture, brutality and dehumanizing actions which their citizens suffer. The Union commended the Tanzanian government for holding an inquiry and several officials who accepted responsibility for torture and murder of suspects carried out by oficials under their control. (sic) This event was without parallel in Africa's recent history.
>
> The Union announced that it had established a volunteers' register for writers who wished to contribute to the African liberation struggle in any capacity... cooks, stretcher bearers, ambulance drivers or combatants. The Union also called on President Sadat to release journalists, writers, students and workers imprisoned after the recent food riots in Cairo.[43]

Soyinka has been a factor in Nigerian politics for some years; in *The Man Died* he records "a bizarre night-visit" during which he was offered a cabinet post.[44] His attention now seems to be turned more to Pan-African and supra-continental issues, but this is partly a trick of the international light which now shines on him. His work in London during 1959 included responses to the Hola Camp scandal and Sharpeville and, through poems such as "Castration Blues," to the injustices endured in the Black Diaspora. It showed that he has long had a sense of responsibility to the continent and beyond. The effectiveness of his international urgings will be tested by the response to the points he put forward at FESTAC as Secretary General of the Union of African Writers.

In the meantime three straws in the wind suggest an international impact: the first, the recognition, by Amnesty International, that Soyinka was prisoner of conscience and the international attention that was focused on him while he was detained; the second, the issue of *Transition* he devoted to the articles about Amin's slaughter, which stands as documentary proof of the willingness of some Africans at least to condemn the mass murderer;[45] third, the "shuttle diplomacy" by which he brought Senegal back into FESTAC after she had withdrawn over a disagreement about the concepts which the Festival was to reflect.[46]

Soyinka as Writer:

Returning to the seminal paragraph, Soyinka records that after leaving Ife he spent his time "writing." Soyinka as writer brings together the Soyinkas glimpsed so far: Soyinka as Yoruba, translating, incorporating, interpreting; Soyinka as academic, lecturing, presenting papers, writing reviews: Soyinka as man-of-the-theatre, writing stage-plays, radio plays, revue sketches, on commenting directions in the theatre; Soyinka as political activist, critic, protester, Third Force, conscience of a nation, of a continent. The list of his publications indicates that his versatility as a writer is even greater than suggested so far. He has written short stories and radio pieces, and the lists I have compiled have not done justice to him as novelist, author of *The Interpreters* and *Season of Anomy,* and as poet, author of *Idanre and Other Poems, Shuttle in the Crypt, Ogun Abibiman* and of poems scattered through the pages of magazines and to the four winds. The quality of his work has already earned him the Jock Campbell Award and other prizes will follow. His writing is always worthwhile and sometimes masterly. Almost all of it bears frequent re-reading and yields new depths on each encounter. It will endure.

The essays, papers and articles in this collection are largely concerned with Soyinka as writer. For the most part the critics and scholars start from the texts, though the importance of the impact of plays in performance has been recognized. My concern in this collection has been to draw together the best of the farflung criticism on Soyinka's work. In the process a variety of perspectives, of views from different angles, from different "periods," has been brought together. In the same process more space than might have been expected has been given to some works, less space than might have been expected has been given to others. This is inevitable in a collection of this sort where quality is important. Another of the results is that the collection has one of the structural features of Soyinka's own work: progress through contrast, juxtaposition of images.

A final comment:

Soyinka's assessment of his current preoccupations as a writer and his vision of Arcadian bliss invite a final comment. Soyinka says that he has become "more and more pre-occupied with this theme of the oppressive boot." A comparison of the post-Prison writing with the work of the fifties and sixties shows that many of the supposedly new elements are, in fact, not new at all. There were Greek interests in Soyinka's work long before *The Bacchae of Euripides.* The cultural assessments apparent in *Death and the King's Horseman* were present, in embryo, in *The Lion and the Jewel.* The critical principles elaborated in *Myth, Literature and the African World* underlay the early essays on "The Future of African Writing" and "From a Common Backcloth." The fact that Jero, who was tried in 1960, was resurrected and metamorphosed in 1973 in a grimmer version of the same dark comic mode points to the continuity of Soyinka's concerns, his integrity, his consistency. It is in the scope, the depth, in what Abiola Irele has described as "the growth and the consequent deepening of his consciousness in its contact with and reaction to the immediate experience of his time and place"[47] that the new elements can be observed. It is also in the confidence of technique which can dispense with the sometimes frantic striving for effect of *The Road,* with the overschematic juxtapositions of *Kongi's Harvest,* and produce *Death and the King's Horseman.* And in "the preoccupation," not the interest that has always been there, but the preoccupation "with this theme of the oppressive boot."

Soyinka's idyll is, it seems, a polygamous, farming life with opportunities for archaeological investigations among local shrines and for "honing three or four poems a year to an exquisite clarity." Of the farming interests there are hints in the recurring imagery of growth and harvest. Of the preference for pologamy there are indications between the lines in the poems "for women." Of the archaeological bent there are some foreshadowings in the historical scenes set in the Court of Mata Karibu and in the decision to treat the interrupted ritual suicide at Oyo. That the poet should "hone," like Ogun "sharpen a blade," like a driven being move in on a target, is only to be expected. That he should "hone to an exquisite clarity" will be a relief to readers. But, on the whole, I think, his readers will deny him his idyll, hand him a typewriter not a hoe, and prevent him from "sliding peacefully into thrifty poetry and polygamous sloth." He disturbs, he disquietens, he delights, he demands attention and now African letters, indeed Africa herself, cannot do without him.

James Gibbs

Zomba

Footnotes

[1] *In Person: Achebe, Awoonor and Soyinka,* Karen L. Morell, (Seattle: Institute of Comparative and Foreign Area Studies, University of Washington, 1975), pp. 113-14. The volume includes Soyinka's paper on "Drama and the Revolutionary Ideal" and transcripts of three encounters.

[2] Wole Soyinka, *Myth, Literature and the African World* (Cambridge: Cambridge University Press, 1976), p. 61. The full sentence reads: "Thanks to the tendency of the modern consumer mind to facilitate digestion by putting in strict categories what are essentially fluid operations of the creative mind upon social and natural phenomena, the formulation of a literary ideology tends to congeal sooner or later into instant capsules which, administrated also to the writer, may end by asphixiating the creative process."

[3] For background of these two **kingdoms**, see, for example, Robert F. Smith, *Kingdoms of the Yoruba* (London: Methuen, 1969). J. Ade Ajayi and Robert F. Smith, *Yoruba Warfare in the Nineteenth Century* (Cambridge: Cambridge University Press, 1964).

[4] Morell, p. 93.

[5] I deduce this from Soyinka's answers to Lewis Nkosi in *African Writers Talking,* ed. Dennis Duerden and Cosmo Pieterse (London: Heinemann, 1972), p. 175. See also O.R. Dathorne, "African Literature IV: Ritual and Ceremony in Okigbo's Poetry,' *Journal of Commonwealth Literature* 5 (1968), 79-91.

[6] *Myth, Literature and the African World,* ix.

[7] See the list of "Translations" in the Bibliography of Soyinka's works.

[8] This, of course, is not a comprehensive list and it might have been more revealing to cite those works in which Yoruba influences *do not* provide foreground interest. For example, the early poems, "Nursery Tail-piece" and "Castration Blues"; *The Swamp Dwellers;* etc.

[9] Compare with what Los says in Blake's *Jerusalem:* "I must create a system or be enslaved by another man's."

[10] Interview with Valerie Wilmer, 'Wole Soyinka Talks to *Flamingo,' Flamingo,* 5,6 (1966), 16.

[11] Wole Soyinka, "Neo-Tarzanism: the Poetics of Pseudo-Tradition," *Transition,* 48 (1975), 44.

[12] E. Bolaji Idowu, *Olodumare, God in Yoruba Belief* (London: Longman, 1962); S.A. Babalola, *Yoruba Ijala* (Oxford: Oxford University Press, 1966).

[13] See, for example, Amos Tutuola, *The Palm Wine Drinkard* (London: Faber, 1952).

[14] Soyinka is confident even when inaccurate. While it is impossible for me to comment on his representation of Yoruba elements, there are a number of points concerning other matters on which he is wrong. For example, Shirley Bassey was born in Tiger Bay, the dock area of Cardiff. She was not born and brought up in London as Soyinka maintains in "African Personality," *Radio Times* (Lagos), 22 January 1961, p. 6. Peter Brook's production, *Orghast,* was not entirely in Ted Hughes's invented language as Soyinka suggested in a discussion at Seattle, Washington. See Morell, *op. cit.* p. 103. these points do not affect his arguments in either case, but they reveal an attitude. A potentially more substantial error occurs in his exegesis of "Humpty Dumpty" in the "Neo-Tarzanism" article already cited. The origin and meaning of this nursery rhyme is still the subject of controversy.

[15] I have no knowledge of Soyinka's financial affairs, apart from that provided by *The Man Died,* and "Ever-ready bank account" which appears in *Shuttle in the Crypt* (London: Rex Collings/Eyre Methuen, 1972), pp. 81-83.

[16] Compare the "blurb" of *Death and the King's Horseman* (London: Eyre/Methuen, 1975), with "The FESTAC Colloquium," *West Africa,* February 1977, p. 280.

[17] See W.H. Stevenson, *"The Horn.* What it Was and What it Did," *Research in African Literatures,* 6 (1975), 5-31.

[18] Wole Soyinka, "Gbohun-Gbohun," *The Listener,* 2 November 1972, pp. 581-83.

[19] Personal communication. "The Fourth Stage" originally appeared in *The Morality of Art,* a festschrift for G. Wilson Knight edited by D.W. Jefferson (London: Routledge and Kegan Paul, 1968), pp. 119-34. The terminology in "The Fourth State"is similar to that used by Wilson Knight, who was Soyinka's professor at Leeds.

[20] *Myth, Literature and the African World,* ix.

[21] See, for example, the important but neglected paper he presented to the International Symposium on "African Culture: History, Values and Prospects," (Ibadan, December, 1960), entitled "The African Approach to Drama."

[22] One of the errors which has crept into the writing about Soyinka is that this play was entitled *The Inventor.* The mistake first appeared in "National Dramatist," *West Africa,* 19 December 1964, 1417. Another error, which appears in Gerald Moore's *Wole Soyinka* (London: Evans, 1971), p. 15, is that Soyinka acted in *The Caucasian Chalk Circle.* In fact, see next item but one on the list, he played Yang Sun in *The Good Woman of Setzuan.* A third example in this area, which has not, as far as I know, been retailed is that the 1965 production of *The Road* was at Stratford on Avon. (See Vladimir Klima, *Modern Nigerian Novels* [Prague: Academia, 1969], p. 52.)
I fervently hope that I have not created or perpetuated any such errors.

[23] Interview recorded at Leeds, May 1973. See also "Gbohun-Gbohun," already referred to.

[24] See Terry Browne, *Playwrights' Theatre* (London: Pitmans, 1975).

[25] *African Writers Talking,* p. 177.

[26] See, for example, interview with Alan Akarogun, *Spear Magazine,* May 1966, pp. 16-19 and p. 42 and Morell, *op. cit.,* pp. 94-97, and p. 105. In the former he advocated two-year official sponsorships of existing performing companies so that a national repertoire could be built up. In the latter he says "national theatre reduces, from what I have seen, people of genius and talent to squabbling children and political fools. That seems to be a disease that transcends any cultural bonds." Soyinka was within four months of having *The Bacchae of Euripides* produced by the National Theatre in London. By that time he, presumably, had had extensive and intimate contact with the British National Theatre.

[27] *African Writers Talking,* p. 174.

[28] The London critics generally failed to respond to the play in R. Joffe's production. Of the thirty-two notices I have traced the most penetrating are those by W.A. Darlighton ("A Case of Believe it or Not,' *The Daily Telegraph,* 3 September 1973) and Albert Hunt ("Amateurs in Horror," *New Society,* 9 August 1973, p. 342-43.

[29] "Ola Rotimi Interviewed," *New Theatre Magazine,* 12, 2 (1972), 5.

[30] I should admit that the grounds for banning the plays do not entirely support my thesis. *The Detainee* and *Kongi's Harvest* are forbidden on political grounds. But *The Jero Plays* were rejected because they might offend religious convictions and constitute a threat to public order. *The Lion and the Jewel* was construed as being obscene and as an attack on tradition.

[31] Interview article in *The Guardian,* quoted by Hunt, see footnote 29.

[32] See *The Man Died,* pp. 155-56. Soyinka was acquitted because of a contradiction in the evidence presented against him. But I have no doubt that, after Chief S.L. Akintola had rigged the elections, Soyinka did hold-up the radio station and did substitute for Akintola's victory address a tape advising Akintola "and his crew of renegades to quit the country." Soyinka had asserted himself in the midst of chaos. After his acquittal he was carried shoulder-high from the court. He had shown up the quality of justice in the Western Nigerian courts, but I do not think that was his intention.

[33] "Still Outspoken," *The Times* (London), 5 December 1969.

[34] Morell, *op. cit.,* p. 86

[35] *Ibid.,* p. 135

[36] The sentence "I prefer the clarity of action," appears in *The Militant* Interview,' *The Militant* (Young Socialist Movement, University of Ibadan), 2, 1 (December 1972), 5.

[37] Wole Soyinka, "The Choice and Use of Language," *Cultural Events in Africa,* No. 78 (1971), 4

[38] *"The Militant* Interview," p. 4

[39] John Agetua, *When the Man Died* (Benin: John Agetua, 1975), p. 41.

[40] *Myth, Literature and the African World,* xii.

[41] Abiola Irele, "The Significance of Wole Soyinka," a paper presented at the Symposium of Wole Soyinka, held at Ibadan, 13 May 1974, p. 5

[42] "Wole Soyinka Appointed Professor," *Daily Times* (Blantyre), 8 January 1976, p. 2

[43] "African Writers Protest," *West Africa,* 7 February 1977, p. 26.

[44] *The Man Died,* p. 52.

[45] The cover of *Transition,* No. 49, bore a drawing of Amin and the words "Karasi: Finish him."

[46] *The Times* (London), 18 January 1977.

[47] Irele, *op. cit.,* p. 2

The Early Writings
of Wole Soyinka

BERNTH LINDFORS

WOLE SOYINKA'S first books appeared only twelve years ago, in 1963. Since that time he has earned an international reputation as one of Africa's most abundantly gifted writers. Prolific and versatile, he has published eleven plays, a collection of satirical dramatic sketches, two volumes of poetry, two novels, a translation of D. O. Fagunwa's first fictional narrative, an autobiographical work based on his experiences in prison during the Nigerian civil war, and numerous essays on literary, social and political matters. What is most impressive about this extraordinary output is not its gross quantity but its fine quality; Soyinka is one of the few highly productive African authors writing in English whose works are original, creative, imaginative and satisfying. He is neither an inveterate autobiographer like Ezekiel Mphahlele nor a reformed "Market" writer like Cyprian Ekwensi nor an incontinent iconoclast like Taban lo Liyong. His imagination, vision and craft distinguish him as a creative artist of the very first rank, as a writer of world stature. Some would say he is the only truly original literary genius that Africa has yet produced.

His prodigious talent has not gone unrecognized by scholars and critics. Three critical books and one study guide on his writings

Research for this essay was done in Nigeria in 1972–73 on a Younger Humanist Fellowship awarded by the National Endowment for the Humanities. I wish to thank NEH and the University Research Institute at the University of Texas at Austin for their support.

19

have recently been published,[1] and he is featured prominently in
nearly every serious appraisal of modern African drama, poetry and
fiction. Indeed, no survey of contemporary African literature would
be complete without at least one chapter devoted to Soyinka's writings. He is already a classic, already a monument in the pantheon of
African letters.

But though his life and works have been subjected to careful academic scrutiny, no one has given much attention to his early formative period as a writer. Little is known about his literary activities
prior to 1960, when he returned to Nigeria after completing a B.A.
in English at the University of Leeds and working for three years in
London as a bartender, bouncer, substitute high school English
teacher, and script-reader at the Royal Court Theatre. Even less is
known about the writing he did before leaving for England in 1954,
and not much has been said about how he spent his year in Ibadan
as a Rockefeller Research Fellow in 1960–61. This article attempts
to fill in a few of these large lacunae in Soyinka's literary career by
examining some of his unknown writings.

Soyinka's first published works probably appeared in annuals or
literary magazines at Government College Ibadan, the elite secondary school he attended before enrolling in 1952 in a preliminary
course necessary for entry into University College Ibadan. It is
known that he contributed to "house" magazines at Government
College,[2] but his contributions have never been exhumed and discussed, probably because copies of these publications are now extremely hard to find. In an interview recorded in August 1962,
Soyinka said:

> I would say I began writing seriously, or rather taking myself seriously,
> taking my *writing* seriously about three, four years ago, but I can only
> presume that I have always been interested in writing. In school I wrote
> the usual little sketches for production, the occasional verse, you know,

[1] Gerald Moore, *Wole Soyinka* (London, 1971); Alain Ricard, *Théâtre et nationalisme. Wole Soyinka et LeRoi Jones* (Paris, 1972); Eldred Durosimi Jones, *The Writing of Wole Soyinka* (London, 1973); James Gibbs, *Study Aid to "Kongi's Harvest"*
(London, 1973).

[2] Information supplied by Dapo Adelugba, Theatre Arts Department, University
of Ibadan. See Soyinka's comment below.

the short story, etc., and I think about 1951 I had the great excitement,
of having a short story of mine broadcast on the Nigerian Broadcasting
Service and that was sort of my first public performance.[3]

One wonders if the story Soyinka remembers as his "first public
performance" was "Keffi's Birthday Treat," a brief narrative broadcast on the Children's Programme of the Nigerian Broadcasting
Service's National Programme and published in one of the earliest
issues of the *Nigerian Radio Times* in July 1954.[4] Even if "Keffi's
Birthday Treat" is a later radio contribution, it may be significant as
Soyinka's first short story to be published in a national magazine.
Earlier stories may have appeared in high school and university publications, but these would not have been available to the general
public. "Keffi's Birthday Treat" was very likely Soyinka's first public
performance in print, if not on the air.

The story is a charming vignette telling of a young boy's attempt
to treat himself to a visit to the University College Zoo in Ibadan on
his tenth birthday. Here is the entire 850-word text, which must have
taken about five minutes to read on the Children's Programme:

> "I'll be ten tomorrow," said Keffi to himself as he lay in bed, staring
> at the ceiling of his home in Yaba. Yes, Keffi would indeed become a ten-
> year-old boy the following day. He had received some presents already,
> he was sure he would receive some more the next day, and finally, there
> was going to be a birthday party for him at seven o'clock in the evening.
> But, of all the presents he had received, there was not one which attracted
> him more than the book which had been sent to him by his big brother
> in England. And of the treats which he had been promised, the most ex-
> citing was the one which he had promised *himself*. The book contained
> beautifully coloured pictures of the animals in the London Zoo, and the
> treat was a trip to Ibadan to see the animals in the University College Zoo.
> As far as Keffi was concerned, Ibadan was merely a street in Lagos!
> So, after breakfast the following day, he went to the nearest bus stop,

---

[3] Cosmo Pieterse and Dennis Duerden, eds., *African Writers Talking: A Collection of Radio Interviews* (New York, 1972). pp. 171–72.

[4] *Nigerian Radio Times* (July 1954), pp. 15–16. Chinua Achebe, who was working
for the Nigerian Broadcasting Service at this time, may have edited this story for
publication.

taking with him his week's pocket money, leaving a note on his mother's bed telling her where he was going, and promising to be back before the party. Keffi had no idea that Ibadan was a huge town and was over a hundred miles from Lagos; he had read of the University College Zoo in the Children's Newspaper, and had determined that some day, he would go and see it for himself.

Luck seemed to be with Keffi: for, as he stood waiting for the bus, he saw a kit-car pull up outside a petrol station, and—was he dreaming? —on its doors was written, "UNIVERSITY COLLEGE, IBADAN." Keffi at once ran towards the driver, begging him for a lift. But when he got to the car, he saw the driver's back was turned, and—his heart began to beat very fast—the door at the back was open! How very exciting to climb *in*, remain very quiet, and surprise the driver by coming out of the car when they got to the college! And this was just what Keffi did. He lay flat on the floor of the car, and waited for the driver to start it. Very soon, he heard the driver's voice. There was also another man, and they seemed to be coming to the back of the car, carrying something rather heavy! Keffi dared not look up, for fear he would be caught. He heard the driver say,

"Just lift it up and throw it inside."

What would they throw inside? Was it a box, and would they throw it right on him? Suppose it was a very heavy object and it was thrown on him; would it break his bones? Or was it a new animal for the zoo? Suppose it was a tiger, fresh from the jungle. Poor Keffi's knees were knocking and he began to be sorry that he ever started on this adventure. Should he scream? But before he could make up his mind, the two men threw the object into the car. It was a motor car wheel, and luckily, only a little part of it caught Keffi on the back. The driver did not even look inside the car, but shut the door, went to his seat and drove off.

Half an hour later, the car pulled up inside a place which looked like a big plantation. Keffi watched the driver get out of the car and after a while, he too crept out. He saw cows grazing in the fields, and a lot of fowls in the special little houses which had been made for them. This amused him a great deal, for the houses even had steps leading from them to the ground! And then Keffi grew very much interested in some vehicles called tractors. These had large iron spades, large iron wheels, large iron teeth and claws, all of which were used in uprooting the ground and felling trees. But he had not yet seen any wild animals, and it was while looking for them that a kind-looking official saw him, enquired where he lived and what he wanted. When Keffi told him, he burst out laughing. After laughing very heartily for a long time, he told Keffi,

"You are a little unfortunate, my boy. The lions and leopards and gorillas have all been taken away for a holiday. They will return after a week.

Will you come back then?" Keffi promised to return after a week, and thereupon the kind gentleman took him home and put him right on his doorstep.

He had spent only two hours away, and when, feeling sure that he had been to the University College Zoo, he told his mother his adventures, he was surprised to see her burst out laughing. When he asked why she laughed, she replied,

"You were very lucky that the driver did not go straight to Ibadan. That was not the University College Zoo, it was Agege Agricultural Station!"

"Next time," Keffi promised himself, "I really shall go to the Zoo."

What is most appealing about this story is the delightful combination of gentle humor, suspense and drama Soyinka manages to achieve in less than a thousand words. He is essentially telling a joke or humorous anecdote but he never allows the comedy to get out of control. He deftly builds up an air of excitement around the boy's escapade, inserts a few good laughs toward the end, and finishes with a punch line which Lagos and Ibadan listeners would especially appreciate. The University College Zoo at Ibadan, which was opened in the early 1950s, has always been a favorite tourist attraction for Nigerians, so Soyinka's story about a young boy's curiosity to see wild animals would have appealed to a wide radio audience, not just to children. "Keffi's Birthday Treat" was topical and entertaining, a harbinger of the creative harvest to come.

Soyinka's first contribution to campus publications at University College Ibadan appears to have been a poem entitled "Thunder to Storm" published in the second issue of *The University Voice*, the official organ of the Students' Union, in January 1953.[5] (Soyinka would have been eighteen years old at this time.) Written in rather jerky iambic tetrameter couplets with occasional slant rhymes and awkward syntax, the poem describes the impact of a brief but devastating tropical storm on a seaside community somewhere in Africa. One could say that "Thunder to Storm" bears a vague resemblance in narrative strategy to eighteenth and nineteenth century English

---

[5] *The University Voice* 2 (January 1953): 21. The poem is the earliest I have been able to trace. It was published six years before the poem Moore cites as "the first of Soyinka's work to appear in Nigeria" (Moore, *Wole Soyinka,* p. 6).

meditative verse devoted to pondering man's relationship with his natural environment, but specific comparisons would be ludicrous because Soyinka's poem lacks art. Indeed, his craftsmanship is so crude and his tone so uncertain that one frequently cannot tell whether some of the comical side-effects are accidental or deliberate. One imagines Soyinka's puckish grin somewhere beneath the fractured surface, but it is conceivable that this ninety-eight-line jingle was actually intended as a serious poem. Certainly it is the most juvenile of his juvenilia. To prove the point, here is the whole catastrophic cloudburst, with every minor typographical disaster preserved:

A low, long rumble from the sky,
That dwindled off into a sigh.
Querying eyes looked up. The sky was clear.
And this of course soon quelled all fear.
No heavy cloud, the day was bright,
So thought they all. but none was right.
Said two young boys, "we'll go for wood,
When we return, we'll have some food."
"I'll hurry home," a woman said,
"I've got to put my babe to bed."
Boasted one man, "I'll win this game,
In chess I have a lot of fame."
The homeless tramp, he laughted and shrugged
He'd had no luck, and on he jogged.
The fishermen upon the sea,
They hauled their nets for all to see.
The rich old man watched them at work,
From his near home, he mused, "what luck!"
About their daily tasks they went
All were happy, all content.

Then hell broke loose; the bright clear sky
Was covered up, dense clouds rolled by.
Quite soon their heavy tears they'd shed
And down below the humans fled.
Huge streaks of lightning flashed about
As if the whole world they would rout.
And down to earth, a march with the wind
'Twas all-destroying, nowhere kind.

But scene of sorrow, sight for mourn.
Dead bodies—torn and mangled
'Neath the cables bent and fangled.
The woman who some time before
Had hurried—making for her door;
The two chess-players who'd been so well
They reached home safe but their home fell;
Two little boys who went for wood
They too were in a happy mood:
The merry tramp for shelter fled
The friendly tree his body bled:
The fisherman who'd worked all day
He did not see the sun's next ray:
The rich old man who'd loved the sea
The sea grew rough and claimed him fee:
The quiet families at home
Thought they were safe; no more they, droam.
Some killed by lightning, some by walls
Some smashed by trees, none heard their falls
Electric wires by trees were cut
Some touched them and—that was their lot!
The homeless wept when morning broke
But what of those who never woke?
They little thought so soon they'd leave
Their loved ones for them to grieve.
The child no more his mum could call;
Why do they poke beneath the wall?
The wife no more her spouse would storm
He'd gone off in a thunderstorm.

It is a wonder that young Soyinka, after composing this uninspired undergraduate doggerel, managed to escape being struck down by one of Shango's thunderbolts!

In 1953–54, his second and last year at University College Ibadan before leaving for Leeds, Soyinka was involved in a number of campus activities which made demands on his literary abilities. As an enthusiastic member of the Progressive Party, a student political organization set up in opposition to the more powerful student Dynamic Party, he took over the editorship of *The Eagle,* an irregular cyclostyled newssheet of campus commentary and humor. Three issues edited by him can be found in the African collection of the

This tree was stubborn, down it went
Poles and cables, them it bent.
This house stood firm, it soon crashed in;
And with the wind went the dust-bin.
Some roofs were slack and off they went
To some far place by the wind sent
Electric wires soon were cut
They'd stood for years, their pride was hurt.
The dead alone were free from this,
But wait! They would not have this bliss.
Into the graveyard the wind marched
And for a mighty tree it searched.
It soon found one—its great shadow
Had sheltered graves—but no ado.
A deafening crash and down it fell.
The ghosts cried out, "This's worse than hell."
Its long stout roots all gave a tug
Up came the graves without a clog.
Its mighty trunk on others crashed
And round the wreckage the wind lashed.

Then came a lull—nerves were on edge
The wind seemed shamed of its sacrilege.
All things stood still, all places quiet;
Was that the end—none could say yet.
But when the people's hopes had soared,
The winds unfurled, the thunder roared.
"We do but rest and muster strength
You'll fell our mighty arm at length."
And so again the elements marched
The ground was sodden where once was parched.
Imams called 'Allah', Christians, 'Lord';
On blew the wind by their stouts bored,
Twisting, felling, crashing, breaking,
Tearing, smashing—all destroying.
"Forgive our sins," they cried with tears
They had not called on God for years.

Spent and weary the wind retired,
So did the rain; the clouds were tired.
Behold the sky—already bright
Could one believe it spelt such plight?
But look below—this is no fun,

Ibadan University library.[6] Each begins with a half-page cartoon (drawn by a student named Bodede) and a column of quips and queries called "Sneezy Nosey Wants to Know." Some of the things Sneezy Nosey wanted to know in Soyinka's years as editor were:

—Why people say, "I'm on the level"—as if a level-crossing is not the same as a double-crossing.

—Why we no longer have poached eggs in the mornings. Or have the game-keepers grown too vigilant?

—If the average 'Dynamic' councillor was drunk when he stood elections. Or have students not heard of the Dynamite, who when reminded that a council meeting was in progress said, "Get away! Do you think I have time for nothing else?"—very illustrative of the 'Dynamic' sense of duty.

—Whether every student knows he is first a student before being a noise-maker and when we will save lecturers the energy expended in begging for silence.

—Whether the use of pyjamas on the Bar Beach was that its variegated colours attracted sea-anemones and agamemnones from their beds into the research nets.

—Whether students know it is hitting below the belt to refer disparagingly to a stewards's office when he is getting the better of you in an affably begun argument over the evil effects or otherwise of drinking ice-cold water after hot tea.

—Whether there is not a great gap between a "gentleman" and a gentle man.

—How many students make one Union and how many Unions make one University College.

—How much you enjoy reading the "Eagle."

Soyinka also wrote an editorial column on page two in which he commented on campus affairs. In his first issue he used some of this space to welcome incoming freshmen and to outline the editorial policy of *The Eagle,* which he called "the cleanest paper for reading in this college":

The policy of the paper differs from the others in this, that we believe more in attacking general faults than in putting individuals to ridicule. This does

---

[6] I wish to thank the librarians at the University of Ibadan, particularly Mr. S. O. Oderinde, for assisting me to locate materials in this collection.

not mean that we never attack individuals; we do this when it is necessary, but never vilely or with personal animosity showing in every line of it. We concentrate on trying to raise the general standard of behaviour among students, and at the same time, give them the most interesting articles to read.[7]

In the first two issues he edited, Soyinka remained true to this policy by using his editorial column to scold fellow students for failing to turn up at meetings on time, to thank faculty and staff for giving student hitchhikers lifts to and from campus, to congratulate the Dynamic Party for its decisive students' council election victory, and to reprimand *The Sword,* another campus publication, for indulging in smear tactics against its critics. However, by the time the third issue of *The Eagle* materialized, Soyinka's patience with the antics of some of his peers had been exhausted by a personal incident which he took very seriously and which prompted him to let loose the full fury of his tongue in an editorial entitled "Reptiles." The piece is worth quoting in toto, for it reveals the impassioned rhetoric of which the nineteen-year-old Soyinka was capable:

I hate snakes. I hate all reptiles with a hatred that is born of fear. That is why I'm writing this. That, in fact, is why I have stayed on this term merely to write this Editorial, which is about the only thing I have done in the production of this issue.

I'd rather face an infuriated bull—then, at least, I can see what's coming to me. But a snake, a vile venomous, slimy, disgusting creature who will strike and disappear before you can say "Jumping Rattlesnakes". . . .

Some days ago, a student killed two snakes and a scorpion—all in one night! He was quite amazed, for he hadn't believed that there were so many reptiles in the Campus. How many people think the same way! And that is precisely what makes reptiles so dangerous. Until the last holidays I, too, did not realize that the college had so many of them. But we do! They exist in shirts and trousers, they browse in the library and behave like gentlemen.

When the BISI TAIWO—BOZO gang, hiding under the cloak of anonimity [sic], scored personal hits off the "Embassy" members, several students said it was "Fair Comments." I ask such students if they will still make the same defence for them when they learn that these cowardly

---

[7] *The Eagle* 3, no. 1 (1953): 2.

creatures, or members of the same 'genus,' wrote letters to friends of the Embassy maligning the members most callously, and concocting stories, compared with which Russian propaganda is child's play. These letters, I may add, were written mostly to girl-friends of the Embassy Clubmembers.

I called them snakes. Yes, only a snake's brain could have thought of a description like "wriggling her waist like a wounded snake." I know that BISI TAIWO is a jilted aspirant, as were many of the horrified "Puritans." But surely it was carrying vindictiveness too far, *to write an anonymous letter* to that girl's principal, embellishing and painting luridly an incident at which civilized people would not have batted an eyelid. What did you hope to gain? The credit of having ruined a girl's career by engineering her dismissal from her school?

Contemptible creatures—too mean to be noticed, too dangerous to be ignored! The fountain-heads of morals, uprightness and virtues. Self-imposed judges, most competent, since, being master of all vices, you can smell a little fault one mile off and, what's better, placard it 120 miles toward the Coast. Your cowardice threw the former Editor of "Bug" into disrepute; for a long time he was thought to be the writer of the anonymous letter. Rather than correct the opinion, you encouraged it, because it put you above suspicion.

But I warn you, stop playing with poison gas. We have enough snakes in this college without your belly-crawlers who fawn in public and strike behind.[8]

Vituperation of this sort, however, was rare in *The Eagle*. Most contributions were light-hearted and amusing, even when they were jabs at the absurdities and bad manners of fellow students. Since many of these pieces were anonymous or signed with pseudonyms, it is likely that a good number were written by Soyinka's friends and acquaintances, but he himself set the dominant tone with his editorials, regular columns and numerous witty vignettes and fillers. One can use his signed contributions as a guide to identification of the articles he wrote incognito. Here, for example, is an unsigned anecdote which is characteristic of his playful style:

SORRY PARTNER

Once upon a time, I went to play tennis on the tennis court (some play it on the table, you know.) Well, my partner was just as good a player as

---

[8] *The Eagle* 3, no. 3 (1954): 2.

I—that is, the very worst. He wielded his racket like a blunderbuss and once or twice sent his racket into the football field. That didn't worry me. It was when I saw that he was a confirmed die-hard sorry-partnerer that sweat began to stand out on my forehead like icicles.

I was embarrassed. Why? Because I was playing just as badly as he and there he was, apologising for every bad stroke he played. In vain I assured him that the essence of tennis is not in apologies, but he insisted, and poured out his Sorrys as if he had all the sorrows of Satan in his pocket.

The short of it was that, in the long run, he became so effusive that I took the offensive. Boy oh Boy! Did I sorry-partner him or did I? When, (he standing at the net) I hit the ball into his rudder, I porry-sartnered him. When, attempting to take a fast one, I skated, jitter-bugged and eventually landed on my cusher, I torry-parsnered him before he could open his mouth. When, (a liver fluke it was), he hit a super-tonic one that took our opponent on the kisser, I Tory-gardenered him. (You see, by this time I didn't know what I was talking again.)

Even when he groaned (as he always did when hitting a ball), I sorry-portnered him. I'm telling you that I very-pestered him so ruthlessly that he capitulated and took refuge in a passing car.

That's what to do to them![9]

Also, as far as anonymous poetry is concerned, one would be willing to swear, based on the evidence of "Thunder to Storm," that the following rhymed lines bear all the earmarks of the wild and Wole idiom:

THE BANJO'S BROKEN STRING

A Hall Three disaster
Hapt after siesta.
Ukele Banjo
Woke with the cry, "My Joe!
I'll betcha my last dime
For high tea it's high time."
He went for a quick bath
Gave his tooth a quick bruth—
That is how he said 'brush'
When his tooth had—but s-sh!
His brush played a bad joke
His false tooth in two broke.

---

[9] *The Eagle* 3, no. 1 (1953): 4–5.

The poor lad his tooth eyed,
Said, "Thou wasth my great pride."
He fixed back the top half
To tea went with a loud laugh.

But worse hapt at tea quaff,
The top part too came off.
My lad thought 'twas sugar
Or hardened vinegar,

And being a good Christian,
He swallowed his pride. When
this Banjo was ex-rayed,
This was the report made:—

"Long after a ray-look
Up and down his stommick,
We found his false fangus
In his oesophagus."
Signed—X-Ray Man, Tagus.[10]

Even if these two attributions are incorrect, even if Soyinka never wrote inspired trivia about tennis or teeth, he must be given credit for having encouraged such nonsense in *The Eagle*. The quality of the humor in the three issues he edited was far higher than that in any of the rival campus publications of his day and infinitely superior to what can be found in similar academic publications in Nigeria today. Soyinka was one of the quickest of the campus wits at University College Ibadan in the early fifties, and he earned his reputation as a clever word-monger by making people laugh. He had an antic imagination.

If one wishes to seek clues to his literary opinions at this period, *The Eagle* provides a few rewarding hints, especially in an article entitled "Ten Most Boring Books," which Soyinka had culled from an American magazine. After reporting that a poll of hundreds of editors, booksellers, authors and librarians in America had revealed that Bunyan's *Pilgrim's Progress,* Melville's *Moby Dick,* Milton's *Paradise Lost,* Spenser's *Faerie Queene,* Boswell's *Life of Samuel*

---

[10] Ibid., p. 6.

Johnson, Richardson's *Pamela,* Eliot's *Silas Marner,* Scott's *Ivanhoe,*
Cervantes' *Don Quixote* and Goethe's *Faust* were regarded as the
ten most boring classics of literature, Soyinka added: "A good choice
I would say, except in Scott's *Ivanhoe* and Cervantes' *Don Quixote.*
How the latter in particular was included in the list beats me completely. And evidently those lucky people have never heard New-
man's *Idea of a University*—oh, maybe it isn't a classic."[11]

It is perhaps significant that Soyinka, as a young student, was
turned off by all but the prose chivalric romances on the list. In the
following issue of *The Eagle* he wrote, under the pseudonym "The
Gallant Captain," a mock-heroic poem which spoke of longing for
the old days of King Arthur when it was possible to rescue damsels in
distress with romantic flair.[12] Soyinka, who had written many gallant
articles in defense of "ladies" maligned, heckled or in some way
abused by his peers at the university, may have responded to the
ideals and courtesies of courtly love, even while perhaps adopting a
more down-to-earth approach in his own personal entanglements. As
well as being a humorist, the teen-aged Soyinka appears to have been
a pragmatic romantic.

The importance of *The Eagle* in Soyinka studies is that it gives us
a bird's-eye view of the vitality, creativity and intellectual energy that
animated this extraordinary young man long before he developed
into a full-fledged writer. We can see a sample of what he thought,
what he did and what he wrote at this very formative period in his
life. He once invented this motto for his contributors:

> A plateful of criticism
> With a spice of witticism
> Makes the correct article
> of food for the "Eagle."[13]

One could say that all of Soyinka's creative concoctions have been a

---

[11] *The Eagle* 3, no. 2 (1954): 5.

[12] *The Eagle* 3, no. 3 (1954): 6. This poem is quoted in full in my "Popular Literature for an African Elite," *Journal of Modern African Studies* 12, no. 3 (1974):
471–86.

[13] *The Eagle* 3, no. 2 (1954): 8.

blend of witticism and criticism, but it is clear from reading his earliest writings that over the years the emphasis has gradually shifted from light witticism to heavy criticism. In his youth he could still indulge in innocent laughter.

After leaving for England in 1954, Soyinka appears to have settled down to his studies for a year or two. At least there is no extant published evidence from mid-1954 until 1956 to show that he continued to engage in such extracurricular activities as creative writing and campus polemics while making the initial adjustment to undergraduate life at the University of Leeds.[14] He occasionally composed humorous "Epistles of Cap'n Blood to the Abadinians" which he sent to his friends Pius Oleghe and Ralph Opara, the new editors of *The Eagle* and *The Criterion,* where at least one of these letters was published in 1955; from this sample it is clear that he enjoyed regaling his friends with tall tales about life in the British Isles:

Hallo Ed.,
   I'm sure you must be hoping that I'm dead—and when I say you I mean of course your readers (usually no more than six or seven) who must be glad that I no longer smear the pages of the "Eagle" with my nib. No such luck, I'm afraid. You ought to know I'm pretty hard to kill. Why, only yesterday a car bumped into me and had to be taken to the Scrap-Iron Dealer, while I walked home with no worse damage than some engine-oil on my trousers.
   Well, I suppose that story is as good as any to begin with but I'm sure you never believe it—just because you fellows never believe me when I'm telling you the truth. You'll want to know what I think of England, no doubt. Well, it's a wonderful place to live in. Even the climate is not unbearable. The only thing I quarrel with in the climate is the frequent gales. These gales, you'd better know, don't come once in a grey sun; they come without warning (except when B.B.C. Weather forecast has remarkable luck) and they are strong enough to blow your teeth into your throat. But I must admit to myself that it does me a world of good to watch men and women (the fatter the better) chasing their hats or shawls for a couple of thousand of yards.

---

[14] The record, of course, may be incomplete. It would be interesting to examine student publications from the University of Leeds to see if any contributions by Soyinka can be found there.

Only yesterday I stood at the bus-stop and one of these gales was fool-
ing around just then. Well, a friend of mine came along, and he stretched
out his hand for a handshake. D'you know what happened? The wind
bent his hand gradually backwards, and before he knew where he was,
he was shaking hands with the person standing behind him. If that doesn't
give you an idea of the strength of these "breezes", nothing ever will.[15]

Though Soyinka did not start writing for the stage while he was at
Leeds, Gerald Moore states that some of his early satirical poetry,
such as "The Other Immigrant," was written there before he obtained his B.A. in 1957.[16] What is not generally known is that Soyinka
also wrote a good deal of fiction in his late undergraduate years. In
1956, for example, he was awarded second prize in the Margaret
Wrong Memorial Fund writing competition for a fiction entry
entitled "Oji River."[17] He also published at least two short stories in
a University of Leeds magazine called *The Gryphon* and contributed
another to *New Nigeria Forum,* a Nigerian students' journal based
in London. Since it would take too much space to reproduce these
stories in full, here is a brief synopsis of each.

"Madame Etienne's Establishment," which appeared in the March
1957 issue of *The Gryphon,*[18] is a hilarious Chaucerian tale of sexual
duplicity. Told in the leisurely, familiar style of a witty confidante,
it describes how a clever Parisian madam contrives to marry a fool-
ish provincial barber in order to convert his barbershop into a pros-
perous rural bordello. This is accomplished without the husband ever
realizing what is going on. Persuaded to believe that she has merely
changed the place into a high-class hair dressing salon, he goes off
to his farm each day, leaving all the hairy details of the new business
to his wife and her numerous buxom assistants from the metropole.
The establishment thrives and becomes a major French tourist attraction. Only toward the end of the story does a crisis threaten.

---

15 *The Eagle* 4, no. 2 (1955): 4.

16 Moore, *Wole Soyinka*, p. 6.

17 *West Africa* (13 July 1957), p. 670. Manuscripts submitted for this competition were to be "not less than 7,500 and not more than 15,000 words," according
to *Universitas* 2, no. 1 (December 1955): 3.

18 *The Gryphon* (March 1957), pp. 11–22. I am grateful to Tony Harrison for
bringing this and the following story to my attention.

Monsieur Etienne returns home early one day and finds Petjones, the ex-Mayor of the town, in the waiting room.

"What are you doing here?" demanded Etienne.

"I came for a hair-cut of course," replied the miscreant.

"A hair-cut?" laughed Etienne. "Why, you haven't a hair on your head!"

It was true indeed. Petjones's head shone with the bald brilliance of fifty years' careless living. But at that moment, it also housed a measure of active matter, which was now working furiously, and eventually succeeded in producing the outrageous lie that, "It was a mere slip of the tongue. I really come here every week for a scalp massage. It is meant to make my hair grow again."

Etienne looked at the man and he pitied him. Then he looked at the terrified girls, and he despised them. He looked all round the room, at the expensive furniture, and the plush-carpeted floor. And he smiled bitterly. For he knew at last what vile methods had been used to pay for the luxury.

He had always considered his business and his name impeccable. But now a huge light shone on the rottenness, and he realised at last the dishonesty of the foundation on which his reputation as a hair-dresser had been built. This was what Valeise had meant by her Parisian methods.

He felt disgraced and polluted for ever, and the veins of anger swelled in the muscles of his bull neck.

"Send Madame to me at once," he snapped at the girls. "I shall be waiting for her in her private room."

Soyinka then allows suspense to build up for a few paragraphs while Petjones tries to take French leave of the establishment. Finally there is the climactic confrontation scene:

Monsieur Etienne wasted no time at all when he stood face to face with his wife. He seized her by the shoulders, and the scared and guilty look on her face confirmed the very worst of his suspicions. Valeise gasped with pain and terror as his powerful fingers dug into her flesh and brought her mercenary face within an inch of his own livid countenance:

"Madame," he spat, "Have you thought of what will happen to us when Monsieur Petjones, and the others you have swindled, discover that you have no means of making their hair grow!?"

It was marvelously orchestrated scenes such as this, scenes which swell up magnificently until Soyinka suddenly deflates the melodrama by letting it burst into comedy, that gave evidence of Soyinka's maturing theatrical instincts. He obviously knew how to keep an audience entertained.

Soyinka's next story for *The Gryphon* was a mock fable set in Africa in the early nineteenth century.[19] Entitled "A Tale of Two Cities," it told of court intrigues and missionary conspiracies in the palace of King Kupamiti of Abeolumo. This young king, an early convert to Christianity, had been persuaded by the missionaries to give up four of his five wives and to take on a private tutor named Oddy Summers so future princes and princesses could be instructed in the ways of Western life. One of the first services Summers is called upon to perform for the royal household is to provide secret assistance for Kupamiti's queen who discovers she is barren. Both are aware that this news must be kept from the king lest the queen and Christianity be expelled from the kingdom. Summers carefully arranges for a twin baby discarded by a pagan village to be retrieved from the forest and pronounced the queen's miraculously conceived son. The strategem works, the bastard heir is christened Prince James, the kingdom rejoices and celebrates the immunity from British taxation that this continuation of the royal line ensures, and King Kupamiti and his queen are presented with a special gift from the British crown to commemorate the historic event and to create an indissoluble link between the dynasties of the two nations. The gift is a bed-warming pan.

Soyinka tells this zany tale with characteristic wit and ebullient imagination. Again he opts for amusing rather than instructing his audience.

The third story from this period, published in the *New Nigeria Forum* in May 1958, also had the somewhat incongruous title of "A Tale of Two Cities."[20] It recounts a harrowing episode in the life of Raymond C. Pinkerton, Esq., a young British civil servant assigned to a colonial post in Lagos. To prepare for his stint in Africa, Pinkerton had heated his London apartment to a super-tropical temperature, had borrowed all the books on African travel and adventure

19 *The Gryphon* (Autumn, 1957), pp. 16–22.
20 *New Nigeria Forum* 2 (May 1958): 26–30.

from the municipal library, and had put in long hours at local cinemas watching Tarzan films. After three strenuous weeks of sweating and swotting, he boards the plane exhausted and soon falls asleep while reading yet another true-life adventure about a "mammoth spider which swallowed a whole cow alive and crushed wooden huts with its tentacles." When the plane arrives in Lagos, Pinkerton is still sleeping, and the official who has come to welcome him, thinking he has been overpowered by the heat, quickly conveys him to his flat and puts him to bed. Pinkerton awakes the next morning puzzled, then alarmed, then terrified and panic-stricken to discover that he and his bed are completely surrounded by a gauzy film tapering to a point directly above him.

> . . . his mind went back to the book which he had read on his plane journey. Spiders! African spiders! A spider which would swallow a cow, and crush wooden huts could surely spin such a web as that. Pinkerton began to sweat. His imagination was fired. He could see it all . . . . The dead of night, and the spider stalks into his room, and finds him lying helpless in his bed. Perhaps the monster had just dined and finds a juicy morsel like Pinkerton too large for dessert. So he spins a web round him, intending to return after he has digested his last meal. That could be any moment now!

In a blind and desperate fury Pinkerton flings himself at the web, finds he can't break through, and struggles frantically to disentangle himself from its clinging folds. When he screams for help, an African steward rushes to his aid and quickly extricates him from the spider's terrifying white shroud, which of course turns out to be nothing more than a mosquito net.

Given this evidence of Soyinka's pronounced predilection for merriment, it is not surprising that three of his earliest plays, all of which date from his London years, were comedies—*The Lion and the Jewel*, "The Invention" (an extravagant political satire), and *The Trials of Brother Jero*.[21] Since his career as a neophyte dramatist at

---

[21] Pieterse and Duerden, *African Writers Talking*, pp. 170–74; Moore, *Wole Soyinka*, pp. 7–15; Ricard, *Théâtre et nationalisme*, p. 228; Jones, *Writing of Wole Soyinka*, p. xiii. For a description of "The Invention," see Charles R. Larson, "Soyinka's First Play: 'The Invention,' " *Africa Today* 18, no. 4 (1971): 80–83.

the Royal Court Theatre has already been traced by a number of commentators,[22] let us now turn our attention to his activities in the months following his return to Nigeria early in 1960.

Soyinka leapt back into Nigerian life with gusto. Awarded a fellowship by the Rockefeller Foundation for research on African drama,[23] he was able to buy a Landrover and travel about Western Nigeria with ease. However, he appears to have spent most of his time in Ibadan where he held a position at the university as research fellow in African drama.[24] From this base he made frequent jaunts to Lagos, at times commuting between the two cities almost daily in order to rehearse with those members of his newly formed acting company "The 1960 Masks," who lived in the capital. Gerald Moore and others have sketched in the outlines of this very busy period in Soyinka's life.[25]

What has not been discussed or even mentioned in the literature on Soyinka is his work in Nigerian radio and television in 1960 and 1961). The *Nigerian Radio Times* (later called the *Radio-TV Times*), a program journal of the Nigerian Broadcasting Corporation, provides a gold mine of information on his performances and productions for the electronic media during this period. As early as March 6, 1960, he was on the air participating in a dramatic reading of his first one-act play, "The Swamp Dwellers," which had been performed in London and Ibadan the year before. His program notes for the occasion yield interesting theatrical data. After giving a brief synopsis of the plot and warning listeners that it would be "futile to seek a central character or action" in this "play of mood," Soyinka describes the earlier performances as follows:

---

[22] See especially Moore, *Wole Soyinka,* pp. 7–9, and James Gibbs, "Wole Soyinka: Bio-bibliography," *Africana Library Journal* 3, no. 1 (1972): 15–22.

[23] Moore, *Wole Soyinka,* p. 9. Moore says Soyinka was awarded a "research fellowship which would enable him to travel widely in Nigeria, studying and recording traditional festivals, rituals and masquerades rich in dramatic content," but an account in Nigeria's *Radio Times* (3 July 1960) states, "A grant was made recently by the Rockefeller Foundation to enable 'Wole to make a survey of Nigerian drama in its modern development." It appears that he was studying modern development in traditional theater.

[24] Gibbs, "Wole Soyinka," p. 16.

[25] Moore, *Wole Soyinka,* pp. 14–15; Gibbs, "Wole Soyinka," pp. 15–16.

"The Swamp Dwellers" was first produced in London at the Annual Drama Festival of the National Union of Students on New Year's Eve, 1958. It turned out that there was nothing significant about the date. We called ourselves the Nigeria Drama Group, but this included a Ceylonese (Tamil), two West Indians, an American with a jaw breaking German name, and three Britishers.

We also had some Nigerians. Miss Francesca Pereira was our First Lady of the Stage—listeners here are already acquainted with her talents.

Mr. Jide Ajayi provided unexpected comic inventions with his creation of the part of a goofy drummer, and Banjo Solaru—of "Calling Nigeria" fame— paralysed the audience for five minutes, during our second performance, by giving vent to a subterranean, earthy, odorombustious belch after the cane-brew swilling scene of the play.

It was the briefest but windiest ad-libbing I was ever priviledged [sic] to hear on any stage.[26]

Five months later, in the *TV Times and Radio News,* an entertainment publication spawned by the *Daily Times* of Lagos, there is a report on Soyinka's first television play, which was broadcast on August 6, 1960. This may be the only account available of this still unpublished play:

The Western Nigeria Television organisation reaches a significant milestone on Saturday August 6. On that day (at 8.45 p.m.) WNTV will screen the first full length play produced in their studios in Ibadan. The play entitled "MY FATHER'S BURDEN" was written by the Nigerian playwright, Wole Soyinka and has been produced and directed for television by Segun Olusola, WNTV Producer.

"MY FATHER'S BURDEN" is a human interest drama about the struggle between an idealistic young man and his father whose philosophy of life, in an age where every man tries to grab the most he can, is "live and let others live."

The part of Chief Nwane, the sixty-year-old father, is played by Nigeria's stage and screen star Orlando Martins.

This will be Orlando's first public appearance on the stage since he returned to this country about a year ago after nearly forty-five years abroad.

Chief Nwane is an aristocrat. He is enlightened, influencial [sic] and a former minister of state. He loves his son, Onya, and sees to it that he is

---

26 *Radio Times* (March 1960), p. 5.

well provided for to enter the world. But Chief Nwane is also pompous, proud, authoritative and blunt. . . .

Wole Soyinka, author of the script, assumes, perhaps, the most burden-some role—that of Chuks, ostensibly Onya's friend. Chuks does not know a thing about Onya's character neither are they of the same tempera-ment. He is no more than Onya's drinking companion.[27]

Soyinka wrote at least one other script which has never been printed. This was a play called "The Tortoise" which was broadcast on NBC radio in mid-December 1960 and again in late January 1961. It appears to have been a rather unusual Anansi story. The first account of it in the *Radio Times* states: "The Tortoise in Wole Soyinka's play is different. This Tortoise is in business—big busi-ness. In actual fact, this story is about the days of prospecting. I know nobody will believe that the Tortoise can ever have any saving grace, but this play is about one Tortoise who turned out to have a heart of Gold."[28] A later account gives more details:

In Wole Soyinka's play, the Tortoise appears under the name of Anansi. The change in name or rather the adoption of a pseudonym has not effected any change in character. The Tortoise is always the Tortoise. One would have expected Anansi (The Tortoise) to be a little bit out of his depth with so much (shoot'n) going on. But no sir! Anansi had his own "one shooters" even if he did not use it too often. He did not have to, you see. After all he had got himself interested in research work and by diligently experimenting with all sorts of home-brewed wine, he had dis-covered the most lethal weapon of all—the Anansi Milk-Shake. You may well ask "what on earth is that?" My answer will be "The first ever in-vented homemade bomb," and the recipe is very simple!

In all his exploits, the Tortoise has always had one family or the other as his target. In this play, it is the unfortunate Ajantala family. Yes, the Ajantalas and the Anansi were perpetually feuding. . . . "You can take all your Western badmen and put them together—the Kelly's, Bill and Kid, Cimarron Kid, Jesse James and all other what-nots—and I tell you that none of their exploits will come near the havoc which the Ajan-talas and the Anansi reaked [sic] on one another. Two out of every three murders which were committed in Plateau Dry-Gulch Saloon could be notched on the one-shooters of these two clans."

---

[27] *TV Times and Radio News* (28 July 1960), pp. 12–13.
[28] *Radio Times* (18 December 1960), p. 3.

That was a long time ago. It all happened in Plateau Mining Town
in the days when stories were *not* stories but part of every-day life. In
other words, it happened ONCE UPON A TIME."[29]

Soyinka's first TV drama, "My Father's Burden," may have been intended as a serious work or a "play of mood" similar to "The Swamp
Dwellers," but this mock "Tortoise" from the Wild West obviously
was meant as a free-wheeling farce. Soyinka was back to his old
antics again, trying to corral belly laughs.

The *Radio Times* also makes mention of one other unknown
Soyinka play entitled "The Roots," which was "played during the
British Drama League" in 1959, presumably in London.[30] No further
details are given but one imagines Soyinka must have been active
in the production since he was still in England at that time. Later, on
September 25, 1960, just one week before the ceremonies marking
Nigeria's full political independence, the *Radio Times* announced
a forthcoming radio production of Soyinka's "Camwood on the
Leaves," which had been "specially commissioned by Radio Nigeria
for INDEPENDENCE."[31] This play, broadcast five years later on
the BBC's "African Theatre" program and finally published in
1973,[32] was introduced in program notes by Abiola Irele as having
been "inspired by some traditional Yoruba songs," especially "one
of the best known traditional songs of the Yorubas, 'Agbe'," which
concerns "Camwood (*Osun*), a bright red dye with which the new
child is bathed."[33] These traditional songs apparently were incorpo-
rated in the play without substantial textual modification by Soyinka.

In addition to writing radio and television playscripts, Soyinka was
quite active in 1960 in developing a new series of radio talks called
"Talking through Your Hat."[34] Several of his light-hearted contribu-

---

[29] Ibid. (22 January 1961), p. 7.
[30] Ibid. (3 July 1960), p. 6.
[31] Ibid. (25 September 1960), p. 6. Soyinka mentions this fact in an interview in
Pieterse and Duerden, *African Writers Talking*, p. 171.
[32] See Shirley Cordeaux, "The BBC African Service's Involvement in African
Theatre," *Research in African Literatures* 1 (1970): 153; Soyinka, *Camwood on the
Leaves* (London, 1973).
[33] *Radio Times* (25 September 1960), p. 6.
[34] Ibid. (3 July 1960), p. 6.

tions to this series were later published in the *Radio Times*: first a hilarious medley of parodies on after-dinner speeches as delivered by a patronizing American, a pompous government minister, a long-winded "small-fry" master of ceremonies, and the oldest alumnus in attendance at the Sir Milton Mackenzie Grammar School Eve of Independence Old Boys' Dinner;[35] then an amusing glance at the lives of lorry drivers and their scrapes with the law (a theme to which Soyinka returned in his play *The Road*);[36] next a personal travelogue telling of the wonders of Paris, "land of flesh and bread";[37] and finally an attack on the concept of the "African Personality," which Soyinka found as demeaning to Africans as previous stereotyped notions of the "African mentality."[38] All these topics, even his serious indictment of the shortcomings of the Negritude ideology, were treated comically.

Although writing for radio and television must have kept him quite busy, Soyinka also managed to find sufficient time in his first months home to play a leading role in a University of Ibadan production of *The Good Woman of Setzuan;*[39] to complete the manuscript of *The Trials of Brother Jero*, which had its première performance in Ibadan that same year;[40] to script, produce, direct and act in his most ambitious play, *A Dance of the Forests*, which had been commissioned for the Nigerian Independence Celebrations;[41] and to publish a number of poems and critical essays in *The Horn*, a University of Ibadan poetry magazine founded a few years earlier by J. P. Clark and Martin Banham.[42]

Soyinka was a regular contributor to *The Horn* between 1960 and 1962. Among his poems dating from this period are two dealing

---

[35] Ibid. (11 September 1960), p. 7.

[36] Ibid. (18 September 1960), p. 7.

[37] Ibid. (4 December 1960), pp. 6–7.

[38] Ibid. (22 January 1961), pp. 6–7.

[39] *Ibadan* 9 (1960): 20; Moore, *Wole Soyinka*, p. 15.

[40] Ibid.

[41] Moore, *Wole Soyinka*, p. 15; Gibbs, "Wole Soyinka," pp. 16–17. Reviews of the performance can be found in *Ibadan* 10 (1960): 30–32, and *African Horizon* 2 (January 1961): 8-11. Moore said it was *Caucasian Chalk Circle*, also by Brecht.

[42] For a history of this magazine, see W. H. Stevenson's article in a forthcoming issue of *Research in African Literatures*.

with aspects of the theater, "Stage" and "Audience to Performer,"
one written in pidgin English, "Okonjo de Hunter," one entitled
"epitaph for Say Tokyo Kid" (a driver and captain of thugs who re-
appears later as a character in *The Road*), as well as the earliest
printed versions of his now famous "Season" and "Death in the
Dawn."[43] His major critical contribution to *The Horn* was a 1960
essay "The Future of West African Writing,"[44] in which he argued
that the real mark of authenticity in African writing was indifferent
self-acceptance rather than energetic racial self-assertion. Early African writing, he claimed, was dishonest because it either imitated
literary fashions in Europe or pandered to European demands and
expectations for the exotic and primitive. The first West African
writer to produce truly African literature was not Léopold Senghor
but Chinua Achebe:

> The significance of Chinua Achebe is the evolvement, in West African
> writing, of the seemingly indifferent acceptance. And this, I believe is the
> turning point in our literary development. It is also a fortunate accident
> of timing, because of the inherently invalid doctrine of "negritude."
> Leopold Senghor, to name a blatant example. And if we would speak of
> "negritude" in a more acceptable broader sense, Chinua Achebe is a
> more "African" writer than Senghor. The duiker will not paint "duiker"
> on his beautiful back to proclaim his duikeritude; you'll know him by his
> elegant leap. The less self-conscious the African is, and the more innately
> his individual qualities appear in his writing, the more seriously he will be
> taken as an artist of exciting dignity.

Soyinka's famous put-down of Negritude ("a tiger does not have to
proclaim his tigritude") apparently originated in this remark on the
duiker and duikeritude, of which it must have been a perversion,
tigers being no more indigenous to Africa than surrealist French

---

[43] "Stage," *The Horn* 4, no. 1 (1960): 1; "Audience to Performer," *The Horn* 4,
no. 1 (1960): 4; "Proverb: Okonjo de Hunter," *The Horn* 3, no. 3 (1960): 6–7;
"epitaph for Say Tokyo Kid," *The Horn* 4, no. 5 (1962): 10–11; "Season," *The Horn*
4, no. 2 (1961): 2; "Death in the Dawn," *The Horn* 4, no. 6 (1962): 2–3. Other poems
of his in this magazine are "Poisoners of the World, Unite," *The Horn* 3, no. 3
(1960): 4–5, 9, and "Committee Man," *The Horn* 4, no. 3 (1961): 10–11.

[44] *The Horn* 4, no. 1 (1960): 10–16.

poetry.[45] In any case, this early articulation of Soyinka's artistic credo is interesting when placed beside the creative writing he was doing at this period in his career. In his serious works Soyinka evidently aspired to create authentic African art of "exciting dignity." His aesthetic philosophy was based on total acceptance of his Africanness.

Soyinka's impressive literary and dramatic accomplishments in London and Ibadan soon won him a measure of recognition in Nigeria. In March 1961, after he had been back home only a year, the twenty-six-year-old author was made the subject of an illustrated feature article in *Drum,* probably the leading African popular magazine in Nigeria in those days. The headline read "Young Dramatist Is Earning the Title of Nigeria's Bernard Shaw."[46] The comparison was apt, probably more apt and more prophetic than the journalist who made it could have realized, for Soyinka hadn't yet displayed some of his most Shavian qualities. He was known primarily as a humorist, a public entertainer, a campus wit, a high-spirited clown. And he was known almost exclusively in his homeland, where he addressed his own people through the most popular of the public media—theater, radio, television and, much less often, print. It was not until 1963, when his first three books were published (two of them in England) that he became—instantly and forever—one of the most important writers in the English-speaking world.

---

[45] Janheinz Jahn quotes Soyinka's later elaboration of this concept at a conference in Berlin in 1964 in his *History of Neo-African Literature: Writing in Two Continents* (London, 1966), pp. 265–66.

[46] *Drum* (March 1961), p. 27.

Tradition and the Yoruba Writer: D. O. Fagunwa, Amos Tutuola and Wole Soyinka[1]

ABIOLA IRELE

I

THE TITLE of this paper is a deliberate echo of that of one of the most celebrated of T. S. Eliot's essays, namely, 'Tradition and the Individual Talent'. In that essay, Eliot defined the relationship of the European writer to the entire literary tradition of European civilization, and sought to clarify the manner in which the work of the significant new talent coheres, as it were, with that tradition and creates a new pattern of meaning within its total framework. Eliot's idea offers, I believe, an extremely profitable perspective for a comprehensive view of European literature not merely with respect to its historical development, but also, and perhaps primarily, with respect to its essential spirit. But what strikes one as significant about this essay is the original understanding which it offers of the meaning of 'tradition'—as not so much an abiding, permanent, immutable stock of beliefs and symbols, but as the constant refinement and extension of these in a way which relates them to an experience that is felt as being at once continuous and significantly new.

I have taken Eliot's idea as my point of departure here because of what I believe to be its immediate relevance to a consideration of the literary situation in Africa in our times. It is my personal belief that what gives a special character to literary creation in Africa today is the movement to establish and to maintain the sense of tradition, the sense that Eliot gives to the word. The essential direction of modern African writing, of the work of the truly significant writers, is towards the definition, in and through literature, of a distinctive mode of thought and feeling, towards an imaginative apprehension and embodiment of an African spirit. And the main motive power in this movement, proceeds from the endeavour of the African writers to work out a new spiritual coherence out of the historical disconnection between their African heritage and their modern experience. In no other area of Africa is the current along which this elaboration in literature of a continuous stream of the collective consciousness from the traditional to the modern so clearly evident, and so well marked out, as in Yorubaland. For while it is true to say that, in other parts of Africa, the writer has been aware of the compelling reality and importance of the essential structure of traditional patterns of life for his experience and for his artistic expression, and has sought either a thematic or formal integration of his work to the specific mode of literary expression which has been associated with these traditional patterns of life, it is only among Yorùbá writers that, to my knowledge,

45

the various levels of this transition from the traditional to the modern
can be illustrated to bring out its full implications. In Yorubaland
we have the extraordinary situation where the vast folk literature,
alive and vigorously contemporary, remains available to provide a
constant support for new forms—for the literate culture developing
within the language itself as a result of its reduction to writing, as
well as for the new popular arts that sociological factors have brought
into being, particularly the so-called 'folk opera'; and beyond these,
to provide a source for the new literature in English, the language
through which the modern technological world made its entry into
the awareness of Yorùbá people and constituted itself part of their
mental universe.

Perhaps the most remarkable feature of the evolution of Yorùbá
culture over the past century or so has been the way in which it has
been able to afford a stable institutional and spiritual groundwork for
the transformation of collective life and feeling for the individual
within this culture, at the critical moment when Western civilization
introduced an element of tension into African societies. Yorùbá culture
has played an integrative role in the process of acculturation which
all African societies have undergone, in such a way that this process
can be seen today as one largely of adaptation, the adjustment of the
native culture with the foreign, the harmonization of two ways of life
into a new entity.

The integrative role of Yorùbá culture in the situation of contact
created by the advent of Western culture is fully reflected in the work
of the Yorùbá writer, not only at the level of content analysis of individual works, which reveals the direct working-out of the process,
but more significantly in the pattern of evolution established by the
inter-connections between the various levels of literary expression in
Yorubaland. It is in this perspective that I would now like to discuss
the theme I have chosen, by reference, to the work of three outstanding
Yorùbá writers, D. O. Fagunwa, Amos Tutuọla, and Wọle Ṣoyinka.
If I have chosen these three, it is because of the intimate relationship
that exists in their work not only by their derivation from a common
back-cloth (to echo Ṣoyinka himself) but also through the active
influences at work from one writer to another all along the line of
development which can be seen running through their writings.

II

The death of D. O. Fagunwa on the very day on which his article
on vernacular literature appeared in one of the Nigerian dailies (December, 1963) is surely one of the most tragic coincidences in literary
history. By an obscure irony of fate, this writer, whose work was
steeped in the mystical world of Yorùbá folklore, seemed to have felt
a premonition of his departure, and to have wanted to leave behind a

final testament of the faith in his vocation which animated his literary career.

But not only his end, his whole career now appears as an irony. While his works enjoyed an immense popularity among the Yorùbá public as evidenced by the publication history of his novels, each one of which has been reprinted no less than ten times, he does not seem to have attracted until very recently the kind of serious attention that lesser writers working in English have had. Even now, the recognition that he is beginning to get as a writer is a grudging one. There is interest in him as a vague fore-runner of Tutuọla, and in a mention of this connection, in his *History of Neo-African Literature,* Janheinz Jahn is able to affirm confidently: 'Tutuọla's source, everyone agrees, is the oral Yorùbá tradition, and he is closer to it than the author Fagunwa, who wrote in the Yorùbá language and influenced him' (p. 23). In an earlier article by Beier, from which Jahn probably derived his impression, we read, after an analysis of a passage of Fagunwa, this surprising comment: 'It is in passages like this that Fagunwa is closest to Tutuọla. *The Palm Wine Drinkard* and *My Life in the Bush of Ghosts* abound with descriptions like this, and they may well have been influenced by Fagunwa'. (*Introduction to African Literature,* p. 191). The whole tone of that comment, as of the article itself, suggests that Beier was concerned primarily with pointing out the achievement of Fagunwa, while taking care to safeguard the foreign reputation of Amos Tutuọla. But the ultimate injustice to the memory of Fagunwa and to the nature of his achievement comes however from his own publishers who seem to have appreciated his value as a source of profitable business rather than as a writer in his own right. In the translation of Fagunwa's novel, *Ogboju Ọdẹ*, prepared by Wọle Ṣoyinka and published by Nelson, the title page and blurb are designed to relegate Fagunwa into the backdrop as much as possible, and to bring the translator into focus; obviously, Nelson are more interested in having Ṣoyinka on their list (with the prospect of good sales that this entails) than in giving the wider world a taste of Fagunwa's creative genius. The cynical attitude of Fagunwa's original publishers with regard to his work is seen at its height in one advertisement of Ṣoyinka's translation I have seen in which they have gone as far as to suppress Fagunwa's name altogether.

I have insisted at this length on Fagunwa's fate at the hands of critics and of his own publishers not simply to give vent to personal indignation, but rather, to make a point which needs to be vehemently made, that his work stands at the head of creative writing in the Yorùbá language and exerts the most pervasive influence on every category of Yorùbá literary expression; to highlight the extreme importance of a proper and serious consideration of his work in the development of a new tradition of Yorùbá literary expression.

The achievement of Fagunwa has been by all accounts a remarkable one. He responded early to the need for a literature in the vernacular, at a moment when a new cultural consciousness began to emerge out of changing social conditions. His work appeared at the appropriate phase in the development of the language itself, from a purely oral to a written one. With about a hundred years of work already expended upon the task of devising a graphic form for the language, and thus giving it, as it were, a more stable character, Fagunwa arrived to consolidate the work already done by furnishing the language with a literature in the secondary (literal) sense of the word—by translating the oral tradition into a written form, and laying the basis for its transformation into a literate culture. In the sense that he was the first to make a new and significant literature of the language, to have given the oral tradition an *extended* literary form, he was a pioneer.

But the term 'pioneer' is inadequate to describe Fagunwa, a writer who was nothing less than a complete artist and indeed a master in his own full and independent right. In an original situation such as that of Fagunwa, it is especially important to consider the exact nature of the relationship between the work of the writer and the particular context in which it occurs, and from this point of view, the achievement of Fagunwa in creating a new literature within the Yorùbá language must be taken as being indeed a considerable one. But beyond this simple fact of Fagunwa's originality, his work needs to be measured in terms of its coherence as a whole, and of the levels of meaning revealed by his use of language, and in this light, he appears to be more than the simple initiator of a forward movement in the development of Yorùbá literature. He is indeed the creator of a particular insight into life. In his work, Fagunwa did more than give new life and effect to the oral tradition which he inherited from his culture; he also created out of the communal material it offered him a distinct personal statement in artistic terms upon the issues of human life.

Thus it would be a grave error to dismiss his work as simple fantasies, or more serious, as naive childish productions. On the contrary, there is maturity of expression and of vision in his work which is as fully adult as the most modern novel, and a seriousness of purpose which fully engages the imagination and the intelligence. For the primary element in the achievement of Fagunwa was the way in which he was able to fill out the restricted outline of the folk tale and to give it the dimension of a developed narrative form, which retains its essence—its allegorical and symbolic quality—while giving it an enduring relevance. This new and original medium one can only call, for want of a better term, the 'mythic novel'.

The novels of Fagunwa are constructed in relation not only to a definite cosmology. His narrative technique flows directly out of the oral tradition; at the same time, it is evident that he strove, even with noticeable strain, to get beyond the limitations of the tradition in the context of an extended literary medium. What Fagunwa has sought in each of his novels is to create a unified sequence rather than a juxtaposition of motifs from the Yorùbá narrative tradition. Indeed, in the series of adventures that make up the narrative scheme of each novel, it is not so much a question of the author putting together separate, recognisable motifs into a sequence as his drawing upon the raw materials in the tradition to create a single extended narrative. There is a genuine attempt at a more elaborate construction of situation, and a certain measure of concern for realising character more fully than in the folk tales. Both his human and super-natural characters are endowed with life, and clearly individualised in such a way that their actions, though proceeding from moral or spiritual attributes that are given at the outset rather than developed, assume that measure of interest necessary to engage the reader. Thus, in *Igbo Olodumare*, the formidable spirit, Eṣù-Kékeré-òde, with which the hunter Olówó-Aiyé has to wrestle, is so vividly realised that the outcome of the contest becomes important for the reader. Moreover, an attempt to give a central unity to the conception of character is apparent in the link between Akàrà Ogùn and Olowo-Aiyé, (the central figures respectively in the first two novels, *Ogboju-Ọdẹ* and *Igbo Olodumare*), who are both hunters of the same family. Above all, in making the transition from the oral tradition to a written literature, Fagunwa brought into play his considerable descriptive power in order to give the necessary imaginative scope to the situations he creates and to sustain his narratives. The opening pages of *Igbo Olodumare* represent a remarkable example of this aspect of his art.

This last observation points at once to what remains the most striking merit of Fagunwa's art—his way with language. He possessed the Yorùbá language to a high degree and employed it with intimate mastery. The tone of his language, as has already been observed, is that of oral narrative which not only gives to his writing an immediate freshness, but reinforced by the use of imagery, contributes to what Wọle Ṣoyinka has called Fagunwa's 'vivid sense of event'. The various shades of living speech give full value to the style of the author who draws the most surprising effects from the structure of the language itself. Repetition, balance of tonal forms, word building, and sustained phrasing in whole passages build up in his works a distinctive idiom in which Fagunwa's personal feeling for language and the rhetoric of Yorùbá oral literature have become intimately fused. Thus, what is significant about his personal use of language is his resourceful exploitation of the communal medium and his ultimate fidelity to its nature, his individual illustration of its peculiar blend of exuberance and gravity.

It should become clear that a consideration of Fagunwa's narrative

technique and use of language provide a lead into the profound meaning of his work as a whole. His language in particular expresses an
attitude, which reveals itself in these novels in the extra-ordinary
sense of humour with which he treats his subject matter. The atmosphere in each novel despite its 'ghostly' character, is constantly
lightened by touches of warm, familiar humour; the most grisly
character is damned from the outset by a laughable name, the most
harrowing situation relieved by some comic interlude. The lightness
of touch confers a certain emotional ease not only to the individual
situations but to the whole narrative train, so that the mind moves
freely in the world of Fagunwa's novels.

This quality of Fagunwa's work is not without significance. For
the humour, the apparent lightness of the imaginative discourse in his
novels are an inherent part of their moral purpose. It is not simply
in the didactic strain of these novels—which in itself constitutes a
value for the Yorùbá—that this significance must be sought, but
rather in the total world view which the novels reveal. Fagunwa's
work reflects a vision of man and his place in the universe. This is
admittedly not a deliberately worked out and consciously articulated
structuring of his novels, but something inherent in their symbolic
scheme and resonance, and which derives ultimately from the culture
that stands as the foundation of his individual imaginative world.

The most obvious characteristic of Fagunwa's world is its fusion
into a comprehensive theatre of human drama of the natural and supernatural realms. His characters exist and move within an imaginative
frame-work whose frontiers are wider and more extensive than that
of the conventional, realistic novel, a universe in which the 'normal'
barriers between the physical and the spiritual world have been dis-
solved. He has created the universe of his novels directly out of the
African, and specifically Yorùbá conception which sees the supernatural not merely as a prolongation of the natural world, but as co-
existing actively with it. Given such a cosmology, the role of the
traditional artist has consisted in transposing the real world in his
work in such a way as to reveal its essential connection with the unseen,
in giving to the everyday and the finite the quality of the numinous
and infinite.

The special position of Fagunwa in this respect is that while his
work relates to this tradition, his art goes beyond it by giving a freshness to the old materials with which it was carried on. His knowledge
of Yorùbá life and customs, combined with the particular effect of
his descriptive and narrative power, gives vividness to the settings of
his novels and lend a strange and compelling quality of truth to his
evocations. The world of spirits, the realm of fantasy, is made familiar
and alive, because it proceeds, in these novels, from an individual
understanding of human life and of the varied moral situations in

which it takes place. It is this element in Fagunwa's art, the continuous extension of human fate and responsibility beyond the confines of the immediate social world into the spiritual, which lends to his work its total impact.

The significance of his work is thus inherent in the symbolic framework and connotations of his novels. A simple but valid interpretation of the pattern of situation in his novels suggests that his forest stands for the universe, inhabited by obscure forces to which man stands in a dynamic moral and spiritual relationship and with which his destiny is involved; in short, a mythical representation of the existential condition of man as expressed in Yorùbá thinking. The tremendous adventure of existence in which man is engaged is dramatised by the adventures of Fagunwa's hunters, who go through trials and dangers in which they must justify and affirm their human essence.

The very choice of the hunter as the central figure in Fagunwa's principal novels and in the human scheme of his narratives is of great importance, for the hunter represents the ideal of manhood in traditional Yorùbá society. There is a real sense in which the hunter can be said to be a 'given' hero in the Yorùbá imagination, as exemplified not only in numerous folk tales, but especially in the *ijálá* poetry, the themes of which are specifically organised in relation to the hunter's perception of the world of nature, and which express the particular ideal that he pursues: the unique combination of physical and spiritual energy that is the privilege of man in the universal order, and which the traditional image of the hunter represents in the highest degree.

There is, then, a humanist vision of a special kind inherent in the symbolic foundation of Fagunwa's novels. They express a sharp awareness of the necessity implied by man's precarious existence for an active confrontation of the world, as well as a triumphant affirmation of man's central place in the entire scheme of creation. It is to this attitude that Olowo Aiyé gives expression in a passage from *Igbo Olodumare*:

> ẹbọra ti o ba fi oju di mi, yio ma ti ọrun de ọrun, emi ọkunrin ni mo wi bẹ, oni ni ng o sọ fun ẹyin ẹbọra Igbo Olodumare wipe, nigbati Ẹlẹda da ohun gbogbo ti mbẹ ninu aiye tan, o fi enia ṣe olori gbogbo wọn. (p. 16)

> (Take care, you daemons, that none of you show defiance towards me, lest he spend his days wandering without rest through the spheres. Daemons of the forest of Olodumare, hear this today from a man, that when the Creator created everything in the universe, He placed man as master over all.)

It needs to be emphasised that we are dealing here not with an influence from an outside source—that Fagunwa's humanism is not

Western or Christian—but that this is an element that proceeds
directly from the very structure of the imaginative tradition from
which his work derives. Contrary to the theories that anthropologists
have peddled, depicting the traditional African as so saddled with
the weight of his existence as to be crushed by it and therefore inclined
to a passive attitude to the universe, the cosmologies of the different
African cultures reveal an intelligence of the world centred upon the
privileged position of man, an imaginative and symbolic organisation
of the world not simply in human terms, but in a comprehensive
relation to man.

For the Yorùbá, the balance of human life, the very sense of human
existence, consists in the dynamic correlation of individual responsibility and the pressure of external events and forces. In the oral
literature, the understanding that human fate is as much a matter
of chance as of conscious moral choice is what determines its social
function—their illustration of the moral and spiritual attributes
needed by the individual to wrest a human meaning out of his life.
In the folk tale, in particular, the imagination is led precisely towards
a vision of the world that privileges the part of human will and responsibility, and by the same token reduces the force of the arbitrary and
the hazardous. It is this element of the folk tradition that is so vividly
drawn out by Fagunwa in his novels. The trials and terrors, the
forces that his heroes confront in their adventures set off on the one
hand the fragility of man, but on the other, by an ironic reversal,
emphasise the very strength of his moral and spiritual resources
through which he triumphs over nature.

When the testamental import of these novels is grasped, the relevance of Fagunwa's fantastic world becomes clear. Our very notion
of fantasy as opposed to reality undergoes a drastic revision, and we
are in a position to understand more adequately the nature of Fagunwa's
art, and to enter more fully into his world. We cannot then demand
from him a narrow realism, either in his theme or in his construction
of character. His imagination is operating at a more profound and
more fundamental level than that of the realistic novel. It is on this
account that one would reject as too narrow the criticism made by
Ayọ Bamgboṣe, that Fagunwa does not develop the psychology of his
characters. [2] Psychology in relation to character belongs to the 19th
century European novel, and has even now been abandoned by the
modern writer, in favour of a probing of the deeper layers of the
human consciousness. It is the work of Kafka, not Flaubert, that is
most representative of the creative development that is responsible
for the peculiar strength of the European novel today: the withdrawal
from a surface exploration of human motivations and their implication in social issues to a more comprehensive and more fundamental
concern with the total spiritual atmosphere in which the human

condition itself is shrouded. The spirits and figures that inhabit Fagunwa's forest and cross paths with his strong willed hunters (Ogboju ọdẹ), are clearly projections of the terrors and obsessions that have haunted the imagination and consciousness of man from the beginning of time, and which remain the active characters of the collective dream of humanity. To this dream of mankind, Fagunwa gives a localisation within Yorùbá culture. More than this, he has invested it with a direct immediacy in his individual transformation of its elements within his personal vision.

Fagunwa's work belongs then to the great tradition of allegorical and symbolic literature, set within the framework of a particular complex of cultural references. His achievement resides in his creation of a form in which the Yorùbá imaginative tradition can be given a translation in modern terms, and in the process acquire new vitality. It is this achievement that lies directly behind the work of Amos Tutuọla who exploited the medium of expression forged by Fagunwa and, because he wrote in English, thereby won international acclaim.

III

There is a great amount of misunderstanding involved in the reputation that Tutuọla has enjoyed outside Nigeria, and especially in Western countries. It was thought that he had created a new form of expression, a new kind of novel, whereas in fact, as has been shown, he merely took over a form developed out of the folk tradition to a new level of expressiveness by Fagunwa. It was even imagined that the universe of his narratives bore some kind of relationships to that which the Surrealists, each in his own way, sought to evoke from the subliminal reaches of the individual consciousness. His limitations with regard to the English language in which he expressed his works were also valorised. I suspect myself that on this point, an element of prejudice was combined in a number of cases with ignorance: one commentator for example welcomed the English of Tutuọla as a welcome change from what he considered the 'pretentious' rhetoric of his more thoroughly Westernised compatriots, as if there was necessarily merit in doing violence to English, and a corresponding demerit in using that language with an acceptable measure of competence! In short, Tutuọla has been admired for his 'quaintness', for the apparent ingenuousness of his style and of the content of his novels.

Now, quaintness, as such, is not and cannot be a value. To make matters even clearer, we must go further and say that on the specific point of language, the limitations of Tutuọla are limitations and constitute a real barrier, sometimes even a formidable one, both for him as an artist, and for his readers. Tutuọla obviously does not dominate his linguistic medium and there is no use pretending that this is an advantage. The truth is that we arrive at an appreciation of Tutuọla's genuine merit, *in spite of* his imperfect handling of English, not because of it.

It is clearly useless to speculate at this stage what the exact nature of Tutuọla's work would have been like, and what his standing, if he had chosen to write in Yorùbá rather than in English. There is however no question that the Yorùbá language lies much nearer the heart of his inspiration and of his sensibility than English, and one cannot help feeling that it would have been preferable if he had written his works in the language that came most easily to him and most naturally, as it were, to his material. The very pressure of the Yorùbá language upon the peculiar idiom which Tutuọla wrung out of the English language may have a fascination for some of his foreign readers, but it is not, to my mind, a satisfactorily creative tension between the two languages that it produces, but rather an imbalance, and a resultant break between the content of his work and its medium of expression which must be considered a serious shortcoming.

There is nothing to wonder at therefore in the poor and often hostile reception which his work has received in Nigeria, especially among literate Yorùbá. This is something that has surprised and worried Tutuọla's foreign admirers. A good part of this reception has admittedly been obtuse, but a little reflection and some understanding of the cultural context in which Tutuọla's work has been received at this end is enough to show that the sudden acclaim showered on Tutuọla could not but make little impression upon a public long familiar with the works of Fagunwa—in other words, with the original thing, presented in the singular felicities of Fagunwa's handling of Yorùbá. It needs to be said and recognised that the shift from Fagunwa in Yorùbá to Tutuọla in English cannot but represent, at least at the first flush, a disappointing experience for the Yorùbá-speaking reader familiar with the work of Fagunwa so that it needs closer attention to arrive at a response to the writings of Tutuọla adequate to his peculiar genius. The temptation to disregard the many pointers to this genius, and thus to miss the true value of his work, is made all the stronger not only by the divorce of the material from its original setting by Tutuọla's use of English but indeed by the very peculiarities of this English which tend to obscure the real qualities and the strength of Tutuọla's imagination. It is but a short step from the initial disappointment to the conclusion that, set beside Fagunwa, Tutuọla is nothing but a poor imitator, an inferior artist who has taken advantage of the historical prestige of English to overshadow the creator and master of the new Yorùbá novel.

This view of the relationship between Fagunwa and Tutuọla is not without a certain element of truth. It is clear that much of the praise and acclaim that have been lavished upon Tutuọla belong more properly to Fagunwa who provided not only the original inspiration but indeed a good measure of the material for Tutuọla's novels. The echoes of Fagunwa in Tutuọla's work are numerous enough to indicate that the latter was consciously creating from a model provided by the former. In some cases, these echoes have the sound of straight-forward transcriptions, not to say plagiarisms. But having said this, it is important to make the only point that seems to me to be significant in the current examination of Tutuọla's debt of Fagunwa, that despite its derivation from the work of Fagunwa, Tutuọla's work achieves an independent status that it owes essentially to the force of his individual genius. The development that he has given to the form he took over from the earlier writer has the character of a brilliant confirmation. It is pertinent here to observe that a writer's use of a medium created before him is of course the most normal thing in literary history—the very essence of the continuity of a literary tradition resides in the passing of forms and means of expression from one writer to another in successive generations. There is thus no disparagement of Tutuọla's achievement implied in pointing out the immediate derivation of his work from that of Fagunwa. It would indeed have been to Tutuọla's advantage if this connection had been discovered earlier, and when subsequently noticed, more overtly acknowledged. This omission in Beier's considerations of the two writers appears to me particularly regrettable, for a more rigorous examination which insisted upon this connection would have brought out the special vigour of Tutuọla's imagination, its considerable sharpness, as it is inscribed within the mythical framework in which, after Fagunwa, he too operates. The point then is that Tutuọla needs to have his case more scrupulously made for him by the critic. For the fact that needs to be made more evident is that Tutuọla possesses a power of the imagination which breaks though the limitations of his language and which, properly considered, compels our adhesion to his vision and our recognition of him as an original artist.

Tutuọla has been discussed enough by comeptent critics to save me the labour of going over his work, and it would appear to me sufficient to indicate here his particular contribution to the Yorùbá narrative tradition within the perspective I have adopted for this discussion. The distinction of Tutuọla, as Gerald Moore has observed, resides in his visionary powers. [3] The Orphic significance which Moore has drawn out of his writing is indeed important, and it is useful to observe that it lies at the end of the high road of myth which his imagination, at one in this respect with that of his culture, traverses with such zest and assurance. But its importance also arises from the fact that it is the dominant element in the individual apprehension of Tutuọla the artist and not, as is the case with Fagunwa, in the indivi-dual expression of a collective consciousness. The difference I am making between the two writers may perhaps appear a specious one,

particularly to readers who have a direct acquaintance with Fagunwa
in the original. But I believe it to be real, and that it is fair to say that
where Fagunwa achieves a personal reorganisation of the traditional
material, and is thus able to put his stamp on this material in his own
writings—aided especially by his gift of language—one feels that with
Tutuọla, there is a total *reliving* of the collective myth within the
individual consciousness. The artist is here at the very center of his
material and of the experience that it communicates. It is not so
much a matter of authenticity, of a literal fidelity to the details of the
tradition, as of the degree to which the artist has assumed the tradition
and so interiorised its elements, its very spirit, as to bring to it, in his
own work, a new and original dimension.

It is perhaps possible to articulate this impression that one receives
from Tutuọla's novels in a more precise way by pointing to the imagery that he employs. The most cursory study of his works shows the
constant recurrence of images built upon the play of light through
the entire range of the colour spectrum. His imagination can indeed
be qualified as being characteristically luminous, for his visual imagery
constantly communicates a sense of brilliant intensity for which the
only parallels one can think of in modern African literature belong to
the work of Senghor and Okigbo. One can point for example to a
passage such as the following from *The Palm Wine Drinkard* to illustrate this special quality of Tutuọla's imagery and its peculiar
fascination:

> She was the Red-smaller-tree who was at the front of the bigger
> Red-tree, and the bigger Red-tree was the Red-king of the Red-
> people of Red-town and the Red-bush and also the Red-leaves on
> the bigger Red-tree were the Red-people of the Red-town in the
> Red-bush.

The 'Television-handed ghostess' of *My life in the bush of Ghosts*
affords another memorable example, among many others, of this
constant engagement of Tutuọla's perceptions and sensibility with
the phenomenon of light.

Tutuọla's imagery suggests the nature of his experience and gives
an indication of the temper of his imagination. His vision is that of a
dreamer, in the sense in which Eliot described Dante as a dreamer;
that is, of a seer of visions. The imagery reflects an unusual capacity
for perceiving and realising in concretely sensous terms a certain
order of experience that lies beyond the range of the ordinarily 'visible'.
And in this ability to give body to the fruits of his unusually productive
imagination, Tutuọla also displays the multiple facets of a sensitivity
keenly attuned to the marvellous and the mysterious.

Tutuọla cannot be considered a mystic in the ordinary Western
understanding of the word because although his visions are personal,

they do not involve a withdrawal from the world, but, on the contrary, in terms of the culture in which his mind functions, a more active involvement with that scheme of reality that binds the everyday to the extra-ordinary in a lively reciprocity. The faculty that generates the kind of events that we meet with in Tutuọla's work is one that is favoured and in specific cases cultivated in the environment which has shaped his mind, so that we can accept Tutuọla's testimony that he set down these events in his books in the order in which he saw them—that his visions are, in truth, *literal*. His novels prolong, in the clearer perspective afforded by art, a feature of the culture to which he belongs that stands out as a norm.

The heightened capacity for vision in this primary sense also accounts for that other aspect of Tutuọla's imagination that impresses itself upon our attention, what one might term its expansiveness. Tutuọla's imagination is not only 'outsize', it tends towards a constant comprehensiveness; it seizes with energy upon any aspect of experience within its range in order to integrate it into the particular tenacity of feeling determined by its own mode of apprehension. There is a cumulative effect in Tutuọla's way with imagery which is akin to the manner of much of African music, which often progresses by an insistent building up of tension. The inner intensity of seeing in the individual progression of his images derives from the extreme precision with which they reveal themselves, and combine with an outer expansiveness to create that impression of a living variousness that we get from his works. There is at work in the densely packed atmosphere of his narratives an unrestricted play of the imagination and at the same time a strong sense of artistic involvement, a deep identification on the part of the writer with the products of his imagining spirit. Tutuọla's individuality resides in this constant movement of his own mind, in this fundamental response of his own creative spirit, to the whole expanse of his imagined universe as it presents itself in his novels.

It is this keen participation by Tutuọla in his own evocations that seems to me to set him off from Fagunwa. In all Fagunwa's stories, a distance seems to separate the characters and events that he presents from the deepest feelings of the author himself. This impression of a dissociation between the narrative content and the writer's response is reinforced by Fagunwa's habit of didactic reflections and constant asides to his audience. The result is that the world Fagunwa presents, despite its vivid realisation, acquires a certain objectivity and the drama that he depicts a certain explicitness whose meaning seems to stand apart from any activity of his own artistic consciousness upon his material. With Tutuọla, on the other hand, we get the impression that he is himself the hero of his own stories, and we feel that they relate primarily to his own immediate sense of humanity and proceed from his own immeasurable appetite for experience rather than from a more general social and moral awareness. There is thus a sense in which one can speak of a contemplative quality that is implicit and immediate in Tutuọla's evocations, and which goes deeper into the spirit of the mythical language which he employs than the works of Fagunwa. In other words, the heroic implication of the traditional mythical vision that informs Fagunwa's work finds in Tutuọla's development the kind of concrete and fully felt realisation that was necessary to give it a new artistic dimension. In his exploration of the governing symbols that translate the Yorùbá perception of the forces that are active in the life of humanity, Tutuọla does not merely provide the general framework of an allegory in which the essential tensions of human life are more or less explicitly denoted, but in the fuller penetration of his creating mind into the very texture of these symbols, restores for us a sense of the fluid connotations that wrap round their central meaning.

Tutuọla's experience, then, is very personal, and his vision particularised; nonetheless, the elements that furnish the substance of his writings derive in a recognisable way from his culture. His work relates in a much freer and more dynamic way to the Yorùbá narrative tradition than that of Fagunwa, but there is the channelling of the elements through the form created by his great predecessor. It is this newly creative use of his inheritance that redeems Tutuọla from the snare into which he put himself by his use of a language which he so imperfectly commands, and which constitutes his work into an important stage in the development of a new literary tradition within Yorùbá culture. Fagunwa has had imitators and followers writing in the Yorùbá language, but none of them manifests the genius of Amos Tutuọla. The point, then, is that it was not imperative that Fagunwa's work should be continued in the Yorùbá language; what was important was that the direction of his work should be maintained, and the true significance of the communal spirit which it embodied.

Thus, despite the varying degrees and different manners in which they express this communal spirit, the works of Fagunwa and Tutuọla belong very much together and complement each other admirably in their reference to a common stock of symbols and their foundation in a world view that is culturally bound. Their work flows out of a distinctive manner of envisaging the world and of comprehending it, and it is precisely in their attachment to this essential foundation that they acquire their universal resonance.

Much of the effort of interpreting and understanding the writings of Tutuọla in Western circles has turned on the application of certain categories of myth analysis, and were Fagunwa to be made more assessible in these circles, there is no doubt that the same approach to his work would be adopted. Clearly these works do provide a striking illustration of the mythical imagination at work, and as such, a fertile hunting ground for the avid Jungian; it is even quite conceivable that they could yield material for a typology of arche-types and their transformations. But it is well to bear in mind that the specific forms of transformation that these symbols undergo in the work of Fagunwa and Tutuọla are determined by their cultural context which gives them their particular shapes and shades, and which, combined with their artistic presentation, brings them alive. It must also be remembered that any direct and automatic assignment of Jungian 'tags' to these symbols as they appear in the works of Fagunwa and Tutuọla gives them a false transparency which reduces the force of the very meaning that is sought in them. They are not just details in a general and abstract scheme, they build up together to express that affirmative purpose which Jung himself recognised as the ultimate purpose of myth. In other words, the significance of the creations and evocations of Fagunwa and Tutuọla lies not so much in their literal correspondence to aspects of the universal mental processes as in their global representation of the complexity of the lived texture of human life: of the human condition in its existential fullness.

IV

If the relationship between the work of Fagunwa and Tutuọla to the Yorùbá narrative tradition and world-view can be considered direct, due to the close situation of the two writers to the well-springs of the culture, no such direct link can be said to underlie the work of Wọle Ṣoyinka, in which elements of the traditional system are integrated into the writer's vision through the mediation of a highly conscious art. This means that in the case of Ṣoyinka, the relationship of the work to the communal spirit passes through a process of personal rediscovery of traditional values and the progressive approximation of the individual artistic personality to the determinations of the collective consciousness.

It is however not an accident that Wọle Ṣoyinka should have come to undertake the only English translation of a Fagunwa novel. Apart from the esteem which the older writer has long enjoyed in his homeland, and which has made his name, in the popular parlance, a 'household word', his novels do reflect the pervasive influence of the culture on all its members which the fact of Western education has, paradoxically, helped to throw into high relief in the awareness of its most sensitive members.

Ṣoyinka's preface to his English version of Fagunwa's first novel[4] is a testimony of his admiration for the work of his great predecessor in the tradition. The two qualities that Ṣoyinka singles out for special praise in Fagunwa's writing are his sense of drama—'his vivid sense of event', as he puts it—and his use of language, qualities that one recognises as belonging also to Ṣoyinka's own works, in which the dramatic effect is carried through a sensitive exploration of language, in this case English, in its various shades. Moreover, the special trait that Ṣoyinka shares with Fagunwa on this question of the artist's response to his means of expression is the same blend of humour and seriousness characteristic of Yorùbá itself, the working out of the deep artistic meaning of the work by taking language through a wide range of expression.

We also know that Ṣoyinka's admiration for Amos Tutuọla is also considerable. The relationship between the two writers who employ English to the older writer, who employs Yorùbá, seems therefore to turn upon Tutuọla himself as a kind of link between Fagunwa and Ṣoyinka, who can be considered the spiritual heir of Fagunwa, and spiritual brother of Tutuọla. This is not to say, however, that Ṣoyinka's work contains any distinct direct echoes of the work of the other two writers. The exception to this is perhaps *A Dance of the Forests,* where the symbolic setting of the dramatic action is the same as in Fagunwa's novels, and where the figure of the 'Half-child' may have been taken over from Tutuọla's *Palm wine Drinkard.* Even here, these are elements that also belong directly to the Yorùbá imaginative tradition.

Where Ṣoyinka stands apart from the two is the extreme individuality of his own art, which proceeds from a developed awareness of the multiple meanings that this art achieves. There is not only an intuitive participation of the artist in his own symbols, but an intellectual direction given to them, as a means of an integrated and conscious artistic statement.

This method of directly employing the materials of the traditional cosmology to engage in a clearly articulate discourse, to make an individual point, is best illustrated in his play, *A Dance of the Forests.* This was his first 'serious' play—in it, Ṣoyinka effected a notable transition from a superficial satirical approach to social problems, towards a deeper concern with the great moral and spiritual issues. His elaborate use of Yorùbá mythology in this play can be explained partly by the need he began to feel from this period onwards to give resonance to his handling of the larger problems of existence, and partly also by the evolution in him as an artist toward some kind of comprehensive framework of thought that would provide a foundation for his own spiritual needs and imaginative vision.

Although *A Dance of the Forests* is not a satisfactory play, it remains a very important work in the development of Ṣoyinka's art, for what he initiates in this play begins henceforth to achieve a refinement both in the expression and in the greater coherence of the experience. The personal elaboration of elements drawn from tradition into a new pattern of meanings attests not simply to a desire on the writer's part to give originality to his work but to a more important artistic preoccupation; it registers Soyinka's quest for fundamental human and spiritual values as they are expressed in the traditional world-view. There is thus an immediate connection between the use of traditional material in his expression, and the development of his individual artistic experience. In this last respect, it appears indeed, from the evidence of *Idanre*, that Şoyinka's exploration of tradition has led him to evolve a personal relationship with the tradition, a kind of poetic mysticism derived from Yorùbá cosmology.

This development begins to unfold in an explicit way in *A Dance of the Forests*. If in this play he does not appear to be in full control of his symbolic scheme—for the dramatic medium certainly does not sustain it adequately—he does succeed in making a statement of importance. It is the first work in which the troubled awareness of the human scene, as exemplified by the African situation, which has emerged as the dominant theme of Şoyinka's work, is given expression at a serious meditative level. The immediate reference of the play, the celebration of Nigerian independence, is presented as a paradigm of not only the African society, marked explicitly by the fact that it is poised at a turning point in time, but also of human society generally, whose moral progress is inscribed within a historical perspective. The play is a consideration of the chances of Africa, in which this historical perspective has taken on an acutely felt dimension, of fulfilling the promise of the moment by a universal renewal of moral and spiritual values. The historical moment assumes, as it were, a cosmic significance.

The direction of Şoyinka's meditation in this play has been indicated by a statement which occurs in one of his essays in which, calling for what he calls a 'historic vision' on the part of the African writer, he develops his point as follows:

> A historic vision is of necessity universal and any pretence to it must first accept the demand for a total re-examination of the human phenomenon.

This clearly is the objective that he set himself in *A Dance of the Forests*. Şoyinka presents a somewhat Voltairean view of History as a record of human follies, of mankind imprisoned within an absurd cycle of blind passions. Forest Head who represents the Supreme deity in this play also acts as a kind of objective judge of human condition, and it is through him that the essential point of the play is put across most clearly:

> ... The fooleries of beings whom I have fashioned closer to me weary and distress me. Yet I must persist, knowing that nothing is ever altered. ... Yet I must do this alone, and no more, since to intervene is to be guilty of contradiction, and yet to remain altogether unfelt is to make my long-rumoured ineffectuality

complete; hoping that when I have tortured awareness from their
souls, that perhaps, only perhaps, in new beginnings. . . .

The true significance of the moment should be the fulfilment of the
little in the past that is genuinely creative, a spiritual regeneration, in
a word. Demoke, the carver and ward of the god Ogún only dimly
understands this, but he is nonetheless significant as the image of the
artist which Şoyinka begins to conceive. The 'historic vision' is
lodged in the consciousness and sensibility of the true artist, who
affords society those momentary insights into the nature of existence
by which a moral and spiritual intelligence of the world is built up.
And it is such intelligence that gives power to man to master his condition in a meaningful way. The play's theme points them to the
larger issues of human experience: time and human will, man's relationship to the universe, the great mystery of life.

With such a weighty theme, it was only natural that the dramatist
should seek for an appropriate and adequate symbolic scheme with
which to represent it. His turning to the Yorùbá 'forest of symbols'
for his presentation of the drama of existence arises specifically from
the local focus of the play, but beyond this fact, the very handling of
the material shows a new understanding of the traditional world
beginning to emerge in Şoyinka's writing. This understanding turns
on his progressive elaboration of a vision of the artist in society, and
of his relationship to its organic life. *In a Dance of the Forests,* it is
through the character of Demoke that we are presented with the first
clear outline of Şoyinka's conception of the privileged position of the
artist, of the creative and sensitive individual, within the human community. As the central human character in the play,—a position
highlighted by his role in the final scenes of the play in which he
appears as the turning point of the choices open to his society—
Demoke serves principally to provide a moral and symbolic focus for
the multiple interactions between events past and present, and between
the characters, human and supernatural, through which the implications of the play are unfolded. In the very ambiguity of his two por-
trayals, there seems to lie a confirmation of the primary value of his
position in the final drama. Demoke maintains a sinister continuity
through a repeated crime between his previous life as official poet in
the court of Mata Kharibu in which he plays a role as the purveyor
of mindless rhetoric which serves to justify a destructive course,[5] and
his reincarnation as a carver. But a new light is thrown upon his new
existence which transforms his dramatic personality and reserves his
earlier significance in a more positive perspective. In his link with
Ogún in his new existence, he partakes of the same boundless impulse
associated with the god and shares the same spiritual endowment of
the hunter, the creative energy which is fundamental to his vocation

as an artist. There is the suggestion that the contradictions of his existence resolve themselves finally into a new insight into his own individual nature and that of his fellow men, a development which transforms him into a true artist, into the live center of the communal consciousness. Art in its deepest sense implies not only a surge of the senses, but also an introspective process.

The myth of the artist as it develops in Ṣoyinka's writings rests on an idea of his role as the mediator of the inner truths that sustain the collective life, and on his function in renewing the fundamental values that govern it. This myth is demonstrated in *The Interpreters,* Ṣoyinka's only novel to date, and a kind of sequel to the play, *A Dance of the Forests.* The novel gives a dimension to the social satires of Ṣoyinka, for where the satirical plays, especially *Brother Jero,* focus upon manners which are the external signs of the disturbing spiritual state of the society, the novel is a direct and comprehensive analysis of that state itself. It seems that Soyinka needed to turn to the narrative form in order to work out this intention, for it allows him extensive scope for analysis and presentation which the dramatic form does not.

The burden of the novel is carried by the character Egbo, in whose spiritual adventure the problem that Ṣoyinka wants to demonstrate is developed. Egbo is presented as an individual who is also unusually endowed, and who is seeking for some kind of fulfilment. His quest all through the course of the novel does not however find any form of adequate realisation not only because his innate strength is never allowed full outer expression, and thus spends itself in inconclusive mystical strivings, but also because he does not himself have a clear understanding of his own powers. His dilemma is not however without meaning, for it not only indicates the means to that complete reformation of the spirit through which, as Ṣoyinka says in an essay, 'the salvation of ideals' can be achieved in social life, but it also emphasizes the heroic and exacting nature of the process. In the tragic divorce of human action from a governing source of values which characterises the social world that Ṣoyinka depicts in the novel, Egbo's groping towards some form of profound and abiding measure of living takes on an exemplary value. His intimations are those of the true artist as Soyinka conceives him—the relentless seeker after the profound meaning of existence.

The Professor, in *The Road,* is a character who also corresponds to this conception, and his quest for the 'word' is, in a sense, an articulation of Egbo's strivings. *The Road* takes up the themes of *A Dance of the Forests* and of *The Interpreters* where they touch upon metaphysical issues. The central problem of life and death dominates the dramatic action, and the whole play turns upon the idea of death as a form of revelation upon life. It is significant that the central character, the

Professor, is presented as a kind of cross between a quack and a madman, and therefore, as essentially an individual outside the norm of society. He does not live or act by the same references as other men, but is moved rather by the force of his inner vision. His progression towards the 'essence of death' seems therefore to be prepared by some kind of illumination of the spirit.

More important still, the world of the Professor is that of the dream, which extends to the universe of myth. His relationship with Murano, the dead Agẹmọ cult masquerader, seems to be his means of insight into a world beyond the visible, and into the connection between life and death, and their essential unity. As with *A Dance of the Forests,* Wọle Ṣoyinka is using in *The Road* the traditional collective myth as the organising principle of his individual symbolic framework and as a channel for his artistic vision. Beyond this immediate factor, the issues upon which Ṣoyinka touches in these plays have a profound human significance which has been perceived and symbolised in the traditional thought systems of the Yorùbá, hence the ready availability of the material with which Ṣoyinka represents his concerns. Thus, without seeking a point by point correspondence between Yorùbá thought and Ṣoyinka's work, we can say that the former serves as a foundation for the latter, that the collective system represents a global reference for the individual artist's expression.

The Road is a kind of fantasy in which the inner questionings and obsessions of the playwright are exteriorised and interwoven with elements of reality in a dramatic 'condensation' of multiple levels of action and symbols. It would be difficult to unravel these adequately for the purposes of elucidation especially as the play itself does not provide a constant framework of references which could serve as reliable pointers to the various stages and direction in the unfolding of Ṣoyinka's meditation. However, what appears to constitute its basic symbolic structure is the fusion of the image of the road with the Yorùbá belief in a transitional stage between life and death expressed in the Agẹmọ cult. The obvious and general connotation of the road as the symbol of the journey through life is merged with the idea of death as a process, a gradual transformation into another form and essence, contained in the Yorùbá myth, to give a broader, more intense conception of life and death as connected and transitional phases in a single and vast movement of the spirit. In other words, *The Road* expresses the idea of existence as a becoming, as one long rite of passage. The Professor's search for the 'word' is not only equivalent to the artists' groping towards its profound meaning, his effort to grasp its hidden principle, but represents as well man's eternal quest for ultimate knowledge.

The general theme of the road as a symbol of human experience—

as an image of life seen as a trial and a progression towards some kind of fulfilment and revelation—seems to command more and more Wọle Ṣoyinka's imagination. His poetry in particular can be summarised as a varied expression—in significant fragments—of this single theme. The first section of the volume *Idanre and other poems* is entitled 'of the road' and the poems in that section are intimately related to those in the third section, entitled 'of birth and death'. Human experience seems to be presented as consisting of a cycle involving life in the constant passage from one stage of organic development to the other, a development that is shot through with spiritual implications. One poem in particular from the third section of the volume holds a special meaning in relation to this general idea—it is the poem entitled 'Dedication'. It is cast in the form of the prayer at the naming ceremony of the new child (ìkomọ jádc), and gathers up in powerful organic imagery some of the traditional ideas associated with the mystery of birth in the framework of the cosmic order:

Camwood round the heart, chalk for flight/of blemish—see? it
dawns!—antimony beneath/Armpits like a goddess, and leave this
taste
Long on your lips, of salt, that you may seek/None from tears.
This, rain-water, is the gift/of gods—drink of its purity, bear
fruits in season
Fruits then to your lips: haste to repay/The debt of birth. Yield
man-tides like the seas/and ebbing, leave a meaning on the
fossilled sands.

In this poem, the vitalism intimated in the previous works is given full expression, and the artist's imagination and consciousness are directed towards an intimate coincidence with the elemental.

It is in the long poem, *Idanre* that we see most clearly this movement of Ṣoyinka's artistic spirit and the role of tradition in its most developed expression in all his work. The poem itself is the record of a personal experience which recalls and extends that of Egbo in *The Interpreters*. In the poem, the natural world becomes a more expressive symbol of vital values: the landscape itself is suffused with the presence of the primal and the elemental, and *Idanre* stands as the concrete embodiment of the Yorùbá myth of origin.

The central section of the poem is an evocation of the saga of Ògún, whose power is for Ṣoyinka the archetype of the artistic endowment, of that intense energy of the mind and of the senses which is the privilege of the creative individual. This evocation indicates the essential spirit of the poem, for the re-enactment of the traditional myth is equivalent to the ritual recall of the gods in the Yorùbá festivals, whose essential purpose is to revitalise the world of creation. The poem represents for the modern artist a means of recapturing

that full sense of life, that intense organic feeling for the universe
which the myth expresses, and which forms the basis of Yorùbá
religion and world-view.   Thus, the experience of *Idanre* is a mystical
one, in which the poet enters into communion with the land and
with its moving spirit.   The poem marks a high point in Ṣoyinka's
relationship to tradition and in his spiritual development.   The collective myth has entered so fully into his awareness, has been so
profoundly interiorised as to provide the very substance of his intimate
experience.   For Ṣoyinka, artistic creation has become a medium for
realising his individual sensibility in and through the collective consciousness.

V

The great French poet, Baudelaire, once remarked that he could
admire only three categories of men: the warrior, the priest, and the
poet.   This is a remarkably 'African' point of view, and more precisely,
these three categories represent exactly the great points of cohesion in
the Yorùbá world view, which is reflected in the work of the three
Yorùbá writers I have been considering, and particularly in the writing
of Wọle Ṣoyinka.   They embody those qualities, and their characteristic vocations dramatise those traits that stand out as illustrative of a
conception of life which seems to serve as the organising principle of
the collective mode of being and of the existential posture in the fundamental African society.   This conception manifests itself specifically
in the Yorùbá context in the discernible cult of intense vitality that
permeates every aspect of the culture and its social articulations, in
the active celebration of the sense of a constant and forceful connection
of man with the springs of life latent in the universe.

But if I have made the reference to Baudelaire, it is not to stress a
similarity of outlook between him and Ṣoyinka, but rather the difference in their situations.   Baudelaire strove to take French poetry
beyond the rhetorical limits within which it was confined when he
began to write, to make it a means of knowledge.   Neither he nor
those poets who followed his lead—from Rimbaud right up to the
Surrealists—were able to find a truly coherent cultural reference for
their visionary aspirations.   The collapse of Christianity as the great
myth of Western culture has forced these poets to create an individual
mythology, each one for himself.   In English poetry, the most striking
example is that of W. B. Yeats; and Eliot's efforts to give a new relevance to Christian cosmology as the source of poetic thought and
feeling for the modern world have not met with any kind of general
response. [6]
The great fortune of African writers is that the world views which
shape the experience of the individual in traditional society are still
very much alive and continue to provide a comprehensive frame of

reference for communal life. The African gods continue to function within the realm of the inner consciousness of the majority of our societies, and the symbols attached to them continue to inform in an active way the communal sensibility. It has thus been possible for our poets in particular to evoke them as a proper, and indeed integral element of their individual imaginings.

It is of course possible to take the view that one of the functions which this return to the African source has served in the work of some African writers has been to effect a cultural differentiation of their creations from those of the metropolitan writers, and thus to afford some kind of psychological satisfaction to the African writer in his striving for an original idiom. There is no doubt that this kind of Africanisation of the content of the literary work implies in some cases no more than a literary pose, a mere decking out of the material employed, lacking the force of a full and genuine commitment of the artistic personality to the African system of ideas and symbols. It is however an entirely different matter where such a commitment can be discerned, where the writer is felt to be creating out of a sense of a responsive connection of his individual imagination to the communal spirit.

I venture to say that the links between the three writers discussed here demonstrate just this latter kind of situation. The work of Fagunwa and Tutuola grow out of a living tradition, and in the writings of Wole Soyinka, we find a personal appropriation and reinterpretation in new terms of Yorùbá cosmology, so that it exists in his work as an authentic mode of vision. The artistic experience of the three writers, taken together, represents a development of the common stock of images in a way that is not only a restatement of their significance in the context of the traditional experience, but also of their continuing truth for modern man. Their work expresses the essence of myth as a comprehensive metaphor of life: as a re-formulation of experience at the level of image and symbol so as to endow it with an intense spiritual significance.

ABIQLA IRELE
Department of Modern European Languages
University of Ibadan, Ibadan

NOTES AND REFERENCES

1 An earlier version of this paper was presented at the weekend seminar on Yoruba language and literature, held at the University of Ifẹ.
2 See his article 'Yoruba Studies today' in *Odu,* New Series, No. 1, April 1969.

3   See his article 'Amos Tutuọla, a Nigerian Visionary' in Ulli Beier (ed.)
    Introduction to African Literature (London: Longmans, 1967).
4   *Ogboju Ọdẹ ninu Igbo Irunmalẹ,* translated as *The Forest of a Thousand
    Daemons* (London: Nelson, 1968.)
5   Demoke's role in this connection calls to mind the character of Demokos,
    whose name he echoes, in Jean   Giraudoux's *Tiger at the Gates* (*La
    guerre de Troie n'aura pas lieu).*
6   For a fuller discussion of this point, see George Steiner, *The Death of
    Tragedy,* Chapter IX.

Demoke's Choice in Soyinka's
A Dance of the Forests

NICK WILKINSON

There are as many interpretations of Wole Soyinka's *A Dance of the Forests* as there are commentators. The source of the wide range of disagreement lies principally in the interpretation of the Half-Child and Demoke's choice in handing it to the mother, the Dead Woman. I should like to add a further way of looking at this play, which, though by no means definitive, seems yet to make some sense.

Soyinka's plays, especially the serious ones, are not linear in their form: each scene reflects on other scenes which both precede and follow it. One scene or part of a scene cannot be looked at in isolation, even if its dramatic context seems to set it apart from the rest of the play. The scene with the Half-Child is dramatically entirely different from the earlier part of the play, with the voices of symbolic spirits speaking through the masked human beings, the grotesque Triplets, and the fierce dancing setting it apart from the more familiar conversations of men and gods. The perilous situation of the Half-Child with all the hostile forces swirling around him also has an immediate emotional appeal and involvement which has been rather lacking so far in the play. These, I suspect, are the reasons why the Half-Child has been seen in special isolation from the rest of the play; Una Maclean[1] views it as representing 'the new nation' of Nigeria at Independence; Eldred Jones[2] regards it as 'a symbol for man's future'. Even Margaret Laurence[3] in an extended and deeply-argued interpretation in *Long Drums and Cannons* restricts herself to the immediate scene and does not relate it to other parts of the play. I intend, therefore, to discuss the Half-Child from its first entrance up to Demoke's decision, and then relate that decision to parallel situations in the play.

The Dead Man and the Dead Woman had both suffered questioning by Eshuoro in disguise, and had been sent off, first the Man, and then the Woman, to be unburdened of her pregnancy. Forest Head announces 'this is the moment / For the welcome of the dead',[4] and the form of this 'welcome' is the possession of the masked human beings by various Spirits, such as of Darkness and Precious Stones. Each Spirit reveals only its malevolent aspects in relation to humankind, speaking in imagery which revolves around blood and death. Only the Dead Woman and the Half-Child return to witness the welcome, the Dead Man having been told to wait until after the human beings have spoken. In fact, he never returns, so that a negative reply to his appeal is implied. As soon as the first Spirit has spoken through a possessed human being, promising 'Heads will fall down / Crimson in their red!'

(p. 73), Eshuoro, disguised as the Figure in Red, enters, presumably to represent bloody death. The Half-Child begins a game of *sesan* in which the Figure in Red joins (echoes of Ingmar Bergman's *The Seventh Seal*, in which the Knight plays chess with Death?). Unhappy, the Half-Child moves away from the game, and then returns to it, saying:

> I who yet await a mother
> Feel this dread,
> Feel this dread,
> I who flee from womb
> To branded womb, cry it now
> I'll be born dead!
> I'll be born dead!   (p. 74)

Later he choruses with the Spirits of Darkness, Precious Stones, the Pachyderms, and the Rivers with the words 'Branded womb, branded womb' (pp. 74–5).

Thus, the Half-Child is clearly associated with the Yoruba concept of the *abiku*, the child born only to die. Soyinka has also written a poem called 'Abiku'[5], on which Gerald Moore[6] comments:

Abiku, though he appears a child, is truly ageless and forever apart, hostile or at best indifferent to our endeavours. Even the warmth of the womb is cloying to him; even an egg-yolk, universal symbol of generation, is only material for the shaping of burial-mounds.

If this is Soyinka's idea of an *abiku*, it is clearly different from the Half-Child, which was not allowed to be born because of the death of his mother while still pregnant. He is not yet an *abiku*, but as subsequent lives follow the pattern of the first (the Dead Man has had three lives as a eunuch subsequent to his gelding) he will be born dead and acquire the character of an *abiku*.[7] As he is not yet an *abiku*, but is merely dead, the game of *sesan* acquires significance; when the Figure in Red wins, it is to claim the Half-Child as an agent of death, that is, to make him into an *abiku*. However, though the Figure in Red wins the game, he does not claim his rights until after the Welcome of the Dead has been completed, that is, after the Ants have spoken. (With the Ants and the Triplets revealing the future for human beings, treating the Half-Child as a symbol of the future seems superfluous.)

The human beings are then unmasked, and the hideous Triplets enter, with the Interpreter (Eshuoro's Jester in disguise) dancing with them. Forest Head addresses them 'You perversions are born when they [human beings] acquire power over one another' (p. 80): the concept of an evil birth linking them with the Half-Child, soon to become an *abiku*. Only after the Third Triplet, representing Posterity nourished on blood, does Eshuoro reveal himself and claim the Half-

Child in his own right, as if to join him with the other blights of man-kind.

The Half-Child tries to reach its mother, and says 'Still I fear the fated bearing' (p. 80), thus emphasizing that it has not yet been properly born. The Dead Woman also says:

> Shall my breast again be severed
> Again and yet again be severed
> From its right of sanctity?   (pp. 80–81)

Her words imply that she will be doomed to being the mother of an *abiku* in all her future lives. Only the child can 'Free me of the endless burden' by accepting her and its own premature death. Ogun, who throughout the play has supported the human beings, especially Demoke, the most worthwhile of them, tries to help her by drawing the child towards her. (Margaret Laurence takes the exactly opposite view, and sees the reunification of mother and child as a confirmation of the *abiku*, with Ogun acting in a malevolent aspect in this case.) To attract the child back, the Interpreter and Third Triplet dance the *ampe* again; then they draw him into the dance and throw him between them. Rola screams and Demoke rushes among them to save the child. Ogun catches the Half-Child and throws it to Demoke, who is left holding it.

The decision on the Half-Child's future thus lies with Demoke, a living human being who has freedom of choice. Forest Head washes his hands of the matter, only asking: 'Aroni, does Demoke know the meaning of his act?' (p. 82). Aroni then says to Demoke:

Demoke, you hold a doomed thing in your hand. It is no light matter to reverse the deed that was begun many lives ago. The Forest will not let you pass.   (p. 82)

If Demoke breaks the *abiku* doom on both the Dead Woman and her Half-Child by allowing them rest, either complete dissolution or a chance of a fulfilled incarnation, he will suffer the malevolence of the Forest under Eshuoro. Eshuoro has managed to manoeuvre himself into a winning position either way: he either gets the Half-Child, to be an *abiku* curse on humankind, or Demoke will be at his mercy. Demoke makes the human choice of restoring the Half-Child to its mother, thereby atoning for the death of Oremole, and bringing the doom of the Forest upon himself.

The Half-Child, then, acts as the agent by which Demoke is faced by a moral choice: between letting things be, or interfering and causing danger to himself. The Half-Child itself is a specific being, tied to the court of Mata Kharibu which we had been shown just before the Dead Couple appeared before Forest Head (unlike the three human beings,

Demoke, Rola and Adenebi, the Dead Woman and the Half-Child had
not had lives subsequent to their death at the Court). The Half-Child's
death was caused by the 'moral' act of his father, the Warrior/Dead
Man, while his salvation rests on the 'moral' act of Demoke. The
balance of the two cases is vital in interpreting Demoke's act.

While Demoke acts to save the existence of two others, the Warrior
takes a moral stand for himself, dragging others with him (his corps of
soldiers), and indirectly causing the death of his pregnant wife. Though
he knows that his soldiers will follow him, he insists: 'They made their
choice themselves. They must do as they decide.' (p. 56). He therefore
commits a crime of power, as represented by the Second Triplet, the
Greater Cause, that of freedom of choice. However, the freedom he
demands is negative, it is the right not to act. For a Warrior, it is a
denial of his proper role, and his emasculation in some sense fits his
moral stance. In fact, at Madame Tortoise's insistence, he chooses
castration against copulation with her. Had he chosen the latter course,
he could presumably have killed Madame Tortoise, whom he saw as
the source of evil at the Court (a reverse Judith and Holofernes?). His
three subsequent lives are said by the Questioner to have been 'foolishly
cast aside' (p. 71). His grievance arises from his still considering his
choice to have been correct, his inability to accept his own responsibility for his state. This is presumably the reason why he is denied the
Welcome, as he could gain nothing from it.

On the other hand, the Dead Woman accepts her own responsibility
for her condition, blaming it on 'My weakness, Forest Head' (p. 69).
Though she seems to have been condemned by Eshuoro, Demoke
accepts her case and manages to save her. At the first appearance of the
Dead Couple, Demoke showed sympathy for her case, though he
refused to take it up immediately, having the 'business' of the death of
Oremole on his mind (soon to be partly relieved when he described it
freely to Obaneji/Forest Head). His parting words to the Dead Woman
on this occasion are prophetic: 'Perhaps we will meet. But the reveller
does not buy a cap before he's invited.' (p. 4) He is 'invited' to the
Welcome; but when it comes to the point, Demoke waits for no
invitation before jumping to help the Half-Child. The action here is
contrasted with the case of the Dead Man, to whom Rola had offered
help 'Even before you ask it' (p. 4) but had withdrawn the offer
because of the Dead Man's embarrassed refusal to explain his position:
'O O O I am so ashamed' (p. 4). (This embarrassment shows he still
considers himself superior to his present condition.) He cannot win his
appeal, because he cannot learn the reality of his case.

Thus Demoke's act is seen as a genuine, but difficult, act of freedom,
made against a background of dire prophecies and revelations of the
human condition. They had been shown to the dead and have presumably affected their living human channels, 'to pierce the encrusta-

tions of soul-deadening habit, and bare the mirror of original naked-
ness', in the words of Forest Head (p. 82). Demoke's act is a positive
one, but it exacerbates the division among the gods (Eshuoro and
Ogun) and sets himself, and perhaps mankind, against the Forest.

Soyinka has therefore shown the difficulties of moral choice, and the
dire implications of even a seemingly 'good' moral choice. The parallels drawn between *A Dance of the Forests* and Nigeria's position at
Independence can then be related to this general idea, rather than
individual symbols or figures within the play: all human history is
gory, and all human decisions have fearful implications. Thus this
approach fits in with the general sombre warning tone seen by all
critics to be the essence of the play.

University of Nigeria, Nsukka

NOTES

1 Una Maclean, 'Soyinka's International Drama', *Black Orpheus*, No. 15
 (1964).
2 Eldred D. Jones, *The Writing of Wole Soyinka*, Heinemann, 1973, pp. 44–6.
3 Margaret Laurence, *Long Drums and Cannons*, Macmillan, 1968, pp. 40–45.
4 Wole Soyinka, *A Dance of the Forests*, O.U.P., 1963, p. 73.
5 Wole Soyinka, *Idanre and Other Poems*, Methuen, 1967, pp. 28–9.
6 Gerald Moore, *Wole Soyinka*, Evans, 1971, p. 93.
7 In seeing the Half-Child as only a potential *abiku*, I differ from Margaret
 Laurence (op. cit., p. 40) and Ulli Beier, 'Review of *A Dance of the Forests*',
 Black Orpheus, No. 8 (1960).

THOUGHTS ON CREATING THE POPULAR THEATRE

K. E. Senanu

Long before I had made up my mind to go and see the Wilson-Opoku production of Wole Soyinka's *The Lion and the Jewel,* at the Drama Studio, the neighbors who owned television sets began to talk about it. They had seen snatches of the production telecast and, no doubt, the flirtatious Gahu dances proved a heady appetizer for them as, I believe, for the many members of the audience who crowded the Studio when I went to see the production. It occurred to me, while I watched the Studio fill up long before the play began and, later, as I observed the enthusiasm of the "Zongo" audience clamoring for a repetition of the seduction scene between the Bale and Sidi, that, at long last, we seem to have discovered in the Wilson-Opoku combination, a group of theatre entrepreneurs who may give the fillip to the development of the popular theatre in Ghana. Mr. Wilson certainly ought to be congratulated on his choice of play; especially as he has proved himself an astute producer before now in his choice of "The New Patriots." Much credit must also go to those who did the publicity work for the production. And, since the theatre's patrons are the best judge of its success, Messrs. Wilson and Opoku deserve praise for the resounding success of this production. They know what is good entertainment for the patrons.

At the same time, the success of the production raises, in a most acute form, a question that must be exercising the minds of those who have paid even a cursory attention to the popular entertainment which has been provided in our playhouses for the past eighteen months or so. The question: what form should dramatic productions which stand any chance of being patronized by more than a mere elite audience, take? Or, if putting it that way makes it sound too prescriptive, what are some of the features of productions which seem to have gone down well with a varied audience and how can those who are interested in the development of the popular theatre in this country "cash in" on these features?

I use the phrase "popular theatre" in two distinct, but closely related, senses. In the first place, I mean any form of stage production which appeals to more than an elite audience. For, let us face it, for the theatre to exist and survive in Ghana, the number of people we manage to get into our playhouses is crucial. And when I used the word entrepreneur about the Wilson-Opoku combination above, I had in mind a business-like approach which keeps an eye on how to get the crowd into the playhouse, both by the play it chooses and the manner it produces it.

But the phrase "popular theatre" has always meant—when applied to those rare occasions when the threatre has been a success in any society—a mode of entertainment as well as a mirror which reflects and reveals something of the body and the soul of a people's life. The theatre is primarily the placing before an audience, that which is seen, that which has body, that which appeals to the senses, that which is "spectacular". But the sensual and the spectacular are there to make visible and clarify that which is hidden. To quote a familiar phrase: "The purpose of a play is . . . to hold the mirror up to nature . . . and to show the very age and body of the time, his form and pressure." A production attracts a popular audience in so far as it both entertains them and holds up a mirror to show them something of the meaning of the life around them.

Judged according to both meanings of the phrase "popular theatre" the Wilson-

Opoku production has been successful. The production has combined the "spectacular"—in the dance, in the libidinous appeal of the wrestling and seduction scenes to the "Zongo" audience—with that which appeals to the intellect, and has drawn a varied audience into the theatre.

The vitality of the play itself depends as much on verbal drama, on wit, on the ridiculous or theatrical proliferation of language, and on grotesque behavior, as it depends on those emotive moments which can only be adequately expressed through music and dance. This is part of the difference between *The Lion and the Jewel* as a working-script and the weak structural material which went into productions like *Obadzeng* several years ago, into *The Dagger of Liberation* some months ago, and into *The Lost Fisherman*. Wole Soyinka's play has a firm story-line; it has solidly drawn characters; it has a verbal wit which continually recalls Moliere to mind; above all, it draws upon mythic and archetypal elements which lie behind human life throughout the world, while it gives these elements a twist and makes them immediately relevant to life in West Africa. And because it employs the basic drives of sex, youthful vanity and pride, wise-old cunning, and braggart cuckoldry, it touches these levels of human "action" most appropriately dramatized by music and dance.

The script itself thus offers a solid basis for a truly popular theatre. It has something to offer as entertainment to those who can only take their amusement in the most direct, sensual and empathic form; but it also appeals to those whose intellect is awake to verbal wit and structural form or, to use a modern jargon, sub-textual meaning.

But although the script has all these potentialities and although the producers, as I shall indicate later, sensed some of these elements and basic drives, the production, as a whole, falls between two stools.

One must admit at once, that the script has some intractable bits—there is for instance that whole section which precedes the Bale's seduction of Sidi. One was painfully aware that the production dragged considerably at this point. The greater part of the dialogue which is interspersed with the bouts of the wrestling could be cut. But this can only be done if the producer is keenly aware of the wrestling match as part of the seduction itself so that the choreography can make the match much more organically related to what both Baroka and Sidi are undergoing. In fact this is just where the production breaks down. For the dance—by which I mean those parts of the production which do not rely on dialogue for communication: i.e., the actual dances, the pantomime, the wrestling, the drumming— instead of becoming the most complex form of expressing what the characters were undergoing, became decorative and illustrative and hardly formed an organic part of the total production.

In the script, Sidi "stages" a pantomime to re-enact the arrival of the photographer from Lagos who had fallen in love with her, taken photographs of the village and given her image a front-page printing in a popular magazine. The magazine, bearing a beautiful image of Sidi, had just been received back in the village and the pantomime is meant to *celebrate* Sidi's joy and pride in her own youthful beauty. The producers, quite rightly, alter the script's demand for a pantomime in which the awkward Lakunle would have had to play the role of the visitor from Lagos. But the problem which the production faced at this point and never quite managed to solve, was to make the traditional dances chosen as a substitute for the pantomime, a *celebration* of Sidi's youth. This would have prepared the way for the finale and contrasted capitulation of youth to old-age cunning at the end of the play.

But, having substituted powerful traditional dances for Wole Soyinka's imitative pantomime, the producers seemed to have called forth a genie which they found difficult to manage. The dances became interludes between the main spans of the action. And because no organic function has been really seen in the script for the dances, although all the hints seem to be there, Mr. Opoku has done very little fresh choreography for the production. The Gahu, which is a flirtatious dance and most appropriate for the scene of seduction, is used even when Sadiku is celebrating her triumph over her supposed impotent husband. And there are very awkward transitions from one drum rhythm to the other and therefore from dance to dance. If the dances were not being merely used as decoration, if they had been structured orgnically into the enfolding action of the play, such errors could have been avoided.

The fact is that neither of the two producers seems to have discovered the basic sub-textual meaning of the play, a meaning which the music and the dance would most appropriately have objectified at the emotive moments suggested by the script.

The problem is a very basic one to the creation of an indigenous and virile popular theatre. Nobody who has given any thought to the matter can doubt that in the dance we already have the most direct, and yet the most complex, form of dramatic and theatrical communication which is both prior to, and transcends, the verbal drama. Even if we were ignorant of this, the popularity of the "dance-spectacle" in our theatres should make us stop and think. That which is done with the body, movement, positions in space, gestures, speak much more clearly and much more directly even to an illiterate audience than the verbal drama.

This is common knowledge. But its implications are only now being rediscovered and utilized by theatre people all over the world. *We* are fortunate here, because our audiences do not need to be educated tounderstand dance,movement, and the use of space, generally, as a much more direct and complex form of communicating thoughts, emotions and attitudes—those things which constitute the subtext of any written script. Faced with a written script like *The Lion and the Jewel* we need the use of all our resources.

Our dances have the scope of expressing the most realistic imitation of action—such as we see in the pantomime of the felling of the trees in *The Lion and the Jewel*—as well as the most abstract form of celebrating that which is happening within us. It is true that we have not yet developed the vocabulary to accurately describe both the movements and the meaning of our traditional dances. But this is the kind of verbalizing which the theatre audience does not need, simply because communication through "that which is done" (dromenon) is immediate and adequate without any further explanation . Nobody who has communed with dancers at a funeral, needs to be told what he has gone through. And the essence of the theatre is this ritual participation.

The question is how to handle a script like *The Lion and the Jewel* so that the verbal communication dovetails smoothly into the "dance-spectacle", and the dance becomes an organic part of the total production. This, I suggest, requires a vigorous attention to the underlying life of the play, the evolving action, the sub-textual meaning which binds all parts of the play together.

Speech, as has been said, is a highly specialized activity in human life. Verbal utterance is the overt issue of a greater emotional, mental and bodily response and it is prepared for in feeling and awareness or in a mounting intensity of thought which the words spoken sometimes reveal. But although speech is a very abstract form of human action its basis in bodily emotion is undeniable. The central problem of the theatre when it handles written scripts is to translate speech, especially at its most translucent, into bodily actions and movements which communicate, as precisely and directly as possible, the emotional basis, the sub-textual meaning of the script.

In *The Lion and the Jewel* we have a script which presents a variation on an archetypal theme: the rivalry—in this case, mainly sexual—betwen *youth* and *old age*. Wole Soyinka makes this familiar theme to the theatre relevant to West African life by making the representatives of youth, Lakunle and Sidi, also the advocates of a very questionable form of progress. When the play opens Sidi is ready to accept some of the new-fangled ways of the comic village school-teacher Lakunle. Her acceptance opposes him; but both Sadiku and the Bale remark the school teacher's influence on her thoughts.[1] Thus in spite of the apparent disagreement between Sidi and Lakunle, over kisses and the bride-price, they both represent youth against the cunning old rake Baroka. At the end of the contest however it is the cunning of old age which wins against youth.

The play thus proceeds by a series of dramatic reversals. In the morning scene, Lakunle and Sidi turn youthful courtship into a battle of wits between the sexes, made grotesque by the flamboyant language of the village school-teacher who is hopelessly in love with the illiterate village beauty. Lakunle comes off very badly in this context and the scene ends with a dance which *celebrates* Sidi's vanity,the triumph of her youthful beauty over ineffectual manhood.

The triumph of course is premature and the Bale, who joins the general celebration with meaningful glances at the flushed village beauty, proceeds to lay his plans for the seduction.

We need not recount the rest of the details of the action on the play. For our concern is with those nodal points of the plot, those moments in the unfolding action, when speech cannot adequately express what the characters are undergoing and when the dance, the bodily movement to music, objectifies the life of the play.[2]

There are four such moments in the course of the play: the first is at the end of the morning scene when Sidi celebrates her renowned beauty; the second, at the beginning of the night scene, when Sadiku performs the spell, followed by a dance expressing her supposed emasculation of the Bale; the third moment is the wrestling-match, between the Bale and his court wrestler in which the Bale effectively demonstrates his prowess and anticipates his seduction of Sidi. The final moment is the dance which celebrates the cuckolding of Lakunle and the marriage of Sidi and the Bale.

These are all ritual moments, moments of *celebration,* which dances, carefully choreographed, ought to project. We become aware of them as we pay attention to the underlying life of the play, to that struggle between youth and old age, between the comic image of the evolue and crafty traditionalism.

The central characters involved in these moments must have the technical ability to make the transition from the verbal drama to the drama as celebration. For them to remain stage-managers, calling for a dance troupe to celebrate what they themselves are supposed to be undergoing is to make the dance merely decorative. Just as in the classical Greek drama, they must be the leaders of the dance. For, as characters in the verbal drama, they are only the focal point of what the rest of the dance-chorus is supposed to be undergoing.

To be aware of the perennial and archetypal drives which are involved in this play is to begin to understand something of its appeal to a varied audience. But it is also to be sadly aware of how amateurish and unstructured most of the directing, the choreography and the performance was. It is true that the producers were faced with a great deal of technical difficulty, i.e. actors whose awareness of their bodies, voice projection and sustained emotional involvement were quite unequal to the demands of the complex roles they were playing. Mr. Opoku, for example, was faced with a stage on which it was extremely difficult to define a meaningful space for dancing. But the central problem which the production never quite solved is to work out a significant and organic relation between the verbal drama and the dance. There is no simple formula for this. Each script will raise new problems. But a producer, on the look-out and plumbing the depths of the script, will take hints and pass them on to a creative choreographer.

If I am right in suggesting that the production of *The Lion and the Jewel* offers a guide-line for the development of a really virile and indigenous theatre, then there is an overwhelming need for a reorientation in the kind of training we give to our professional performers. I have no doubt in my mind that the roots of that training must be in the dance. We cannot therefore have a separate dance-school and theatre-school recruiting students with differing qualifications as in the case now at Legon. This is a very outmoded system of training people for our indigenous theatre. The results of this system are obvious in the production under review. On the one hand, we have dancers whose bodies are trained and expressive but who are incapable of playing roles in the verbal drama: and, on the other hand, we have people trained for playing roles in the verbal drama who are scarcely aware of what they are doing with their bodies.

It is true that in spite of its many technical shortcomings the Wilson-Opoku production of *The Lion and the Jewel* offers a very entertaining evening—thanks to some superb sense of timing and performance from George Awoonor-Williams, as Lakunle, and to the "dance-spectacles". But success in the theatre is not fortuitous; it requires conscious artistry and hard work. And unless dance research, dance teaching, academic study of the theatre and the drama go hand in hand with performing, there is no hope of our getting rid of the mess in which most productions in our playhouses find themselves. Of course we can choose to continue imitating the sterile forms of the verbal drama: but then, we must reckon with empty auditoriums.

---

1. In fact it is because she is first seduced by the glamorous ways of the city, which Lakunle advocates, that she later capitulates to the old Bale who speaks, at the crucial moment, in the very tones of the village school-teacher.
2. In some ways the play itself celebrates this potency and superiority of the dromenon, the thing done, over the thing said. The Bale seduces Sidi foremost by demonstrating his prowess in the wrestling match. This is why the wrestling ought to be choreographed to make explicit its sub-textual meaning. Mr. Opoku does not take much trouble over this match which becomes drawn-out and tedious.

Soyinka's Brother Jero:
Prophet, Politician and Trickster

Richard Priebe

Relatively little critical attention has been given to Wole Soyinka's short comedy, *The Trials of Brother Jero*, despite the fact that much of the action is generally considered quite successful as comedy. The play is usually dismissed as a rather conventional farce, saved somewhat by the effective interplay of pidgin and conventional speech, but ruined by a weak ending.[1] As will be shown, much of the impact of the play is lost on the non-African critic. This is not to say a non-African cannot enjoy the play, but merely that the awareness of certain cultural facts serves to elucidate the implicit universality. Neither is this to say that a different critical standard must be employed, for once we are aware of some of the echoes contained in this play the task of the critic will be no different than it would be for any other play.

Before we look at some of these echoes it will be helpful to examine one of the ways the play is structurally held together. As an audience we become active participants in *The Trials of Brother Jero*. The play opens with Jero speaking directly to us, telling us about himself. We learn that he is "A prophet by birth and by inclination" and has worked his way up against a lot of competition from others in his field as well as the modern diversions which keep his "wealthier patrons at home." In short, he tells us that he views his work as a profession that happens to be his chosen one by virtue of his extraordinary ability to gain money and power through his practice of it. Three of the five scenes in the play begin in a similar fashion with Jero addressing us and confiding in us secrets of his business. Since Brother Jero has told us much more than he would dare tell any of his usual patrons, this does more than merely set the point of view from which we are going to view the rest of the action. We are conned into letting him lead us through a day in his life and even into conspiring with him as he moves his other pawns around.

This relationship of Jero to us is central to any analysis of the comedy, and we will continually return to it as we examine the play more closely. For the humor in this play is the result of Soyinka's having woven three things into this pattern of which we are so integral a part. We will first look at Jero as a trickster figure; then we will look at the political satire in the play; finally, we will examine the social satire.

Trickster stories are extremely common throughout all of West

Africa. In fact, the trickster may be seen as a popular hero whose triumphs are due more to "shrewdness and cunning . . . than . . . steadiness and industriousness, as in European tales." [2] In West Africa he usually has the attributes which Herskovits ascribes to Legba, the Dahomean trickster. Legba is a major diety in the Dahomean pantheon and was chosen by his mother, the creator, to be the linguist of the gods.[3] We are told "that while he dupes others, he is rarely duped himself. His activity, again, is calculated, highly conscious. His acts are rarely impulsive, but for the most are directed toward the achievement of a well-defined end. He knows socially accepted values even when he behaves contrary to them; he is in no wise the source of them." [4]

The relation of this figure to Jero becomes quite clear when we compare Jero with the Yoruba counterpart to Legba, Eshu-Elegba. The prophet Jero, like Eshu, is something of a mediator between men and god(s). Yet even though they act as representatives of god (s), they are independent spirits, subservient to no one The similarity of these two can be noticed from the moment the curtain rises, for Jero's dress bespeaks a veritable personification of Eshu. His hair is described as "thick and high" and his appearance "suave." Soon we learn of his general attraction to women and of theirs to him. Eshu is also always depicted as having long hair. In fact, in sculpture his hair is often shaped as a phallus indicative of his association with libidinous energy. Moreover, Jero's divine rod can be seen as corresponding to the club that Eshu carries, an object which is also symbolic of general, as well as sexual, power and aggression.[5]

Susan Yankowitz sees Jero's control of his flock as paralleling Amope's domination of Chume. Her conclusion is that Soyinka shows "religion itself is an emasculating force that supports man's impulse to escape the responsibility of his manhood." [6] While this element of false religion is satirized in the play, it should be understood in terms of the significance of the trickster figure in Yoruba society. Joan Wescott's comments on Eshu are particularly illuminating here:

> . . . he is the principle of chance and
> uncertainty . . . By postulating Eshu-Elegba,
> the Yoruba compensate for the rigidity of
> their social system on the one hand, and
> externalize responsibility for any
> disruption that might occur on the
> other. . . . Thus the autonomous Eshu, a
> creature of instinct and of great
> energy and power, serves a dual role:
> as a rule-breaker he is, as it were,
> the spanner in the social works, and

> beyond this he is a generating symbol
> who promotes change by offering oppor-
> tunities for exploring what possibili-
> ties lie beyond the *status quo*. He is
> also a satirist who dramatizes the dangers
> which face men and the follies to which
> they are prone. . .[7]

In light of this we can see that Jero is not simply a rogue to be scorned, but a figure to be admired. Our relationship to him is thus as paradoxical as his dual role. At the end of the play Chume cries out: "O God, wetin a do for you wey you go spoil my life so? Wetin make you vex for me so? I offend you?" The implicit answer to his question is simply, "Nothing." The element of chance has been at work in the form of Jero and with Chume's life it has unfortunately played havoc. In this there is no question of right or wrong action, for chance is clearly amoral.

We would undoubtedly be very hard-pressed to find any specific trickster tales that Soyinka has drawn on for this play, but that is beside the point. What is important is that he has created Jero out of a relatively large oral tradition in which such figures play a major role. Such a tradition quite obviously establishes which comic patterns work well and which figures are most successful in a story. Stories which are not very good are simply forgotten.

Jero lives by outwitting others. There are moments when his tricks get him into trouble, but in the end he is in control of things. He almost gets caught by Amope at the beginning, but manages to slip away. Later Chume catches on to his tricks and almost gets back at him, but Jero's mind as well as his feet are too fast for his opponents, and we see in the end that Chume will be carried off to the lunatic asylum. Much of our attachment to Jero can be accounted for in this archetypal pattern. Quite simply, we enjoy seeing someone manipulate others with his wits.

It is no accident that Jero is the most articulate character in the play. Nor, for that matter, is it merely coincidental that Legba is the linguist of the gods. Both these tricksters use their linguistic talents to exercise power and gain control over people. Note, for example, how Jero handles the politician in the last scene. The man at first has no time for Jero, but Jero has observed him closely and discerned his weakness. Furthermore, he knows just what to say to convince the politician that he controls his political future:

> Indeed the matter is quite plain.
> You are not of the Lord. And yet such

is the mystery of God's ways that his
favour has lighted upon you . . . Minister
. . . Minister by the grace of God . . .
[*The Member stops dead.*]
     Yes, brother, we have met. I saw
this country plunged into strife. I
saw the mustering of men, gathered in
the name of peace through strength.
And at a desk, in a large gilt room,
great men of the land awaited your decision. Emissaries of foreign nations
hung on your word, and on the door leading into your office, I read the words,
Minister for War . . .

In short, Jero says exactly what the politician wants to
hear. The choice and rhythm of the words serve as devastatingly
effective rhetoric, yet Jero removes any doubts the politician
might have about this through his flair for dramatic exits and
entrances. The play closes with the politician lying prostrate
before him, fully convinced that Jero is indeed a prophet.

The action of the play mainly centers around Jero's scheming
to get out of paying Amope for the white velvet cape she sold
him. To do this he figures it is worth relinquishing the power he
exerts over Chume through not letting him beat his wife. In the
end he must go further and quite literally sacrifice Chume
himself, but in the process he also gains power over a more
important person, the politician.

Now this is where our active participation in his scheming is
important. For despite Jero's very strong archetypal appeal
we could quite simply react against him when we see him destroying Chume. Naturally we feel Amope deserves everything
she gets, but Chume is simply a helpless fool. A look at the asides
in the scene we have just been discussing shows again that our
sympathy is controlled. Jero opens the scene by commenting on
the politician. Through Jero's eyes he too appears as something of
a fool. Jero dares us to doubt that he can draw him in to his
flock. The result is that we rather anxiously await seeing the ras-
cal at work again. Later he brags to us of his success: "By tomorrow, the whole town will have heard of the miraculous
disappearance of Brother Jeroboam. Testified to and witnessed
by no less than one of the elected Rulers of the country. . ." The
childlike quality of this bragging reduces the act to merely
a prank at which we can laugh. Moreover, we are prepared for
his final aside to us: ". . . It is a pity about Chume. But he has
given me a fright, and no prophet likes to be frightened. With
the influence of that nincompoop I should succeed in getting

him certified with ease. A year in the lunatic asylum would do him good anyway." A rather harsh judgment for Chume, but since we are seeing this all through Jero's eyes we are almost inclined to accept this amorality.

The fact that we do qualify our acceptance of Jero's behavior is important. As amusing as this scene is, we are left with a rather uncomfortable feeling concerning the way in which we have been amused. Jero, after all, has not completely controlled the point of view throughout the play. Had he done so, we would have had a rather straightforward comic play, very closely patterned after the trickster tales but lacking much of the dramatic irony and political satire that we find here.

Scenes II and IV are almost totally dominated by Chume and Amope. The one time in these scenes that we do see Jero he is in the position of making a somewhat humiliating escape from Amope. The absence of Jero's guidance at the beginning of these scenes enables us to develop a more personal perspective of the couple. We come to feel real empathy for Chume in his plight as a henpecked husband, however comic it is, for there are no redeeming qualities in his shrewish wife. By the time he leaves in Scene II we feel we would like nothing better than to see him thrash her. What is of interest to us here is the light this sheds on Jero's personality.

Jero, as we discover in Scene III, is really the cause of Chume's emasculation. Our knowledge of this, along with the view we have just had of Chume, give rise to one of the most comical dialogues in the play. Here we actually see Jero control Chume's desire to beat his wife. It is at this point that the political satire becomes rather evident. Jero's actions are a travesy of the behavior expected of a politician. Instead of ministering to Chume's need, he utilizes it to control him. Through his aside to us we learn that the same situation is true of everyone in his congregation: the man who wants to become chief, the couple that wants to live to an old age, the lady who wants children, and so on. As Jero explains to us earlier in this scene, knowing how to keep people dissatisfied is the key to power. Once people realize that they don't need you, you lose control over them.

The political machinations of Jero are exactly what we would expect of a trickster, though the opposite of what we would wish for in a politician. Like Eshu, Jero is extremely interested in money [8] as demonstrated by the fact that he sacrifices Chume for the one pound, eight shillings and ninepence he owes Amope. But money is only a means to the power that Jero enjoys, the manipulation of people. Now we expect a politician to manipulate people, but for social rather than personal ends. Eshu and

Jero are completely asocial, and their actions serve only their own vanity.[9]

Since *The Trials of Brother Jero* is one of Soyinka's earliest plays it is very likely that it was written prior to Nigerian independence in 1960. This being the case, the play is an interesting foreshadowing of the political events which followed independence. As we hear of the competition Jero has had in gaining control of his section of the beach, we think of the great political scramble wherein many tried, in the phrase then popular, to "get a piece of the cake." Two Nigerian novels of the sixties, Cyprian Ekwensi's *Jagua Nana* and Chinua Achebe's *A Man of the People,* appear to be rather accurate reflectors of the political milieu. As we can see in these novels, the attempts by the prophets to gain their beaches through the use of "women penitents to shake their bosoms in spiritual ecstasy" varies only slightly in style from the tactics employed by the politicians to get their "cake." This thrust at the avariciousness of the politicians is very obviously echoed in the later comments on the "penitent" who believes he will be the Prime Minister of the yet to be created "Mid-North-East State" and the member of the Federal House who sees in Jero his chance to become Minister for War.

We can see Jero then as a perfect parody of a politician. This trickster realizes that style is everything. Thus, he set out to create a spectacular image of himself as witnessed by his white velvet cape and the name he chose for himself: Immaculate Jero, Articulate Hero of Christ's Crusade. Compare this name with the one which Nanga took in *A Man of the People:* Chief the Honourable Dr. M.A. Nanga, M.P., LL.D. Such empty titles were, by the way, not at all uncommon. We can see that Soyinka's comment is, with the addition of irony, much like the journalist's in Achebe's book. "Na waal Nothing fit passam."[10] For the goal of the politician would seem to be some type of political security comparable to Jero's artificial apotheosis at the end of the play.

In line with this image, Jero is aware that how you say something is often more important than what you say. We have already looked at Jero's talent as a rhetorician, but one further comment is noteworthy. Towards the middle of Scene III we see Chume in a situation where Jero has left him alone with the congregation. One of the women falls into a religious paroxysm. After stumbling blindly for a few moments, Chume slips into the appropriate rhetoric and gains control of the congregation. It is obvious that the humor in this scene stems in part from Chume's unconscious parody of Jero. But in doing this Chume is also burlesquing popular political rhetoric of a chicken in every pot.

The social satire parallels the political satire and is of some interest, though it is not nearly so integral to the comedy. Part of the problem here is that it is not so evident to one unfamiliar with the rather rampant sectarianism in Nigeria.

After the missionaries had established a strong footing, Nigeria went through a situation similar to the great revival waves in America in the 19th century. Many people got caught up in the new religion. Rivalries broke out within, as well as between sects. The result was that by the 1960's almost every town in southern Nigeria had at least one sect which had formed from people who had broken away from the Baptists, the Anglicans, or any of the other larger sects. Then, as in America, Elmer Gantrys and Brother Jeros began soon to create even more sects. Some insight into this can be gained from Soyinka's novel, *The Interpreters*. There we see another prophet, Lazarus, whose personality, though different and perhaps more complex than Jero's, elicits several comments from Sagoe about how religion is good business.[11] Sagoe's cynicism in respect to religion is not at all uncommon among Nigerian intellectuals.

We have then the comedy of a religious fraud, the humor coming from the discrepancy between what he is and what he professes. He ministers to no one but himself, but being both the trickster and the politician that he is, we greet Brother Jero's escapades with laughter. Look at the situation in Scene IV where Amope is trying to flee from Chume's wrath. She pounds on Jero's door yelling, "Let me in or God will punish you!" Jero replies, "[sticking his fingers in his ears] Blasphemy." No one in the play could be less sincere in saying this, but it isn't Amope to whom this is said. She doesn't even hear him. It is to us—the fact that he has already told us that he is a fraud only serves to heighten the humor. We laugh because of our conspiracy with him.

In using a trickster figure as the central character in the play, Soyinka introduced a mechanism for controlling the temperature of the satire. Throughout, the satire stays at a mild level, never getting so hot that we are unable to laugh at the folly that we ourselves have become involved in. Yet it is, after all, this folly that has resulted in Chume's being led to an insane asylum, and despite our intimate association with Jero, we see too much of ourselves in Chume to rest comfortably in our laughter.

Notes

1 See Susan Yankowitz, "The Plays of Wole Soyinka," *African Forum*, Vol. 1, No. 4 (Spring 1966), pp. 132–33. Also see Margaret Laurence, *Long Drums and Cannons* (London: Macmillan, 1968), p. 23.

2 William Bascom, "Folklore and Literature," *The African World*, ed. Robert A. Lystad (New York: Frederick A. Praeger, 1965), p. 482.

3 Melville J. and Francis S. Herskovits, *Dahomean Narrative* (Evanston: Northwestern University Press, 1958), p. 37.

4 *Ibid.*, p. 101.

5 Joan Wescott, "Sculpture and Myths of Eshu-Elegba, the Yoruba Trickster" *Africa*, Vol. 4 (1962), p. 348.

6 Yankowitz, *op. cit.*, p. 132.

7 Wescott, *op. cit.*, p. 345.

8 Joan Wescott points out (p. 345) that the Yoruba have a saying that 'Elegba hides behind cowries.' Eshu sculptures are always covered by strings of cowries (an old form of money) which attests to the belief that Eshu has something to do with all transactions of money.

9 It is interesting to note here that Eshu sculptures are almost always found with a small mirror strung around the neck. The mirror, of course, symbolizes vanity (Wescott, p. 346). While Jero does not have such a mirror on his body, the stage directions at the beginning of Scene III call for a mirror among the few objects on stage.

10 Chinua Achebe, *A Man of the People* (New York: Anchor Books, 1967), p. 18.

11 Wole Soyinka, *The Interpreters* (New York: Collier Books, 1970), pp. 175 and 193.

KONGI'S HARVEST (A REVIEW)

Boyd M. Berry

Kongi's Harvest, Wole Soyinka's latest play, has predictably created a sensation at Dakar, where it was presented at the Negro Arts Festival. For Soyinka has chosen a topical subject, African nationalism, and whether he likes it nor not, his hysterical Kongi has probably been judged as much in terms of Nkrumah's ejection, for example, as by artistic merit. This reviewer is largely unfamiliar with African politics and the traditional values upon which Soyinka apparently bases so much of his work. Consequently, these remarks of an unabashed outsider of necessity concern only the clarity and coherence of the play considered, perhaps unfairly, outside its social context.

As mounted in the Arts Theatre at the University of Ibadan—that is, without the final scene, called "Hangover", and with considerable confusion attending its conclusion—the play depicts for the outsider what sort of harvest a man reaps if he sits alone on top of a mountain. That is Kongi's situation through the greater part of the play; he descends, at its conclusion, to a harvest festival at which he is presented not with the expected new yam, but with a decapitated human head.

Kongi, as several characters in the play remark, is a *poseur,* a man who thinks of the world as watching him at all times. He sits upon his mountain, looking out on the world, and at the same time, he is visible to that world. Such an approach to living seems to have taken its emotional toll. Kongi is hysterical, and in the final scene, he delivers in mime what we are told is a four-and-a-half hour speech, while the affairs of the world—the preparation of the new yam, and the noise thereof—completely submerge the words of the speech. The speech is pure gesture, devoid of sound, unheeded by the world. The gestures, full of fury only, are those of a man out of all emotional control.

Ranged in various more or less defined sorts of opposition to Kongi are at least three characters. The first of these is Oba Danlola an old and obstinate, fiery, traditional leader. He is in detention as the play opens, presumably for opposition, and one of the major actions of the play involves bringing Danlola to present Kongi with the new yam—to renounce in effect his traditional authority in the feast. The old order passeth, and Danlola finally consents.

The outsider is not really competent to judge Obas generically. One imagines that, as sketched, Danlola is a stock traditional figure, and he seems a pleasant enough fellow. Yet, at one point, two characters liken him to Kongi in the important matter of posing. To the uninitiated there seems little obvious point in the comparison not because Danlola does not pose, but because his posing does not seem to have produced hysteria. This point may also be made in terms of the notion of "isms" developed in the play. Kongi rules a land called Isma, and his devotion to "isms" seems to be a function of his posing. Danlola, poseur though he may be, can't really be said to participate in this fondness for "isms". We have only the bare, unqualified assertion of Danlola's likeness to Kongi, and nothing visible on the stage to support the statement. Surely, here Soyinka has either led us considerably astray, or has failed entirely to carry us with him.

Apparently, Danlola's nephew and heir, Daodu, is also ranged against Kongi and his "isms". "Apparently", because we see Daodu do precious little. He is a bar fly, a habitué of Segi's Night Club, and Segi's present lover. Segi is a sort of Herculean whore, Kongi's former mistress about whom terrifying stories circulate: she destroys men, the suggestion is, sexually. It does not appear to what extent

Kongi's present, highly disorganized condition is owing to his experiences with her. Nor is it clear whether it is Segi or Daodu who has the upper hand in their relationship. When he is not drinking Segi's beer, Daodu raises champion yams on a farm settlement which runs a sort of loose competition to the Kongian establishments, outdistancing them every time. It is his yam which is selected at the concluding festival, pounded, and presented to all but Kongi. Obviously, in the matter of harvest Daodu and his yams are separated from Kongi and his human head by the distance between life and death. However, Daodu at one point in the play announces a platform of resistance to Kongi which is predicated upon very nearly universal hatred and, to follow the metaphor, human heads. Segi opposes his position, pleading for a loving approach to one's fellow men, but, like so much in the play, the point of this conversation remains obscure. One is left to speculate whether Segi here asserts her basic domination of Daodu, or whether Daodu is to be viewed as the "developing character" who grows out of his hatred, or whether it is all a horrible joke, Segi's words of love sullied by her profession. At any rate, Daodu's program of hatred seems clearly opposed to his benevolent yam growing, and we never see him do anything which resolves the issue.

Segi may also be placed in opposition to Kongi, but if it is difficult to determine Daodu's and Danlola's positions, with Segi the problem is hopeless. Primarily this is true because we see her do even less than Daodu. She never acts unambiguously in such a way as to disprove the persistent story that she destroys men. Her relation with Daodu is so undefined as to shed little light on this matter. For much of the play she maintains silence, which she breaks most noticeably with her passionate appeal for universal love. Here, her destructive tendencies seem open to question. Her other major action, completely at odds with her profession of universal love, concludes the play. Facing Kongi directly, she presents him with the decapitated head of her father. As staged, the confrontation is Symbolic with a capital S; in view of the obvious sexual overtones of the harvest festival, one immediately suspects that Kongi's particular harvest results from cultivating the likes of Segi, that if one resorts to her one can only get abominations. Here again Soyinka may have led us astray. If Segi is a champion in the pitched battle between the sexes—engaged in the good fight Soyinka has portrayed in *The Lion and the Jewel*—destroying men as rumor reports he does, Soyinka has carried us a long way from African nationalism in that final scene. For in that case, Kongi, and also Danlola and Daodu, are mere tools in a perverse fertility rite, and the trouble with Africa lies not in its dictators, but in its whores.

In view of the series of major interpretive alternatives suggested above, one is forced to conclude that *Kongi's Harvest* is, to the outsider, an incoherent sprawl. Alternative, and mutually exclusive interpretations are not artistic ambiguity. Soyinka sets us on a number of scents, which pursued, lead in no single direction. We are led into every briar patch in the area, along widely divergent and mutually exclusive paths, and end by running in very small, perplexed circles.

Against such a view of the play two objections might be raised. First, some of the suggestions about the meaning of various actions might be termed over-ingenious. Such an objection must be at least partially granted; yet, Soyinka himself must bear partial responsibility for this critic's over-zealous application. Soyinka has the true dramatist's gift of making actions seem significant. His imaginative use of action and language effectively commands the audience "look here, this is important, and you should watch carefully". When a comparison of

two characters is underlined by considerable discussion of the comparison, when a
dumb character finally speaks, when a passive character finally acts, we cannot
choose but suspect the situation is important. Perhaps Soyinka is too good at
getting our attention, with the result that we are fascinated by the non-essential as
well as the essential.

On the other hand, it might be objected that a man as unfamiliar with African
politics and culture as this reviewer cannot form a proper opinion of such a play.
This too is a formidable objection. Still, drama is a public form of art, if it is
anything, and an artist like Soyinka should decide whether he wants to reach
anything larger than a purely Nigerian or African public. It would seem that an
artist tries to order parochial events in such a way that they have more than a
parochial significance. In presenting the uninitiated a dramatic experience with
African politics Soyinka only confuses, and one can only suspect that he is
confused himself.

The matter of Right and Left Ears of State exemplifies the outsider's difficulties
very nicely. Those two remarkably named characters are introduced as the
henchmen of Kongi's Organizing Secretary. They are a grand "sight gag"—the
conception funny enough to demand our attention, and we expect that they will do
something amusing. Instead, they disappear mutely into the backroom of Segi's
Night Club, never to re-appear. We later learn that they have been killed in
retribution for Kongi's politics. Their memory lingers on, however; we can't really
believe that we have lost them so early; moreover, various characters employ
"ear" phrases which recall their names to us. As a result, when in the last scene,
the head is presented to Kongi, we, without Soyinka's stage note stating whose
head it is, recall, even if only for a brief moment, our old friends the Ears. Our
attention, in other words, is at least partially distracted at this important point by
the strong expectation that the Ears will prove interesting. Soyinka must reckon
with the fact that he can arouse our interest, and in nonessential matters, handle
that talent carefully. It is a great disappointment to realize finally that, in the
interests of coherence and clarity, many fascinating dramatic touches in *Kongi's
Harvest* should, like the Ears of State, be more fully developed, carefully
subordinated, or lopped off.

Language and Meaning in Soyinka's *The Road*

D. S. Izevbaye

Although *The Road*[1] is one of Soyinka's most exciting plays, it is also a 'problem' play because not only does it raise the question of linguistic communication and apprehension in the theatre – like all the major plays except perhaps *Kongi's Harvest* – it is itself about the problem of communication. Because Soyinka writes mainly plays, a form which requires direct and instant communication with an audience, it is natural to prefer the more accessible of the plays to the obscure. Against this background even a favourable and proficient review of *The Road* in the pun-loving *T.L.S.* seems to hold an unintentional scare for the reader of Soyinka's works in its ironic title, 'Keep Off the Road.[2] In a more deliberate objection to the 'general obscurantism' of the play, a reviewer of the *text* makes a virtue of simplicity by arguing that *The Road* is 'unfortunately not vintage Soyinka'. *The Road* is, of course, vintage Soyinka, in the sense that we find in it both a development of recognizable Soyinka themes and a tightly evolved structure in which the carrying out of Particulars Joe by the thugs is the only scene where the seams probably show as a 'change of scene'. The subject of death by the road which Soyinka presents in *The Road* first appeared in the early poem, 'Death in the Dawn'. But the subject had become a preoccupation by the time he published *The Road*. Apart from being the starting point for the play, death by road is the main structural device for *The Interpreters* published that same year, when he also published his poem on the death by road of Segun Awolowo.[3] Taken together, 'Death in the Dawn' and the Segun Awolowo poem bring out the usual ambivalence in Soyinka's treatment of this subject. Together the poems show the satirical and the spiritual attitudes which we find in the play. *The Road* is important among Soyinka's works, not merely because of the themes and attitudes in it, but because in this play Soyinka achieves an unequivocal success in the union of theme and dramatic technique, an experiment which he first attempted in *A Dance of the Forests* (1960). It is this balance of message and method which makes the play a successful communication, not in the sense of something immediately and wholly understood, but in the sense of a play which satisfies our sense of dramatic rightness. *The Road* is itself a dramatization of the limits of language. So a stylistic analysis in which we examine the relationship of characters deployed down a linguistic ladder from Professor the talkative one to Murano the mute one would tell us only part of the story, not only in the usual theatrical sense in which visual items complement dramatic speech, but because in this play that which is heard is challenged by that which is seen. The main tension between these two modes of communication is established from the start.

The opening 'scene' dispenses with words altogether, but it displays some of the terms on which the play asks to be understood. It communicates the mood wholly through setting and mime. The road, the corner of a church, and an old mammy waggon now used as the 'Aksident Store' are not merely the physical setting but communicate, through their usual everyday associations, the religious and social dimensions of the play. Their constant presence on stage sustains this function: the road links the spiritual and the satirical aspects of the play by being the agent of death as well as the path along which the dead passengers are carried to their church funeral. However much we are consciously unwilling or unable to link the opening scene with death, the sprawling, motionless figures lying close by the Aksident Store must appeal to our subconscious by their likeness to death before the comedy takes over. After this a mime rapidly suggests some motifs of the play: Murano the tapster disappearing into the dawn, Samson the idler prying uncertainly after him, then poking a spider's web in frustration after failing in a lonely, desperate attempt to wake his companions.

In contrast to this visually received communication of the first 'scene', the first words of the play show how much value we may place on verbal communication:

> SALUBI: Six o'clock I bet. I don't know how it is, but no matter when I go to sleep, I wake up when it strikes six. Now, that is a miracle.
> (*He gets out his chewing stick, begins to chew on it.*)
> SAMSON: There is a miracle somewhere but not what you say. Maybe the sight of you using a chewing stick. (p. 2)

It is worth pointing out how, from the start, Samson's disarming wit elevates him above our censure of characters in the play. The laughter provoked by what he *tells* us clouds the fact that from what we have just *seen* of the three who are awake so far only Murano has washed his face. But more important is the disagreement over language and how Samson

is used to demonstrate how easily language may be devalued. Although his
jocular definition of 'miracle' is the immediate means for criticizing
Salubi's use of the word, the values by which we judge such words in the
play has been visually communicated to us at the beginning of the play
when a church occurs as part of the setting. The whole scene prepares us
for the first appearance of Professor who enters brandishing a road sign
and announcing its discovery as

> Almost a miracle . . . dawn provides the greatest miracles but this . . .
> in this dawn has exceeded its promise. (p. 8)

Because of his ridiculous dress and the comic atmosphere which
prepares for his entry the cloud of laughter which greets Professor would
sweep away almost all our willingness to take his 'miracle' seriously. But
not totally, or for long. His language soon becomes a means of recreating
and heightening an experience. The 'wonder' he now offers us is as
arresting as the earlier 'miracle' seemed absurd:

> PROF.: Come then, I have a new wonder to show you . . . a madness
> where a motor-car throws itself against a tree – Gbram! And showers
> of crystal flying on broken souls.
> SAMSON (*suddenly alarmed*): Wait! What was that about an accident?

Professor leaves the usually cheerful Samson distressed. As audience,
we too have become disturbed about our initial comic response to Professor.
In serious scenes like this, essential communication goes on between
Samson and Professor in spite of the intellectual gap between them. We
are not left in total darkness either, for even if we are not always able to
interpret his words consciously and immediately, their religious associations
register sufficiently to control our response:

> You are afraid? There are dangers in the Quest I know, but the Word
> may be found companion not to life, but Death. Three souls you know,
> fled up that tree. You would think, to see it, that the motor-car had tried
> to clamber after them. Oh there was such an angry buzz but the matter
> was beyond repair. They died, all three of them crucified on rigid
> branches. (p. 11)

The last sentence here has always had a profound significance in another
and more orthodox context. And there is nothing in the passage itself
which denies our giving it this significance and our serious response,
although there is much perhaps to offend orthodoxy. Professor's acknowledgement of 'dangers in the Quest' comes from his rejection of orthodox
Christian doctrine of the Incarnation when he announces that 'the Word
may be found companion not to life but Death'. This I take to mean that
the Word was not made flesh, but all flesh becomes associated with the
Word during the process of decomposition. It is this acceptance of the

Yoruba view of flesh dissolution in place of the Christian doctrine of the Incarnation which brings Professor into association with drivers whose trade involves death, and with *agemo*, described by Soyinka as 'a religious cult of flesh dissolution'.

It soon becomes clear that the rejection of his Christian background is the point of departure for the evolution of Professor's philosophy, and the point of reference at every stage in his Quest. Even his defection appears modelled on Paul's conversion – a reversal which emerges especially from his account of his fiery scourge of palm wine bars in his youth (p. 68). This religious background becomes the language through which we understand the dramatic unfolding of Professor's experience. Parts of his story come through only in brief accounts and imprecise snatches of history, like accounts of the incidents which caused him to leave the Church. But an immediate grasp of the story of the past is not essential. The primary function of the religious language which we are given is not explication but evaluation, and it also helps us to understand the action of the play both at the level of plot and at the more difficult level of the meaning of the Quest.

Our understanding of the plot and of characters' motives would not be complete without this religious background. We may see the drivers' recognition and acceptance of fear as the means for judging Professor's obsession with death, because their fear comes naturally from their constant contact with death. But Professor's Quest is not merely intellectual. It has emotional sources as personal as those of the drivers' fear. He is feeling his way through the evening of his life towards not just death but also the achievement of that divine status which he apparently lost by his fall from ecclesiastical grace. This fall is represented in the play as guilt over embezzled Church funds and as blasphemy against Church dogma, especially on the interpretation of the Word. Professor's rejection of Christian theology appears to be final but is really equivocal. Although he builds his shack in competition with the church after his apparent excommunication, he insists that the Church cannot cast him out. However the contradiction in his position does not affect his single-minded Quest. What he calls his rehabilitation is merely the attainment of one type of grace at the loss of another, and is his non-Christian restatement of the doctrine of the fall and redemption.

Secondly, the meaning of the Quest is gradually defined for us because Professor tries to relate the language of the religion which he has left behind to the idiom of the religious cult of death which he has just found. Thus he sets out with a vague idea of what he is looking for and a general idea of where it may be found. This obsession with language and death, the only certainties of his career, makes him a madman in the eyes of the

other characters in the play. He is separated from the drivers by language,
and especially by his power of interpretation. He can see beyond the
merely literal and is contemptuous of statements which are merely
accurate, as he makes clear while preparing a police statement on the
accident at the bridge for Kotonu:

> ... have I spent all these years in dutiful search only to wind up my last
> moments in meaningless statements. What did you see friend, what did
> you see? Show me the smear of blood on your brain. (p. 56)

Professor's written record of Kotonu's report which follows this speech is
metaphysically rewarding for him although it is also a parody of pedantry:

> KOTONU: It (i.e. the lorry) was a full load and it took some moments
> overtaking us, heavy it was.
> PROF. (*writing furiously*): It dragged alongside and after an eternity it
> pulled to the front swaying from side to side, pregnant with still-
> borns. Underline – with stillborns.

Professor's use of language shows, not his love for the sound of words
only, but his platonic view of people and events. To Samson the accident
victims on three branches would have been just three dead *people*. For
Professor they become three figures each hanging from a tree, just as the
back of the doomed lorry is filled, not with people, but with stillborns.
For him language does not merely describe the immediate, particular
event, it reveals the archetypal figures and primary ideas behind it. The
dramatization of this exploratory function of language emphasizes the
difference between *The Road*, which deals satirically and tragically with
the use of langauge, and *Kongi's Harvest*, which deals with its abuse. In
Kongi's Harvest the excess of words generated by propaganda techniques
is ridiculed in the royal anthem about the 'harvest of words / In a penny
newspaper'. A kindred fullness in Professor's language suggests that
perhaps he is one of those characters created out of the artist's need to
purge his passion for words, and held at a distance satirically. But though
Professor is satirically treated in parts of the play, he does not prostitute
his talent like Adenebi and the Fourth Aweri, neither does he succumb to
its hypnotic effects as Sagoe does while seeking psychological release in
words. Professor's gift of words is effectively part of the plot, and is not
merely a guide to his character.

Since language is theme and medium in the play, Professor's Quest
begins as an adventure in language. Because he has not found the Word
when the play begins he cannot give us a precise definition, and he uses it
in shifting and frequently bewildering contexts. He predetermines its
character, however, by fixing it with a familiar label although he allows
himself a certain range of ambiguity to allow for interpretation and to

enable him to correct his errors by adjusting his meanings. We can detect
the process by which he discovers the Word by outlining the three main
contexts in which he uses it.

Professor begins by treating the Word in the ordinary sense of words in
a language, especially printed words. This leads him to collect all printed
matter within reach – newspapers, fallen road signs, and even pools
coupons. He does not, however, pretend that everyday words are identical
with the Word. Apparently it is the equivalence of sound and the rough
correspondence of meaning which assure him that ordinary words are a
means of achieving the Word. When he erroneously pulls up an erect
road sign with 'BEND' on it, he admits that this is not the Word. But he
hangs on to his spar of error in the absence of a usable alternative because
'every discovery is a signpost . . . eventually the subterfuge will be over,
my cause vindicated' (p. 12). This insistence on the value of error gives
'BEND' an ironic relevance for his reasoning throughout the play, just as
his quest for broken words in order to find the unbroken Word points to
his adoption of unorthodox means for the end he seeks. The duplicity in
this method is further dramatized in the uprooting of the sign: 'this word
was growing, it was growing from earth until I plucked it . . .' (p. 8). The
language through which Professor presents the road sign as a growing,
living thing also expresses the death he has dealt his golden goose; his
subsequent attempt at 'replanting the tree of life' (p. 21) surely represents
not only his recognition that language cannot function effectively without
at least a minimum of nourishing context, but also his own transplant,
being his symbolic acceptance of his need for this new shack community
to which he has been drawn by 'a sympathy of spirit' as replacement for
the Christian community from which he has been uprooted.

The agricultural metaphors which Professor employs leads to the next
stage of discovery by defining the context in which the Word may be
found. Death is described as a harvest (as Soyinka himself frequently does
in his poetry), and the meanings gained at the scene of an accident are the
offerings or leavings of the hungry god. Professor is therefore continually
'gleaning loose words from the road' (p. 85), and the bundle of assorted
papers on his table is his 'granary . . . the select harvest of a faithful
gleaner' (p. 63). His faithfulness here ironically recalls his defection –
which is why he 'missed his way'; but it more immediately refers to his
steadfast watch at his new station for road deaths to lead him to the Word.
The Word is therefore connected with death and the earth. Professor says,
in answer to Samson's question, that the Word may be found 'where
ascent is broken and a winged secret plummets back to earth' (p. 45). The
stages of the spirit's progress outlined here suggests the influence of
Ogboni thought on Professor. The ascent is the spirit's aspiration towards

its maker, Olorun the father, while the plummeting back to earth is the return to Ogboni, the earth, the mother of all life.[4]

In the third type of context, the two earlier meanings with which the Word has been associated lead to what is obviously the object of Professor's Quest – the Word as a divine power manifesting itself in potent utterance. This recalls what has been described as the Ogboni use of the earth cult as a means not only of preparing for death but also of gaining power,[5] and transmitting it verbally. We find such a verbal demonstration of divine power in *The Interpreters* (published, like *The Road*, in 1965), when Bandele, the most god-like and adequate of the characters in the novel, stands,

> old and cruel as the *ogboni* in conclave
> pronouncing the Word
> I hope you all live to bury your daughters.[6]

Bandele's curse is of the same order as that of Professor who seeks to damn Salubi with an imprecation by wielding the Word: 'May the elusive Word crack your bones in a hundred splinters!', although Salubi gets more than he deserves. It is true that before leaving the Church Professor had a similar view of the Word as a sword of fire burning people by the ear (p. 68), but in his later interpretation the Word is neither the incarnated Word nor the breath of the Christian God but the word of wrath, corresponding in its baleful properties to the Yoruba *oro*.

If these contexts provide a guide to what Professor seeks, by asking whether he has found the Word and whether what he has found is of any value,[7] we would be seeking to understand the statement of the play. When Samson puts the first question to Professor, Professor admits that Murano could not reveal much, as we may well expect. For Murano, the *agemo* masquerader knocked down by Kotonu's lorry and nursed back to partial life by Professor, has been entrusted with the secret of the Word, but is therefore 'forever silenced', like many such figures in literature who, on their return from limbo, are forbid to tell the secrets of their prison-house. Professor has been seeking to know the unknowable through language, a clumsy tool outside the field of ordinary knowledge. We can see even from the idiom of the drivers and layabouts that there are areas of experience best communicated in terms which are primarily non-verbal. For example, Kotonu's problem is explicated mainly through the rituals and emblems which contribute to the language of the drivers. Although we hear of Kotonu's sensitivity through the mouths of the characters, its most convincing and dramatic demonstration comes when Samson shows how the sensitive accelerator foot of Kotonu can distinguish the penny he is standing on from a shilling. It is this self-indulgence with

feeling that has kept Kotonu safely on the road for so long after others are
gone into the oral records of praise poetry. It is right for such a sensitive
driver to have 'No Danger No Delay' as the emblem of his lorry. But
Kotonu does not really speak the language of the drivers, for the emblem
shows only the faith in his sensitive foot. Samson's indignant complaint
that

> When other drivers go out of the way to kill a dog, Kotonu nearly
> somersaults the lorry trying to avoid a flea-racked mongrel. (pp. 18–19)

seeks to make us understand Kotonu's accident as a failure to communicate
this trade mark to the gods through the reach of ritual and sacrifice. The
main irony of the play is that Murano, knocked down by Kotonu, represents the drivers' god confronting the driver who would not sacrifice, and
frightening him off the road. But the casualty list ritualistically chanted
by the drivers on their remembrance day is also an ironically appropriate
emblem of their values. It is a reminder of the actual effect of sacrifice.
But as Jones points out, it is also a potent memorial,[8] the source of the
assurance behind the verbal swagger of Say Tokyo Kid and the drivers'
capacity to endure and enjoy life through a ritual deadening of feeling.
Kotonu's desire for this ability explains his willingness to take over the
trade of Sergeant Burma whom he admires for his lack of feeling:

> KOTONU: Sergeant Burma was never moved by these accidents . . .
> SAMSON: He wasn't human.
> KOTONU: But he was. He was. A man must protect himself against the
> indifference of comrades who desert him. (p. 21)

Kotonu has therefore come as client to Professor who is trying to evolve a
philosophy that should enable him to 'cheat fear by foreknowledge'
(p. 94).

From the beginning of the play up to the point when, by turning from
language to ritual, Professor admits that this foreknowledge cannot be
acquired merely by waiting for a verbal revelation of Murano's secret, he
is shown to be out of touch with the true idiom of the drivers. But from
his first appearance *we* are made aware of the superiority that ritual has
over language for making certain kinds of communication, because of the
way Professor treats every action as ritual. He ironically occupies an
extreme position of the drivers' belief in the value of ritual when he treats
every object as the mask of an archetype, and every action as a mime of an
experience which can be entered into only by mimetic evocation. Thus
when he comes upon Samson on an elevated chair playing at being rich, he
takes the physical elevation as a sign of superior enlightenment. We
would recall this scene later on when Professor pores over 'certain cabalistic
signs' so difficult he assumes they are not by human hands until Samson

tells him they are pools coupons and thus brings him to admit that his education is incomplete. The earlier scene expresses the basic interaction and conflict between ritual and language in the play. Professor's appeal to Samson, 'Tell me you who sit above it all' (p. 9), deflates for us the man of words. But because we are in the theatre and the relentless progress of action moves us to make an immediate application of words to their situation before we have had time to reflect on their irony, we also accept Professor's rebuke of Samson for cutting himself 'from common touch with earth'. And we would not be wrong in doing so. Samson has also cut himself from touch with earth – not in the way that Professor haughtily keeps himself aloof from the common herd because of his supposedly superior insight, but by shying away from things of death – for earth is the place of death, as the contexts of Professor's words show us. Professor's words have the power to darken the mood of a scene, and the scene changes from Samson's song of life ('God I go chop life make I tell true', p. 6,) to his talk of death ('It's just like you to rob a dead man' and 'Your father's decomposing corpse', pp. 12 and 13). The darker tones which now mark Samson's speech do not, however, show that he has come to accept death as an important fact. He talks of the late Sergeant Burma as if he were alive still, and thus causes Salubi to point out that 'Sergeant Burma is dead'. The words and the whole incident look forward to that scene in which Samson manoeuvres himself into crossing the gulf to dead Sergeant Burma while innocently playing at his game of life.

Gerald Moore points out that in scenes like that in which Samson becomes possessed by the 'spirit' of Sergeant Burma, Soyinka makes an economic use of setting and characters to extend the theme of the suspension of time or death and so does more than solve production problems of time, space and cast.[9] In addition to the visual and verbal means of communication that have been discussed earlier, spirit possession is part of the 'mask idiom' which makes up the third and major area of communication represented in the play. Kotonu's experience of Ogun possession is presented more as an experience re-lived in the present than as a flashback. This not only gives it the immediacy of a recalled experience, it also communicates directly to the audience the traumatic hold which it still has on Kotonu. Its structural position also intensifies the main motif of the play: Kotonu, like Murano, whose transition agonies he has experienced, is in a state of limbo, a state marked by the lassitude for which Samson constantly upbraids him. The transition ecstasies which Samson and Kotonu experience are linked with that of Murano in the sense that they all result from some form of communication with the dead. Just as Kotonu under the mask screams with the agony of possession, so Samson screams for forgiveness at unwittingly identifying with Sergeant Burma.

Both sufferers anticipate Murano who 'suffers from gutturals like a love-crazed frog' when Professor restores him to the state of possession and so brings the living into active communion with the dead.

What Professor discovers by this resort to ritual is that Murano, the wine-bearing god who inspires conviviality but reveals little, has now become the *agemo* masquerade who inspires terror, for the dancing mask is now in continuous communion with the other world, and 'the dance is the movement of transition'. Murano's dance is a means of making death apparent. That is why the drivers cringe with dread at Professor's resurrection of their god. The popular indignation at sacrilege which Say Tokyo Kid voices by asking, 'Do you want to go blind with things you should not see' (p. 94), has been anticipated in Professor's similar warning to Samson who would spy on Murano: 'Those who are not equipped for strange sights – fools like you – go mad or blind when their curiosity is pursued' (p. 45). Death is of course the prescribed punishment for sinning at the tree of knowledge. 'Samson with an ass's head', whose lion-hearted curiosity prompts him on, is restrained from actually sinning at the forbidden tree by the threat of blindness. On the other hand, Professor shows by his words that he understands the consequences of sacrilege. He can ignore them because he considers himself equipped with superior understanding. His role of philosopher among fools implies two religious traditions defining his relationship to others in the play. The drivers belong to the popular tradition of Ogun worship and their instincts are mainly self-protective, their god being essentially a tutelary deity, as we see from their attempt to make Professor their patron and protector.[10] Professor behaves as if he belonged to a clerical elite. He plays the *babalawo* to Salubi and Samson and claims his divination dues. In defiance of the threat in the *oro* song (p. 28), he is not content with merely seeing and paying obeisance, he must seek understanding. But his desire to understand lacks the usual intellectual disinterestedness of a *babalawo*, even though he insists he would not 'foul up eternal beads of cowries with minted commerce' (p. 63). That is why he ignores rituals enacting the penalty for irreverence. The ritual similarity between the prophetic end of Part One and the end of Part Two is quite emphatic. At the end of Part One, Salubi almost gets killed for spying on Murano. The message is not intended for Professor – who can be trusted to ignore it in any case – although it is a rehearsal of the fate that will overtake him at the end of the play. Its function is to prepare us to accept the rightness of Professor's death by prescribing the penalty for sacrilege in dramatic form.

It would not be satisfactory however to reduce the play's statement to mere satire on sacrilege. What makes the play tragic rather than satirical is the closing speech which, like Egbo's experience in *The Interpreters*, is

the divine boon won by the traveller who 'beards the gods in their den'.[11]
The Word which Professor has found is similar in purpose to Bandele's
Word of judgement. For this speech to be seen for what it is – a map of
the experience of the characters in the play – the final movements of the
mask before it 'dies' in the last scene should be visually reminiscent of the
gradual sinking of the mask at the end of the possession of Kotonu – at
least sufficiently so to suggest a link between the experience of Kotonu
and the knowledge of which Professor speaks in this scene. It would be
noticed that the speech is largely based on the report of Kotonu's experience (since Murano could not reveal much):

> Be even like the road itself. Flatten your bellies with the hunger of an
> unpropitious day, power your hands with the knowledge of death. In
> the heat of the afternoon when the sheen raises false forests and a
> watered haven, let the event first unravel before your eyes. Or in the
> dust when ghost lorries pass you by and your shouts fall on deaf panels
> and the dust swallows them. Dip in the same basin as the man that
> makes his last journey and stir with one finger, wobbling reflections of
> two hands, two hands, but one face only. Breathe like the road. (p. 96)

The dust of the ghost lorries, the multiplying faces, and the 'one shadow
cast by all the doomed' are insights lent by Kotonu and held in language
by Professor. We are reminded of the rehearsal for this speech in that
scene where Professor feverishly takes down his interpretation of Kotonu's
dictated experience. Its metaphors belong primarily to the drivers' world.
It is evident from these metaphors that the state of the road determines
the character of the drivers' god, and one may glimpse the physical
features of the land through these metaphors. The controlling image is the
snake or serpent, which not only hints at the treachery of the god, but also
the image for the uneven and winding road:

> Be the road! Coil yourself in dreams, lay flat in treachery and deceit
> and at the moment of a trusting step, rear your head and strike the
> traveller in his confidence, swallow him whole or break him on the earth.

The above quotation combines the literal subject, the road, with the
speaker's interpretation of his experience of this road, in the single image
of the snake. It uses the symbolic language of myth as a means of en-
compassing all its experience, for it is in the character of myth to express
in a single image a complex or coherent experience.[12] The language of the
play is logical because its metaphors are functional rather than convenient
or decorative. It may seem unusual, for example, for the road to be
described as a woman when all along it has been identified with the male
god, Ogun. But the road is also a woman because it is that aspect of the
Earth Mother which endures the treacherous destruction of human life
described by Professor as a menstrual waste:

> Below that bridge, a black rise of buttocks, two unyielding thighs and
> that red trickle like a woman washing her monthly pain in a thin river.
> So many lives rush in and out between her legs, and most of it a waste.
> (p. 58)

Taken along with the earlier image through which we are made to see a
loaded lorry as 'pregnant with stillborn',[13] this image of the frigid woman
suggests the need to earth Ogun so that his vital energies may prove
creative rather than wasteful.

Professor's speech hints at human neglect of road conditions, although
this is blurred by his treatment of the phenomenal world as if it were only
a shadowy projection of the spiritual world in which he lives. When he
describes the road sign which he pulled out as he would describe a plant
(p. 8), it is partly because it has been hidden from sight by surrounding
growth for a long time. At this level Professor's speech describes the essence
of social reality. It shows an understanding of the character of the environment and it presents the sympathetic union of characters and landscape in
the play. But the effect of environment on character is presented not as a
simple social statement, but as a condition for survival. The spiritual
questions raised in this final speech makes it more than a simple social
statement. The speech is complex and it works in an almost insidious way.
The exhortations are made to look like the conditions for survival, so that
the whole speech seems a benediction spoken at an initiation of the
children of the road. But the invitation is contradicted by negative values
like 'treachery and deceit', so that the opening sentence, 'Be like the road,'
now opens out the other option – the possibility of free will which enables
the characters to choose what they will be. The criticism is thus turned
both ways – against the characters as well as the conditions to which they
respond. The characters are pulled into this ironic vision through the
image of the road (both the geographical item and the mythical being)
which acts out its dual role of patron and destroyer. This dual role makes
a simple, clear-cut statement undesirable.

A simple statement is thus usually avoided in Soyinka. The two
extremes of a situation are usually held in balance by a mediating device –
a Yoruba technique which he adopts in *The Interpreters* where the need to
balance Orunmila's bowl of order with Esu's circle of chance does not
allow him to award either of the two divinities exclusive ownership of
either the circle or the lines of divination:

> . . . the eternal war of the first procedure with the long sickle head of
> chance, eternally mocking the pretensions of the bowl of plan, mocking
> lines of order in the ring of chaos.[14]

In *The Road* we have been prepared for the ambivalence of the last speech
by Soyinka's use of the mediating device of the spider, which is more

easily understood than the road because at first it sticks out as an almost mechanical symbol to which we refer the different characters for evaluation. It never remains static, however, because although it starts as a mere complement to the meaning the road suggests, it soon develops into a dramatic item directly involving one of the main characters in its fate. Thus the most revealing 'cant' in the play is spoken by Kotonu to parry Samson's thrust at him for lying in wait like a spider for its prey: 'The road and the spider lie gloating, then the fly buzzes along like a happy fool . . .' (p. 34). This reveals not only the unseen deadly side of Kotonu and the road, but also Samson's relationship to passengers. The compassionate driver's boy who herds shocked passengers away from the death pit is also the importunate tout who lured them into the lorry trap in the first place:

> (*Samson finds himself doing a running battle with a fly . . . he takes the fly to the spider's web, throws it in, and stays to watch the spider seize it, a satisfied grin spreading over his face.*)
> SAMSON (*obviously slightly drunk*): Got him? A-ah, he understands the game all right. Easy as chucking an unwilling passenger into a lorry. (p. 91)

The wine which Murano bears makes possible this exposure of Samson's weak underside. Samson's involvement with the spider and the fly makes us now know exactly how to take Professor's definition of truth as 'scum risen on the froth of wine' (p. 70).

Like the incident of Kotonu's accelerator foot, Samson's battle with the fly shows that the means by which the audience understood are only partially verbal. Often music, physical motion, and physical symbol become the most striking mediators between the play and the audience. This is the basis of Soyinka's claim for the theatrical appeal of *A Dance of the Forests*. The play is generally held to be difficult to interpret but, according to Soyinka, it is the cooks and stewards who come night after night to see it.[15] A similar dramatic appeal is present in the motor park foolery and masquerade play of *The Road*. *The Road* communicates at two levels. At the immediate, theatrical level Professor is the 'professor' or 'conjurer' who communes with spirits, as well as the stereotype, so strong in popular Nigerian imagination, of the learned man who like Paul has gone mad with too much learning. Both types are socially identifiable. At this level Professor's image is mainly a device for theatrical appeal, and his 'meaningless' but impressive rhetoric would make sense. But social realism is not the intention behind Professor's image. It is rather that other side of him, the 'madness' of the intellectual so obsessed with learning that he remains blind to flesh and blood, or the inevitable 'madness' of the figure of satire, which points the realism behind the portrait. Here Soyinka is working within the Yoruba dramatic tradition in which masquerade representations of certain social types are made, quite often with a satirical slant; this explains how a serious play can be made from such light materials as we find in *The Road*. But we ought to balance the image of Professor as an absurd character with the tragic figure of the condemned man who speaks the word of truth in the end.

The meaning of a play can merely be limited, not exhausted, by a literary interpretation of the play. Its most important meaning is intuitively received. If the response is adequate to the play's appeal, much of its power may remain inexplicably felt and its meaning apprehended only subconsciously. The cerebral activity of the critic of a dramatic text thus becomes merely a disciplined attempt to explain the presence and workings of this power and meaning in a rational manner. The critic thus becomes, in relation to audience, what Professor has been to the layabouts.

NOTES

1. *The Road* (London, O.U.P., 1965). All references are to this text.
2. *Times Literary Supplement* (10 June 1965), p. 476.
3. 'Segun Awolowo: He Who Was', *Sunday Express* (Lagos) (25 July 1965), p. 6.
4. Peter Morton Williams, 'The Yoruba Ogboni Cult in Oyo', *Africa*, XXX (1960), p. 373.
5. Morton-Williams, op. cit., p. 372.
6. *The Interpreters* (London, Heinemann, 1970), p. 251.
7. Cf. Margaret Laurence, *Long Drums and Cannons* (London, Macmillan, 1968), p. 63.
8. Eldred Durosimi Jones, *The Writing of Wole Soyinka* (London, Heinemann, 1973), pp. 62–3.
9. Gerald Moore, *Wole Soyinka* (London, Evans, 1971), p. 60.
10. This is the main intention of the praise song on p. 86.
11. *The Interpreters*, p. 127.
12. For a similar view of the Yoruba language see Adebayo Adesanya, 'Yoruba Metaphysical Thinking', *Odu* (Ibadan), No. 5 (n.d.), p. 37; and cf. Soyinka, 'Language reverts in religious rites to its pristine existence eschewing the sterile limits of particularization', 'The Fourth Stage', in *The Morality of Art* (London, Routledge and Kegan Paul, 1969), p. 124.
13. This image, which suggests Professor's view that man is not fulfilled until he dies, should be taken along with his picture of Murano resting his big toe on the chrysalis and his belief that fulfilment (the imago) awaits the cracking of the chrysalis.
14. *The Interpreters*, p. 225.
15. Interview by Olu Akaraogun in *Spear Magazine* (Lagos) (May 1966), p. 19.

The Asphalt God

RONALD BRYDEN

What kind of Commonwealth Festival would it have been had Ian Hunter defined it originally as a display, not of distinguishing national inheritances, but of shared historical experience? Something small, poorer and more embarrassing, no doubt, but perhaps more interesting. The Burlington House exhibition would have forfeited its treasures of African and Asian antiquity. There would have been more items like the Sydney Symphony's opening concert of Elgar, Parry and Vaughan Williams, and fewer to draw lunch-hour crowds, hoping against hope that the Sierra Leone National Troupe's ladies might defy the Metropolitan Police and the elements, to Trafalgar Square. That pointedly uninvited guest, the ghost of empire, would have stalked the festivities like Banquo, its topee tucked underneath its arm, shaking its crimson cock-feathers. But in the contemporary arts we might have suffered a good deal less folksy romantic nationalism and been startled by more things like *The Road*.

The fascination of Wole Soyinka's play (snatched from the official program by Stage Sixty to make a fringe event at Stratford East) is its assimilation into specifically Nigerian terms of a universal modern phenomenon, brought by imperialism — petrol transport. In other words, it's about the real modern Nigeria: an enormous, inchoate territory whose ancient units of tribe and religion are being supplanted by the new patterns of technology — above all, by the system of rough, weather-pitted roads along which thousands of ramshackle, picturesquely named lorries speed goods and passengers hundreds of miles to market.

A community of free-lance lorry-drivers inhabits a tumbledown night-shelter run by a white-bearded, frock-coated eccentric called the Professor. His hold over them is multiple — he runs their lives, forging the driving-licences they need to gain employment, selling spare parts for their decrepit machines, advising them in their encounters with the police, providing an accommodation address. In addition, he offers a refuge where they can smoke hemp and supplies them nightly with illegal palm-wine, brewed by a deaf-mute protégé he once rescued from a wrecked hearse. But his power over them clearly does not end there. Once a minister in the Christian chapel next door, he is now a seeker after some new, greater revelation, and his drivers wait reverently for it — the Word of a God who will dispose their comings and goings, account for all accidents, extend beyond their horizons, give their lives purpose and nobility, prepare their deaths.

Meanwhile they sit gossiping, waiting for evening and the palm-wine bootleg- ger, acting out the sagas of the road, its famous smashes, the great names it has reaped: Muftau, who drove an oil-tanker non-stop from Port Harcourt to Kaduna, Sergeant Burma, who handled his lorry like a toy and claimed to have been cheated overseas of a VC; Cimarron Kid, 'Humphrey Bogart', Akanni the Lizard, Kotonu, a driver known for his skill from Lagos to Monrovia, wants to escape his vocation before he joins this pantheon. He too waits on the Professor's revelation. In the end it comes, the god reveals itself. It is the Road, the great dusty snake in whose life all theirs are contained, in whose coils death lurks at every bend.

It's a play of poetry and atmosphere rather than action, modelled perhaps (Soyinka read English at Leeds, and spent 18 months as a play-reader for the Royal Court) on O'Neill's *The Iceman Cometh*: there's a strong resemblance between the ragged drivers watching for sunset and the releasing palm-wine and those twitchy Bowery derelicts awaiting the gay, fatal Hickey. It's a disadvantage for English audiences that some of this poetry's obscure in idiom and imagery — you need a sharp ear and a smattering of West African mythology. But when communication fails there's a stunning set by Ken Calder and some striking masks to contemplate, and even through an unevenly professional production the power and sophistication of the play leap out at you. To appreciate its vivid audacity, you need to ask who in Britain could paint an equivalent picture of our own surrogate religion of the car, with its votive badges, costly unguents and tiger-gods with annual feasts of blood.

A NIGERIAN ORIGINAL

Penelope Gilliatt

Every decade or so, it seems to fall to a non-English dramatist to belt new energy into the English tongue. The last time was when Brendan Behan's "The Quare Fellow" opened at Theatre Workshop. Nine years later, in the reign of Stage Sixty at the same loved Victorian building at Stratford East, a Nigerian called Wole Soyinka has done for our napping language what brigand dramatists from Ireland have done for centuries: booted it awake, rifled its pockets and scattered the loot into the middle of next week.

The Road in performance is tough work for local hearing, but after cleaning my ears out and reading the script I am quite sure that it is the work of a man with an intensely interesting body of plays to come who already writes like an angel. If the accent of his actors is unfamiliar, then the answer perhaps is that we might learn it, as Americans are learning Merseyside and as every filmgoer in England long ago mastered the voices of Chicago and the Bronx. The foreignness of the matter is something else: it is the jar of originality, distinct and audacious. The compressed phrases often creep up from behind, or buck like a hose of water, and they compound common ribaldry and upper metaphysics in a way we're not used to.

If a man is going to talk like John the Baptist now, an English audience expects him to do it in the accent of a T. S. Eliot clubman; no wonder Soyinka's characters are confusing, these illiterate bums lobbing comic insults at one another and at the same time worrying about the Word and the meaning of meaning. It is like finding the spirit of Professor Ayer lodged in a funny gardener at the Whitehall.

The looming invisible hero of the play is the road itself, as it appears to a band of lorry-drivers and passenger-touts and floggers of spare parts. Sometimes the road is their livelihood, manageably under their feet; sometimes it takes on the opposite anthropomorphic meaning and becomes their destroyer, more alive than they are, buckling up so that their break-toes tread on air and their bodies fall into its maw with no more sovereignty than crumbs obeying gravity. This alternating active-passive sense of themselves, which almost palpably multiplies by two the number of presences on the stage, has an impact rather like the quarter-tones in Indian music: it is a dimension that can be learnt, a commonplace from another landmass that oddly relates to experimental art here.

● ● ●

Soyinka's play is mystical-satirical, one foot in the limbo of dissolving flesh that is called *agemo* and the other firmly up the rump of modern Nigeria. The chief character, named Professor, is a mischievous visionary in frock coat and top hat who makes his entrance waving a road-sign that has obviously been catastrophically ignored. Accidents are his meat, both spiritually and commercially. They provide him with striking reasons for spouting about death and the Word, which he looks for patiently in antique bundles of the *Daily*

Mirror, and at the same time they allow him to run a profitable business forging licenses for replacement drivers.

Samson, a passenger-tout bereft of a job because his driver has suddenly gone into a coma of transcendentalism and given up the wheel, is enthralled by the memory of a contest in religiosity that Professor once had with a visiting bishop. But he can also see the sage to be a fair idiot, for in spite of being literate, the man mistakes football pools for heavenly signs. A policeman called Particulars Joe, face shiny with bribes, is as impressed as anyone by the old boy's Biblical sense of theatre; but when Professor starts talking grandly about welcoming a spell in jail as a chance to contemplate, the cop has enough independence to point out that prison is the least solitary community in the world.

Verbal exchanges here are about the most liberating experience available. Materially the choices are few, between driving, cadging passengers and thugging for a politician ("thug" in "The Road" becomes an indispensable verb). Politics, like the Church, are essential, sacrosanct and ludicrous. They are also, in Samson's phrase, a way of making the parish hot soup. The play functions as much through its humour as through the drugging dances and drum-music; the jokes are its way of swivelling back into the objective. They are made with a horse-sense undismayed by a diet of sermons and Government gobbledygook and they display an effortless command of rudeness. Samson can play endless lazy variants on the subject of a friend's stink.

The narrative of the play undeniably goes rather like a stalling lorry. Obscure hubbubs build up, and suddenly release an energy that lurches the torpid engine forward. The last brakeless run downhill, with a demonic dance and a surprise stabbing, represents a rush of plot that seems theatrically a mistake. It is also true that the cast is sometimes hesitant and amateur. But the director, David Thompson, has all the same performed a signal feat for a remarkable play; and so has the designer, Ken Calder, who has devised a dump for live souls around the back of a defunct lorry with a chapel window proffered over it like a jujube.

THE EXIGENCIES OF ADAPTATION: THE CASE OF SOYINKA'S *BACCHAE*

K. E. SENANU

The Bacchae which Euripides (480-406 BC) wrote towards the end of his life, while he was in self-exile in Macedon, has always been recognized for its astonishing power, for the classical simplicity and rigor of its structure, and for the remarkable nature of its homage to traditional beliefs from a man who has spent the greater part of his writing career expressing his scepticism and showing up the absurdity of the Gods and their behavior according to received ideas.

In general terms Euripides dramatizes in this play the conflict which Nietsche has observed at the basis of all Greek drama, the conflict between the Apollonian and Dionysian principles in life, between light and darkness, between reason and ecstasy, between control and liberty, between male and female. In more specific terms Euripides is concerned with the complementary nature of these principles and the difficulty in discerning the limits of the one against the other. He suggests the precarious balance which exists between these pairs of principles by staging a conflict between Pentheus, the ruler of Thebes, and his cousin Dionysus, the son of Zeus and Pentheus' aunt Semele: a new God, whose worship involves, as Pentheus sees it, the overthrow of all decency, self-respect and control.

The precarious nature of the balance which subserves normality is represented by the simple but symbolic setting of Euripides' play. Pentheus' palace which faces us center stage stands at the meeting point of two ways: one leading to the city, the other to the hills of Cithairon. The palace is sustained by a balance between the civility, the control and rationality of established polity, and the ecstasy, the freedom and the mystery of the wild open country. Euripides' Pentheus is unconsciously aware of this precarious balance, expressed through the attraction which Dionysus, this new-fangled God obviously created by the wily old priest Tiresias for his own material benefit, exerts upon him:

> So; you *are* attractive, stranger, at least to women—which explains, I think, your presence here in Thebes. (p. 210) 1

he confesses. But, as a ruler, he must restore order to a city suddenly deserted by its womenfolk running in pursuit of some orgiastic rites in the hills. Therefore, in spite of the warnings of Tiresias and Dionysus himself, whom he tries to imprison without success, Pentheus mobilizes his army against the worshippers of this new God. Dionysus tempts him with safe-conduct to spy on the orgies of these female celebrants of the new cult before his attack on them. When he yields to this temptation we are aware that this is a surrender of integrity from within, a yielding to the attraction of that which he has consciously been opposing, an upsurge of that potential danger which the precarious balance has hidden so far from sight. Pentheus is led, grotesquely dressed in the costume of the female celebrants, to his death, torn to pieces by his own mother, Agave, and his aunts. The play ends with a lamentation for Pentheus, sacrificed by members of his own family who have been maddened by their resistance to the new God. The guilty members of the family go into exile under the curse of Dionysus, and the final note of the play is on the inscrutable ways of the Gods.

Soyinka calls his adaptation of *The Bacchae* "a communion rite." It seems to me (i) that the three major changes that he makes to Euripides' play help to define what he means by a communion rite, and (ii) that the adaptation serves his purposes as a playwright after *Madmen and Specialists* and before *Death and the King's Horseman*. I shall look at these changes in detail before I turn to the broader issues raised by the adaptation.

The three major changes involve (i) the nature of Pentheus' reign, (ii) the redefinition of the role of Dionysus and (iii) the transformation of the end of the play from a threnos of lamentation to a muted celebration, including a sudden recognition or an epiphany.

Soyinka's conception of Pentheus' reign is suggested, at the very opening of the play, by the setting. For the classical simplicity of Euripides' setting he substitutes the baroque intensity of a palace standing upon a charnel-house, visually represented by the line of skeletons which dip steeply into the earth and the sweating labor of slaves on the threshing floor. In this setting, the way, or more accurately, the road to the countryside has disappeared. The herdsman who brings the jug of wine and the smell of ripening grapes to the slaves is within the city walls when the play opens. Pentheus confesses to Dionysus later that he knows little of Thebes beyond the city: "Almost nothing of the country, come to think of it" (p. 288), so that the precarious balance between city and country, symbolized by Dionysus' attraction for Pentheus, is played down. In fact, instead of the "effeminate beauty" of Euripides' Dionysus, Soyinka talks of "a being of rugged strength and of rugged beauty" and prepares the way for the *manly temptation* - i.e., the flattery, through which Dionysus later inveigles Pentheus to his death.

With no knowledge of the country and concentrating all his energies on his civic responsibility, Pentheus has established a tyranny which involves a perversion of religious rites into a cruel and meaningless sacrifice of slaves as scapegoats. It is in this area of the perversion of religion that Soyinka offers a profound reinterpretation of the nature of Pentheus' failure as a ruler and suggests the radical cause of tyranny.

In the opening scene Tiresias impersonates an old slave and takes on the role of the annual scapegoat for the cleansing of the state. As a priest and prophet of the state religion, he knows he is inevitably implicated in the leadership of Pentheus' realm. The tyranny which Pentheus' rule involves is expressed by the suffering of the slave as a scapegoat on behalf of the entire realm. This is an obligation which should rightly devolve on the leadership of the realm, or more accurately, on the spiritual leadership of the realm. In other words, the leadership that exerts control is also duty-bound to provide liberty. The paradigm case of liberty is the ecstasy that Dionysus symbolizes. And the most radical form of tyranny is suffered when the scapegoat, in the person of the slave, is made to undergo the ecstasy on behalf of the realm. Ecstasy with its attributes of cleansing and purification is truly such when it proceeds from a willingly accepted sacrificial death - not an imposed death on an unwilling and helpless slave. It remains meaningless suffering and death, with no prospect of a new life or a new beginning, unless it is willingly undertaken. For the scapegoat sees his death as oppression, the imposition of the tyrant's will upon *his will*. His given life is in no way available for the renewal of the realm. The only condition which ensures such a renewal is the willingness of the giver. This is why renewal is the unique prerogative and privilege of the leader and the ruler. And it is for this reason that Soyinka dramatizes this *movement of transition* elaborately in this section of the play.

When the slaves see the future of their old comrade, impersonated by Tiresias, led to the yearly sacrifice, they threaten rebellion, for they recognize in this yearly sacrifice the depth of tyranny. Of course Tiresias, the seer, has anticipated this in taking on the role of the old slave. IIe confesses to Dionysus that his ultimate aim is not simply to prevent rebellion but to make renewal available:

> I have longed to know what flesh is made of. What suffering is. Feel the taste of blood instead of merely forseeing it. Taste the ecstasy of rejuvenation after long organizing it ritual. When the slaves began to rumble I saw myself again playing that futile role, pouring my warnings on deaf ears. An uprising would come, bloodshed, and I would watch, untouched, merely vindicated as before - as prophet. I approach death and dissolution, without having felt life . . . its force . . . (pp. 243-44)

But Soyinka also dramatizes this inevitable involvement of leadership with sacrificial death in order to ensure social renewal through the role he gives to *the leader* of the slaves on the advent of Dionysus. He is the first to recognize and to try to give vocal acknowledgement to the God. Of course, on one level, he has been waiting for the revolution which should end the political tyranny of Pentheus. Hence his fellow slaves restrain him, and remind him of the fate of the helots of the days preceding the coming of Christ. But the leader does not see the coming of Dionysus in exclusively political terms, although that is the primary reality of his life. When he addresses the followers of Dionysus he calls them fellow aliens, emphasizing his sense of dispossession. However, it is he who leads the Bacchantes into the chant and the dance which expresses the spiritual reality that the coming of Dionysus means. Soyinka takes a great deal of trouble in defining the music and the dance which dramatizes this moment of the play. He talks of "the emotional colour and temperature of a European pop scene without the usual tawdry commercial manipulation of teenage mindlessness." He talks of the control of the leader as emanating "from the self-contained force of his person expressing a deepening spiritual presence," and to this he adds "the energy of the black hot gospellers who themselves are often first to become physically possessed." In addition, drawing upon the incantatory rhythm of his *Idanre,* he provides some of the most carefully structured verse for this portion of the play. And at the climax the rhythm enacts an emblematic sacrifice, a tearing from limb to limb of the leader of the slaves, now become the leader of the liberated celebrants of Dionysus. Thus through the aborted role of Tiresias and the fully integrated role of the leader of the slaves, the nature of Pentheus' failure as a ruler is dramatized and the spiritual dimension of leadership is suggested.

The second large area of transformation we notice in the adaptation of Euripides' play affects the role of Dionysus himself. Euripides has presented Dionysus as the opposite, but complementary, principle of Pentheus' insistence on rationality, decency and civility. Soyinka eliminates the feminine attractiveness of Dionysus but emphasizes the intoxicating nature of the ecstasy that comes with the breakdown of control. In the temptation scene Dionysus does not play on Pentheus' curiosity. He offers him two mirror images of the release which the new God brings. It is significant that these two tableaux draw attention to both the liberation from class and political constraints on the one hand, and to spiritual renewal on the other hand. The one tableau presents the amusing tale of Heredotus concerning the marriage ceremony of Hippoclides and Agariste, the daughter of the tyrant of Sicyon in which, under the influence of wine, the bridegroom shocks his aristocratic in-laws by his irrepressible and vulgar dance and willingly forfeits his bride. The second tableau presents Christ's first miracle at the marriage of Cana. Although it is suggested that these two images of the influence of the new God tempt Pentheus into accepting the cup of wine offered by Dionysus, Soyinka adds an extra dimension to the role of Dionysus in the temptation scene. Dionysus insists that the *images of release* through wine are illusory. They are imitations of the reality. And to face that reality, he flatters Pentheus:

Dionysus:	You are a king. You have to administer.
	Don't take shadows too seriously, Reality
	Is your only safety. Continue to reject illusion.
Pentheus:	I do.
Dionysus:	You found me out. I have the gift
	Of magic, conjuring. But reality
	Awaits you on the mountains.
	Are you still afraid?
Pentheus:	No. What do you suggest?
Dionysus:	Come with me to the mountains. See for yourself.
	Watch the Maenads, unseen. *There are risks*
	A king must take for his own people. (emphasis mine)
Pentheus:	Yes, yes, that is true. (p. 287)

It is possible to argue that Pentheus accedes to this awful responsibility of risk-taking under the influence of the wine and, therefore, that his sacrifice does not release the true ecstasy, does not constitute the movement of transition, which releases new life. But even if this were true (and the evidence for Pentheus' drunkenness at this point is ambiguous: on the one hand, he refuses to put on the women's Bacchic dress and insists on his armor; on the other, when he is actually dressed in this Bacchic costume he mistakes it for his armor), Soyinka has underlined this aspect of the death of Pentheus, instead of simply suggesting as Euripides does, that Pentheus surrenders as a result of an invasion from within or as a result of the collapse of the precarious balance that his reign implies.

However, there is an even more significant reason for suggesting at this point that Pentheus' acceptance of his role implies a recognition of the responsibilities of the leader. For it is such an acceptance that makes meaningful the transformation of the end of the play into a celebratory rite of communion symbolizing rejuvenation instead of the threnos for irretrievable loss we have in Euripides.

Dionysus assures Tiresias after his timely intervention to rescue the priest from the lashes of his bloodthirsty functionaries in the first scene, that there would be real ecstasy in Thebes. The sacrificial death of Pentheus fulfils this promise. The blood that flows from that death not only soaks the land into new fruitfulness, it becomes a fountain of wine. The real blood and the illusory or symbolic wine are united in this sacrifice.

In the quotation given above, Dionysus urges Pentheus to ignore the illusions of ecstasy he has presented to him and to concentrate on the real responsibility of kingship. I have suggested that Dionysus seems to be flattering Pentheus, offering him a *manly temptation*. It is the God's ambivalent way of urging what in fact should be the reality of Pentheus' royalty. What seems flattery turns out to be the truth. For there are indeed risks that a king must take for his people. And in taking these risks, the political leadership and the priestly, sacrificial leadership are once more united.

Students of Soyinka are aware that in *Madmen and Specialists,* which he probably conceived while in detention during the civil war from August 1967 to October 1969, the proliferating tyranny and violence are partly the result of the initiation of both the cynical old man and the idealistic young specialist into the cannibalistic rites of the God As. For the young specialist, especially, the access of power to practice death on all who oppose him including his father, comes out of the liberation from the taboo of eating human flesh. Once this taboo has been removed, the sacredness of human life disappears and a reign of terror is unleashed. This is a perverse form of the unity of the political and "spiritual" priesthood. For instead of defining a self-sacrifice which enables rejuvenation, it ordains death as the ultimate reality. There seems to be no way out. The pessimism and despair of *Madmen and Specialists* has been remarked by many commentators and Soyinka has himself called the play an exercise in exorcism.

If the ultimate reality is death and the power to inflict death, as the young specialist in *Madmen* believes, then we can see how *The Bacchae* offers an opening for coming to terms and making meaning of this inexorable fact. There have been prototypes of the scapegoat figure in some of the earlier plays: Eman in *The Strong Breed,* for instance, who had to learn to face death. But the scapegoat figure, in as far as he is a victim who painfully learns to accept sacrificial death on behalf of others, is not a satisfactory answer to the fact of suffering and death. It is only when death is freely chosen as a process of transition which ensures new life, that death is truly circumvented. And this can only be done by someone in authority, upon whom, it cannot be said, the process has been imposed. What the music and the dance of transition, which first emerge in the adaptation of *The Bacchae* and are then fully explored with indigenous material in *Death and the King's Horseman,* symbolize is the ecstasy, the ineffable joy and peace which accompany this process of renewal through a freely chosen suffering and death. Pentheus, as ruler and sacrificial priest, provides the true image of what Soyinka suggests. African leaders should be like him instead of like the Kongis and, worst still, the young Specialist. The Elesin, the Horseman in Soyinka's next original play after *The Bacchae,* roughly adumbrates the pattern. But the almost impossible nature of the process is dramatized in the Elesin's inability to resist adulation - which is an inbuilt feature of leadership roles in Africa - and his very human desire to take a last sip of the cup of life even at this crucial moment of transition. The temptations within and without which assail the leader in the desert are complexly dramatized in this play. But the play itself has a simplicity of structure which is new in Soyinka. I believe the adaptation of Euripides has not only contributed to this clarity of form but met the exigencies of resolving the crisis of faith which *Madmen and Specialists* represents.

1. Quotations from Euripides' *The Bacchae* are taken from the Arrowsmith translation in *Greek Tragedies,* Vol. III, ed. David Grene & Richmond Lattimore (Chicago: University of Chicago Press, 1960). Soyinka's adaptation called *The Bacchae of Euripides* is available in Vol. 1. of *Collected Plays* (London: Oxford University Press, 1973). Page references are to these two editions.

Amateurs in Horror
Albert Hunt

At the end of Wole Soyinka's version of *The Bacchae,* there's a severed head on a stick in the middle of the stage. The head belongs to Pentheus, the king of Thebes, who wouldn't dance and wouldn't drink, but who spied pruriently on the rites of the Bacchantes. It's been torn from his body by his mother Agave, acting in drunken ecstacy. As she emerges from her frenzy, she is confronted with the reality of what she has done. The moment is, apparently, one of total despair. But then, from the head, there gushes a red fountain. "Again blood, Tiresias, nothing but blood," says Kadmos, a former king. But Tiresias replies: "No, it's wine." The head on the pole forms a phallus. But, to Wole Soyinka, it's not simply a primitive fertility symbol. It's a real head on a stick, and as such it's part of his own, unhappy, lived experience.

Wole Soyinka was born in Nigeria. Not long ago he spent two years in solitary confinement. His crime was that he had tried to visit Colonel Ojukwu to persuade him not to set up a separatist Biafran state. "It was a hopeless task," Soyinka said later. "Ojukwu too was a power-seeker. He, too, is a guilty man, his immense blunder overshadowed only by the far greater crime of the massacre of the Ibos." Soyinka refers to "two elitist states, swimming along the same sewer of reaction, two very complacent regimes in which the seeds of revolution would have perished alike."

The two "complacent regimes" were led by two highly civilised black men, both of whom had been educated in British army establishments at Eaton Hall, Hythe and Warminster. Together they presided over an orgy of genocide, which was connived at by a distant god in the shape of a benign white man with a pipe. And when the orgy was over, the vacuum was filled by weekend entertainments on Bar Beach, the Sunday playground of Lagos, in the form of public executions. "We're back to Roman decadence," said Soyinka. "To watch these bloody circuses in the name of public morality is to unite and identify with the guilty men of power." And he added, "The war no longer united people in stoicism; so they're trying to unite them in bestiality and guilt by the titillation of the power-cravings of the meanest citizen."

It's against this slice of contemporary reality that Soyinka's version of Euripides must be seen. The "guilty men of power" are represented in the play by Pentheus. With his stern, puritan sense of morality, he sees the women in the hills, practising the rites of Dionysius, as a threat. But he is also unhealthily fascinated and excited by them. He goes out to spy on them, his presence unleashes the violence, and he is torn to pieces.

There are two points to make about this confrontation between Pentheus and the Bacchantes. In the first place, in Soyinka's play the violence is not an intrinsic part of the Dionysiac rites. Dance, drunkenness, ecstacy, sexual license, orgy—these belong to Dionysius. But the violence is let loose only when the Bacchantes are menaced. When herdsmen approach them, the Bacchantes rise up and tear the cattle limb from limb; and when Pentheus is discovered, spying from a tree, he too is brutally destroyed. In both cases Soyinka makes it clear that it is the interference of the "power-seekers" that provokes the horror.

Secondly, this is no simple confrontation between the rational man of society and the liberating impulses of irrationality. Pentheus may consider himself in control, but Soyinka emphasises that his apparent rationality is itself irrational, obsessive. It is his lack of reason, his obsession with the Bacchantes, that leads directly to his destruction.

In much of this, Soyinka follows Euripides closely. His lived experience in Nigeria has illuminated rather than transformed the myth. But in two opening scenes, that are linked directly with Soyinka's final image, Soyinka sets the Greek myth inside the framework of his own response to Nigerian reality. He does this, not by "modernising" the play, but by adding one image and sharpening another.

The image he adds is that of a chorus of male slaves. At the very beginning of the play, they shamble through the audience, linked to each other by chains that clang as they walk; and on the stage they form themselves into a shuffling circle that evokes images from the concentration camps. This chorus exists throughout the play as an added dimension. The chains that, according to Dionysius, bind Pentheus's spirit are made concrete around the wrists and ankles of these slaves. The Bacchantes are seen by the slaves, and by Soyinka, as a *politically* liberating force.

The image that is sharpened is that of the wine. In an additional opening scene, that has been described by several critics as superfluous, the Herdsman and the Slaves share a jug of wine, that is passed round the group. (In the National Theatre production this sense of communion is totally lost). Wine is identified in the scene with joy and fertility. "There is heaven in this juice," says the Slave Leader. "It flows through my lips and I say, now I roll the sun on my tongue."

And so when, at the end of the play, the severed head gushes wine, which the slaves, as well as the Bacchantes, drink and are drenched in, Soyinka is using the wine as a concrete image of rebirth. Soyinka confronts us with a cycle. Out of the horror has gushed the wine: but out of the wine has come the delirium. And out of the delirium, the horror. And out of the horror, the wine . . .

Soyinka stares unblinking at the contradiction. But he ends by asserting the rebirth. And what gives him the right to assert the rebirth is that he has lived with the horror. The play's final affirmation is wrested out of his experience of the nightmare: his play is subtitled, "A communion rite."

"As a writer," Soyinka has said, in an interview in *The Guardian,* "I have special responsibility, because I can smell the reactionary sperm years before the rape of a nation takes place." Soyinka has, in recent years, been present at the rape of a nation. And his experience of this rape has translated itself into an expression of astonishment and wonder that, out of the most terrible mutilation, joy can still emerge.

This, then, is the play Wole Soyinka has written. But the trouble is that, in the staging of his play by the National Theatre at the Old Vic, Soyinka has come into direct collision with the unyielding amateurism of the British professional theatre. The company that presents Soyinka's play contains a drummer who can't drum, dancers who can't dance, and actors whose only concept of narrative acting is to begin every speech in the flat clipped tones that used to characterise British war movies, and then to rise in a gradual crescendo towards uncontrolled emotional wallowing. Where the play calls for ecstacy, the girls in the chorus offer a well-bred imitation of a hop at the local disco; and where the play calls for horror, we're given a crude imitation of a Madame Tussaud head, out of which spurts pink paint. The strength of Soyinka's final assertion is frittered away in a grotesque attempt, by this production, to express release.

What this production demonstrates yet again is the stylistic illiteracy of what is generally accepted as the best in British theatre. Faced with a text that calls for precise and strictly meaningful gesture, for narrative clarity, and for a theatre language built on ritual, the director has opted for imitation orgies, fake horror, and whooped up excitement. It isn't so much that he has failed to find the right answers as that he has shown himself completely unaware of what questions to ask.

MEDIATION IN SOYINKA: THE CASE OF THE KING'S HORSEMAN

D. S. IZEVBAYE

In this essay I intend to argue that the principle of mediation is fundamental to Soyinka's dramatic art, especially his dramatization of the tragic experience. I shall propose as the key figure in the pattern of mediation developed in *Death and the King's Horseman* not the familiar mythic figures in Soyinka's works, like Ogun, the candidate proposed in "The Fourth Stage" as the Yoruba tragic protagonist, or Sango, the rival god of lightning whose fiery temperament disqualifies him for the tragic role, but *Esu Elegba,* the principle of uncertainty, fertility and change, and the one god who makes possible the reconciliation of opposites which we associate with mediation.

In "The Fourth Stage" Soyinka describes Ogun as *the* tragic actor because he alone among the gods fulfils the Nietzschean requirement for the superman who has will enough to cross the abyss. The primitive irrationality of Ogun is opposed to the sanity and serenity of Obatala, as Nietzsche's Dionysos to his Apollo. Ogun is a mediator between two states of being. There are other forms of mediation to which his qualities do not apply, but it will first be necessary to show why mediation is so central to Yoruba cosmology and consequently to the style of Soyinka's art.

The three-part structure which is often implicit in the cosmology of Soyinka's work reflects the three-part organization of Yoruba political and religious systems: the judicial, the religious and the executive arms of government; the world of the unborn, the world of the living and the world of the dead in religion. (see Morton-Williams, 1964: 243-61). Soyinka turns to this cosmology to explain his intentions in *The Road* (Soyinka, 1975ᵃ: 117), and he ends his most recent play, *Death and the King's Horseman,* with a similar allusion to "the dead . . . the living . . . the unborn". Twice, before the publication of this play, Soyinka had attempted an explication of what remains implicit in Yoruba ritual and philosophy, that there is a "fourth area - the area of transition . . . the area of the really dark forces . . . the area of stress of the human will" (Soyinka, 1975ᵇ, 117-18).

It is Ogun's ability to dare this region that qualifies him for tragic stature. But he is not the only figure who mediates between the other areas of existence. Other beings listed by Soyinka include cripples and albinos who are held in holy awe for their physical deformities, and wandering spirits like Abiku. Soyinka is here merely articulating a widely held belief: the women Cassandra, Clark's Orukorere and Armah's Naana are gifted with second sight; and an abnormal looking child pictured in Verger's book (Pierre Verger, 1957: plate 136) qualifies to be considered "a supernatural being" because he has chameleon eyes starting from their sockets, a hanging lower lip and a pyramidal forehead. These beings are thus either in constant motion between the different realms or they permanently inhabit the area of transition and are in a constant state of passage. Iyaloja says of the proposed union between Elesin, who stands at the threshold of death, and the mystery market girl, that "the fruit of such a union will be neither of this world nor of the next. Nor of the one behind us . . . [but an] elusive being of passage."

But mediation is not only this kind of link between planes of existence as in *The Road*. It is also a reconciliation of opposites through either a finding of correspondences, as in the human-divine matching in *The Interpreters,* or the comparable political methods of Kongi and Danlola. The mediator can be a person, (a carrier or a trickster), an act (the dance in *The Road*) or a structure (the relationship between audience and performer, or the arrangement of Ifa divination furniture in which Esu is an essential companion of his opposite, Orunmila). Thus, although Soyinka does not actually use the word mediation or mediator in his writing, the presence and operation of the principle is implied in his description of the different forms of this device; the dance is "the movement of transition" in *The Road*, theatre is a "technique of interaction" (Soyinka, 1975: 65), and many of his protagonists are "twilight creatures," beings who have to "breach or cross this gulf over and over again," thus illustrating the phenomenon described as "human will under stress." As a result of this view his key characters are usually intermediaries: Lazarus, Murano, Aroni, the Kadiye, Eman, the Organizing Secretary, Si Bero and Elesin.

The device leaves its mark on Soyinka's language too, for it owes its vibrant quality partly to this feature. It is present in the love of paradoxes, punning, *double entendre*, and also the transposed attributes in this quotation from *The Interpreters*: "the *logic* of nature's growth was bettered by the *cabalistic* equations of the *sprouting* derrick." Mediation is thus useful as a principle of balance and moral judgement, even in his use of language. Such paradox is present in the traditional religious order, especially in the ordering of Ifa divination furniture. In the hymn to the creation of the gods in *The Interpreters*, Kola's canvas celebrates "the eternal war of the first procedure with the long sickle head of chance, eternally mocking the pretensions of the bowl of plan, mocking lines of order in the ring of chaos." In this description of the divination board and the sculpture of Esu the circles and the lines become the mediators between the certainty of Orunmila and the disorder of Esu, so that neither god enjoys complete control of the Yoruba cosmos. The result of this balance of forces is not disruption but a cosmic dance.

It is this same principle which gives *A Dance of the Forests* its title. In this play Soyinka treats drama as an art of mediation. It borrows its language and form from the procedure of the judiciary, its medium from the dance. The main questions that may be asked at a first reading of *A Dance of the Forests* is at what point in the play did this "dance" actually take place? The abortive festival planned by the Town Dwellers never takes place, so the "dance" is both the penitential progress of the three humans (a progress which makes the character grouping somewhat reminiscent of that of *The Tempest* in that Prospero/Forest Father leads the three men of sin to redemption and self-knowledge through the agency of Ariel/Aroni). The central dramatic episode is "the trial" of humanity, in which the forests (the spirits of the palm, the pachyderms, the ants, rivers and volcanos) give testimony against the humans. It is after this that the triplets, the figure in red, the Interpreter, and the half-child "dance" for the humans. This play within the play has the structure of a judicial procedure in the employment of advocates, a prosecutor and witnesses, as well as the use of Oro, the punitive agent in traditional Yoruba society. A hint in this direction has been given when the first scene opens with a legal phrase; "Will you take my case, sir?" The dance is the mediator for linking the three aspects of the play, the legal idiom, the political occasion for the play and the religious interpretation of its action. The relationship of dance and religion is made obvious not only by the important place of dance in religious ritual but by the fact that it is the means of moving between planes of existence in *A Dance of the Forests*, as in *The Road*.

In the earlier play the link between the judicial and the religious aspects of the play is brought out by the interventions of Ogun and Eshuoro in the judicial procedure of the "dance" episode. Such interruptions occur frequently in the drum and dance incidents of later plays; they constitute the dramatic moment of these plays and signify the moment of truth for the characters. In *Kongi's Harvest* such a moment occurs when the Superintendent stops Danlola's drums and when Daodu "split/The gut of our make-believe". In *The Road* Murano's mask-dance is interrupted by Kotonu's accident and later by the indignant action of Say Tokyo Kid. Since the dance is described as "the movement of transition" in *The Road*, its interruption implies an arrest at the point where the dancer remains in transition.

This is the state of paralysis in *Death and the King's Horseman* where action is impossible and where fulfilment is frustrated for the protagonist who, unlike Soyinka's late father, cannot be celebrated for having "danced and joined the ancestors." That Elesin has arrived at the state of transition is suggested in the confusion in the mind of Joseph who cannot tell whether the chief is living or dead: the drumming "sounds like the death of a great chief and then, it sounds like the wedding of a great chief." The white man's intervention in the rites of passage is the historical stopping of the drums. It is presented off-stage to heighten its dramatic impact on both Olunde and the audience:

> OLUNDE: The drums. Can you hear the change? Listen. (The drums come over, still distinct. There is a change of rhythm, it rises to a crescendo and then, suddenly, it is cut off. After a silence, a new beat begins, slow and resonant.) There. It's all over . . . my father is dead. His will-power has always been enormous.

This is the main dramatic irony of the play, for at this point Elesin is neither dead nor has his will-power been proved to be enormous. This decline in the stature of Elesin comes in the Fourth Act of this classic Five Act play after we have witnessed the tragic, Ogun-like courage of Elesin in the climactic Third Act. The function of the fifth Act would be not only to bring about the usual resolution to tragic action but also to bring out the trickster side of the hero's personality - his quick tongue and failure of nerve. The five Acts alternate between the world of the white men and the world of the Africans, and dance is the mediator of both these worlds. Each of the first four Acts opens and closes with the action of dancing, thereby creating a basis for comparing and contrasting both worlds.

Death and the King's Horseman is thus an extended image. It dramatizes the interruption of the psychic and cultural harmony of traditional Oyo society. Its protagonist is an accomplished dancer and his entry involves drummers and praise-singers. When the play opens his dance is "no longer of this earth." The opening scene presents the Yoruba as a people who have had a vision of the void and whose values are an attempt to overcome it. The harmony of their world is imposed on their fear of chaos:

> If [our] world leaves its course and smashes on the boulders of the great void, whose world will give us shelter? . . . In your time we do not doubt the peace of farmland and home, the peace of road and hearth, we do not doubt the peace of the forest.

Part of this hope is expressed in the election and initiation of an "intercessor to the other world" whom they address as "you who now bestride the hidden gulf and pause to draw the right foot across." They thus seek a balance between the material world and the spiritual.

When the stage lights come up on the opening scene of the play, they would fall, significantly, on

> a passage through the market in its closing stages . . . stalls are emptied, mats folded . . . bolts of cloth taken down . . . and piled on a tray.

The symbolism of this setting is as important as that of the dance which occupies such a central role in the play. The cultural importance of the Yoruba market has been discussed by more than one writer:

> In a close relationship with the *Afin* in sharing the centre of the town is the main market which was held in front of the *Afin*, where the Oba could watch from a reasonable distance the regular assembling of his people. (Ojo, 1966: 40).

The Yoruba market appears to have the symbolic value of a microcosm. This is suggested by two facts. First, while the major Oba are addressed as *Alaiyeluwa* (Owner of the world and of life), the minor Oba who are founders of their towns have the title, *Oloja* (Owner of the market) (Fadipe, 1970: 160). Second, there is the common Yoruba saying, *Oja L'aiye, Orun n'ile* (the world is a market, heaven is home). This attitude is reflected in Elesin's flippant boast, "this market . . . is my roost . . . where I have known love and laughter away from the palace," as well as the earnest song of the market women, "We shall all meet at the great market", and the description of Iyaloja as "mother of multitudes in the teeming market of the world."

The rich and colorful cloths in the market - damask, *alari, sanyan* and

cloth of indigo - are the material equivalent of the honor and glory
awaiting the people's emissary to the other world. The rich cloths and
sexual favors generously offered to Elesin are meant to honor him for
daring to bridge the gulf. The spiritual world is thus spoken of in material
terms: honor is not an abstract idea, but is represented in concrete terms
by the advance of rich food and cloths, since the Yoruba like "man in any
environment must eat before he can philosophise" (Ojo, 1966: 205).
Dishonor has its material expression also. Elesin's disgrace is felt to be
tragic because it is couched in language which makes us feel it as a
physical experience. When he fails in honorable deeds the imagery of
sweetmeats and rich cloths with which he has been honored changes into a
picture of the elder who "has no more holes in [his] rag of shame"
stepping "in the vomit of cats and the droppings of mice" [to] fight them
for the left-overs of the world." A similar image is used in *Oba Waja*
where the Oyo people ask, "shall the commander of the horse/Re-
main behind to eat earthworms and centipedes?" Honor comes too late
restored to Elesin, and the final vision of him among the ancestors which
we are given is actually a dreadful curse:

> His son will feast on the meat and throw him bones. The passage is clogged with
> droppings from the King's stallion; he will arrive all stained in dung.

The key to Elesin's failure would be found in his excessive love of the
material world symbolized by clothes and sex. It is significant that in the
crucial third Act when Elesin is being put through his paces by the Praise-
Singer, who is both the voice of tradition and the spirit medium for the
late Alaafin, it is the reminder of his vows as well as the good life which
Elesin has enjoyed (good food, fine clothes), which prefaces the ritual test
of his preparedness for his spiritual role

> PRAISE-SINGER: . . . . . . If there is
>   Weight on the loose end of your sash . . .
>   . . . if your sash is earthed
>   By evil minds who mean to part us
>   at the last . . .
>
> ELESIN: My sash is of the deep purple *alari*
>   It is no tethering-rope.

Having been assured that Elesin is not tied down by love of material
things, the Praise-Singer drops the imagery of clothing and feasting from
the ritual and gradually replaces it by that of pathfinding, of striving and
endeavor: of horse and dog as guides, of finding one's way in the dark, of
the elephant rushing into the forest and the albino making his way
through the dark. Believing that Elesin has fulfilled his vows, the Praise-
singer pronounces a song of praise: "How shall I tell what my eyes have
seen . . . oh how shall I tell what my ears have heard?"
    If Elesin's preparedness for his role seems assured by the end of Act
Three, his failure in Act Four would seem to have been caused by the
intervention of the white man, and the reproach of Olunde and Iyaloja in

Act Five would seem a little harsh. But the first Act already shows Elesin's paralysis when he "enters along a passage before the market." He remains spiritually in this state till the end of the play when Iyaloja informs us that "he is gone at last into the passage." Between his first appearance at the market and his death he makes little progress. The white man's intervention in Act Four has been foreshadowed in the first Act by two minor interruptions of his dance. The first occurs when he halts the lyric grace of his dance by his surprising invocation of the "Not I" bird.

This break in the dance is part of his dramatic style, as he earlier stopped his dance to feign annoyance with the market women. But the dramatic irony of the "Not I" bird incident exposes his alienation from his world. Although Elesin explains that the "Not I" bird refers to the fear of death, it also ironically implies an anathema since it is the act of warding off evil by snapping the fingers round the head, as the farmer does in Elesin's tale, to ward off penalties for an unintended abomination. Elesin in a speech of dramatic irony "unrolled my welcome mat for him to see."

The other interruption of Elesin's dance is caused by his lust for an unknown girl glimpsed amidst the market stalls. She is his fatal Cleopatra. The encounter is actually a reversal of the one between the Complete Gentleman and the pretty girl, as the ominous phrasing of Iyaloja's warning suggests: "Elesin, even at the narrow end of passage I know you will look back and sigh a last regret for the flesh that flashed past your spirit in flight." This yearning for the girl is like the backward glance which turned Lot's wife into a pillar of salt. Soyinka detests all forms of womb-yearning. That is why, at the height of Elesin's strength, the Praise-singer finds it necessary to utter an incantation to ward off the danger of an infantile regression: "No arrow flies back to the string, the child does not return through the same passage that gave it birth."

If Elesin fails to attain the grandeur which makes Ogun the hero of "the Fourth Stage," his circumstances are close enough to that of Ogun for him to show a full awareness of his responsibilities as a being of transition. Nevertheless, in spite of the Nietzschean echo in his profoundly ambiguous excuse in the speech to his bride, its sexuality exposes a weak strain in his personality: "I needed you as the abyss across which my body must be drawn." So although Elesin functions well in his institutionalized role as a kind of scapegoat, when the time comes for him to confront his fate he lets himself be ruled by his trickster motives and blames his failure of nerve on "the alien hand [which] pollutes the sources of will."

An African historian has pointed out how widespread and popular this explanation of social change in Africa can be. When the Yoruba say "*Aiye Oyinbo at aiye baba wa*," they mean to divide their history into "the colonial period and that when power lay with our fathers" (Atanda, 1970: 221). Elesin adopts this interpretation of history. But his tragedy can also be explained in terms of the trickster trait in the personality of the nonconforming individual. Joan Wescott suggests that *Esu*, the Yoruba trickster-god, is a means of explaining the difficulties of conforming, and he serves as an agent of continual change and readjustment (Wescott, 1922: 353). In Duro Ladipo's dramatization of the Elesin affair, the Oyo

People assign the responsibility for change to *Esu*, the "confuser of men [and] the god of fate".

The concept of *Esu* as a folkloric explanation of uncertainty and the threat of individualism to social order must have been encouraged by the social pressures of the past. It has a mythical rather than contemporary reality. Johnson the Yoruba historian notes that at one time delay or reluctance on the part of chiefs who are expected to accompany a dead Alaafin had such grave moral implications that members of the offending official's lineage would rather strangle him than suffer the stain of ignominy. But he could add that by the end of the nineteenth century when he compiled his history "all the men now refuse to die and they are never forced to do so" (Johnson, 1921: 57). The Oyo period which provided the material for *Oba Waja* and *Death and the King's Horseman* had become less demanding on her citizens than the plays emphasize. Voluntary suicide had become little more than an "act of love" by citizens. (Morton-Williams, 1967: 56, and Atanda, 1970: 228).

Factors making for change in Oyo after World War II included "the economic and social developments which accompanied colonial rule" (Atanda, 1970, 225). It is worth noting that this factor is given its historical importance in Achebe's *Arrow of God* where the social disaster is as much a result of economic activity as of the stubbornness of the priest or the blundering of the white man.

The difference in the treatment of this theme is revealing especially since both protagonists, Elesin and Ezeulu, operate in identical circumstances, including the importance of their religious and political offices as mediators, the confusion in their minds at certain moments as to their relationship to the other world, their perception of the advantage of letting a son learn the wisdom of the enemy race, their dependence on the moon for their roles and the intervention of the white man who thus causes an eclipse in their fortunes. Ezeulu is ruined for insisting on what he considers right and honorable for himself and his god; Elesin, whose speech to the bride is a self-criticism that might be profitably applied to Ezeulu, suffers for being more attached to the material world than to his "peace of mind [and the] honour and veneration of his own people."

Soyinka and Duro Ladipo alter historical facts such as dates and the fate of the hero. Both seem to lean on oral traditions, especially the surviving conventions of myths and transition rituals, instead of strictly imitating the lines of the historical development of events as Achebe tries to do in his novels. As in myth, periodization seems less important to the dramatists than general historical significance. For example, 1946 is given as the date for the original historical event at Oyo. Soyinka takes his plot back to the War years. But the Alaafin under whom the Horseman in question would have served died in 1944, and was succeeded by another Alaafin in 1945, although Olunde, in Soyinka's play, says the action of the play occurs about a month after the King's death.

Soyinka's note informs us that some of his changes were made for "minor reasons of dramaturgy." Two points ought to be made from the point of view of the audience. First, the historical incident in which the *Olokun-esin* lives on would have been too untidy for tragic form, since it does not encourage the dramatist to focus and control the values of tragedy. Elesin's despair in the play is heightened by his almost futile suicide. But his suicide is partially restitutive - that is, he is not allowed to live on to feed on the corruption which he has created. In the second place, the four novels of Achebe have sought to demonstrate that the colonial intervention in African societies provided an opportunity for abandoning the harsh ethical values of the past for more materialist values.

The situation which emerges from this interpretation of African history would make mimetic art unsatisfactory to a writer like Soyinka because such art upholds a decadent "ethic of reconciliation" to the existing situation. Soyinka accepts the view of drama as a communal art not in the sense of conforming to the values of its time, but in the sense that as "a revolutionary art form", the magic of the drama should be used to work the playwright's end upon the senses of his audience by "a conscious exploitation of the innate activity of man, play-making, in the service of the larger historic process" (Soyinka, 1975[b]: 63).

For Soyinka the kind of theatre which seeks to recreate the physical conditions of traditional festival theatre is not the only medium favorable for audience participation. The proscenium barrier can be crossed if the playwright treats the modern theatre as "two fluctuating halves of the same unit both manipulated by a commonly shared dynamic." The dramatic action is thus a mediation between audience and performance, and "a direct operation of moral and sensual forces" (Soyinka, 1975[b]: 63-79 passim). Soyinka gives a comically graphic but symbolic account of the bridging of the gulf between performers and audience at a Cuban theatre during the revolution. A sudden panic in the theatre revived for him the problems of illusion and reality in the theatre and raised the issue whether the audience could have been distinguished from the revolutionary performers in the ensuing confusion.

Soyinka demonstrates this theory in *Death and the King's Horseman* where the play-acting of the girls breaks down the barrier between illusion and reality for Sergeant Amusa, and almost gets him to do their will by joining in the act. *Death and the King's Horseman* itself contains a more complex form of mediation between the play and its readers in the conduct of the debate between Mrs. Pilkings and Olunde on the cultural value of self-sacrifice. To clarify the true character of what Jane Pilkings describes as "a barbaric custom," Olunde shows how the Prince of England's journey to the colonies at great personal risk helps to ensure "sanity in the midst of chaos" for Englishmen serving in the colonies. The story of the ship captain is used to provide a subtle justification for self-sacrifice in Oyo. The ship captain's sacrifice saved "the innocent people around the harbour" from "loaded ammunition [which] had caught fire" or "those lethal gases they've been experimenting on." In this Oyo state policy ensures that the cease of majesty dies not alone. The general groan, sometimes intensified by palace plots and intestinal conflicts, had to be alleviated in the past by the voluntary suicide of the most favored of the king's officials, so that before the reign of Alaafin Atiba, even the Crown Prince had to pay his price (Morton-Williams, 1969: 61)

In this play Soyinka stresses the importance of honor for the well-being of man by pointing out the need for transcendence of material goals. Without this, there would be nothing left but a gulf of anguish which Elesin would have had to endure had he lived, or an emptiness represented by the figure of Pilkings capering at the Resident's fancy ball without recognizing his alienation from the costume he has borrowed and the culture from which it is borrowed.

An ethical code which would uphold death before dishonor is necessary if the tragic gesture of an Olunde is not to degenerate into the play-acting of a Pilkings. From the portrait of masquerades in *Things Fall Apart* and *A Man of the People* we know that such a change is possible when the younger generation of maskers begin to lose sight of the functions performed by some of the masks of their fathers as mediators between the material world and the spiritual. The difference between the two generations is a difference between the ritual of the King's Horseman and the entertaining masque at the Residency.

BIBILOGRAPHY

(A). Soyinka, Wole,   (a)   *Death and the King's Horseman*
                                London, 1975.

                          (b)   "Drama and the Revolutionary Ideal"
                                and three interviews, *In Person:
                                Achebe, Awoonor and Soyinka,* ed. Ka-
                                ren L. Morell, Washington, 1975, 59-
                                130.

                                "The Fourth Stage: Through the Mys-
                                teries of Ogun to the Origin of Yoru-
                                ba Tragedy," *The Morality of Art*, ed.
                                D. W. Jefferson, London, 1969, 119-
                                131.

       Ladipo, Duro.   "Oba-Waja" in *Three Yoruba Plays*
                                (translated by Ulli Beier), Ibadan,
                                1964.

(B). Atanda, J. A.   "The Changing Status of the Alaafin
                                of Oyo Under Colonial Rule and
                                Independence," *West African Chiefs and
                                their changing status under Colonial Rule
                                and Independence*, ed. Michael
                                Crowder and Obaro Ikime, Ife, 1970,
                                212-30.

       Fadipe, N. A.   *The Sociology of the Yoruba*, Ibadan,
                                1970.

Johnson, Samuel   *The History of the Yoruba*, London,
                            1921.

Morton-Williams,
    Peter.   "The Yoruba Kingdom of Oyo, *"West
                            African Kingdoms in the Nineteenth Cen-
                            tury,* ed. Daryll Forde and P. M.
                            Kaberry, London, 1967, 36-69.

Ojo, G. F. Afolabi.   *Yoruba Culture* Ife and London, 1971.

Wescott, Joan.   "The Sculpture and Myths of Eshu-
                            Elegba, the Yoruba Trickster: Defini-
                            tion and Interpretation in Yoruba Ico-
                            nography," *Africa,* XXXII (1962),
                            336-53.

Soyinka's New Play

Gerald Moore

On a wide, bare stage a lone figure dances to the antiphonal singing of male and female choruses. He dances from the condition of life towards the condition of death. He has moved beyond words and is now "darkening homeward' to the urgent music of other voices. From the balcony above him the Praise-Singer, who had earlier spurred him along the path of transition his dancing feet must tread, now seems at the last to hold him back:

> Elesin Alafin. I no longer sense your flesh. The drums are changing now but you have
> gone far ahead of the world. It is not yet noon in heaven: let those who claim it is
> begin their own journey home. So why must you rush like an impatient bride: Why do
> you race to desert your Olohun-iyo?

This long scene is the center of Soyinka's new play and it is compelling theatre. Here is the purest expression to date of that African form of the tragic trance which Soyinka has long striven to realize in his art. The physical isolation of the Elesin upon the stage matches his psychic isolation as he prepares to abandon life and join his dead lord. But the Elesin, the King's Horseman, does not yet die. For the play is based on that well-known episode when the intervention of the District Officer prevented the Alafin's chief attendant from following him into the ancestral world.

The chief about to die takes the young bride intended for his son; and the son, about to live, embraces the death intended for the father. Only when confronted with the body of the son who has died to redeem the honor of his blood, does the Elesin strangle himself with the chains of his new bondage. For the alien intervention is not so much the cause as the precipitant of the tragedy. It collaborates with the sensual weakness which has already caused the Elesin to take a young bride on the very threshold of his own death, thus postponing the embrace of the shadows to embrace human flesh once more. As the Iyaloja, leader of the women, reminds him:

> I warned you, if you must leave a seed behind, be sure it is not tainted with the curses
> of the world.

This carnal involvement with his son's betrothed is one of the details Soyinka has added to the historical event, not only to heighten its dramatic content but to enrich its meaning. By making the Elesin a collaborator in his own undoing, Soyinka leads the audience away from sterile cliches about "culture conflict" towards a more subtle understanding of the event, turning it into a critique of the whole process by which Africans consented to the undermining of their vision of the world. The Elesin himself puts his finger on the wound:

> We know the roof covers the rafters, the cloth covers blemishes: who would have
> known that the white skin covered our future, preventing us from seeing the death
> our enemies had prepared for us.

Soyinka's premiere production makes bold use of the magnificent new theatre at Ife, which was initiated with this event. He has opened out the play, exploiting

126

the Elesin's isolation on the forestage and pushing his choruses of marketwomen and praise-singers into the side balconies. The effect is to heighten the Elesin's role as carrier of a chosen death for the community. His failure is thus a communal catastrophe, evoking more anger than pity. The Masque scene in which a spooky parade of colonial dummies in "white-face" greet a visiting English prince to the excruciating strains of a local brass band, is also played to splendid advantage on this big stage. But the sheer volume of air separating the players from each other and from us did create problems of audibility on this first night.

Fortunately Jimi Solanke, who has to carry the bulk of the play in the role of the Elesin, turned in what must be the performance of his life. His expressive body and eloquent dancing were matched by a voice of great range and flexibility. Not a word was lost, and each word in the rich verbal texture of this beautiful play was made to work within our understanding. Other fine performances gave promise that the revival of the play early in the New Year will be an event which should send many trekking back to their origins in Ile-Ife.

Soyinka directing "Elesin" in Rush Theatre (Chicago) rehearsal of *Death and the King's Horseman* in 1979.

Soyinka's "Beggars' Opera"

Mario Relich

"Call it the *Beggars' Opera* if you insist. That's what the whole nation is doing—begging for a slice of the action."

These words from the character called the Disc Jockey introducing the *Opera Wonyosi* set the tone of Wole Soyinka's Africanized version of Bertolt Brecht and Kurt Weill's *Three Penny Opera.* With a generous dash of peppery relevance, Soyinka has converted it to a fable about Nigerian expatriate racketeers and "security advisors" in the twilight days of Bokassa's Central African Republic.

The opening-night audience of the academic establishment of the University of Ife, and other prominent figures, was itself not dissimilar, *mutatis mutandis,* to the audiences that Brecht, and John Gay before him in the *Beggars' Opera,* lampooned by holding up a mirror to their defects.

Soyinka's version was his directorial debut as new Head of the Dramatic Arts Department. He therefore struck close to home when one of the gang of fake beggars turned out to be a professor "undergoing a refresher course" while on sabbatical. The professor was played with hilarious subservience by Kole Omotoso, a novelist, dramatist, and real-life academic in his own right.

As for the beggars' leader, his crafty cynicism echoes Brecht's original every step of the way, with a grotesque variation of his own when he explained about one of the "costumes" he was renting out: "That's the cheerful cripple—victim of modern road traffic. We call it the Nigerian special."

Soyinka himself directed the "arias" from the side of the stage, sometimes sporting a black leather jacket, at others covered in priestly robes. This was uncharitably construed as narcissism by some, especially as he ordered the whipping of the beggar-professor at his first appearance, but actually it was an ironic parody of Brechtian alienation-technique.

Though Soyinka's songs were entertaining enough in performance, they were eclipsed by such retained Kurt Weill favorites as "Mack the Knife" and "Pirate Jenny." Brecht's lyrics, however, seem light-hearted when compared to the rage behind Soyinka's. Especially hard-hitting was a song alluding to the clearance of cement-bags from Lagos harbor: "A man's lungs for clear air is meant/not for breathing in clouds of cement and overtime pay comes to mere chicken-feed/when the cement tycoon has filled out his greed." At the end of one song, a wonyosi-clad actor from the audience ostentatiously "sprayed" a twenty naira "Murtala" note on the singer's forehead.

The title of the "opera," in fact, hints at the mockery of the absurdly prestigious value attached to imported lace in Nigeria, especially of the flimsy and very expensive kind called "wonyosi." As his gaoler tells Mackheath: "I like lace you know. But you look as if the police dogs and barbed wire had been fighting over it."

Other targets of Soyinka's ire were righteous bloodlust at public executions and the recent decree against societies. The anti-secret society decree was defended by the emperor-designate's Nigerian military advisor, played with superbly supercilious disdain by Femi Euba, a veteran of Soyinka's productions. The beggars put "Colonel

Moses" on trial and reached the droll verdict that the army itself was guilty of behaving like a secret society. To support their verdict, they cited the alleged fact that all the anti-civilian riots of recent years, including the burning of Fela's "Kalakuta Republic," had been officially attributed, as they repeatedly cried out in unison, to "unknown soldiers."

There seemed to be no area of Nigerian public life left untouched but, fortunately, relief from laughter at one's own expense was provided by "Boky's" Napoleonic antics—a worse plague than any Nigerian reality, however grim. Soyinka's exploitation, as the program note puts it, of "Bokassa's timely stride backwards into pre-history," proved to be a cleverly amusing substitute for the Victorian Jubilee climas in Brecht's play.

Boky was at his most outragious when he drilled his goon-squad with encouraging words like: "I am an egalitarian. If I were not an egalitarian I would not be among you dregs, you scum, you *residue de bidet!*" He also expatiates on the "mother country": "Our mother country, not content with being the cradle of revolution, is also the cradle of culture. If you are not cultured, you are not French."

Despite uneven performances (with the exception of Gbemi Sodipo, who was outstanding as Anikure, the beggars' boss) and the pace lagging a bit on opening-night, the Ife drama students succeeded in entertaining capacity audiences three nights in a row. The play itself is minor Soyinka, but then neither was the *Three-Penny Opera* Brecht's best work, and its continued popularity is mainly due to Kurt Weill's unforgettable music.

Soyinka's achievement is that he has reactivated its explosive satire. The consequence is a searing exposure of the boom-time mentality. But let Mackheath have the last word on this dilemma afflicting much of humanity at all times: "The smell of money endows the dumbest Nigerian with instant intelligence."

The Fox's Dance

The Staging of Soyinka's Plays

Annemarie Heywood

The reputation of Wole Soyinka rests perhaps most firmly on his work for the theatre. His plays have proved themselves on the stages of three continents. Indeed it can be held that his gifts are essentially dramatic, and that even his poetry and fiction draw their vitality from a dramatizing imagination. His lyrical poetry usually suggests an incantatory voice, or the voice of a character in monologue. *Death in the Dawn*[1] and *Abiku*,[2] for instance, are voiced introspections, monologues, in which the poet's musings are distanced via a persona, an assumed mask and voice which is not entirely that of the poet himself. *Malediction*,[3] *Civilian and Soldier*,[4] and *Dedication*[5] suggest declamation or incantation within a given situation without which they would lack meaning.

Although it is cinematically rather than theatrically conceived, *The Interpreters* too has this dramatic rather than narrative quality.[6] Soyinka surrenders historical, sociological, or biographical sweep for a brisk succession of evocative scenes which range freely through past, present, and future. Sekoni's background, for instance, is established in a montage of brief snippets of dialogue, spanning many months, between two sections of interior monologue, followed by the slightly expanded scene of his return to Ijoha. Soyinka neglects the established techniques of introspection and authorial elucidation for establishing the inner life and the social attitudes of his characters. Instead we have episodes of almost pure dialogue interspersed with vivid evocations of setting rendered in the stylistic register of the character through whose mind they are experienced. Thus Sagoe provides the 'voice' for the satirical, irreverent, and frequently coprophiliac descriptions of the social milieu, whereas Egbo's style dominates the evocations of numinous nature and numinous woman. We find here a central strategy of contrastive characterization built up by the evocation of externals – dialogue, gesture, and mien; yet the characters, even though they are brilliantly defined and differentiated, are not given much depth; nor do they develop significantly. They are in fact masks or voices in an adventure of ideation, a dialectical exposition of possibilities. Like masks, they each represent one possibility only. This may be a complex and profound possibility, but it neither varies nor changes.

Put differently, Soyinka anatomizes the complex situation confronting his representative characters, idealistic and creative young graduates in post-independence Nigeria. They need to 'find new laws for living', and the complexities and ambiguities and choices are fully voiced through their personae. There is no resolution through conflict or action. The two main action set pieces are arranged around two catalytic characters, the Aladura Lazarus and Joe Golder, representing respectively the challenge of the unknowable, and the challenge of the unspeakable. They serve as tests of response. When the exposition is complete, the action stops abruptly in a tableau, each character frozen in an emblematic pose. The reader is left with an intolerable open paradox – 'the choice of a man drowning' – a disequilibrium calling for commitment and action.

It is significant to note that the later plays end in this way too. In *A Dance of the Forests* Demoke had actually made a choice in seizing the Half-Child and giving it to the Woman:

> Darkness enveloped me, but piercing
> Through I came
> Night is the choice for the fox's dance.[7]

There is no such resolution in the later plays. *Kongi's Harvest* ends in a cacophonic re-statement of the conflict: 'A mixture of the royal music and the anthem rises loudly, plays for a short time, comes to an abrupt halt as the iron grating descends and hits the ground with a loud final clang.' The 'loud final clang', as well as the 'abrupt halt' also close *Madmen and Specialists* which ends with a revolver shot, followed by a brief passage in mime: the beggars' chant 'stops in mid-word and the lights snap out simultaneously'. In *The Road* the dying Professor's peroration adds no insight, merely re-states the enigma, whilst the spinning mask sinks lower and lower 'until it appears to be nothing beyond a heap of cloth and raffia'.

These endings leave us in the air, discomfited and unbalanced, uneasy. Important issues have been raised, yet they are not raised within the framework of a closed system which determines their resolution. The resolution of such issues is what customarily distinguishes tragic action from life. Soyinka, like the dramatists of the absurd, prefers to articulate in an ethical no man's land. The clowning and the paronomasiac dialogue too belong with this genre. Yet Soyinka does not chart private ontological anxiety. His writing remains communal, his concerns social, even political. In this he is, I think, most closely akin to Brecht whose 'sort of theatre, its liveliness and freedom, not so much his purpose or intentions' he was commending as early as 1962.[8]

It cannot be denied, however, that such an open-ended dialectical exposition creates problems for the audience. The critical response to Soyinka has of late been increasingly exasperated. His 'enigmatic obfuscations' have recently been forcefully attacked by Bernth Lindfors.[9] Such attacks are, I believe, demonstrably based on limited or mistaken expectations. Thus Lindfors praises the lucidity of earlier plays which are written in the realist idiom. *The Lion and the Jewel, Brother Jero, The Swamp Dwellers,* and *The Strong Breed* are localized in setting and illusionist in idiom. Here the greatest stylistic problem in staging is likely to be the

relatively simple one of complete authenticity in the evocation of a West
African locale.

The more weighty plays which take their shape from inner dialectic are
sharply criticized by Lindfors. In the progression from *A Dance of the
Forests* ('arty structure', 'plotless plot', 'incoherence') via *The Road* ('a
defiantly difficult play which makes no compromises with instant intel-
ligibility') to *Madmen and Specialists* ('a multi-faceted cryptograph') he
diagnoses a growing 'tendency towards meaningless frivolity which robs
his work of any serious implication' (about the very last thing to fault in
this profoundly nihilistic exploration of the deadly follies of the political
animal!) and wonders for whom these plays are written – 'just for Western-
ized Yoruba eggheads . . . for a cosmopolitan international elite, or . . .
simply for himself?'

Whilst attacking the 'histrionic razzle-dazzle' of the basic articulation,
Lindfors concedes that even the plays he condemns make brilliant theatre.
Soyinka, he says, 'can apply a very slick surface to the roughest or least
substantial of narrative foundations', and his 'plotless plots . . . could be
enjoyed as a series of well-paced theatrical happenings' without making
much sense. This is, surely, not quite good enough. The difficulty of the
obscure plays arises from their idiom, or basic strategy, which is not well
served by illusionist production and 'character'-acting inviting empathy.
These plays are best plotted for production as masques or cabaret, with
characters conceived as masks, dialogue as choral, movement and gesture
as emblematic.

A Dance of the Forests appears incoherent only if one's expectations are
geared to narrative articulation and character development. But this play
is a spectacle and more closely akin to *Comus*, *The Magic Flute*, or Ravel's
L'Enfant et les Sortilèges than to, say, *A Midsummer Night's Dream*,
comparison with which it might invite. The mode in production should be
surrealist and shun that leaden mimesis which can only stultify the poetic
exposition of meaning.

Of all Soyinka's plays it is theatrically the most demanding. It requires
a set and scenery which can effect the transition from one world to another
by almost instantaneous transformations. A separately lit back scene is
necessary for the transitions from forest to primeval glade, and from forest
to the court of Mata Kharibu. The scenery must offer instant visual clues
to the order of reality it evokes: drably 'natural' for the mundane forest
with its sound-effects of 'beaters' and engine noise; supernatural and
mysterious for timeless spirit-forest which is co-extensive with the former,
but charged with mystery, power, and significance, particularly in the moist
primeval glade which forms the setting for the ordeal; and lastly the
barbaric splendour of Mata Kharibu's court in the past.

Similarly, the characters are drawn from four distinct levels of abstraction or 'reality', a number of them appearing as themselves, but in different

forms, at two levels. Costume, make-up, and gesture therefore have to be contrived to make such crossers of the boundaries instantly recognizable, whilst at the same time suggesting the nature of their change.

Within the mundane forest we meet three orders of being: present-day humans; two revenants who must be instantly recognizable as such; and, in certain scenes, Murete the tree-imp who belongs to the spirit world. In the numinous forest we meet three of the humans; the same humans in a previous incarnation; the revenants as ghosts, and as incarnations; and a host of spirits, some of whom assume temporary disguises. The terrible Triplets, grotesque symbolic masks, are perhaps yet another category. The forest-dwellers should be symbolically garbed and masked or painted; their movements should be abstract and deliberate. The entire sequence needs to be carefully choreographed and scored so that the gravity and significance of the ordeal can be fully appreciated by the spectators as occurring at a deeper level of insight where human evolution over the centuries is on trial. It is further desirable to indicate degree in the masking: the hierarchy of authority and power should be reflected in the relative 'importance' of the masks. Ogun and Eshuoro are equal adversaries; Forest Head outranks them. Since his speeches, especially at first, are mild and he exerts no more power than a master of ceremonies, the spectators may suffer some perplexity which should be resolved by visual cues.

Forest Head is one of the boundary-crossers, in that he is first seen as Obaneji among the humans. Since he is masked in the forest scenes, it would be necessary to indicate his identity by a characteristic code of gesture, gait, and bearing, for voice and face will be modified. The second category of the boundary-crossers are the restless dead whom we meet first as ragged revenants, then as they were in life eight centuries back at Mata Kharibu's court, and lastly once again as ghosts. As ghosts they should not, of course, be masked, but costumed in cobwebby tatters and corroded remnants of armour. The third group are the humans who reappear at Mata Kharibu's court in a previous incarnation: Demoke, Rola, Adenebi, and Agboreko. They should be instantly recognizable, yet transformed to match the splendid and mannered mode of the historic world.

It is clear that the play makes considerable demands on the actors, particularly of versatility in projecting different modes of stylization in gesture and movement. The forest spirits should ideally be dancers and move with choreographed eloquence and precision. I like to imagine their style as characterized by kinetic distortions: a slightly slowed motion which in scenes of conflict bursts into formal movements of great speed and eloquence. Music and dance enrich the texture throughout, and should underline the passage of the action through levels of significance, as the folly of a generation is judged against an age-old history of 'cannibalism' and chosen individuals are offered insight into their repetitive destructiveness. From such insight alone might spring evolution, the only guidance to be offered by the guardians of the earth. As an argument the play is brilliantly articulated; but an audience which is confused about the levels of reality – timeless, past, and present: spirit, ghost, and human – is likely to remain confused. A highly disciplined and visually lavish production on a stage equipped for instant transformations is necessary for a realization that will translate this play fully on to the stage.

Whereas *A Dance of the Forests* demands sophisticated professionalism in stagecraft, costume, and make-up, as well as accomplished acting styles, *Kongi's Harvest* could be performed by amateurs, provided the direction stresses the patterns of similarity and contrast on which the satirical comedy largely rests. One could do much worse than follow Brecht's directives to actors and directors of the epic theatre. *Kongi's Harvest* is total theatre, brilliantly structured to articulate a dialectical confrontation of old and new, not so much through dramatic action, as by theatrical means. The 'meaning' is communicated by design, music, costume, style of gesture, and delivery over and above the dialogue within the plot.

Basically we are faced with a design in triptych form. The old and the new, Danlola and Kongi, facing each other across their synthesis, the club, Daodu and Segi's world whence originate the moves which activate both Kongi and Danlola towards the climax. The production demands a static set with three distinct acting areas, separately and characteristically lit and furnished. The final Harvest Festival will of course exuberantly occupy the entire acting area, although the various groups of characters may still be symbolically stationed on their previous locations.

Only thus can the central satirical pattern of similarities and contrasts, and the dialectical structure of the argument, be graphically conveyed and the importance of the Daodu/Segi section as the proposed synthesis be instantly recognized. The comic parallelism of Danlola and Kongi, which should come over almost like an inkblot picture, generates a bitterly ironical groundswell to the lyrical and farcical goings-on. They could be seen as static tableaux, each dominated by a central autocrat demanding superhuman status, given to histrionics, peevish rages, and behaving like a jealous prima donna. There is the same concern for image; the same preoccupation with protocol, dress, and emblems; the same claque of praisers and flatterers: the same static, self-perpetuating quality. Both are surrounded by a 'court' of dignitaries and functionaries, yet essentially isolated; both are guarded by the Carpenters' Brigade. There is even an attendant clown in each section: Dende and the Fifth Aweri. None of this is to deny that the audience will, and must, prefer Danlola to Kongi – but it should prefer him for reasons of style. Danlola's outmoded autocracy has a human, relaxed quality; it is also radiant with history, tradition, ritual, richly evocative: whereas Kongi's dictatorship is inhuman, grotesque. But Danlola's charm will overwhelm the play unless the parallels are underlined and Daodu's thematic importance stressed.

A naturalistic acting style is inappropriate. Danlola and Kongi are types; as simulated people they lack all depth and interest. Personal charm in Danlola or a psychologically credible form of megalomania for Kongi would be equally distracting. These characters demand to be 'narrated' in the epic style to use Brecht's terminology, rhetorically projected in the third person, so to speak. A similar stylization is required in the crucial Daodu/Segi exchange. When it is played as a 'love scene', that is, if an illusion of reality is attempted, actors and audience are equally ill at ease. This problem disappears if the scene is conceived as the emergence and development of a new motif to oppose directly the hitherto dominant Danlola/Kongi confrontation – the fullest statement, that is, of the positive values to set against their sterility. The dialogue should be spoken very formally 'as poetry' – perhaps best previously recorded on tape in a soft voice, and played back while the characters remain in an immobile tableau of Segi kneeling to the robed Spirit of Harvest. The break between heightened and normal dialogue is clearly discernible in the text. Similarly, Daodu's praises of Segi in the nightclub should not be spoken by him, but sung by the juju guitarist.

In the productions I have seen, Danlola elicited the audiences' sympathies, Kongi their derision; Daodu and Segi remained a romantic ornament. Yet they are thematically central. The play shows that there is little to choose between the two autocrats who have everything in common except style and the weight of tradition. Danlola is moribund, Kongi is a killer: Daodu is life. Kongi harvests death: Daodu, with his farmers' commune, harvests life. He is Danlola's rightful successor, but he is one with the common people too. (There are interesting parallels here with *Henry IV*). He challenges Kongi, not as the pretender, but as a revolutionary leader. If Daodu fails to emerge as the answer, the play loses much of its coherence and becomes a series of satirical sketches.

It may be worthwhile to indicate briefly how this stylized content might be reinforced in production. Music is all-important. The play could happily be expanded into a musical with a score as full of pointed contrast, grave nostalgia, and lyrical mockery as the text. Even a conservative realization demands versatility: traditional drumming and singing for Danlola; electronically amplified military march music for Kongi; amplified juju, with its synthesis of sounds and instruments, for Segi's Club. The movement of the actors on the stage is to some extent determined by the music, but should be pointedly choreographed to become another expressive instrument. In Danlola's area it should be static, or else engaged in the easy yet formal swirling of traditional dancing (In a student production we stressed the danced elements and dressed Oba Danlola's court in stiff *gbarye* dress which swirls out heavily: the dignified circling of Danlola's supporters in their gorgeous swelled-out robes suggested planetary analogies which were entirely apt). On Kongi's side movement is regimented, angular, machine-like. Drill and marches;

leaping-up and sitting down. Kongi's own outbursts should suggest a robot out of control. In Segi's Club there should be constant swaying motion. The vegetation and snake imagery of the songs suggests the rhythm: sophisticated juju, and on-the-spot subtle swaying and rippling, cool.

Costume and colours also underline the contrasts: traditional robes for Danlola (exotic fantasies are out of place), a certain dusty splendour of colour, muted deep dyes. Kongi's adherents should all be uniformed, like himself: stark white and khaki; the Organizing Secretary in a grey suit, the New Aweri likewise in uniform (in Soyinka's own production they wore gown and mortarboard!). Costumes in Segi's Club should be stylish, but plainly cut; the colours electric, bright, but harmonious.

The lighting needs to be separately controlled for the rapid scene changes in the mid-section. It too should reflect the contrast with mellow warm light, suggesting oil lamps, for Danlola; a hard white brilliance, as of fluorescent strips, for Kongi; and fairy lights in Segi's Club. Gesture and delivery should be suited to the pattern: utterance in Danlola's section is rich, cadenced, modulated, humorous; gestures hieratic, yet relaxed. In Kongi's section a staccato quality prevails: tight angular gestures, 'pointlessly angry'; even the discordant chorus of the Reformed Aweri should have a shrill and peevish pattern. In Segi's Club the voice rhythms are natural, even in the lyrical passages; movement relaxed, poised, cool.

Kongi's Harvest seen in this way has a very coherent and simple basic articulation. The two most recent plays, *The Road* and *Madmen and Specialists*, are more complex. In spite of their realistic surface and an action which is for the greater part comic, even farcical, they are felt to encode a disturbingly elusive oracular message. *The Road* is localized and must aim at verisimilitude in evoking Nigerian community life around a motor park. *Madmen and Specialists* is not anchored to any specific locale: it could be set in the hinterland of any modern ideological war. The Earth Mothers, chorus of 'unformed minds in deformed bodies', intelligence officer in search of power and control, and Socratic teacher/therapist are modern archetypes and could be translated into any location. Otherwise the two plays have much in common. Both revolve around a central 'mad' guru with his band of would-be initiates. The Professor of *The Road* is more eccentric, his speeches oblique and cryptic; in *Madmen and Specialists* the Old Man's drift is plainly towards sanity, scepticism, and humanism. But the conception has become more nihilistic: the Old Man's followers are also his tormentors, and his therapeutic exercises can be subverted for propaganda and brainwashing purposes. Murano, the returned-from-death vatic mute of *The Road*, has been replaced by the chorus of the Earth Mothers. Both plays are substantial and serious, yet their surface glitters with grotesque wit and comic invention.

The Road, by virtue of its local references, demands a stylized naturalism of staging and acting. The characters are partly recognizable portraiture, partly symbolic; their speech cadences are specifically Nigerian and need to be sensitively reproduced, yet a 'dialect' naturalism would be distracting. Say Tokyo Kid and Particulars Joe, for example, are witty stylizations of familiar types – yet actors and director should not be tempted into essaying a Stanislavskian verisimilitude. The pattern is still choric. The characters are still masks or mouthpieces in an adventure of ideation. Every effort must be made to combine local colour with pace, wit, and thematic phrasing. The flashback to the masquerade should be clearly marked as occurring in a different dimension, through lighting change and by stylized, perhaps slowed, motion. The problem here is similar to that posed by *A Dance of the Forests* with its multi-dimensional frame of reference. Yet *The Road* is delightful quite simply as comedy, and this freshness must remain dominant. We are in the world of absurd clowns where the laughter is shot with the hysteria of chaos.

Madmen and Specialists is more abstract, the characteristic dialectic at its tautest stretch yet. The prophet/sacrifice has evolved into a more fully overt role of teacher/healer/sacrifice. Though the nature of his dogma/therapy is only stated obliquely, it is plainly concerned with self-knowledge, scepticism, and sanity. The paradoxical climax is potently nihilistic, yet extraordinarily energizing, more so than in any previous play. There is enough fun and 'business', movement and surprise, to entertain any audience. It may be tempting because of this to treat the play as a vehicle for virtuoso character-acting and a plethora of illusionist 'business'. Inevitably the outcome would be an entertaining conundrum. I should like to see the play done in cabaret style, very rhythmical, tightly choreographed and scored, with stylized characterization. The Mendicants and the Earth Mothers to be rehearsed as choral units, their speeches not so much dialogue addressed to one another (in the illusionist manner) as articulated themes addressed to the audience. Against these choric arbiters – humanity and the Earth – the conflict between son and father, cannibalism and humanism, political and individual sanity, should enact itself as a dialogue of principles. Again, as in *Kongi's Harvest*, a single set should be used with differentiated arenas (say, surgery, sanctum, and open place), so that the three interacting and conflicting interpretations of men's needs can be appreciated as co-existing without resolution. A monotonous yet relentless rock or West African drum rhythm might run on throughout, into which are woven characteristic themes for the Mendicants' chant and the Earth Mothers' utterances. Ideally the Mendicants would provide their own percussion with crutches, beggar's bowl, hand-slapping on the floor, etc.

Two of the characters emerge as more than types, Aafaa and the Old Man, superb parts for skilled actors. Great tact is necessary in interpreting them. Even here a distancing stylization is essential: to invent a plausible history and convincing psychology for these characters would disrupt the pattern as a whole. It is sufficient that their rendering should be coherent, and consistent with their function within the action as a whole. They are not so much invented men as mouthpieces for arguments in the complex exposition of an ideological trap.

The easiest temptation in interpreting Soyinka's brilliant dramatizations of ideas for the stage is to develop their surface realism; for actors to lose themselves in the vividly differentiated parts; for audiences to relish the rich evocations of the familiar and the sparkling fun of it all. That way perplexity about 'meaning' is inevitable. The remedy lies in interpreting the text like a musical score; in disciplined, stylized modes of acting; in alertness to the currents of ideation, as well as to the sparkle of recognition.

NOTES

1. Idanre (London, Methuen, 1967), p. 10.
2. ibid., p. 28.
3. ibid., p. 55.
4. ibid., p. 53.
5. ibid., p. 24.
6. I am probably here leaning on the distinction drawn by James Joyce via the young Stephen in *Portrait of the Artist as a Young Man*, where he states that the dramatic writer effaces his own personality from his work, impersonalizes and distances his ideas and emotions in purely imaginary projections.
7. *A Dance of the Forests* (London, O.U.P., 1963), p. 85.
8. Dennis Duerden and Cosmo Pieterse, *African Writers Talking* (London, Heinemann, 1972), p. 173.
9. In a conference paper read to the Association for Commonwealth Literature and Language Studies, Makerere, 1974.

Third-World Drama: Soyinka and Tragedy

ANDREW GURR

Novels, being what John Updike calls a 'non-urgent' form of creative writing, are limited in the ways they can be useful to a world of accelerating social change. The novel form, invented in a slower age than ours, is still uniquely valuable for exploring the human psyche, for extending, in George Eliot's phrase, our sympathies. As Naipaul said in 1971:

... you might go on endlessly writing 'creative' novels, if you believed that the framework of an ordered society exists, so that after a disturbance there is calm, and all crises fall back into that great underlying calm. But that no longer exists for most people, so that kind of imaginative work is of less and less use to them. They live in a disordered and fast-changing world, and they need help in grasping it, understanding it, controlling it. And that is how the writer will serve them.[1]

Enlarging our understanding, extending our sympathies, these are the unique values which keep the novel as a socially useful form on offer in the world's intellectual markets today.

But like any form its limitations need to be recognized as well as its values if it is to be used properly. The philosophy underlying the aim of extending our understanding is the nineteenth-century (and Biblical) humanitarian presumption that to understand all is to forgive all. It is by no means an unquestionable axiom. It can be used to enervate or paralyse, to justify inactivity. It is one basic reason why the novel form is non-urgent.

I have argued about the enervating nature of the novel as a literary form elsewhere.[2] Philosophies implicitly resistant to change lie behind other forms as well, of course, and most powerfully behind one of the oldest of all, tragedy. Since Nietsche it has been examined mainly as a corpse in the western world, but it still shows striking signs of life occasionally, and most vividly in the third world, where traditional and modern (western) meet. I think we should seek to understand the implications of such signs of life, whether or not we forgive them.

In the twentieth century Brecht was the western world's most eloquent enemy of the idea of tragedy. He paraphrased Marx's eleventh thesis on Feuerbach when he wrote of his own idea of drama, that it

Editor's Note: This article is a revised version of one with the same title that appeared in *Joliso* (Nairobi), II, 2 (1974), pp. 13–20.

should be 'an affair for philosophers, but only for such philosophers who wished not just to explain the world but to change it'.[3] His hostility to tragedy was based on two articles of faith: that the present condition of society is basically bad, and that humanity is capable of enforcing change for the better through its own agency. As he put it in his anti-Aristotelean *New Organum*, the art of tragedy described by Aristotle existed to explain the ways of the gods to men, to describe the powers operative in a static, unchanging cosmos. It allowed or acknowledged that man had little control over his individual destiny, let alone the capacity to impose change on society and alter its direction. Looked at in this way, Greek tragedy and all drama which shares the Aristotelean outlook can be seen as descriptive like the novel, explanatory in Brecht's term, and therefore open to the objection made in the Feuerbach thesis.

Greek and even Shakespearean tragedy, which has been probably the most potent form in the west, based themselves on a world view which was essentially static. The pace of social change in both societies was so slow as to be imperceptible. Within them, individuals might be made to change, but not the whole structure. It followed therefore that the miseries and the injustices of human existence called for explanation, not revolution. Hope was usually found in extra-terrestrial form. The gods were essentially the expression of a hope that order, control, justice did in fact lie behind life's seeming chaos. True virtue therefore lay in fatalism, in resigning oneself to the demands of one's destiny or to the will of the gods. The common shape of virtue in Greek tragedy was stoicism; in Shakespearean tragedy it was something like Christian patience, the readiness being all.

In the third world, the most rapidly changing segments of the earth, social change is more than a fact; it is an axiom of government. Equally axiomatic is the active participation of human agencies in bringing it about. If the nineteenth century was the one in which God died, the twentieth is the one in which, as Stephen Spender said, the only general belief is in progress.[4] Faith in human progress, even Brecht's espousal of it as a possibility, is not really reconcilable with the view of the cosmos which tragedy embodies.

In Europe today tragedy, like religion, walks in some strange disguises. It ought to have been banished. Fifty years ago I. A. Richards claimed that a religion which promises a life after death cannot mate that promise with tragedy. George Steiner more recently said the same thing of Marxism: 'The metaphysics of Christianity and Marxism are anti-tragic. That, in essence, is the dilemma of modern tragedy.'[5] Such pronouncements have not stopped either Christians or Marxists from trying to hang on to tragedy as a living concept. To take only two recent examples: Ivor Morris in his book *Shakespeare's God* writes that 'the dispassionate inquiry into man's secular condition, as it is the proper undertaking of the tragedian, must also be a true religious function'.[6] In *Modern Tragedy* Raymond Williams says: '. . . in our own time, especially, it is the connections between revolution and tragedy – connections lived and known but not acknowledged as ideas – which seem most clear and significant.'[7] Tragedy is a blanket term which, when stretched to cover both religion and revolution, is likely to get torn.

With dispute of that order in Europe, the survival of a substantial concept of tragedy in the third world seems improbable. But cultural exchange and conflict throw together some strange bedfellows. In modern Africa traditional literatures, evolved as they have been in relatively static social situations, tend to owe more philosophical allegiance to fatalism than to progress. Even Wole Soyinka, committed social critic as he is, can write of Yoruba tragedy as a thoroughly meaningful concept in the modern world. As he put it in 1969, 'that wrench within the human psyche which we vaguely define as tragedy is the most insistent voice that bids us return to our own sources'.[8] In one of his rare academic essays, published in the Wilson Knight Festschrift, Soyinka writes about the essence of Yoruba tragedy and its relationship to the Yoruba view of life. As a rationale for the world view implicit in *Idanre*, and more importantly perhaps in *The Strong Breed*, it provides a useful opportunity to assess the appropriateness of Brecht's criticism of tragedy.

Soyinka deals chiefly with the two primal figures in Yoruba cosmology, Obatala and Ogun. The story of Obatala's imprisonment is the basic Yoruba creation myth. Essentially it tells of his captivity under Shango, god of thunder, with the help of Eshu, god of fate and confuser of men, and the consequent freeing of Ogun, god of war. Obatala submits patiently to his confinement because he has been told his destiny is to suffer. The whole story represents a cycle of cosmic balance, from the peaceful rule of Obatala, through Ogun's wars during the captivity, and back to peace with Obatala's release. This cycle or counter-balancing of cosmic forces is the explanation why things are the way they are – why the blind, the hunchbacked exist, and why wars happen. Ogun's myth, the counter-force to Obatala, to which Soyinka ties himself, is the dynamic, activist one. Ogun is the figure of the rebel-creator where Obatala is the orthodox creator. Throughout his essay Soyinka makes comparisons of these figures and their stories with the Greek pantheon and with the Christian drama of the Passion.

Obatala's myth is a creation myth in the sense that it provides an explanation for the flaws in some of the god of creation's products. Its form is the familiar anthropomorphic one of the suffering god who goes through a cycle of punishment and redemption, following what has been called the archetypal tragic pattern. The flaws happen when

Obatala is tricked into getting drunk. His captivity, expiation, and redemption follow from this error. As Soyinka describes it, the Obatala story is

... not the drama of acting man but that of suffering spirit ... Yoruba myth equates Obatala, god of purity, god also of creation (but not of creativity!) with the first deity Orisa-nla. And the ritual of Obatala is a play of form, a moving celebration whose nearest equivalent in the European idiom is the Passion play. The drama is all essence – captivity, suffering and redemption; Obatala is symbolically captured, confined, and ransomed. At every stage he is the embodiment of the suffering spirit of man, uncomplaining, agonized, full of the redemptive qualities of the spirit of endurance and martyrdom ... It is a drama in which the values of conflict or of the revolutionary spirit are excluded, attesting in their place the adequacy and inevitable aftermath of harmonious resolution which belongs in time and human faith.[9]

Elsewhere Soyinka points out resemblances of the Obatala myth to Greek tragedy as well as the Christian Passion play.

This passage is characteristic of Soyinka's dense and brilliantly incisive essay, not least in its open preference for the 'revolutionary spirit' of Ogun over the suffering spirit of Obatala. He distinguishes Ogun as the god of creativity rather than of war, a dynamic principle where Obatala is the figure of fertile peace. Ogun commands war, has iron for his instrument, and includes craftsmanship in his sphere of influence. He comes nearest in Yoruba mythology to the Greek figure of Prometheus. 'Obatala is the placid essence of creation, Ogun the creative urge and instinct.'[10] As Soyinka presents it, the creative torment of Ogun preceded the cosmic balance ruled over by Obatala.

... the drama of the syncretic successor to Orisa-nla, Obatala's 'Passion' play, is only the plastic resolution of Ogun's tragic engagement. The Yoruba metaphysics of accommodation and resolution could only come *after* the passage of the gods through the transitional gulf, and the demonic test of the self-will of the explorer god in the creative cauldron of cosmic powers. Only after such testing could the Yoruba harmonious world be born, a harmonious will which accommodates every material or abstract phenomenon within its infinitely stressed spirituality.[11]

Ogun is Soyinka's favourite, the god of the dynamic forces in society and above all of the creative and suffering artist. As god of iron he patronizes the forge, producer of the artefacts of war and art:

Ogun is embodiment of Will and the Will is the paradoxical truth of de-structiveness and creativeness in acting man. Only one who has himself undergone the experience of disintegration, whose spirit has been tested and psychic resources laid under stress by the most inimical forces to individual assertion, only he can understand and *be* the force of fusion between the two contradictions. The resulting sensitivity is also the sensitivity of the artist and he is a profound artist only to the degree to which he comprehends and expresses the principle of destruction and recreation.[12]

Beyond the paradox of destructiveness and creativeness there is a further and more important paradox in Soyinka's allegiance to Ogun, in the union between the stasis of tragedy and the dynamism of the rebellious spirit. Soyinka recognizes this paradox, and tries to reconcile it with Yoruba metaphysics:

[Ogun's] acting is . . . a contradiction of the tragic spirit, yet it is also its natural complement. To act, the Promethean instinct of rebellion, channels anguish into creative purpose which releases man from a totally destructive despair, releasing from within him the most energic, deeply combative inventions which without usurping the territory of the infernal gulf, bridge them with visionary hopes.[13]

He seems to suggest that the 'visionary hopes' (and the 'revolutionary spirit') of the Promethean rebel are an antidote to the despair of the tragic victim. But even these hopes rely on a recognition of underlying cosmic harmony in a seemingly chaotic world:

Yoruba myth is a recurrent exercise in the experience of disintegration, and this is significant to the isolation of Will among a people whose mores, culture, and metaphysics are based on seeming resignation and acceptance but are, experienced in depth, a statement of man's penetrating insight into the final resolution of things and the constant evidence of harmony.[14]

This again is stasis, acceptance of an ordained status quo. Man is smaller than his fate. The cosmos has an underlying frame of order. Art thus exists as an explanation, 'a statement of man's penetrating insight' into the underlying frame of order.

An exclusive concern for understanding, for achieving a fundamental sympathy with the human psyche, was the keystone of the philosophy of the greatest of the nineteenth-century European writers.[15] It is also central to Greek, Christian, and Yoruba tragedy, or at least to the currently standard view of them. Understanding in this sense, focussed in the glass of tragedy, is ultimately enervating. Soyinka himself describes its implications:

It is true that to understand, to understand profoundly, is to be unnerved of the will to act. For is not human reality dwarfed by the awe and wonder, the *inevitability* of this cosmic gulf? . . . Suffering, the truly overwhelming suffering of Sango, of Lear, of Oedipus, this suffering hones the psyche to a finely self-annihilating perceptiveness and renders further action futile and above all, lacking dignity. And what has been the struggle of the tragic hero after all but an effort to maintain that innate concept of dignity which impels to action only to that degree in which the hero possesses a true nobility of spirit?[16]

Soyinka says these things in the course of an analysis of traditional Yoruba culture and the traditional Yoruba explanation of cosmic order. We should perhaps make allowances both for that and for the fact that it was written as a compliment to Wilson Knight. Certainly Soyinka's plays and poems which deal with modern Nigeria do not directly invite comparisons to be made between the traditional and the modern situations. Nor has he written anything so elementary as, say, the Ijimere dramatization of the Obatala story.[17] And yet I think it can be seen that the Yoruba tradition and its kinship with the philosophy of tragedy conditions him too.

Soyinka's attitude to tragedy is paradoxical, and might be called ambivalent. It is an admissible position in itself, perhaps, especially when it is a gesture to Wilson Knight, whose gift for paradox is not unknown. But there are similar underlying suppositions in his plays and poetry too. They are not conspicuous in the way that Ijimere's are, but they are probably all the more important for being inconspicuous. If we set aside the satirical plays like *Kongi's Harvest* and *Brother Jero*, we often find a strongly expressed desire to accept fate and destiny, a desire entirely consistent with the essay on Yoruba tragedy. *The Strong Breed* reaches its climax, or tragic catastrophe, with the hero's acceptance of his role as 'carrier', the inherited job of scapegoat for the year's troubles. The play ends in a mood very close to what Soyinka says is the mood of the Ogun mysteries:

In the Ogun Mysteries the drama is 'Passion' of a different kind, released into quietist wisdom, a ritual exorcism of demonic energies. There is no elation, not even at the end of purgation, nothing like the beatified elation of Obatala after his redemption, only a world weariness on the rockshelf of Promethean shoulders, a profound sorrow in the chanting of the god's recessional.[18]

Quietist wisdom, resignation, and acceptance of one's fate are close to being the same thing in this context. They are all close to determinism, the view that would say, for instance, that Hedda Gabler had no real control of her life, and that her suicide was inevitable given her character and social situation.

Brecht's answer to this would have been the brutalist one that Hedda is a fiction, that fiction in itself is nothing but a lie, and that the audience is what matters. If the audience were to walk out of the theatre convinced that Hedda's fate was inevitable then nothing would be accomplished. Audiences should walk out convinced that her death was unnecessary. A better society would not drive its people to suicide, so what is needed is a change towards a better society. Even Chekhov, not usually thought of as a revolutionary dramatist, held this kind of view.

He once said of his aim in writing his plays:

I only wanted to tell people honestly: 'Look at yourselves, see how badly and boringly you live!' The principal thing is that people should understand this, and when they do, they will surely create for themselves another and better life.[19]

It was Chekhov's central reason for presenting futile lives in his plays, and explains why he refused to have a hero whom the audience could identify with.

The philosophies inherent in the Greek, Christian, and Yoruba forms of tragedy are not the only instruments of fatalism, of course. Camus's essay *The Myth of Sisyphus*, a central document in the philosophy of the Absurd, upholds as the supreme virtue of the Absurd hero an absolute clarity of vision. Sisyphus facing the endless task of rolling his rock up the mountain knows absolutely that his fate is endless. Utterly devoid of hope, like Oedipus in his blindness he sees reality and nonetheless concludes that 'all is well'.[20] Here is not so much the opposite of the 'visionary hopes' of Soyinka's Promethean rebel as the reverse side of the same coin. Both figures are resigned to their fate, frozen in the paralysis which comes from 'profound understanding'. From a Brechtian point of view, understanding or not, they are kin to Estragon and Vladimir in Beckett's play. We have some cause, perhaps, to regret that Brecht died before he had finished his counter to *Waiting for Godot*.

Brecht's and Chekhov's aims of stimulating and provoking their audiences out of a frame of fatalism both stemmed ultimately from their faith in a human agency, in the capacity of humankind to change its ways and its systems for the better. An automatic adoption of traditional literary forms, whether European or African, is a denial of this faith.

University of Leeds

NOTES

1 A. Rowe-Evans, 'V. S. Naipaul' (an interview), *Transition*, No. 40 (1971), p. 62.
2 'Third-World Novels: Naipaul and After', *JCL*, VII, 1 (1972), pp. 6–13.
3 'Theatre for Pleasure or Theatre for Instruction', *Brecht on Theatre*, translated by J. Willett, Methuen, 1964, p. 72.
4 Stephen Spender, *The Destructive Element*, Cape, 1935, p. 202.
5 *The Death of Tragedy*, Faber, 1961, p. 324.
6 *Shakespeare's God: The Role of Religion in the Tragedies*, Allen & Unwin, 1972, p. 59.
7 *Modern Tragedy*, Chatto & Windus, 1966, p. 64.
8 'The Fourth Stage', *The Morality of Art: Essays Presented to G. Wilson Knight by His Colleagues and Friends*, ed. D. W. Jefferson, Routledge, 1969, p. 119.

9 ibid., pp. 127–8.   10 ibid., p. 120.
11 ibid., p. 123.   12 ibid., p. 126.
13 ibid., p. 123.   14 ibid., p. 127.
15 *JCL*, VII, 1 (1972), pp. 6–8.
16 'The Fourth Stage', op. cit., p. 129.
17 Obotunde Ijimere, *The Imprisonment of Obatala and Other Plays* ('English version by Ulli Beier'), Heinemann, 1966.
18 'The Fourth Stage', op. cit., p. 132.
19 Quoted by E. J. Simmons, *Chekhov: A Biography*, Cape, 1963, p. 581.
20 *The Myth of Sisyphus and Other Essays*, translated by J. O'Brien, Knopf, New York, 1955, pp. 89–91.

Dramatic Theory of Wole Soyinka

Ann B. Davis

Wole Soyinka has developed an innovative theory of drama which provides workable new theoretical constructs for contemporary dramatic criticism and validates the ritual approach to drama by universalizing its insights. However, Soyinka's theory has not been studied by other dramatic theorists, nor has it been analyzed by critics of Soyinka's dramatic and literary works. The reasons for the dearth of attention to a theory of such significance are two-fold. First, since the essay and speech in which the theory is most fully developed have been published only in respectively, a *festschriften* volume dedicated to G. Wilson Knight, and the proceedings of an African studies seminar,[2] neither of which is relevantly indexed, scholars concerned with dramatic theory have not had access to the works in which Soyinka's theory is articulated. Secondly, and more problematically, since neither the essay nor the speech focuses exclusively on dramatic theory, those writers who have commented on either have failed to recognize the significance of the dramatic theory developed. Their concern as literary critics studying Soyinka's dramatic and literary works has resulted in approaches which view the theoretical insights of the writer in isolation and exclusively in relationship to his plays, novels, and poetry. Such approaches, although frequently providing insights into Soyinka's non-theoretical writings, have nonetheless obscured the primary value of his dramatic theory and thereby further hindered access by scholars in both the fields of dramatic theory and African literature. Further, the problems of access are compounded by the fact that the theoretical insights of the essay and speech constitute a theory only when the two works are correlated, although each is relevant to a variety of theoretical issues in isolation. The understanding of either work as an articulation of aspects of a dramatic theory requires that it be seen first in relationship to the other work, and secondly in relationship to the writer's other statements on dramatic theory.

Soyinka's theory of drama is constructed on reformulations of the terms of previous ritual approaches to drama and is most usefully discussed in relationship to the earlier theories which it modifies. The tradition of dramatic theory linking ritual and drama extends from the origin of western dramatic theory in Aristotle's *Poetics* to nearly all modern dramatic criticism in English, and has manifested a unique concern with discussing dramatic import in terms of audience affect. This concern with audience affect requires that the discussion of ritual theories of drama include analysis of the concepts of audience affect which have been developed by various theorists, as well as an examination of their concepts of ritual and drama.

The two earlier ritual theories of drama most useful to an understanding of Soyinka's theory are the theories of Friedrich Nietzche and G. Wilson Knight. Both Nietzsche and Knight reconsider the link between drama and ritual which was originally suggested by Aristotle, and develop concepts of audience affect which contrast with that of Soyinka. In the *Poetics* the only relationship posited between ritual and drama is that Aristotle finds the historical origin of tragedy in the dithyramb.[3] This historical link is distinctly peripheral to Aristotle's central functional definition of tragedy which does, however, depend on a concept of audience affect—the achievement of a catharsis of pity and fear.[4]

Like Aristotle, Nietzsche's theory of drama is essentially a theory of tragedy. However, unlike the dramatic theory of Aristotle, that of Nietzsche is based on a postulated relationship between ritual and drama. Neitzsche assumes Aristotle's contention that tragedy developed from the Dionysian dithyramb,[5] and postulates that in tragedy, ritual dithyramb becomes symbolic of universal and individual conflicts.[6] As noted by Michael Hinden, Nietzsche's concept of audience affect is that in the experience of drama the individual achieves a "subliminal perception" of a communal consciousness. This perception is achieved as the audience member realizes that the dramatic conflict parallels his internal psychological conflict both as an individual and as a member of a social group. At the same time a conflict is paralleled "within the 'world will' between the principles of fusion and individuation."[7]

Contemporary dramatic critics such as G. Wilson Knight have accepted Nietzsche's concept of a metaphorical link between the experience of ritual and that of tragic drama, yet extend the relationship beyond Nietzsche's exclusive concern with Greek ritual and drama to also consider Elizabethan, neo-classic, Wagnerian, and modern drama. Modern theorists have focused on psychological conflicts other than that emphasized by Nietzsche in their discussions of dramatic significance and audience affect. Knight discusses ritual in psychoanalytic terms concentrating on psychosexual conflict. He posits that, "Ritual and drama are agents; as civilization advances the agency becomes more psychological but its action persists," [8] and argues that, "Nietzsche's two principles which correspond on the human plane to the sexes, female, and male, can be found at work within the context as well as the form of Greek tragedy."[9]

Like Nietzsche and Knight, Soyinka is concerned with a metaphorical rather than a historical link between the experience of ritual and the experience of drama, and stresses audience affect. Soyinka's theory differs most obviously from those of the earlier theorists in its rejection of their exclusive concern with the relationship betwen ritual and tragedy. His theory is a theory of drama which focuses on contemporary drama, while Nietzsche develops a theory of Greek tragedy, and Knight develops a theory of drama based on a reconsideration of Greek tragedy.

Soyinka's theory further departs from those of earlier theorists in its use of a broader concept of ritual than that utilized by Nietzsche and Knight. The theory is also unique in that it focuses on the dynamics of social and psychological processes within the dramatic experience, whereas the theories of Nietzsche and Knight are concerned with the dramatic experience only in terms of individual psychological processes. Like Nietzsche and Knight, Soyinka is concerned with defining the experience of drama in relationship to ritual, which he views as its historical and most frequent contemporaneous source. However, unlike the earlier theorists, Soyinka is equally concerned with defining the experience of drama in relationship to revolutionary, or liberating, social consciousness.

Soyinka postulates that in the experience of theater, revolution, and ritual, the individual first loses a sense of individuation to communality, either of audience, cultural value or mythic consciousness. By drawing comparisons between such experiences as his initial reaction, the developing dramatic action, audience response, revealed cultural value, and a sense of mythic awareness, he creates a new sense of individuation based on a renewed awareness of communal values and beliefs.

Since Soyinka's theory of drama treats the experience of drama in relationship to ritual and revolutionary consciousness, an understanding of these relationships is requisite to an appreciation of the theory. Essentially Soyinka views ritual as that which drama incorporates to develop social consciousness, and his theory of drama outlines the dynamics of this process.

Soyinka's concept of ritual as the source of drama is based on the assumption of a broad definition of ritual, and a set of postulates regarding the nature of the experience of ritual. The definition of ritual assumed by Soyinka is indicated in his speech, *Drama and the Revolutionary Ideal,* where he states, that "ritual is the language of the masses," [10] refers to ritual as a universal idiom,[11] and links ritual to other forms of cultural behavior by positing that the ritual form has evolved from tradition and history as well as from myth and magic.[12]

Soyinka's use of the term "ritual" in this speech is in the trend of usage identified by Edmund Leach as that in which "ritual" is used interchangeably with the term "custom," to "denote any non-instinctive predictable action or series of actions that cannot be justified by a 'rational' means-to-ends type of explanation." [13] On the basis of Soyinka's statements it can also be suggested that he would concur with Leach's use of the term "ritual" to denote the communicative aspect of culturally defined sets of behavior, although it is unlikely he would subsume aesthetic aspects of behavior under the term "communicative" as Leach does. Soyinka's use of the term "ritual" to denote aesthetic and communicative aspects of behavior then obviously contrasts with the use of the term by Knight and Nietzsche to denote a more highly specified set of customs historically associated with the activities of the Dionysian cults.

In his treatment of the relationship between ritual and drama Soyinka correlates this inclusive definition of ritual with a set of assumptions regarding the nature of the experience of ritual. These assumptions are based on Soyinka's re-interpretation of Nietzsche's theory of drama in terms of Yoruba rite. Like Nietzsche, Soyinka considers ritual experience in terms of the experience of self as individual and the experience of self as part of a community. However, Soyinka's concept of community differs from that of Nietzsche in that it is developed from ontological postulates of Yoruba metaphysics which assume "three major areas of existence." In addition to the "world of living," which would correspond to Nietzsche's sense of community, Yoruba metaphysics postulates, "the world of the unborn," and the "world of the dead." To these three "worlds," Soyinka adds a fourth mediatory world which he calls, "the area of transition," and defines as:

> the chthonic realm, the area of the really dark forces, the really dark spirits, and it is also the area of stress of the human will.[14]

The significance of this ontology becomes apparent in Soyinka's discussion of Ogun rites in the essay *The Fourth Stage* where the discussion of a particular rite serves as a model of ritual experience generally. Here Soyinka suggests that in the experience of the Ogun celebratory rite, the participant simultaneously loses his sense of individuality in the communal experience and parallels this "routing of individuation" with the experience of Ogun. He is thus able to bridge the gulf of tensions created by the feeling of loss of self in the experience of communal joy by paralleling this experience with that of the deity's. Ogun surrendered his individuation, yet "reassembled himself" organizing the bridge of art and technology between deities and man, as the participant bridges the tensions between sense of individuation and joy of communality and "recreates a self" through poetry and dance. The poetry and dance, then, as "celebrative aspects of the resolved crisis of his god," suggest that the individual, by paralleling his experience with that of the deity, finds in the deity's resolution a solution to his dilemma, and by poetry and dance creates as an individual from a renewed mythic awareness. Absorption into mythic consciousness and with that consciousness, the individual's drawing of parallels between his experience of absorption and the mythic experience of Ogun are the dual aspects or sources of the aesthetic solution, or creative experience in which the celebrating of the resolved crisis of the god, resolves the crisis of the individual.[15]

This description is given to serve as a model of ritual experience generally because of inferences drawn from the postulated ontology and the correlative symbolic importance Soyinka attaches to the Ogun myth. In *The Fourth Stage,* Soyinka first posits a "parallel" relationship between the deities and the living, and the ancestors and the unborn and the living, in that a parallel area of transition divides the deities from the living, as divides the unborn and the ancestors from the living. This parallelism then indicates that the relationship of the deities to the living is potentially symbolic of the relationship of the ancestors and the unborn to the living.

Secondly, Soyinka argues that both birth and death are, "acts of hubris," in that with these acts one risks dissolution in the area of transition in the passage from one area of existence to another. He then suggests that all other human acts are "lesser to these ultimates of the human condition and creative will." [16] Although not entailing the same degree of risk, other acts are seen to follow the same pattern as that of the passages from the world of the unborn to the world of the living, and from the world of the living to the world of the dead.

The process of passage from one area of existence to another, i.e. of action which results in successful change, is then given to entail four stages. First, one must risk change; second, one must find a symbolic parallel to this risk in which change is achieved; third, one must celebrate the successful change in the symbolic parallel; and fourth, by the celebration one achieves change. Whether the change is from one area of existence to another, or one level of awareness to another, Soyinka posits that the experience of change is the same in terms of the process involved; that is, in terms of the ritual form.

Soyinka finds the Ogun myth to be the prototype for his description of the ritual process in that bridging the gulf between the deities and mankind:

> was not only Ogun's task but his very nature, and he had first to experience, to surrender his individuation once again (the first time, as a part of the original Orisa-nla Oneness) to the fragmenting process, to be resorbed within universal Oneness, the Unconsciousness, the deep black whirlpool of mythopoetic forces, to immerse himself thoroughly within it, understand its nature and yet by the combative value of the will to rescue and re-assemble himself and emerge wiser, powerful from the draught of cosmic secrets, organizing the mystic and the technical forces of earth and cosmos to forge a bridge for his companions to follow.[17]

On the basis then of the description of the ritual experience as typical of human acts in which change is achieved, and the re-telling of the Ogun myth, Soyinka implies that for an individual to effect desired change, he must lose his previous sense of self in communal consciousness, and then develop a new sense of self by aesthetically or technically organizing the awareness gained by the self of communal consciousness.

The implication Soyinka draws from this model of human action and human change processes is that drama is the most potentially revolutionary art form because it always potentially embodies the ritual form. He contends that the potential revolutionary character of drama is inherent in the fact that theater is "the most social art form." [18] The basis for this contention is found in his statement that:

> The theater is simply but effectively in its operational totality, both performance and audience, and there exists already in this truth a straight forward dynamic of drama . . . A tension, if you prefer the word, an active, creative, and translatable

tension which need not be announced in words or action (from the auditorium) but which occasionally spills over into the manifested response referred to as audience participation.[19]

In the experience of drama then, it is the performance which forces the individual audience member into a communal consciousness and also provides the material from which a new sense of self may be created. As audience member he experiences his responses to the performance both as shared and individual and finds analogues for this experience in the experience of the protagonistic forces.

Soyinka suggests that drama effects change through the incorporation of the recognizable rite,[20] and in addition, he theorizes that dramas effect change through the use of universal rituals,[21] audience participation,[22] and satire.[23] This group of techniques can be further expanded by the examination of Soyinka's own dramatic works with the aim of identifying ritual aspects or those elements which would function in performance to establish and then break habits of thought or acceptance.[24] Such identification assumes, of course, Soyinka's use of the term "ritual" to denote aesthetic and communicative aspects of culturally patterned behavior.

Soyinka's use of Yoruba festivals in his plays has been discussed by Deirdre La Pin[25] and Oyin Ogunba[26]. Ogunba also treats Soyinka's use of Yoruba expressions and songs,[27] while Bernth Lindfors discusses the significance of Yoruba proverbs in Soyinka's plays.[28] Soyinka does not, however, simply draw upon patterned behavior from examples in Yoruba society. The utilization of a universal sacrificial ritual is identified by Steven Moyo to be evident in *The Road*[29] and one could also discuss *The Strong Breed*[30] in terms of its realization of a universal purgation ritual. Soyinka has also utilized Greek myth and drama in his most recent play, *The Bacchae of Euripides: A Communion Rite.*[31] Soyinka's *The Bacchae* is both an adaptation of Euripides' *The Bacchae*[32] and a re-interpretation of the Dionysos myths. In this drama by the addition of a character, The Slave Leader, and a slave chorus, Soyinka has created a drama focused on the dynamics of social upheaval from Euripides' original ambiguous play.[33] By doing so, Soyinka has rendered in symbolic dramatic terms his contention of a link between ritual and liberating social consciousness. In Soyinka's *Bacchae* the Dionysian dithyramb, which as previously noted is considered by Aristotle and Nietzsche to have been the historical origin of drama, is recreated. Central to the symbolic import of Soyinka's drama, as to Euripides, is conflict between man and nature, as symbolized in Dionysian rites. However, in Soyinka's drama this conflict is also realized in terms of conflicts whithin a caste society. In the play, Dionysian ritual is utilized by slaves to overthrow an oppressive social system. This social conflict in turn becomes symbolic of what Soyinka terms "the universal need of man to match himself against nature,"[34] in that both struggles are shown to demand solidarity, forceful challenge, and sacrifice.

Greek myth and ritual are also of significance to Soyinka's most recent novel and to his poetry. The novel, *Season of Anomy,*[35] incorporates the Orpheus myth, and close analysis of his poetry reveals a structure of imagery developed on the correlation of allusions to Greek matricidal myths and dramas to allusions of Yoruba myth.[36]

It is also apparent that Soyinka incorporates contemporary patterned social behavior into his drama at a number of levels. In addition to utilizing universal stereotypical characters, such as Jero in *The Trials of Brother Jero*[37] and Kongi in *Kongi's Harvest,*[38] Soyinka includes specifically Nigerian stereotypical characters such as Amope, the woman trader in *The Trials of Brother Jero,*[39] Lakunle, the school-teacher in *The Lion and the Jewel* who is supersaturated with bourgeois western values,[40] and Say-Tokyo Kid, the lorry-driver cowboy of *The Road.*[41]

Soyinka also uses literary character stereotypes in such plays as *Kongi's Harvest* and *Madmen and Specialists*.[42] Perhaps due to the influence of Knight's psychosexual theory of drama, female characters in these plays have a symbolic function which is similar to what Knight attributes to Lady Macbeth and witches in *Macbeth* and Clytemnestra and the Erinues in the *Orestia*. Knight states that it is through these female characters that, "we watch sexual principles flowering out into the wider engagement and interlocking of human ideals with the numinous and the supernatural."[43] Certainly the use of women as symbols of the supernatural is not unique to Aeschylus, Shakespeare, or Soyinka, given the ubiquity of the belief that women are closer to nature and therefore are closer to its mysteries. However, what is of interest in Knight's analysis is the suggestion that it is through sexual conflicts in the *Orestia* and *Macbeth* that political struggles are seen in a broader perspective. Similarly, it can be said that in Soyinka's *Kongi's Harvest* it is through the relationship of Daodu and the mysterious Segi and the actions of Segi that the political struggles between Daodu, Danlola, and Kongi can be seen within a cosmic framework. Whether seen as a distinct character or force motivating Daodu, Segi becomes symbolic of a super-human demand for justice. Likewise, in *Madmen and Specialists* it is through the relationships of the earth mothers and Si Bero and The Old Man, that the forces of human destruction expand and interlock with forces of cosmic justice.

In addition to utilizing contemporary patterned behavior in the form of stereotypical characters, Soyinka also incorporates stereotypical situations drawn from contemporary and literary contexts. *Madmen and Specialists* opens with a dice game, while *Kongi's Harvest* begins with a committee meeting, and *Jero's Metamorphosis* [44] opens with Jero dictating a speech to his secretary. However, as is true of the characters, the significance of these immediately recognizable situations is not their inclusion itself, but that their inclusion elicits a set of expectations which Soyinka soon challenges. The stakes in the dice game of *Madmen and Specialists* are not money, but body parts, while in the committee meetings of *Kongi's Harvest* there is not only a failure to resolve any questions, there is a failure to discuss any issues, but particularly those of significance to the society. Similarly, Jero is soon shown to be not a conscientious composer of sermons, but concerned rather with self-preservation and profit.

In addition to establishing and then contradicting audience expectations through the use of specific rites, myths, aspects of Yoruba culture and language, literary allusions, and stereotypical characters and situations, Soyinka also uses dramatic techniques and word-play. Flashbacks are important elements in both *A Dance of the Forests* [45] and *The Road*. In *A Dance of the Forests* what initially seems contemporaneous action with its own motivation is given to have its origin in historical and cosmological action through the use of flashback. Similarly in *The Road,* Kotonou's reluctance to drive is first given to have been caused by witnessing an accident in the main action of the play, while in flashback it is given to have been caused by his having been the hit and run driver who killed Murano. Similarly, Soyinka uses direct address monologue to open *A Dance of the Forests* and *The Trials of Brother Jero* and by this technique establishes audience expectations which the subsequent action modifies.

The pattern of establishing and violating audience expectations is also apparent in the wide range of Soyinka's techniques which can be called "word play." For example, in *Madmen and Specialists* morphological units are abstracted from the context of value-laden words and are given meanings which contrast with the original words in The Old Man's speech:

. . . you cyst, you cyst, you splint in the arrow of ignorance, the dog in dogma, tick
of a heretic, the tick of politics, the mock of democracy, the mar of marxism, a tic
of the fanatic, the boo in buddhism, the ham in Mohammed, the dash in the criss-
cross of Christ, a dot on the i of ego, an ass in the mass, the ash in ashram, a boot in
kibbutz, the pee in priesthood, the peepee of perfect priesthood, oh how dare you
raise your hindquarters you dog of dogma and cast the scent of your existence on
the lamp-post of Destiny you HOLE IN THE ZERO OF NOTHING![46]

A similar technique frequently used by Soyinka is the cliche with a modified ending.
In *The Road* this technique is evident in Salubi's prayer, "Give us this day our daily
bribe," [44] while in Jero's *Metamorphosis* it is found in Jero's first speech, " . . . it
behooves us to come together, to forget old enmities and bury the hatchet in the head of a
common enemy . . . ,"[48] and in *Madmen and Specialists* the technique is evident in the
Old Man's speech, "That the end shall . . . justify the meanness." [49]

It is then apparent that Soyinka's concept of ritual experience and definition of ritual
are of value to the critical analysis of diverse aspects of Soyinka's dramatic works.
Soyinka's discussion of Edward Albee's *Who's Afraid of Virginia Woolf?*, Ben
Caldwell's *The Fanatic*, and Imamu Baraka's *The Slave Ship*, also demonstrates that his
approach is of value to the study of plays which otherwise seem very dissimilar.[50]

Furthermore, his treatment of the plays of Arnold Wesker, Alton Kumalo's *Thembo*
and Lewis Nkosi's *Rhythm of Violence*, demonstrates that the liberating social
consciousness Soyinka believes results from the experience of drama may be thwarted if
an author rejects the use of ritual. As Soyinka notes, all of these plays, "are concerned
with the revolutionary salvation of their victims." [51] However, he contends that in each of
these plays the author has imposed a resolution rather than developed a logical
conclusion from the presentation of contrasted ritual behavior within a social context. On
this basis he contends that such plays are patronizing and condescending and suggests
that:

> The would-be exponent of a proletarian or peasant culture must acquire the
> humility to immerse himself in aspects of that culture that can provide a foundation
> for the emergence of new forms, not approach his subject with the convictions of an
> alien and dubious enlightenment.[52]

Soyinka's theory of drama is then of value for its contributions to both dramatic
theory and dramatic criticism. The contribution to dramatic theory is the development of
an approach to drama which does not focus exclusively on tragedy, utilizes an inclusive
concept of ritual, and treats a broad range of social and psychological processes within
the dramatic experience. As has been demonstrated, the theory also provides useful
concepts for both analytic and evaluative criticism. However, despite the evident value of
the theory certain limitations are apparent. The manner of exposition of the theory itself
presents certain difficulties. Soyinka's statements on dramatic theory are, as previously
noted, most fully developed in a highly reflective essay on the aesthetics of celebrative
rite and drama, and in a speech on drama and revolutionary consciousness. These
sources are supplemented by materials found in the author's numerous essays on
literature and theater, various published interviews with Soyinka, and Soyinka's
dramatic, narrative, and poetic works. That a theory of drama is presented in these works
appears undeniable; however, it seems equally apparent that the theory as it is developed
is not accessible in the way it might be were it presented in a single theoretical essay.

The problems of working from a wide variety of complementary sources are further
complicated by the complexity of the author's style. In addition to frequent use of

parenthetical expression and allusions to an extremely wide range of literary materials, Soyinka's essay style is also characterized by a high frequency of multiple meanings. For example, in the passage "In vain we seek to capture it in words, there is only the certainty of the existence of this abyss—the tragic victim plunges into it in spite of ritualistic earthing,"[53]—the phrase "in vain" can be understood to mean "without effect or avail; to no purpose."[54] It can also be interpreted to mean "arrogantly" or "being excessively proud." The second interpretation is given plausibility by the understanding that "excessive pride" is frequently cited as a tragic flaw.

Since the analyst of Soyinka's theory must frequently work from "secondary" or connotative meanings, the task of analysis is often more akin to that of literary than philosophic analysis. It could be said, however, that Soyinka's style in discussing dramatic theory is itself typical of the ritual school, since the very same difficulties of parenthetical expression, varied allusions, and connotative meanings face the analyst of *The Birth of Tragedy*. Yet at least the essential elements of Nietzsche's theory are developed in this one work.

With these initial limitations in mind, certain other weaknesses of Soyinka's theory may also be identified, many of which it shares with other ritual theories of drama. First, although it seems Soyinka views drama as a type of ritual activity which may function to create revolutionary consciousness by incorporating into its form other types of ritual activity, his use of the term "form" is somewhat ambiguous. In discussing *The Fanatic* he states:

> . . . the author had achieved a successful integration of form, that is ritual, and matter (story), character, conflict, social moralities within a dynamic of revolutionary tension.[55]

This statement would seem to imply that ritual is the form of drama, or that ritual form is the same as dramatic form. However, later in the same speech he seems to imply that the ritual form is simply one form available to the dramatist by saying the dramatist should:

> . . . find a language which expresses the right sources of thought and values, and merge them into a universal idiom such as ritual.[56]

Yet Soyinka does appear to equate ritual and dramatic form in the sense that a ritual form may become, in its adoption by a dramatist, a dramatic form and suggests that if the ritual form is not the only possible dramatic form it is the most frequent and most viable form.

The ambiguity evident in the discussion of ritual form and dramatic form is indicative of the tendency in Soyinka's discussion of ritual and in those of other ritual theories to emphasize the ways in which drama and ritual are similar, while providing little clarification as to the ways in which they differ. The distinction between the two forms, although obvious to the theorist, may then by the force of his argument become obscured to the reader. In terms of Soyinka's argument, this difficulty is also apparent in his discussions of change and creativity. However, discussion of the distinguishing characteristics of these experiences and activities would not negate the contention of similarity. Such discussion could instead clarify the posited similitude by identifying distinguishing characteristics and specifying precisely why such characteristics have no bearing on the argument.

It also seems apparent that an important limitation of ritual approaches to drama is the implicit tendency to isolate drama from other art forms by comparing it to non-aesthetic activities. By his emphasis on the aesthetic aspects of Ogun rites, Soyinka could be said to escape this charge. However, the question immediately arises with respect to his discussion of drama and revolution. Although the terms developed are given to be useful in the discussion of drama, they are in a sense limited to drama in that one either must develop another set of references for the discussion of other arts or to be content to consider them simply in dramatic terms where they are given to be "less like ritual." It is not suggested that the apparent relationships of drama to other verbal and other performing arts must be a primary concern for the dramatic theorist, but rather that the appearance of such relationships seems more ignored than denied or clarified by ritual dramatic theorists.

Finally, although Soyinka's theory of drama illuminates the nature of the dramatic experience and can provide terms for the discussion of any drama, the extension of its implications for dramatic criticism is easier for certain plays than for others. For example, in an application of Soyinka's theory to the work of Athol Fugard one could speak of the ritual form in relationship to the sociological idioms employed as Soyinka himself does in his discussion of *Who's Afraid of Virginia Woolf?* Such an analysis, since it would be focused on plays in which struggles inherent in a social situation are developed to a logical resolution, could examine whether the dramatic conflicts are those inherent to the social situation and whether their development leads to a logical resolution.

Certain limitations of Soyinka's theory of drama are apparent. However, it is also evident that the limitations identified—ambiguous usages, the exclusive focus on the similarities between ritual, drama, and liberating social consciousness, and the fact that the theory seems of more use to the analysis of certain plays than to others—all indicate ways in which the theory could possibly be expanded. The limitations identified do not indicate any fundamental weaknesses in the theory, but rather suggest that elaboration and clarification of certain aspects of the theory would be of value.

The analysis of Soyinka's theory of drama demonstrates that the theory contributes an innovative and coherent theoretical construct to the ritual school of drama and dramatic theory generally. Soyinka's theory also provides useful terms and constructs for both analytic and evaluative practical dramatic criticism. The theory is of clear value for the study of Soyinka's dramatic works but is also of use to the criticism of his novels and poetry, and to the study of other dramatic and literary works. On the basis of a study of Soyinka's dramatic theory it is apparent that Soyinka must not only be considered a leading contemporary dramatist, but also an outstanding dramatic theorist, whose contribution to the ritual theory of drama is an assertion of its relevance to world drama and the understanding of contemporary dramatic experience.

Footnotes

[1] Wole Soyinka, "The Fourth Stage: Through the Mysteries of Ogun to the Origin of Yoruba Tragedy," *The Morality of Art,* ed. D.W. Jefferson (London: Routledge and Kegan Paul, 1969), pp. 119-133.

[2] Wole Soyinka, "Drama and the Revolutionary Ideal," *In Person: Achebe, Awoonor, and Soyinka at the University of Washington,* ed. Karen L. Morell (Seattle: University of Washington African Studies Program, 1975), pp. 61-88.

[3] Kenneth A. Telford, *Aristotle's Poetics: Translation and Analysis* (Chicago: Gateway, 1961), p. 9.

[4] *ibid.,* p. 11.

[5] Friedrich Nietzsche, *The Birth of Tragedy,* trans. Francis Golffing (New York: Doubleday, 1956), p. 26.

[6] Michael Hinden, "Ritual and Tragic Action: A Synthesis of Current Theory," *Journal of Aesthetics and Art Criticism* (Spring 1974), p. 359.

[7] *ibid.,* p. 8.

[8] G. Wilson Knight, *The Golden Labyrinth: A Study of British Drama* (London: Phoenix House, 1962), p. 4.

[9] *ibid.,* p. 8.

[10] Soyinka, "Drama and the Revolutionary Ideal," p. 87.

[11] *ibid.*

[12] *ibid.,* p. 76.

[13] Edmund Leach, "Ritual," *Encyclopedia of the Social Sciences,* ed. David L. Sills (New York: Crowell, Collier and Macmillan, 1968), Vol. 13, pp. 520-521.

[14] Soyinka, "Drama and the Revolutionary Ideal," p. 89.

[15] Soyinka, "The Fourth Stage," p. 134.

[16] *ibid.,* p. 132.

[17] *ibid.,* p. 129.

[18] Soyinka, "Drama and the Revolutionary Ideal," p. 65.

[19] *ibid.*

[20] *ibid.,* p. 126.

[21] *ibid.,* p. 77.

[22] *ibid.,* p. 80.

[23] *ibid.,* p. 126.

[24] *ibid.,* p. 127.

[25] Deirdre La Pin, "The Festival Plays of Wole Soyinka," M. A. Thesis, Wisconsin, 1971.

[26] Oyin Ogunba, "The Traditional Content of the Plays of Wole Soyinka," *African Literature Today,* No. 4, p. 2-18, No. 5, pp. 106-115.

[27] *ibid.,* No. 4, pp. 2-18.

[28] Bernth Lindfors, "Wole Soyinka and the Horses of Speech," *Essays on African Literature,* ed. W. L. Ballard (Atlanta: Georgia State University, Spectrum Monograph Series in the Arts and Sciences, Vol. 3, June 1973), pp. 79-87.

[29] S. Phaniso C. Moyo, "Soyinka's *The Road,*" *Ba Shiru,* Fall 1970-Spring 1971, pp. 89-92.

[30] Soyinka, *The Strong Breed* in *Wole Soyinka: Collected Plays,* Vol. 1 (London: Oxford University Press, 1973), pp. 113-146.

[31] Soyinka, *The Bacchae of Euripides: A Communion Rite* in *Wole Soyinka: Collected Plays,* Vol. 1 (London: Oxford University Press, 1973), pp. 233-307.

[32] Euripides, *The Bacchae,* trans. Phillip Vellacott in *Euripides: The Bacchae and Other Plays* (Harmondsworth: Penguin, 1954), pp. 181-228.

[33] Varying interpretations of Euripides' *Bacchae* are discussed by Phillip Vellacott in the introduction to his 1954 Penguin translation.

[34] Soyinka, "Introduction," *The Bacchae of Euripides: A Communion Rite* (New York: W. W. Norton, 1974).

[35] Soyinka, *Season of Anomy* (New York: The Third Press, 1973).

[36] Ann Davis, "Some Aspects of Susanne Langer's Aesthetic Theory as a Method of Literary Analysis: An Approach to Soyinka's "Abiku," typescript, 1974, pp. 5-7.

[37] Soyinka, *The Trials of Brother Jero* in *The Jero Plays* (London: Eyre Methuen, 1973), pp. 7-44.

[38] Soyinka, *Kongi's Harvest* (London: Oxford University Press, 1967).

[39] Soyinka, "Drama and the Revolutionary Ideal," p. 92-93.

[40] Soyinka, *The Lion and the Jewel* (London: Oxford University Press, 1963).

[41] Soyinka, *The Road* (London: Oxford University Press, 1965).

[42] Soyinka, *Madmen and Specialists* (Ibadan: Oxford University Press, 1971).

[43] Knight, *The Golden Labyrinth*, p. 77.

[44] Soyinka, *Jero's Metamorphosis* in *The Jero Plays* (London: Eyre Methuen, 1973), pp. 47-92.

[45] Soyinka, *A Dance of the Forests* (London: Oxford University Press, 1963).

[46] Soyinka, *Madmen and Specialists*, p. 76.

[47] Soyinka, *The Road*, p. 6.

[48] Soyinka, *Jero's Metamorphosis*, p. 47.

[49] Soyinka, *Madmen and Specialists*, p. 72.

[50] Soyinka, "Drama and the Revolutionary Ideal."

[51] *ibid.*, p. 72.

[52] *ibid.*, p. 86.

[53] Soyinka, "The Fourth Stage," p. 123.

[54] *The American College Dictionary* (New York: Random, 1966), p. 1341.

[55] Soyinka, "Drama and the Revolutionary Ideal," p. 77.

[56] *ibid.*, p. 87.

Complexity and Confusion in Soyinka's Shorter Poems

RODERICK WILSON

The purpose of this article is to evaluate the thirty-six shorter poems in the volume *Idanre and Other Poems*.[1] The discussion does not attempt to deal with 'Idanre' itself, since both the length of the poem and the use of a formal mythology demand a separate study. The guiding assumption here is that Soyinka is a poet who tries very hard to link together many areas of experience, in order to achieve a complex statement of a complex response to life, but I have found that in so doing he often fails to work out the experience as fully or as clearly as necessary in the language of a poem. Sometimes the verbal skills succeed chiefly in drawing attention to themselves and, by extension, to their deficiencies. I divide the poems into three groups for discussion: first, those with serious weaknesses of articulation; secondly, those which exhibit similar weaknesses to some extent, but are thought nevertheless to survive as poems; and, thirdly, the fifteen poems which are felt to show Soyinka at his best.

The poems in the first group are 'Dawn', 'The Hunchback of Dugbe', 'The Last Lamp', 'Easter', 'Fado Singer', 'Luo Plains', 'The Dreamer', 'To My First White Hairs', 'Song: Deserted Markets – To a Paris Night', 'Her Joy is Wild', 'Bringer of Peace', 'In Paths of Rain', 'I Think it Rains', 'Night', and 'Malediction'. These poems are further sub-divided and considered in relation to whichever of three main weaknesses they exhibit: inadequate working out of images and metaphors, slightness of theme, and insufficiently full presentation of the theme or experience involved. The poem 'Dawn' (p. 9), the first in the section 'of the road', falls into the first of these sub-divisions. The poet's sense of pervasive sexuality is what is most immediately apparent, in the way in which he views the coming of day and the responses of plants to the light. Closer examination, however, shows that this view of growth and response is not at all precisely worked out. 'Breaking earth' implies the palm's thrusting up into the air, and the pun in 'spring-haired elbow' conveys both new growth and a coiled energy. There is a tense expectancy, but the 'elbow' is not after all attached to anything and the image remains disembodied. The palm is given in its assertive masculine role, 'piercing / High hairs of the wind', and the sexual imagery is continued from the beginning of the four-line stanza onwards. But, from this point in the poem the role of the tree is reversed, becoming apparently female, with the sun as 'lone intruder', the life-bringing god of light, stealing in to make love to the earth and its plants. The change of sex on the part of the tree marks, not a complex insight, but rather a confusion in the imagery, and although in such a characteristically new-minted compound as 'night-spread', with its connotations both of night covering all and more specifically of bed-spread, Soyinka's gift of taut compression is shown, the poem scarcely recovers from the central confusion in its imagery.

Three poems in the next section of the book, 'lone figure', also seem to suffer from inadequately developed figures and images. 'The Hunchback of Dugbe' (pp. 18–19) is a mixture of the imaginatively moving and the gratuitously decorative. The reader is, for example, stopped short by such an image as 'pigeon eggs of light', but the stopping-short is a hindrance to the poem. The first three stanzas of the poem are clearly the best, reminiscent of Thomas not merely in subject-matter; but in the succeeding stanzas the fragmenting effect of violent images becomes a serious fault, for the essential human nature of the hunchback disappears under the weight of Soyinka's uncontrolled imagery. 'The Last Lamp' (p. 20) is equally fragmented in its imagery. It is built upon a surgical image and a para-sexual suggestion which again stick out more for their own sake than for any job they might have done in the poem. The rather obvious punning of the 'dye / And shroud', the light fading from the brightly-coloured clothes of life and the pale clothes of death alike, needs to be more convincingly integrated into the structure of the poem. One is, finally, unsure of the meaning of the last two lines of the poem, which appear to constitute sound at the expense of sense, and although the poem has some sharply observed individual details it obviously has too many weaknesses. The last of these three poems, 'Easter' (p. 21), seems merely to be an elided play on words and notions, and again the omissions result in imprecision, whilst the religious suggestions seem simply pretentious.

The three remaining poems in this sub-division, 'Fado Singer' (p. 47), 'Luo Plains' (p. 13), and 'The Dreamer' (p. 17) seem to amount to no more than exercises in unrelated imagery. 'Fado Singer' is inferior to the rather similar poem, 'Black Singer', which will be discussed in the second group of poems, and once again the fault is one of lack of control. The poem is a surrealist attempt to express through words the texture and essence of the singing, but is merely a chain of images and half-developed metaphors. In the first stanza, for example, one finds the lines 'My skin is pumiced to a fault / I am down to hair-roots, down to fibre filters / Of the raw tobacco nerve'. There is here the sense of a process of reduction of some kind, leading to the theme of giving birth, but finally all the words lead us into obscurity. The elemental threshing about proceeds through the fifth stanza, in such lines as 'Oh there is too much crush of petals / For perfume, too heavy tread of air on mothwing / For a cup of rainbow dust', and when the narrator declares 'I would be free from headlong rides', the reader cannot but agree. 'The Dreamer' similarly is an exercise in sounds, in rhymes and metres. One is aware that there are sacred and regal elements in the poem, but the essential situation has not been presented but rather refined out of existence. There is a sense of loss, the loss of the 'fruit in prime', in all its shades of meaning up to the metaphoric fruit of Christ, but beyond this the poet seems just to be playing with notions and pun-like assonances, for example, 'bowed the boughs' and 'throes and thrones'. The metrical variation is superficially attractive, but there is in the end a debilitating imprecision which the unassimilated influence of Yeats at the close only makes worse. 'Luo Plains' is, like 'The Dreamer', more an exercise than an achievement. Its static pictures reveal very well Soyinka's strong visual imagination, but this very static quality, partly enforced by the participles, together with the predilection for certain words (e.g. 'honed' of the preceding poem in the collection, 'Around Us, Dawning', becomes 'hone' in this) and the tendency towards insufficiently explored images like 'alchemist sun', all go to make the poem slight in achievement. The parts and levels of meaning, descriptive and metaphoric, fail to join up, and the apparent echo of Lorca's surrealism in the last stanza is not assimilated to any valuable poetic purpose.

The second main fault among the poems of this group, that of triteness of theme, is only present in the poem 'To My First White Hairs' (p. 30), but as in the poems already discussed, a superficial facility with words is being used to cover up deficiencies in the meaning. In this case it is not a failure to organize the figures fully but a basic limitation of significance in the poem's statement. The poem shows on first glance a clever use of language, at once humorously elemental and attempting to place the ageing of man in the context of mutable nature, and age *qua* wisdom is to be ironically undercut by the concluding invocation. Yet the point is slight, and the poem remains a piece of bravura writing. It is perhaps the most obvious example of a certain self-conscious cleverness on Soyinka's part which is capable of spoiling his work at times.

The remaining poems in this group of what must be termed Soyinka's failures, have more substance, but again there is a fragmentariness of details, this time in the inadequate presentation of the experience. 'Song: Deserted Markets – To a Paris Night' (p. 33), the first in the section 'for women', is damagingly ambiguous. What, for example, is the meaning of the seeds in the first stanza? Are they purely literal? Whose is the 'long night of pain'? What is the 'ebony grain' of the third stanza, and why a 'night for a life' in the fourth? All these questions and others remain unanswered, and the nature of the pain involved in the poem is never made clear. The title may be intended to suggest that when the business of the day is over, the individual cry is heard, or in another way that within socio-economic man is an isolate human being, in search of both meaning and response. Even if the 'meaning' is to be found in a suggested mood, it is not coherent here. 'Her Joy is Wild' (p. 35) is likewise almost entirely private in its meaning. The mannered emphasis, stanza by stanza, on 'wild, wild' is annoyingly bardic. The world of the poem, with the senile chieftain and the unnamed rite, remains beyond the poem itself. 'Bringer of Peace' too (p. 37) suffers from a lack of definition of the central experience: the identity of the 'you', the 'bringer of peace', is not made plain. There is a vague sense of the 'I' figure being trapped, but again without a clear reason implied in the poem.

'In Paths of Rain' (p. 39), 'I Think it Rains' (p. 43), and 'Night' (p. 46) are similarly poems about elemental processes which somehow participate in human crises, yet once again the human situation and the meaning of the natural phenomena in each context is obscure. The first is turgid with a sense of growth, momentary being, and movement, but to no over-riding purpose; the second is again a process poem that tries without success to be more. Though it is more clearly organized than 'In Paths of Rain', the meaning of the 'knowledge' with which the tongues are to hang heavy when loosened by the rain is not clear. What are the 'closures on the mind' in stanza three? What are the 'cruel baptisms' of the last stanza but one? 'Night' is equally obscure. 'Exarcerbation' is presumably a misprint for 'exacerbation'. What is the relationship between the poet and night? The nature of the pain is as obscure as that in 'Song: Deserted Markets – To a Paris Night', and the attention is left to wander over the insistent plethora of adjectives ('mercuric', 'subtle', 'jealous', 'incessant', 'serrated', 'warm', 'dappled', 'faceless', 'silent', 'misted', and 'muted'). The last poem in this group, 'Malediction' (p. 55) is better than most of the other poems so far considered, in the sense that it is clearer. The curse of the title is presumably pronounced upon the unnamed woman for some act of rejoicing in relation to the war, for expressing joy when grief was demanded. Yet, for all the offensiveness of her behaviour, the curse itself seems scarcely less so, unpleasantly excessive and far-reaching as it is. The language, with its revelling in alliterations ('crossed in curse corrugations', 'thin slit in spittle silting . . .'), merely draws attention to its own manner, and makes the poem a parade of verbal fireworks.

In the second group of poems, which comprises 'For the Piper Daughters', 'By Little Loving', 'Prisoner', 'For Fajuyi', 'Around Us Dawning', and 'Black Singer', the infelicities of the first group are less noticeable. There is still a partially too-private quality in the experience in the first four, and in the last two, occasional uncontrolled images can still be found, but these poems are less flawed than those

already examined. 'For the Piper Daughters' (pp. 27–8) is notable for
Soyinka's lively humour in such a line as 'Riddle him with lethal pips',
and for the effective use of an Elizabethan cadence in 'I would not have
you cruel . . .'. Enough of the poem emerges to make it effective as a
late Romantic 'O temps, suspend ton vol!' in another key, a praise of
warmth and fecundity which the speaker knows will not last even
while he asks for it to do so. In 'By Little Loving' (p. 41) and 'Prisoner'
(p. 44), the reader is again forced, however, to grope with incomplete
success for the full situation involved. The pain that the narrator
sought to cure 'by little loving' is too vaguely given, but presumably
it is some failure in love. Yet the poem is moving in the way in which
it shows a man in such circumstances coming to seem to himself an
accident of flesh. One is not, however, sure of the validity of the
speaker's drawing 'man's eternal lesson' from his own individual
plight. Another way of looking at the matter, however, would be to
say that the speaker is showing that one cannot live without such
'cords of closeness' and that therefore some degree of suffering is
inevitable, but the universal conclusion still seems inflated, and the
poem is finally weakened by the obscurity in the situation at the end.
'Prisoner' and 'For Fajuyi' (p. 54) are more obscure, and although
something of the meaning emerges, there are too many unresolved
questions. For example, in the first, what are the 'intimations' of the
third stanza? The theme is apparently that of man as the prisoner of
time, but the situation in stanzas three and four, with the death of a
'far companion' and the breaking of a potsherd, is too vaguely
presented. There is a moving sense of loss at the end, when '. . . sadness /
Closed him, rootless, lacking cause', but the central figure and his
experience remain too elusive for the poem to be fully effective. 'For
Fajuyi' is likewise obscure in its situation, for it is not possible to say
what the 'Honour late restored' and the 'trial / Of Death's devising' are.
Although one has a sense of the omnipresence of death and the demanding 'miser earth', a sense of weeds rampantly covering the temporary
paths of man, the nature of the central figure is too shadowy to make
the poem completely coherent. Perhaps the meaning is simply that the
value of the journey of the 'pilgrim feet' is in the journey itself, but one
still needs to know more about what is going on in the poem.

In the second sub-division of the less seriously flawed poems,
'Around Us Dawning' (p. 12) and 'Black Singer' (p. 36), though they
suffer from some lack of control in imagery, they are nevertheless more
successful as a whole than the four just discussed. 'Around Us Dawning'
explores the paradox of human autonomy and contingency, the
situation being that of man as an independent creature whose own
invention, the jet-plane, subtly modifies its inventor's nature. The
invention 'spurns companionship with bird', and in its solitary being

is an analogue of man's alienated consciousness. The imagery of the poem, however, contributes only variably to this central exploration: the image 'passive martyrs', for example, seems less integrated imagination than uncontrolled fancy. 'Black Singer' plays around with the idea of the voice heard being like a vine coiled around the night, and the voice as wine poured out of 'A votive vase, her throat'. Wine and voice are 'Dark, lady / Dark in token of the deeper wounds', remembering the 'cruel phases of the darksome wine', the painful historical experience of the black race. Yet despite this strongly moving quality there are still weaknesses of poorly worked-out imagery in the poem. The 'bled veins of autumn' seems a merely startling phrase, for neither vine nor 'votive vase' can in any sense be conceived of as capable of producing 'echoes' inside veins. The second stanza is clear and moving, but in the third confusion returns: 'Fleshed from out disjointed' is an unhappy phrase apparently unrelated to anything else in the poem; the 'light shrapnels' is a pointlessly obtrusive image; and the use of words like 'darkling' and, in the penultimate stanza, 'darksome', is precious. Compassionate though it is, the poem is spoiled by a lack of discipline, which is shown finally in the description of the 'wine's indifferent flow', when it is surely the response of the world which is indifferent and not the flow of the voice.

The fifteen poems in this volume which may be regarded as almost wholly successful can best be considered in groups according to their central themes. The themes are taken to be those of religious awareness and birth, the image of woman, death, external nature, and war. 'Koko Oloro' (p. 23), the first in the section 'of birth and death', is a simple and touching children's chant, a perceptive and rhythmic, dramatic presentation of mood, character, and social context, showing that Soyinka can write simply on occasion. The human voice reaches out to the known yet unknown reality of the numinous in the everyday environment. The poem which follows, 'Dedication' (pp. 24–5), is also a fine piece of work, affirming that man must be true to the life within himself, that he must be fruitful. This need to be 'earthed' is a central tenet in Soyinka's poetry. 'To One in Labour' (p. 38) presents the theme of gestation in terms of the queen ant. The poem obviously must be taken into account in considering Soyinka's theme of the image of woman: she is mainly seen as a child-bearer and has no apparent intellect. Her solitude in the experience of pregnancy is movingly rendered in the lines '. . . In solitude / Of catacombs the lethal arc contracts, my love – / Of your secretions', and the sturdy capacity for survival is there too in the lines '. . . spathe and spire survive / Subversions of the human tread / Or mind . . .'. The image of the 'Queen insealed / In the cathedral heart, dead lovers round / Her nave of life' is an unusual and lively metaphor, the queen in both cases being shut off from further sexual relations and the lovers being 'dead' in different senses. 'Abiku' (pp. 28–9) shows a darker side of the theme of birth. It has its roots in a specific tradition of folk belief, that of the child which dies and returns again and again to the womb. Yet here the experience, unlike those in several of the poems in the first group, is completely available to us by reading the poem. The image of the spider stands out, but unlike some of the images prominent in earlier poems, this one is fully integrated into the poem. Even while we may deny the literal truth of the experience presented in the poem, we respond fully to the realized dramatic truth of the abiku spirit mocking its human victims.

The different kinds of pain presented in the last two poems lead, as suggested, to a consideration of how women are imaged in Soyinka's poems. Soyinka has great compassion for the particular sufferings of women, and although he sees no intellectual side to women in his poems, they are never regarded as mere sexual objects. In 'Psalm' (p. 34) for example, the concern is with a human sexual relationship involving mutual fulfilment. The here-and-now holiness of human affections is both part and paradigm of the cycle of nature's birth and re-birth. The first line, with its noticeable rhythmic memory of Housman's 'The half-moon westers low, my love', places the sadness and standing-away from life of Housman in an ironic light, whilst the bringing together of the terminology of plant life and religious mystery gives the poem a wide application. The language is beautifully consistent throughout with all the levels of meaning needed: the beauty of the woman's shape is ruined by pregnancy, but this happens in order that new life may come into being, and the cornstalk is similarly bowed with the weight of the coming harvest. The individual man and woman are subsumed in the symbolic meaning of their fulfilled relationship, and life itself is praised in them. Both formal similarities and its placing in the collection make it clear that the poet intends this poem to represent the obverse of the life-view in the preceding and, I believe, unsuccessful poem, 'Song: Deserted Markets – To a Paris Night'. Taken together they represent a strong if limited awareness of the nature of woman, fulfilled or otherwise, the insight of the one modifying but never denying the validity of the insight into the other.

The awareness of death and pain, therefore, is never very far away from celebrations of birth and fulfilment in Soyinka's poetry, and the poems 'A Cry in the Night' (pp. 25–6) and 'A First Deathday' (p. 26) establish the connection in satisfying ways. The first acts as a counterweight to the poem 'Dedication', and the two make a pair of equally valid insights, constituents of a negative capability. In 'A Cry in the Night' human grief is inconsolable, without meaning beyond its own existence, and without redress. It is a tribute to the poet's control, particularly his control of stress, that he is able to make the reader believe what he says here. The human figure of the mother in her agony is, like the figures in 'Psalm' and 'To One in Labour', realized with a dramatic power. The poem 'A First Deathday' (p. 26) which follows, demonstrates again a complex but wholly consistent voice. The poet is dramatically related to us, both as presenter of, and participant in, the experience. The first two stanzas place the experience (the death of a child at about the time of its first birthday) in a religious context, which is in turn mocked by the irony of the last stanza. It is the mockery of one who will in future be able neither to mock nor believe, and we are certainly as interested in the narrator's experience of the experience as we are in the experience itself. The poem can be termed a miniature drama for the three voices of consolation, interpretation, and desolation.

Yet death must also be seen in its more violent and sudden aspects, leading man to question further the nature of the universe in which he lives. The poem 'Death in the Dawn' (pp. 10–11) is one of the best in the opening section of the book, despite the undisciplined imagery of the first and second lines of the first stanza. The 'naked day' is a challenge to man as an active being, going about his daily occasions full of life. Then in the fourth stanza comes the arresting description of the cockerel's death as it crashes into the car's windscreen. This rite, the sacrificial death of a white cockerel, is presumably futile because it has not prevented the human death which the narrator encounters soon afterwards. Yet the full meaning of this rite cannot be grasped unless we view the road and the phenomena of life and death associated with it in terms of its Yoruba god, Ogun. The sense of a religious context is being played off against the knowledge of what 'man's Progression' may imply, and our awareness of man, says the last stanza, must include an awareness of him as accident-stuff. Each item in this synthesis of traditional and western questions the other: man may be both master and victim of his invention in a humanly self-sufficient universe, and at the same time may be the creature of a complex god. Is this, the last two lines enquire, what universal man and the individual narrator may come to? 'In Memory of Segun Awolowo' (pp. 14–15), with similar subject matter, continues the process of questioning the nature of a reality in which sudden fatal accidents can happen, and the ascribing of the fault to him of the seven paths, to a god, paradoxically only makes man's fate more baffling. We only name gods, the poem seems to be saying, in order to get a grip on chaos. The grey presences with which we are left at the end, which 'wander still / Adrift from understanding', seem to mean several things: they are literal ghosts perhaps, surviving apparent death; they are our memories of known and loved people, and theirs of us, after death. Their meaning is arguably not precise enough, and the attempt to generalize in stanzas five to seven is again not quite worked out. 'Death the scrap iron dealer', however, unifying as it does the rural personification of death with an image of urban technological waste, is the sign of the poem's fairly successful fusing of new and traditional ways of seeing man's mortality, with each view questioning the other. 'Post Mortem' (p. 31) may then be seen as a coda to these poems on death: it is ironic, the poem says, that we should use the dead body to try to find ways of preserving our own lives longer, instead of recognizing death as a fact of our experience.

Reality, in these first three sub-divisions of the group of successful poems, is seen, therefore, to be ambiguous: it does not exclude the possibilities of religious meaning, but beliefs are continually being questioned. What then of the physical world in which man's joys and sufferings take place? The poem 'Season' (p. 45) provides the context. It is deceptively straightforward, seeming to celebrate the growth and fruitfulness of the life-ritual of the harvest, with a fine sensuous power which presents nature in texture and rhythm. The repetition of 'rust', however, gives the clue to the deeper meaning, suggesting both decay and the promise of something new beyond. The 'wilted corn-plume', like the rusted artefacts of man, is both sign of decay and prelude to new growth. The life of nature, therefore, imitates the craft of man's life, but in reality is drawing man away from his accustomed interpretations of decay into a necessary awareness of its function in the scheme of things. The poem is thus about the nature of paradox as much as it is about a paradox of nature.

At the heart of Soyinka's awareness in this book is the greatest pain of all, that of war, and in particular that of civil war. 'Ikeja, Friday, Four O'Clock' (p. 49) is a deeply compassionate poem, relating the sense of ambiguous growth in 'Season' explicitly to death by means of the image of the gourds. The dead, or those in the trucks who are soon to die, bring the fruits of human anger clearly home to us, and there is no religious consolation here. The imagery of the crop as a religious offering is developed ironically into that of a feast, but in the profit and loss account of war there is 'No feast but the eternal retch of human surfeit'. Despite this basically available pattern of meaning, there are unfortunately incomprehensible details, such as the retraction of the hands, and in the final stanza the gathering up of the 'Loaves of lead, lusting in the sun's recession' for the 'recurrent session'. Although the gathering up of loaves suggests Christ's feeding of the multitude, it is difficult to see a clear meaning here, and the poem is partly damaged by this overloading of the imagery. In 'Harvest of Hate' (p. 50) the view ranges wider, to consider the sense of loss and destruction of everyday reality in war. Again, despite the obscurity of some individual details (e.g. 'And rashes break in kernelled oil'), the poem is powerful in its depiction of the disruption brought by war and the loss of the young. The last two stanzas are especially moving in their sense of a longed-for peace and of the historical guilt of the fathers which has involved the children and deprived all of harmony.

'Massacre, October '66'[2] (pp. 51-2) and 'Civilian and Soldier' (p. 53) are among the best poems in the collection. Both in individual words ('shards' in the first) and in tone and rhythm (in the second), there is a strong reminiscence of Owen.[3] 'Shards' suggest two meanings: first, that of some fragment of a larger unity, and secondly the shards with which gardeners cover the holes in flower-pots. Something is broken, therefore, but some new growth is to be nurtured. The central meaning, that of fracture, is amplified by the phrases 'shredded in willows' and 'stained glass / Fragments on the lake': nature, once thought of as a meaningful whole, with perhaps a religious significance, is now experienced as fragmentary. The life-giving sun itself is divided. The phrases of fragmentation lead the attention to the symbolic level of the experience: beneath the dying and broken external reality, one searches for a sense of meaning, for a 'mind at silt-bed', and the swim in the lake at Tegel in Germany and the philosophical search are one, metaphorical and literal levels working perfectly together. There is, however, no discoverable meaning in the deaths of those thousands, so far away and yet so near, and the narrator swims in seasonal decay. Even the gardener's labour is futile, as the 'seasoned scrolls' of leaves fall 'Lettering the wind'. Yet this scene, so full of decay, is termed an 'idyll sham', because the placing of the suffering and the deaths in the context of non-human nature is felt to be an evasion of the full horror. The acorns ape 'the skull's uniqueness', but the explosive shattering of them takes the narrator and us right to the heart of the matter: the acorns may be shattered as part of the seasonal process, but the sudden breaking of men's skulls, which they resemble, is agonizingly pointless, and any search for a 'mind at silt-bed' has to reckon with this fact. The metaphor is maintained: the whirlwinds of war crop more heads than pigs crop acorns, and the numbering of the dead is more immeasurable than the numbering of literal acorns. In the midst of disruption, pictures of the personal life return, but the love for a stranger leads the mind back to the agony of loss that is at the heart of the metaphoric structure of the poem. The seventh and eighth stanzas are then the elegiac climax, an anthem reminiscent in cadence and syntactical control of Owen, resonant, honest, angry, tender, and moving.

The final stanza is ambiguous, but perhaps may be construed as follows: the land, the seasons, and all the terms which have served in the poem both as literal setting and metaphoric action, are terms which enable one to express one's sense of the chaos of human life in a particular historical context, without covering the essential isolation of man with any pathetic fallacies. In the midst of chaos, the search for meaning is still of value and can 'stay' the mind in its inner season of despair.[4] The narrator is, therefore, both distant from the events, and thereby enabled to meditate on them, and at the same time painfully involved, and is enabled by distance and involvement to be both particular and universal.[5]

'Civilian and Soldier', strongly reminiscent of 'Strange Meeting' as it is, inevitably suffers by comparison, but the confrontation between soldier and civilian is sharply done, if without all the richness of meaning of Owen's meeting between enemies. The soldier's 'plight' is that he has ceased to be a full man, and it is the difficult job of the poet to try to help us all to be just that. Though the 'bunches of breasts' suggest not an image of fruitful life but rather a dismemberment appropriate to the world of the soldier, the poem survives and reaffirms the vigorous tenderness of Soyinka at his best.

What general conclusions may be drawn now about Soyinka's poetry? It is above all a poetry of movement, of life in process, and the sense of growth is expressed by means of syntactical mobility, sensuously particular imagery, and varied rhythms and forms.[6] It is a body of work very varied in scope and uneven in achievement, but the best of these poems dramatically enact their meanings. A study of poems and plays together would surely show their common basis of complex awareness: a poetry which maintains and explores Soyinka's sense of the paradoxes and disparates of experience.

University of Ghana, Legon, Accra

NOTES

1 Methuen, 1967; page references in parenthesis are to this volume.
2 Though Soyinka's deep concern with the specific historical events indicated by the title (the massacre of some 30,000 Ibos in Northern Nigeria, October 1966) must, of course, be recognized, it is just as important to notice that he goes beyond the delineation of history to the philosophical interpretation of it. One can be excessively concerned with tying the poet to a social-prophetic role whilst failing to give enough attention to the details of poetic language. K. R. S. Iyengar, in *Africa Quarterly*, IX, 2, pp. 182–4, surely falls into this trap when he lays stress on Soyinka's immediacy in such terms as '... fresh from contact with the blood of actuality', and limits his remarks on Soyinka's language to such uncritical plaudits as 'whirling incandescence'.
3 Reviewing *Idanre and Other Poems* in *African Affairs*, LXVIII, p. 176, Elizabeth Isichei has also found a link between Soyinka and Owen in 'Civilian and Soldier', which she links with 'Strange Meeting'.
4 Cf. Gerald Moore, *The Chosen Tongue*, Longman, 1969, pp. 198–9: 'Again,

it is the control acquired in creating his more rarefied and reflective works that helps Soyinka to receive and render the full shock of these events. While his intellectual honesty demands acceptance of them as facts, only his skill as a poet enables him to render an account of them that goes beyond a mere cry of anguish or despair.'

5 K. R. S. Iyengar, op. cit., p. 184, makes this point when he describes Soyinka as the 'Yoruba poet who is also universal man'.

6 Elizabeth Isichei, op. cit., notes in Soyinka '. . . a prodigal command of language which one sees seldom, successions of brilliant images disciplined within the lyric form'. I have argued that in many of the poems such discipline is lacking, though the individual images are often startling.

Mr Wilson's Interpretation of a Soyinka Poem

Dear Sir,

There are three basic objections to Mr Wilson's article on Wole Soyinka's shorter poems in *JCL*, Vol. VIII, No. 1. The author displays a very limited notion of the way in which figurative language works; some of his literary and critical judgements are a little categorical; and he fails to engage with, or even perceive, the various frames of reference set up by some of Soyinka's poems. I propose to discuss Wilson's reading of one of these poems: the poem 'Dawn', which the author believes to exhibit 'serious weaknesses of articulation' (*JCL*, VIII, 1, p. 69).

We may take up my first objection, and assume that figurative language radiates meaning through epithets, images, and symbols. Wilson, on the other hand, tends to identify an image with *one* particular meaning: the 'lone intruder' with the sun. Now, in this instance, Soyinka has already mentioned a 'lone' palm-tree (*Idanre and Other Poems*, p. 9, line 2), and the family relationship between the words 'spikes', 'piercing', and 'tearing wide' clearly establishes an association between the image of the 'lone intruder' and the palm-tree. The palm-tree and the sun are both, in their different ways, 'tearing wide/The chaste hide of the sky'. Similarly, both tree and sun are 'Breaking earth', and both objects are being used by the poet as emblems for creative energy. To cite another example, Wilson maintains that the image 'A spring-haired elbow' 'remains disembodied', and that 'the "elbow" is not after all attached to anything . . .' But the image is sensuous, and imaginative: it suggests the movement of the palm-fronds; the ascending curve of the tree-tops, with the lone palm at the apex; and the rather mystical union of the fronds with the 'High hairs of the wind'. If the figurative language works in this imaginative way, and if the images used set up coherent patterns of meaning, then the poem is absolved from Wilson's judgement (rather a categorical one) that it suffers from a 'central confusion in its imagery' (*JCL*, VIII, 1, p. 70).

Wilson does not ask why Soyinka images the palm-tree as a phallus, 'piercing /High hairs of the wind', bearing 'the pollen highest' and 'tearing wide /The chaste hide of the sky'. The tree obviously radiates one source of creative energy, standing erect and 'aflame with kernels'. These kernels, and the shafts of early morning sunlight, combine to suggest the presence of the 'Blood-drops in the air'. But, why a phallus? Part of the answer might well be that Ọlọ́run, the Yoruba God, handed a palm-tree to Orìṣà-nlá when he sent this divinity to 'equip and embellish the earth' (E. B. Idowu, *Olódùmarè*, 1962, pp. 20–21). Idowu says that Ọlọ́run (Olódùmarè) ordered this so that 'its juice would give drink, its seed would give oil as well as kernels for food'. The palm-tree's fertility ensured the survival of the Yoruba divinities and people, and it seems to stand here as, amongst other things, an emblem for the creative essence inherent in Ọlọrun's universe. The god bestows life, and Soyinka uses a sexual metaphor to convey this notion, in an obvious and practical way, to his readers. We cannot afford, as critics, to overlook these references.

The coming of the dawn marks the coming of inspiration for the Yoruba poet, and that in a rather special way, because the Yoruba traditionally believed that the sun always rose at Ile Ifè, the cradle of their civilization (G. J. A. Ojo, *Yoruba Culture*, 1966, pp. 194–5). Ọlọrun bestows this power, this inspiration, because he controls the motions of the heavenly bodies and the daily rising of the life-giving sun. The morning salutations of the Yoruba often embody an understanding of this idea, and Soyinka's powerful and sensuous poem pays homage to it. The ending of the poem, indeed, clearly establishes this religious frame of reference, and it is a pity that Mr Wilson did not examine it more closely. There, 'a god' is 'Received, aflame with kernels'. The primary reference is to the sun, and one of the Yoruba words for the sun is 'orun' (W. Bascom, *Ifa Divination*, 1969, p. 149). Thus, Soyinka's brilliant poem concludes with Ọlọrun, and his minister, sustaining the Yoruba people. Mr Wilson also errs by not pursuing, or even implying the presence of, the Ogun references in the poem. Soyinka habitually uses this divinity as his symbol for the union of both creative and destructive powers. (These powers are pervasive in the universe, and its creatures. In our poem, the 'tearing wide' of the sky – a rather violent image – suggests a similar duality in human nature.) In his essay 'The Fourth State' (*The Morality of Art*, ed. D.W. Jefferson, 1969, pp. 119–34), Soyinka tells us that Ogun worshippers carry 'A long willowy pole', and that 'it is topped by a frond-bound lump of ore which strains the pole in wilful curves and keeps it vibrant'. One of Ogun's symbols, then, is the palm-tree /phallus, and the fronds image 'his wilful, ecstatic being'. Soyinka goes on to describe the Ogun dance as:

... an explosion of the forces of darkness and joy, explosion of the sun's kernel, an eruption of fire which is the wombfruit of pristine mountains, for no less, no different were the energies within Ogun whose ordering and control by the will brought him safely through the tragic gulf. (*The Morality of Art*, pp. 133–4).

Ogun embodies the creative, fertile principle, and he embodies a titanic will, the will to 'act' and to 'dare'. That is why this Soyinka poem challenges the Yoruba people: challenges them to respond to their heritage, and to go forward and create. I believe that these references are very obviously enshrined in Soyinka's complex and moving poem.

Mr Wilson's criticism of this poem (and possibly of others) has suffered because he has not understood these various frames of reference. (For him the poem betrays an 'inadequate working out of images and metaphors'.) The larger question remains: should he have been expected to understand them? Let me say that the ideas that I have been expounding are important in the whole corpus of Soyinka's work. The Yoruba 'traditions' inform Soyinka's poetry, and they must be taken into account, and properly studied. We accord this privilege to our English poets, and it is a privilege that should be extended to Wole Soyinka.

> Yours faithfully,
> M. J. Salt,
> Dept. of English,
> Fourah Bay College,
> University of Sierra Leone,
> Freetown, Sierra Leone.

POETRY AS REVELATION: WOLE SOYINKA

D. I. Nwoga

One of the functions which poetry is well equipped to perform is that of giving us a new perception of the world in which we live. It can do this at three levels. First, it can sharpen our senses in terms of either making us aware for the first time or sharpening our awareness of the physical phenomena observable in nature. This is a purely aesthetic though quite important contribution. Many people have either not cared for the rainbow or never bothered to appreciate its beauty till they read a description of it or saw a picture of it. A second level has to do with the obtaining of insight into things—seeing other dimensions beyond our mere perception of their surface reality. This in a way is a drawing together of things often thought of separately. For example, a farmer may think of rain happily in terms of providing water for his crops and the civil servant see it unhappily as making the day too wet for going to the office. The poet by drawing the two reactions together may deepen a unified insight into rain. He may also provide other dimensions and possibilities of attitudes. He may open our consciousness to the deeper social and psychological implication of human situations. At a third level is a greater awareness of inter-relatedness of objects and situations, both of their static existential natures and at the dynamic level of cause and effect. Poetry as revelation is directed at achieving any or all of these three levels of new vision. It enlarges our perceptions and reactions and gives us new meanings. It establishes for us a new reality; it provides a new background to our understanding and judgement of particular things, actions and situations and directs our wills and planning for the future. The conception of poetry as revelation, I think, dominates Wole Soyinka's functioning as a poet.

What I want to do in the following paper is to explore the implications of this conception of poetry as revelation by considering Soyinka's work under two aspects: (a) the manner of perception of reality and the poetic style which appear characteristic of his poetry, and (b) the content of subject matter in the poetry and the central meaning and significance of Soyinka's vision.

Perception and Presentation

Wole Soyinka has turned out to be a prolific poet. His early published poetry was comparatively meagre before he turned to drama in which he made his name. He had published seven plays before his first collection of poetry, *Idanre and other Poems,* came out in 1967. He had also had a novel, *The Interpreters,* published in 1965. He had been a prolific writer generally but his determined attention to poetry was a later development. And now he has published more poetry than any of the other poets of Nigeria.

Soyinka's earliest published three poems, though they are not included in *Idanre and other Poems,* are satisfactory beginning points for our inquiry. Soyinka had earlier expressed dissatisfaction with the great attention paid to one of them, "Telephone Conversation," which tended to put him in the group of those treating the racial conflict theme. The other two poems, "The Immigrant" and "The Other Immigrant," also offered possibilities of interpretation in the racial conflict category. The three poems are satiric sketches derived from Soyinka's experience in England in the late 1950's.

"Telephone Conversation" is a dramatic monologue. A "coloured" person is responding on the telephone to an advertisement for a room to let. He is satisfied with the

173

accommodation. His well groomed voice makes him acceptable to the landlady. He is however aware of racial prejudice and thinks he should point out that he is coloured. And here the drama starts, for the landlady does not want a coloured tenant and yet has to appear not to have any uncivilized racial prejudice. In the end the achievement of the poem is its witty dramatic approach, a pleasant change from the nagging seriousness of the racial conflict theme. The relaxed ironic wit of the coloured applicant raises him to a higher level of humanity than the artificial culture of the white landlady.

Though peripheral to the central drama, one of the achievements of this poem is the insight it gives us into the confused sensibility of the landlady:

> 'Madam,' I warned,
> 'I hate a wasted journey—I am African.'
> Silence. Silenced transmission of
> Pressurized good-breeding. Voice, when it came,
> Lipstick coated, long gold-rolled
> Cigarette-holder pipped. Caught I was, foully.
> 'HOW DARK?' . . . I had not misheard. . . . 'ARE YOU LIGHT
> OR VERY DARK?'

Here we see a picture of artificiality struggling to be taken as genuine. What is more important, the picture is presented not through an analytic exposition but a barrage of succinct perceptive images: important because this method of presentation is to be the crux of Soyinka's technique.

The "Immigrant" poems are interesting contrasting sketches of two students. One, suffering from an inferiority complex, sees himself as looked down upon by the white race represented by a girl in a dance hall, and takes out his revenge by taking a prostitute home. The other is full of superiority, refusing communication with the common people of England—bus drivers, cleaners, etc.—with whom he comes in contact and also refusing new ideas; looking for spiritual support in the present in a future when he will be a "big shot" back home in Africa. These poems do not have the sophistication and rich texture of the "Telephone Conversation." There is a lax, languid movement of words. And yet there is evidence of a total revelatory perception of the characters within these poems. And occasionally the flash of intricate insight in succinct imagery can be seen in lines like:

> He felt the wound grow septic
> (Hard though he tried to close it)
> His fingers twitched
> And toyed with the idea,
> The knife that waited on the slight,
> On the sudden nerve that would join her face
> To scars identical
> With what he felt inside.

This describes the moment of tension when "The Immigrant" had been refused a dance by the white girl whose "face exchanges/Vulgarity/For his uncouthness." The Other Immigrant" in his mental superiority thinks:

> My mind would open to
> The niceties of judgement
> To fine distinctions in a thought

If such did exist.
But only fools can doubt
The Solve-all
Philosopher's stone attributes
Of Up-Nasser-Freedom-for-Africa
The height and end of all
So shout with me!

                                                    (*Black Orpheus*, 5, pp. 9-11, 12)

With the significant exception of "Requiem," most of Soyinka's earlier anthologised poems are collected in *Idanre and Other Poems*, so I shall use that text for the study of my theme.

Idanre opens appropriately with "Dawn." "Dawn" itself opens with what I consider an obscure allusion "Breaking earth upon/A spring-haired elbow." (Perhaps this may refer to the myth of the sun being an earth being from whom the light emerges when he wakes in the morning, lifts himself on an elbow, and opens his armpit?) Within the poem an occasional appositional image is difficult to fit into the poem. For example, "Blood-drops in the air" may stand in apposition to "pollen"—a good image but I fail to see its context. But when some of the problems both of language and imagery have been admitted, the poem itself is an effective presentation of dawn both in its physical beautiful appearance and its deep significance.

First, the emergence of the sun is seen in a sharper picture of its rays piercing through palm fronds and the clouds of the sky:

. . . . one
A palm beyond head-grains, spikes
A guard of prim fronds, piercing
High hairs of the wind . . .

Within this overall image, there are individual perceptive images—the sun as a palm in appearance, palm fronds described as "prim" as if guarding the sexuality of the palm, moving clouds seen as "High hairs of the wind." The total picture not only gives us a vivid picture of the physical appearance of the sun, it gives it a sexual overtone. This sexual overtone becomes explicit in the later part of the poem in which dawn is given significance as necessary for supplying energy for life and growth in nature.

. . . . steals
The lone intruder, tearing wide

The chaste hide of the sky

O celebration of the rites of dawn
Night-spread in tatters and a god
Received, aflame with kernels.

                                                    (p. 9)

In this one poem, areas of reality involved range from the purely natural to the deeply mythical through the human. Nature, man and gods are inseparably welded in the imagination that perceived the scene. This is not merely a case of using images from other levels to decorate or illustrate an action at one level but an integrated vision which reveals an inter-related dynamism of significance. In the first stanza the sun *is* a palm, in the last stanza it *is* a god, the sun is a "lone intruder" that rapes the "chaste hide of the sky"; so that at the end "kernels" is not a metaphor for the god's sperm but *is* sperm.

In this poem then, in addition to the presentation of a visual picture which prepares one to better enjoy an interesting sunrise, there is the revelation of a physical natural phenomenon as being a dramatic ritual of major significance. The exclamation "O celebration of the rites of dawn" both expresses the sense of awe which the poet feels before the event and defines the nature of the event as "religious rites."

"Death in the Dawn" used to be considered a difficult poem. But I think these broad ideas of Soyinka's mode of perception and method of poetic presentation open the way to easier understanding and appreciation. It is the quick transition from one level of reality to another presented in quick sudden images that has to be prepared for. Dew seen as "dog-nose wetness of the earth," weak early morning rays of the sun seen as "faint brush pricklings," low mists as giving to pedestrians the effect of "cottoned feet" and so on. Then we come to the end of the poem with its shocked shattering revelation—man is seen as one, the inventor, the poet observer, and the person killed in the car accident and a statement is made about the excitement and the danger of man's inventive progress.

> Brother,
> Silenced in the startled hug of
> Your invention—is this mocked grimace
> this closed contortion—I?

(p. 11)

The rich texture which characterises poetry of this type is well illustrated in the extract. "Silenced in the startled hug of/Your invention" not only says—"Killed in an encounter with a motor vehicle" but adds the ironical note of the Frankenstein archetype, helped by the humanisation of the will of the vehicle in the description "startled hug." A hug is normally associated with friendly human beings and the attachment of the descriptive "startled" makes the vehicle into a suddenly deviant person performing an act of affection towards a destructive result.

The mode of cosmic revelatory perception described here is pervasive in Soyinka and gives rise in his poetry to imagery that is striking because of the distance between the object being described and the source of the imagery with which it is described. Soyinka is not the first to adopt this approach to perception and image. Leopold Senghor has described its nature and prevalence in traditional poetry. The implication then is that Soyinka to a large extent shares the type of imagination which was characteristic of the most intense of traditional poets.

I might indicate that strong beautiful poetry is not an automatic result of this approach. Soyinka's main equipments, we have indicated, are his imagination which can perceive objects and situations with illuminating cosmic integratedness, and his ability to construct and combine images which recreate these perceptions of his imagination. Either of these faculties could err either by not being fully brought to play on a situation or by their action being in excess of the possibilities of the situation. Then we would have either a poem which is struggling to have a significance which is not warranted by the object of the poem; or a poem which strains the bounds of language, that is, a poem which becomes turgid with words in an attempt to create the images for its expression. The one consists in trying to impose on an object more solemnity or meaning or reality than the normal person, i.e. the enlightened reader will take; the other, of writing in a language which makes it impossible for the images to be freely felt.

In *Idanre* for example, in Section II of the title poem, the protagonist looking back to the drinking place, sees the wine-girl and her breasts. He is oversolemn, I think, in the following description:

> Darkness veiled her little hills poised
> Twin nights against the night, pensive points
> In the leer of lightning . . .   (p. 63)

The phrase "In the leer of lightning" is a good example of successful personification—we get an impression of lightning as a dirty old man peering naughtily at Oya's breasts. But the images which describe the breasts, because they are purely physical, emerge as comic exaggerations instead of significant insights. Perhaps such solemn images would have been quite successful if they had been used in the context of breasts as either maternal or sexual objects.

On the level of language, a poem like "Prisoner" is an example of turgidity. Eventually a significance does emerge of some person who has survived all sorts of conflicts and desertions but is defeated by the death of the will to action. But one has to search intensely for any significance at all—perhaps the images are couched in such abstract and esoteric verbiage. It is as if overwhelmed by a perception, the poet is trying to overwhelm us with words. The jerky introduction of images is not the problem—one grows to expect it; it is their unclarity. The same type of abstract and esoteric language is effective in the poem, "To My First White Hairs," but its effect is derived from the language being part of a design of mock-heroic humour:

> Hirsute hell chimney-spouts, black thunderthroes
> confluence of coarse cloudfleeces—my head sir!
>   scourbrush
> in bitumen, past . . .

describe his deceived pride in his young black hair just before he discovers the grey hairs.

> Sudden sprung as corn stalk after rain, watered milk weak;
> as lightning shrunk to ant's antenna, shrivelled
> off the febrile sight of crickets in the sun—
>
> THREE WHITE HAIRS! frail invaders of the undergrowth . . .(p. 30)

This is mock solemnity aided by exaggerated language. The effect is different from the disturbing exaggeration in style and volume of the language of "Prisoner":

> In the desert wildness, when, lone cactus,
> Cannibal in his love—even amidst the
> Crag and gorge, the leap and night tremors
> Even as the potsherd stayed and the sandstorm
> Fell—intimations came.
>
> In the whorled centre of the storm, a threnody . . .   (p. 44)

It is not often however that Soyinka falls into either of these dangers of far-fetched perception of reality or turgidity of language. His successes are many and constitute a large body of poetry of rich texture.

His achievements in the description of nature appear not only in whole poems like "Dawn," "Luo Plains," and "Season," but also in incidental images in other poems. There is the description of morning in "Death in the Dawn":

> . . . Now shadows stretch with sap
> Not twilight's death and sad prostration;

of the effect of light rain in "Bringer of Peace"(p. 37):

> You come as light rain not to quench

But question out the pride of fire

. . . .

You come as light rain, swift to soothe
The rent in earth with deft intrusion

and of rain drops on ashes in "I Think it Rains" (p. 43):

I saw it raise
The sudden cloud, from ashes. Settling
They joined in a ring of grey; within,
The circling spirit

The same detail in observation and infusion of extra dimensions can be seen in descriptions of things and people. To illustrate briefly, in "The Last Lamp," there is a striking image of light at night as "A pale/Incision in the skin of night." The whole of the poem "Around us, Dawning" is an insightful and strangely terrifying picture of a jet plane in flight and the dangers of air travel, starting with the striking personification of the plane:

This beast was fashioned well; it prowls
The rare selective heights
And spurns companionship with bird . . .(p. 12)

In "The Hunchback of Dugbe," a rather light poem with serious overtones, many exquisite effects are created with this imagistic perceptiveness—the hunch on the thin outcast is seen as "An ant's blown load upon/A child's entangled scrawl," or as " . . . his vast creation egg/His cement mixer born/On crossed cassava sticks"; and there is the amusing apostrophe of the man as:

The calmest nudist
Of the roadside lunatics. (p. 18)

Taken singly, it might be possible to reduce what I have said so far to Soyinka's usage of the traditional devices of poetry—simile, metaphor, personification, and so on. Let me therefore summarise three points I have been trying to make in identifying Soyinka's peculiar character as a poet. One is the pervasiveness of these devices by which they become, not embellishments, but an overwhelming mode of perception. Images transcend the status of means of expression to become the means of vision. The second is the scope of the sources of imagery. Again, here, it is not only that the range of reference covers the widest field of reality—mythology and the supernatural, man and nature—but that Soyinka quite consistently presents us with images which do not merely establish and describe by the nearness of referent to object, but go beyond to illuminate and surprise because of the distance between referent and object.

The third point is that the images join in the essential reality of the object. C. M. Bowra, in *Primitive Song,* explains how the primitive use of symbols differs from that in civilized poetry. One of these differences is that

though these lucent, concrete images may be said to symbolise something beyond themselves, such as the processes of fertility, they are not wholly separate from it but partake of its essential nature. In most modern symbolism a symbol may indeed embody much that is important to what it symbolises, but it is separate from it, as the Cross embodies many Christian associations but is not the same as Christianity. But primitive symbolism asserts a real identity . . . if not as exactly identical, at least as different examples of a single thing, which is both natural and supernatural and perfectly at home in the familiar world.

(Mentor edition, 1963, p. 239)

Soyinka's images share the nature of this primitive symbolism. The dawn, the emergence of the sun through the night sky, *is* fertilisation, earth receiving "a god . . . aflame with kernels."

The peak of Soyinka's achievement in this regard in one continuous poem is of course "Idanre." The speed of composition is significant. Soyinka says in the "Preface," "By nightfall the same day, 'Idanre' was completed"—all 26 pages of the poem. The organisation of the poem is even a more significant confirmation of the idea of total vision. "Idanre" is a convoluted poem. In one of the notes at the end of the book, Soyinka explains the Mobius Strip as "a mathe-magical ring, infinite in self-recreation into independent but linked rings and therefore the freest conceivable (to me) symbol of human or divine (e.g. Yoruba, Olympian) relationships." The thematic implications of this idea I will explore later. I have introduced it here because of its relevance to the movement of the poem. A simple description would be that the poem moves with the same type of flashback technique that operates in his novel, *The Interpreters*. The present is perceived and presented within a system of concentric circles which touch both the limits of the past and the bounds of the future.

Idanre's seven sections start with *deluge* . . . and end with *harvest*—an apparently logical development of a natural phenomenon. But the second section, . . . *and after,* which starts by putting us already into the night before harvest, suddenly takes us back in time to near the beginning—to mythical times:

> Vast grows the counterpane of nights since innocence
> Of apocalyptic skies, when thunderous shields clashed
> Across the heights, when bulls leapt cloud humps and
> Thunders opened chasms end to end of fire:
> The sky a slate of scoured lettering
>
> Of widening wounds eclipsed in smoke . . . .(p. 66)

The third section, *pilgrimage,* is transitional, describing the physical and mental movement of the protagonist and Ogun, his mentor, to the fourth section, *the beginning.* Here we have the beginning of things, both the pre-mythical time when chaos was the environment and the gods were by themselves, and then the creation of nature by Ogun. Here also we begin to return to more recent times, to the beginnings of human history in the legend of Ogun and the people of Ire. The section, *the battle,* stays within legendary times when gods fought for and with men. With the sixth section, *recessional,* we return to harvest night and finally in *harvest* to the putative present, "A dawn of bright processions."

This criss-crossing of perceptual time span is counterpointed by the interplay of forces at various levels of reality. For example, in section one, *deluge* . . . , the thunder and lightning of rain-storm are first established in descriptive images from mechanical implements and natural elements:

> The flaming corkscrew etches sharp affinities
> . . . .
> When roaring vats of an unstopped heaven deluge
> Earth in fevered distillations, potent with
> The fire of the axe-handled one . . . (p. 61)

With the last quoted line there is introduced another level of reality: "The axe-handled one" is of course Sango the Yoruba god of lightning who is sculpturally represented as

holding a double-headed axe, symbol of his magic thunder-bolt. And indeed much of this
section becomes a description of deluge in terms of a conflict between Sango and Ogun,
the Yoruba god of iron. This is so successfully done that there is not sense of falsified
mystification when protection from lightning through the lightning conductor is described
in mythical terms as follows:

> Low on his spiked symbols
> He [Ogun] catches Sango in his three-fingered hand
> And runs him down to earth. Safe shields my eaves
> This night, I have set the Iron One against
> All wayward bolts.   (p. 61)

It is successful because it is part of a complete action. The symbol is reality, the poem is
not a description of a mere natural rainstorm. The sky and the earth interplay in a
fertilising process; Ogun and Sango interact; at the centre of all these activities is man
who must attune himself to these interactions, and so the section concludes:

> In gale breaths of the silent blacksmith
> Cowls of ashes sweep about his face. Earth
> Clutches at the last rallying tendrils
> A tongue-tip trembles briefly and withdraws
> The last lip of sky is sealed
>
> And no one speaks of secrets in this land
> Only, that the skin be bared to welcome rain
> And earth prepare, that seeds may swell
> And roots take flesh within her, and men
> Wake naked into harvest tide.   (p. 62)

One could go on illustrating this point in "Idanre." There is, for example, in the whole
poem, the perception of a girl serving wine at a roadside inn as a real girl (Section I), as
the goddess Oya who has sexual daliance with Ogun (Section II), as the eternal Earth-
mother (Section VII). There is the vivid and exciting lacing together of an electric storm
and the conflict and integration of Ogun and Sango:

> The unit kernel atomised, presaging new cohesions
> Forms at metagenesis. Ogun lay on tension wires
> Slung in hammock, sail-wing birds of night
> Nested in his armpits, through pylon rungs flew
> Braids of veins, nerved wings and sonic waves
>
> In the blasting of the seed, in the night-birds'
> Instant discernment, in the elemental fusion, seed
> To current, shone the godhead essence;
> One speeds his captive bolts on filaments
> Spun of another's forge . . .   (p. 64)

Electric wires are the hammock of Ogun, electricity is Sango's "captive bolts,"
harnessed lightning, and the two conflict and integrate to give rise to a new beneficial
reality.

At the risk of oversimplifying what I have said so far, let me conclude this section
with this summary. It is generally accepted that "when a poet uses simile and metaphor
he directly or indirectly compares one thing to another in a way that deepens our

understanding of his subject." My suggestion is that Soyinka's poetry undertakes the task of going beyond this deepening of understanding of a subject into a revelation of wider realities. The dividing line between image and object is practically indistinguishable. One object, person or situation is illuminated by and becomes part of a range of objects, persons or situations spanning the natural and supernatural cosmos.

Content and Meaning

There is no denying the relevance of Soyinka's writing to contemporary realities in Nigeria and Africa and beyond. In *Idanre* there is a whole section of six poems devoted to events in Nigeria in 1966 and several other poems provoked by and commenting on situations provoked by political and social events. In his introduction to "Idanre," Soyinka says that the poem "lost its mystification early enough. As events gathered pace and unreason around me I recognised it as part of a pattern of awareness which began when I wrote *A Dance of the Forests*. In detail, in the human context of my society, *Idanre* has made abundant sense." (p. 58) His later poetry in *Poems from Prison* and *A Shuttle in the Crypt* have been even more directly involved in experiences with a socio/political base.

It would be a gross limitation of the achievement of Soyinka in his poetry, however, to see it as only a commentary on current problems. His poems, even the ones most directly political, contain a world view and a significance which transcend their objective sources. As I have indicated elsewhere, fruitful commentary can best come from an integrated vision, satisfactory criticism arises from a total vision of reality which supplies the background to the perception of particular situations. For comment to rise above the expression of individual pique it has to be embedded in a conception of what life is or should be. Hence the value of poetry as revelation.

Incidentally, it is perhaps this that explains Wole Soyinka's theoretical rejection of Negritude as a literary doctrine while himself being one of the African poets most immersed in both the traditional mythology and the local reality. What is not integrated into the total contemporary and eternal reality he considers artificial and dissipation of the mental and emotional energy necessary for understanding today and planning for tomorrow.

What follows is an attempt to explore the dominating characteristic of the world as presented in Soyinka's poetry and the meaning derivable from this conception of reality. Soyinka has himself hinted at these in his explanatory note on the Mobius Strip: "A mathe-magical ring, infinite in self-recreation into independent but linked rings and therefore the freest conceivable (to me) symbol of human or divine (e.g. Yoruba, Olympian) relationships . . . and even if the primal cycle were of good and innocence, the Atooda of the world deserve praise for introducing the evolutionary 'kink'!" (pp. 87-88). Atooda, he explains, was "slave to first deity. Either from pique or revolutionary ideas he rolled a rock down onto his unsuspecting master, smashing him to bits and creating the multiple godhead." (p. 87)

All this sounds esoteric and fanciful, and I hold no brief for Soyinka's prose style which I think is too tortuous and impressionistic. But the implications of the images used in the explanation become clear when we look at the content of his poetry. It will be helpful to divide Soyinka's poetry into two groups. Though all the poems are to a large extent reflective, two types of objects/situations provoke his poetry—those that may be described as natural or at least unself-willed situations or objects, and those situations or objects which are the results of man's purposive action. To whichever type a poem belongs, whatever the subject of the poem, there is the same content of a world or ideas engaged in a crucial dramatic and mostly ironic conflict, a vision of violent interaction, creating in the reader a paradoxical revelatory awareness of "revolution" as the essence of growth.

I have already used extensive illustrations from the poem "Dawn." I will mention here however that in this first poem of his first collection, Soyinka never uses the verb "to be" or any of its forms. All the verbs in the poem are of vigorous and mainly violent actions—breaking, spikes, piercing, bore, teasing, steals, tearing and received. His reflections on natural situations bear out the implications of this choice of verbs. In "Death in the Dawn," the very title carries the ironic juxtaposition of opposite ends of the spectrum of life, and the phenomena of daybreak are all active agents:

> Let sunrise quench your lamps, and watch
> faint brush pricklings in the sky light
> Cottoned feet . . .
> . . . Now shadows stretch with sap
> Not twilight's death and sad prostration (p. 10)

Like some others of the early poems of Soyinka—perhaps the outcome of early romantic agony—this poem ends on a note of startled recognition of the tragic irony of life in man's unwitting creation of his own destruction. But that crucial element of vigorous action permeates the poem. In "Around us, Dawning," the mountains constitute a threatening existence to the aircraft:

> The mountains range in spire on spire
> Lances at the bold carbuncle
> On the still night air. (p. 12)

The very next poem "Luo Plains" contains this presentation of lake and plains:

> For she has milked a cycle of
> Red sunset spears, sucked reeds of poison
> To a cowherd's flute. The plains
> Are swift again on migrant wings
> And the cactus
> Flowers the eagle sentinel. (p. 13)

The sexual voracity of the lake is not much muted here and though the swiftness is perhaps of the appearance from the travelling aircraft, the attachment of the speed to the plains carries through.

Scattered through the poems are such descriptions of natural settings, of outspoken Abiku children; there are reflections on untimely death and loneliness, of rain storms and seasonal changes and night and day. And the conflicting vigour of their operations as seen by Soyinka is perhaps understandable from Soyinka's presentation of what he calls "apocalyptic visions of childhood and other deliriums" in "Idanre," Section II. One gets the impression from this section that his childhood imagination was filled with terrible visions of cosmic conflict:

> Portents in unquiet nights
>
> Where sprang amoured beasts, unidentifiable,
> Nozzles of flames, tails of restive gristles
> Banners of saints, cavalcades of awesome hosts
> Festival of firevales, crush of starlode
> And exploding planets   (p. 66)

There was not only this picture of cosmic violence. Even among these childhood deliriums there entered the prognostication of ironic transformation of the right order:

> Later, diminutive zebras raced on track edges
> Round the bed, dwarfs blew on royal bugles
> A gaunt *ogboni* raised his staff and vaulted on
> A zebra's back, galloped up a quivering nose–
>
> (p. 67)

The same violence, the same irony, enters both Soyinka's world of political action and his symbolic mythical world. The depth of feeling evoked by his group of poems entitled "October '66" comes largely from the juxtaposition of the terrible pictures of death and slaughter with images of objects that were designed for fruitful use. In "Ikeja, Friday, Four O'clock," the "laden trucks" carrying soldiers for extermination are juxtaposed with "gourds for earth to drink therefrom," and we have the following contrasts:

> No feast but the eternal retch of human surfeit
> No drinks but dregs et reckoning of loss and profit

leading to the end of the poem with its ironic injunction:

> Let nought be wasted, gather up for the recurrent session
> Loaves of lead, lusting in the sun's recession.   (p. 49)

This is one of the few poems of Soyinka in which he uses rhymes (the first set though is purposely a deceptive rhyme of "therefrom" and "form"), and I also think this was a deliberate heightening of effect by the contrast of form and content.

The next poem in the sequence "Harvest of Hate" is one of Soyinka's most pleasant poems to read and yet one of his saddest. There is not acerbity but a reflective sorrow deriving from the wasteful destruction of promise:

> For wings womb-moist from the sanctuary of nests
> Fall, unfledged to the tribute of fire.
>
> . . . .
> There has been such a crop in time of growing
> Such tuneless noises when we longed for sighs
> Alone of petals, for muted swell of wine-buds
> In August rains, and singing in green spaces.   (p. 50)

Violence, irony, sadness—but these are the materials with which Soyinka reveals his optimistic meaning. These are the qualities of the world which he sees, but he is not a post-mortem surgeon, he is a diviner. As he asserts in "Idanre":

> Let each seek wisdom where he can, life's
> Puppetry creaks round me hourly
> Trunks and motions in masquerade grotesques
> Post-mortem is for quacks and chroniclers
> Who failed at divination.   (p. 78)

The "wisdom" which he finds, and what I think emerges from his poems and gives significance to them, is recognition of the cyclic nature of death and resurrection, of destruction and new creation. If then the situation is catastrophic and largely sad, the informed vision holds on to the promise of renewal.

The dirge "For Fajuyi" (p. 54) illustrates this point. One knows from other sources (especially *The Man Died*) that Soyinka had great admiration for Lt. Col. Fajuyi, the first Military Governor of Western Nigeria. The poem gives expression to this admiration, to the sense of loss, and to the irony of the fate of the Yoruba occasioned by that loss in characteristic Soyinka imagery:

> Honour late restored, early ventured to a trial
> Of Death's devising. Flare too rare
> Too brief, chivalric steel
> Redeems us living . . .
>
> Weeds triumph. Weeds prowl the path of sandals
> Thonged to mountains . . .

But inspite of this deep sense of loss, the conclusion is not completely sad or despairing.

> Who seeks breath of him
> Tread the span of bridges, look not down to gravestones.

Gravestones record the past but bridges form a continuing link between the past, the present, and the future. Fajuyi's death then will have a continuing meaning and out of that catastrophe there is created a hope.

It is the vital spirit of the poet that strengthens this awareness of the situation. The strength of that spirit, a spirit which refuses to be defeated by the "masquerade grotesque" of life constitutes a source of the optimistic reaction from Soyinka's poetry. The vigour of his poems, even the ones that appear to give no hope from the content, leads to this inference of optimism. But Soyinka gives definite expression to the existence and functioning of the creative revolutionary spirit defeating convention in a few poems. His poem "Abiku" is too well known to need comment. In "Idanre," in the middle of one of the most terrifying visions of cosmic oppressiveness, Ajantala, the *enfant terrible* is introduced as the symbol of hope:

> Opalescent pythons oozed tar coils
> Hung from rafters thrashing loops of gelatine
> The world was choked in wet embrace
> Of serpent spawn, *waiting Ajantala's rebel birth*
> *Monster child, wrestling pachyderms of myth* . . .   (my italics) (p. 67)

But it is the hymn of praise to Atooda that gives clearest confirmation of this validity of revolutionary action. The evolutionary kink that drives humanity out of its settled cycle and gives new hope of new directions:

> Rather, may we celebrate the stray electron, defiant
> Of patterns, celebrate the splitting of the gods
> Cannonisation of the strong hand of a slave who set
> The rock in revolution—and the Boulder cannot
> Up the hill in time's unwind.
> . . . .
> All hail Saint Atunda, First revolutionary
> Grand iconoclast at genesis . . .   (pp. 82-83)

The primal deity is split into a thousand godheads and we may "glory in each bronzed emergence."

Conclusion

I have used *Idanre and other Poems* almost exclusively for this study, partly for the convenience of more limited material, and partly because it is the first collection of Soyinka's poetry—and for most poets a first collection of this type contains the poet's exploration of his universe and his position in it. (Christopher Okigbo's poems between 1960 and 1964, for example, represent this kind of exploration.) My conclusion from the study is that Soyinka achieves a major success in a coordination of poetic style, material content and significance. All these proceed convincingly from an imaginative perception of reality incorporating the mythical, human and natural worlds, a vision emanating from a vigorous revolutionary spirit that will not yield to the oppressive conventions of fate and human willfulness.

In Detentio Preventione in Aeternum: Soyinka's *A Shuttle in the Crypt*

C. TIGHE

The books we need are the kind that act upon us like a misfortune . . . that make us feel as though we were . . . lost in a forest remote from all habitation – a book should serve as the axe for the frozen sea within us. (Franz Kafka, letter to Oscar Pollak.)

Writing about atrocities, whether they are on a large or a small scale, presents the problem of finding a language to describe and discuss them. Many writers have testified to the problem: Hannah Arendt had difficulties in reporting Eichman's trial in Jerusalem, Peter Weiss grappled with trying to portray Auschwitz in *The Investigation*, and Arthur Koestler, after his long imprisonment, said that he was tormented by nightmares of his own murder before a large and unconcerned crowd, because of his failure to find

. . . an expression of the individual's ultimate loneliness when faced with death and cosmic violence; and . . . inability to communicate the unique horror of his experience.[1]

The image is illuminating. Unless an adequate language is found for dealing with the experience of atrocities, writers find (as Koestler did with his lectures) that they go totally unheeded and are shrugged off without too much effort. Tadeusz Borowski, a Pole who lived through Auschwitz and Dachau only to gas himself at the age of twenty-seven, wrote:

I wished to describe what I have experienced, but who in the world will believe a writer using an unknown language? It's like trying to persuade trees or stones.[2]

In talking of what he calls 'Totalitarian Literature', A. Alvarez may be quite right when he claims that, despite all attempts, 'police terror and the concentration camps have proved to be more or less impossible subjects for the artist'.[3] The main problem in Soyinka's *The Man Died* and *A Shuttle in the Crypt* is that of creating a language for describing twenty-five months of solitary confinement and all its attendant horrors and dangers.

Any attempt to come to grips with the poems must start with *The Man Died*. Many of the poems would make no sense at all unless one knew in detail about the civil war and the events recounted in the prison notes. Soyinka says that the poems are a 'map of the course trodden by the human mind'[4] during his two years of solitary confinement, and that they reflect his dogged insistence that he should survive at all costs. He also points out that we are not presented with the actual struggle against a vegetable existence. Though he barely hints at it, we are presented with the fight for his sanity. Nevertheless, I am not convinced that either *The Man Died* or *A Shuttle in the Crypt* were conceived purely as works of literature, or that they are solely memoirs of what contortions the human mind can be put to by inhuman oppressors. There is a strong element of self-advertisement, almost 'monument erecting', for the powers of his survival. It may be simply the process of the prison experience engendering a survival-by-ego attitude, or it may be a post-imprisonment reshaping of the effects of the experience. *The Man Died* carries the marks of both these possibilities, but *A Shuttle in the Crypt* is a fascinating and more honest sketch for *The Man Died*.

The poetry shows clearly that Soyinka's mental health was a fragile thing. The 'Animystic spells' were designed to induce a state of self-hypnosis by constant repetition, and while the original 'spell' had some sense, preserved and consolidated something of Soyinka, often he found it impossible to shape his thoughts clearly, so that the 'spells' served to preserve a feeling or a mood, rather than a meaning:

My memory at last proves tenacious. That 'mantra' will serve. Utter words, order moods if thoughts will not hold.[5]

The 'mantra' referred to reflects this difficulty:

> Fragments
> We cannot hold, linger
> Parings of intuition
> Footsteps
> Passing and re-passing the door of recognition.[6]

The exhortation 'Utter words', looks straightforward enough, but the very act of writing caused Soyinka terrible trouble. The uttering of words does in some ways channel and order thought, and in a situation where communication is completely sealed off, words and the very idea of language itself can take on some very strange aspects. For Soyinka the act of writing was an admission of loneliness and a tribute to the work of his tormentors. At the same time he was haunted by the belief that a thought did not exist until it was written down and given shape. Language was the only means he had of preserving his sanity and yet to actually use his gifts as a writer was to break his stoic-isolationist resolve: 'I need nothing. I seek nothing. I desire nothing.'[7] It may be that 'Not to create or think is best'[8] but this abstention will not preserve his sanity or help him make sense of his situation. To find that he was credited with a 'Confession' was a subtle damnation and a logical extension of the 'plastic surgery' already done on his public image:

> Confession
> Fiction? Is truth not essence
> Of Art, and fiction Art?
> Let it rust
> We kindly borrowed his poetic licence.[9]

Soyinka has always been obsessed with words and the image of himself using words; the figure he cuts in prison is as much a problem of
Ideals as it is of the correct posture, the noble stance, and the appropriate verbal noises. I don't mean that Soyinka is not an idealist or that
he has nothing to say, but that his imprisonment has not helped to
correct his tendency towards verbosity. The diction of these poems
('solecisms', 'palanquins', 'interstices', 'reversion', 'suturing') is awkward and strained. The high number of equally strained puns and the
generally mystic atmosphere give the impression of imitation poetry
and of 'difficulty'. Soyinka's attitude to his own poetry is ambivalent,
since to occupy the mind with absolutely nothing and to withdraw in
upon himself was one alternative, and it is only through a twisted kind
of logic that he managed to justify his own existence and the desire to
write. His awkwardness in explaining this desire makes it plain that he
had compromised his image of himself. When Soyinka writes of the
Creation he has his own problems in mind:

What then, what was this need to materialize in poor second-mould copy
such outward manifestations of the pure Idea! Why break the invisible
chrysalis of essence, that one unassailable Truth. Truth, because there was
no copy, no duplicate, no faulted cast, not even a bare projection from an
alien mind of that pure idea? For there were no *other* minds. No faker. What
was this need to turn materialist? Uncertainty? Ego? Narcissism? Re-
assurance? Loneliness said the Holy Writ. A fear that thought was Nothing,
and a fear of Nothing which could only be allayed by the thought made
manifest . . .
   Not to create or think is best. The pauses leave the Crypt a little darker
than before. Creation is admission of great loneliness . . .
   I need nothing. I seek nothing. I desire nothing.
   Not even loneliness. A mess known as the world was created to cheat
the loneliness of the one pure essence. So witnesseth the Holy Writ, faking
it a virtue . . .
   I create, I re-create in tune with that which shuts or opens all about me.
Dawn or dusk. Darkness or light. Concrete bars and iron gates.[10]

To emerge from the 'deeper bowels of the Void' and to write does not
alter the situation. If anything, while it attempts to preserve sanity, it
undermines that sanity since the 'mind butchers are in no way appeased',

the imprisonment continues, and the image of Soyinka the idealist is forced to realize that he has made a compromise. This awkwardness and confusion are rare in *The Man Died* since most of that book has been put through a kind of post-imprisonment ego-blender which disguises the real moments of doubt and fear.

A Shuttle in the Crypt is more honest in its confusions than *The Man Died*. The fears and doubts are not resolved in the poetry and we have to accept this state as an integral part of the prison experience. It is difficult to know which of the 'mantras' work and which fail; often there is a huge gap between the 'spell' itself and the rationalization of that 'spell':

But one may also be the moon and hold sway over danger, aloft though tossed and ravaged in murky depths. Somehow separate essential self from the twin reflection and make all harrowing phases more sensory sympathy. My shadow is trapped but not my essence. Repeat. My shadow is trapped but not my essence. Now cast a new spell in case of renewed assault.[11]

The 'spell' exists almost without reference to the explanation, and, if anything, diverges from it rather than otherwise:

> Old Moons
> Set your crescent eyes
> On bridges of my hands
> Comb out
> Manes of sea-wind on my tide-swept sands.[12]

The explanation is far too easy, too assured and logical; the idea of the trapped shadow waiting and inventing 'mantras' for the free essence does not ring true. If anything the poem comes out of the failures of the 'free essence', and the explanation does a very bad disguise job for the trapped 'shadow'.

Something of the same can be seen in 'Roots'. Significantly this poem opens with 'Phases of Peril' and it is Soyinka's prayer that his hold on reality will be sufficient to enable him to keep his sanity. In this the particular pleas within the poem are dissipated, since Soyinka tends to produce and concentrate upon images which detract from the main theme; he is too easily side-tracked by things like:

> . . . Arouse the captive breaths
>
> Of springs and vaulted lakes. . .[13]

It certainly sounds impressive, but what does he mean by 'vaulted lakes'? Soyinka continually finds it easier to talk of ideas, to chase words and images and create fine sounds than he does to talk of his situation. I am not suggesting that he is shirking his responsibilities,

but that he finds it exceptionally difficult to say anything straightforward about his reaction to imprisonment. The 'Animystic Spells' are
another example, and both *The Man Died* and *A Shuttle in the Crypt*
show an inability to write about himself without becoming too concerned with his own image of himself and retreating behind a thicket of
explanations, none of which explains very much. Soyinka finds that the
subject of his imprisonment is fascinating, but that his innermost experiences were so painfully compromised that it is impossible for him
to approach them.

The fact that the poetry had a definite function makes it difficult for
us to come to grips with it:

> Eyes
> That grow as stamens need
> A yeast of pollen. Shun
> Visions
> Of the unleavened, look sooner on the sun.[14]

> Hold
> As they, bread as breath
> Is held and spent, discarding
> Weights of time
> In clutching and possessing – yokes of death.[15]

> Light the old hearths
> With salt and oil, with tubers
> Camwood, chalk and antimony
> What they tell us, these
> Dark ancestors of doom?[16]

These poems are literally incantations understood only by Soyinka. It
is not just the struggle to find an adequate language to describe what is
happening but a struggle to admit the internal effects. The language
that emerges is not successful, but it is as valid as any other through its
attempts at honesty and honest portrayal.

While Soyinka's attempts to write were a compromise, his attempts
not to write, to cut himself off from his surroundings and withdraw
into a void were both frightening and unacceptable:

Still, there being nothing worse to do, Pluto tried to discover tunnels even
from the netherworld into deeper bowels of Void. At the best, it was
mesmeric: the mind's normal functioning seized up, the day eased out in a
gentle catalepsis. At worst it lay within that darkest ring of recreative
energies, revolving on its axis, turning its spoor in the gossamer dust of
infinity . . .[17]

When Soyinka reached the tenth day of his fast he wrote:

> I anoint my flesh
> Thought is hallowed in the lean
> Oil of solitude . . .
> I anoint my heart
> Within its flame I lay
> Spent ashes of your hate –
> Let evil die.[18]

In *The Man Died* he writes of this experience:

I felt a great repose in me, an enervating peace of the world and the universe within me, a peace that truly 'passeth all understanding'.[19]

That he should have come so near to destroying himself haunted Soyinka, and that he should come so close to forgiving the 'mind butchers' brought him to a low level of despair:

I have returned again and again to this night of the greatest weakness and lassitude, to the hours of lying still on the stark clear-headed acceptance of the thought that said: it is painless. The body weakens and the breath slows to a stop.[20]

All Soyinka's alternatives were frought with danger and it was a case of choosing the lesser danger and ensuring the survival of the body, if nothing else. The fact that he did survive mentally intact is a tribute to his determination.

Most of the poems in *A Shuttle in the Crypt* are concerned with statements of belief. The 'Four archetypes' illustrate the plight of the visionary, the exile, and the intellectual and are a direct comment on Soyinka's own position. They reach out to *A Dance of the Forests* and *The Detainee* and they illustrate some of the ideals and some of the stranger confusions of the other prison poems:

> . . . are saints not moved beyond
> Event, their passive valour tuned to time's
> Slow unfolding? A time of evils cries
> Renunciation of the saintly vision
> Summons instant hands of truth to tear
> All painted masks, that poison stains thereon
> May join and trace the hidden undertows
> In sewers of intrigue. Dear Mrs Potiphar
> You seek through chaos to bury deep
> Your scarlet pottage of guilt, your grim manure
> For weeds of sick ambition.[21]

'Truth' is loaded with irony, but the final weakness, the physical bondage as opposed to the 'dreams of fire', does not ring true. The vindication that time will provide would certainly not be sufficient for this

particular Joseph. It is a very particular view of sainthood and martyrdom.

'Joseph' is no stranger than 'Hamlet'. Hamlet is presented as a
wavering intellectual, passionless, afraid of error, dangerous to the
condition of the state, encased in a 'gallery of abstractions' and incapable of positive action. It takes violence upon the Prince to prod
him into action. His delay 'Bred indulgence to the state's disease'. The
poem can be read as a criticism of Soyinka's fence-sitting colleagues at
Ibadan or as a justification for the violent overthrow of the 'diseased
body politic'.[22] That Hamlet's violence should be a reaction to violence
upon himself is not only a criticism of those whose ideals are not as
strongly held as Soyinka's, but also a pointer to his own advocacy of
violence of the last resort in *The Bacchae* and *Season of Anomy*; it also
refers to the Cockroach's ironic claim: 'Yet blood must flow, a living
flood . . .' and 'Oh I know my lore, I've heard the poets.'[23] The Cockroach twists Soyinka's own views to defend mass murder and genocide.
Soyinka's point is much the same as Solzhenytsin's:

A man will always wait silently and submissively for better times, clinging to
whatever small blessings he may still enjoy. But when he has nothing more
to lose and is ready to turn and fight, it is more often than not too late since
he is already at bay or a captive who can do nothing but beat on the stone
walls of his cell.[24]

It is too late to retaliate, and there is a strong element of regret that he
had not used violence:

> It took the salt in the wound, the 'point
> Envenom'd too' to steel the prince of doubts.[25]

Soyinka once remarked to Albert Hunt:

As a writer I have a special responsibility, because I can smell the reactionary
sperm years before the rape of a nation takes place.[26]

Having smelled the sperm he is not happy with his own reaction or the
conduct of his colleagues.

Like many other poems in this volume, 'Hamlet' reaches its climax
with a pun (many of them are much worse than this one). Usually the
puns are a method of side-stepping the real questions that the poetry
raises, a sheepish, grinning, half apology for what is being said. It is as
if he finds his subject far too painful to discuss seriously and dismisses
it with a pun, avoiding any attempt to articulate fully what he feels. At
times the puns express an attitude of 'well this isn't a serious poem
anyway so . . .', an avoidance and apology for dragging unpolished and
angry feelings before an audience; two examples are the pun on
'creepers' (page 64) and the last effort of desperation in 'Orphans of the
world / Ignite!' (page 65). The final pun in 'Hamlet' reveals an emo-

tional undercurrent, which makes it impossible for Soyinka to write without the protection of a joke. It is a far cry from 'Civilian and Soldier' where he had no doubt at all about his reactions:

> ... No hesitation then
> But I shall shoot you clean and fair.[27]

'Gulliver' too has its puns. It opens as a fairy tale, 'Once upon a ship-(of state)-wreck . . .' where local politics are a storm in an 'egg-cup', and where the King's statement is a veritable shower of Joycean puns:

> From Us the Lillywhite King Lillypuss
> To you obfuscating Blefuscoons
> From Us the Herrenyolk of Egg
> To you Albinos of the Albumen...[28]

It all leads up to Gulliver's attempts to work for arbitration in the war and his reasons for leaving Lilliput; the parallel with Soyinka's experience is obvious:

> The fault is not in ill-will but seeing ill
> The drab-horse labours best with blinkers
> We pardon him to lose his sight to a cure
> Of heated needles, that proven cure for all
> Abnormalities of view – foresight, insight
> Second sight and all solecisms of seeing –
>
> Called vision.[29]

A thread of question and answer runs through these poems. The end of 'Joseph' leaves the idealist in a very weak position; 'Hamlet' is the idealist forced into action; in 'Gulliver' the idealist pays for his action and becomes an exile; and in 'Ulysses' the image of the self as idealist is said to be an illusion in spite of all his trials and wanderings:

> ... our lighted beings
> Suspended as mirages on the world's reality.[30]

It is not surprising that after his imprisonment Soyinka felt 'rootless'. The experience was almost incommunicable, and to return home must have been something of an anti-climax:

> I never feel I have arrived
> Though love and welcome snare me home.[31]

In this light, *The Man Died* is very much a re-assertion of personality and character.

> I never feel I have arrived, though I come
> To journey's end.[32]

> The quest
> Is all, endless
> The home-coming
> Respite
> Before the gathering of the outward crest.[33]

In the same way that 'A Cobweb's Touch in the Dark' and 'Roots' tend to consist of a string of images without any real connections, 'Ulysses' includes a string of obscure puns:

> . . . tossed thorn
> In matriseas – mud consummation. I trail
> A sea-weed cord to hold your breaths to mine
> Prime turd among a sea of faeces . . .[34]

At other times the puns show him wanting to say something and yet refraining through the creation of a bitter pun:

> . . . evil is impenitent, evil feeds
> Upon the wounds and tears of piety
> O Wall of prayers, preyed upon
> By scavenger, undertaker.[35]

'Purgatory', the 'central experience', is remarkably thick with puns. Soyinka takes a vicious swipe at Marvell's 'Vegetable love', and his 'observation squad' imparts 'Wet timbres to dry measures of the Law'.

> For here the mad commingle with the damned.
> Epileptics, seers and visionaries
> Addicts of unknown addictions, soulmates
> To the vegetable soul, and grey
> Companions to the ghosts of landmarks.[36]

Soyinka's best poetry arises when he treats his own situation obliquely. When he is writing specifically about himself the portrait is not necessarily an accurate one; the punning, the ego, the lack of concentration and the pain all obscure what Soyinka is really trying to write about. When he writes about the madmen, the fears he had for his own sanity and the difficulties he has in trying to write about his own experiences are clear:

> Your wise withdrawal
> Who can blame? Crouched
> Upon your ledge of space, do you witness
> Ashes of reality drift strangely past?

I fear
Your minds have dared the infinite
And journeyed back
To speak in foreign tongues . . .

. . . tell these walls
The human heart may hold
Only so much despair.[37]

Here the people that Soyinka wants to criticize are in the background, and the criticism is far more effective and successful than his introduction of The lizard and The ghoul into 'Live Burial':

Flushed from hanging, sniffles
Snuff, to clear his head of
Sins – the law
Declared – that morning's gallows load were dead of.[38]

Apart from the awkwardness of the verse, this introduction of personalities detracts from the fact of a Live Burial and produces a note of personal animosity, which though it may be accurate in terms of actual events, spoils the original poem.[39] The strength of the earlier version was in the anonymity of the prisoner and the silent torture by the guards:

The voyeur:
Times his sly patrol
For the hour upon the throne
I think he thrills
To hear the Muse's constipated groan.[40]

The sparse but vicious parody of the doctors' bulletin and the flat, stark tone of the opening stanza, make grim poetry of Soyinka's misery:

Days pass, weeks, months. Buoys and landmarks vanish. Slowly, remorselessly, reality dissolves and certitude betrays the mind.[41]

This effect is denied by his attempts to jibe at the individual guards. 'Live Burial' falls into the same trap as 'Roots' and dissipates itself (in the final draft) with side issues.
Solzhenytsin wrote:

Descriptions of prison tend to overdo the horror of it. Surely it is more frightening when there are no actual horrors; what is terrifying is the unchanging routine . . . The horror is in forgetting that your life – the only life you have is being destroyed . . . This is something that cannot be imagined: it has to be experienced.[42]

It is precisely when Soyinka is not trying to give us the horrors that he

is most effective. His attempts to describe the beatings end up as
attempts at overworked and cheapening indignation or subside into
jibes and grim, punning humour. It is understandable, but when he is
trying to write about other people's situations we get this:

> And some have walked to the edge of the valley
> Of the shadow; and, at a faint stir in memories
> Long faded to the moment of the miracle of reprieve
> To a knowledge of rebirth and a promise of tomorrows
> And tomorrows and an ever beginning of tomorrows
> The mind retreats behind a calloused shelter
> Of walls, self-censor on the freedom of remembrance
> Tempering visions to opaque masonry, to rings
> Of iron spikes, a peace of refuge passionless
> And comfort of gelded sanity.[43]

It is not brilliant poetry, but it is effective. Soyinka is most successful
in talking about himself when he is talking about other people. Here
he is aware of the problems of finding a language and he does not
debase the experience with exhortations to participate in the horror.
The same sort of idea can be seen at work when Soyinka suddenly
realizes that his situation and that of the hanged men is almost identical:
'. . . at this wake / none keeps vigil. None.'[44] In 'Vault Centre' the
absence of horrors and the concentration upon the pigeons above the
cell make the tragedy eloquent enough without any forcing:

> League of sun-gleaners, coursers
> On golden chutes, air-gliders feather-vain
> On wind-currents, you have fed –
> Richer than ravens bald Elijah,
>
> With arcs and eights, death-dives
> And love-duets, frilled parabolas
> Curved beams and vaulting on my air-ceiling –
> This still centre of our compass points.[45]

In 'Procession' Soyinka openly despairs of being able to say anything
about the hangings, and the image which Koestler speaks of (his own
death before a large uncomprehending and unconcerned crowd) is
reversed. He finds himself 'Floating on lakes to cries of drowning.'[46]
He survives but:

> What may I tell you? What reveal? . . .
>
> What may I tell you of the five
> Bell-ringers on the ropes to chimes
> Of silence?
> What tell you of the rigors of the law?[47]

NOTES

1 Arthur Koestler, 'On Disbelieving Atrocities', *The Yogi and the Commissar*, Cape, 1945, p. 94.
2 Quoted by A. Alvarez, *The Savage God*, Weidenfeld & Nicolson, 1971.
3 ibid., p. 208.
4 *A Shuttle in the Crypt*, Rex Collings/Eyre Methuen, 1972, p. vii.
5 *The Man Died*, Collings, 1972, p. 187.
6 *A Shuttle in the Crypt*, p. 68.   7 *The Man Died*, p. 256.
8 ibid.   9 *A Shuttle in the Crypt*, p. 60–61.
10 *The Man Died*, pp. 255–8.   11 ibid., p. 187.
12 ibid., and *A Shuttle in the Crypt*, p. 69.
13 ibid., p. 2.   14 ibid., p. 67.
15 ibid., p. 66.
16 ibid., p. 56; sometimes it is possible to follow the development of an image and something of the general sense of the spell (e.g. the seed image, pp. 53, 56, 67, 69, or the incense boat, pp. 55 and 70) but it is a very vague 'sense'.
17 *The Man Died*, p. 255.   18 *A Shuttle in the Crypt*, p. 19.
19 *The Man Died*, p. 252.   20 ibid.
21 *A Shuttle in the Crypt*, p. 21; cf. Genesis, 36, 37, 39.
22 There are several examples of anti-university poetry: 'From / Beds of Worms / Ivory towers uphold the charnel house', p. 63.
23 ibid., p. 11.
24 A. Solzhenytsin, *The First Circle*, Harvil/Collins, 1969, p. 482.
25 *A Shuttle in the Crypt*, p. 22.
26 A. Hunt, 'Amateurs in Horror', *New Society*, 9 Aug. 1973, pp. 342–3.
27 *Idanre and Other Poems*, Methuen, 1967, p. 53.
28 *A Shuttle in the Crypt*, p. 25.   29 ibid., p. 26.
30 ibid., p. 29.   31 ibid., p. 85.   32 ibid.
33 ibid., p. 66.   34 ibid., p. 28.   35 ibid., pp. 34–5.
36 ibid., p. 38–9.   37 ibid., p. 18.   38 ibid., p. 61.
39 'Live Burial' first appeared in the *New Statesman*, 23 May 1969.
40 *A Shuttle in the Crypt*, p. 61.   41 *The Man Died*, p. 152.
42 *The First Circle*, op. cit., p. 200.   43 *A Shuttle in the Crypt*, p. 39.
44 ibid., p. 50.   45 ibid., p. 40 (cf. I Kings, 17).
46 ibid., p. 46.   47 ibid., p. 42.

A Comment on Ogun Abibimañ

Omolara Ogundipe-Leslie

Quickly to say that this is accessible Soyinka poetry, a change in the use of language and the impaction of image and thought. The immediate associations are with his own *Idanre* and Senghor's *Chaka*. But despite verbal echoes and similarity of mode at points, Soyinka's poem explores a different state of mind.

Soyinka's writing has become doubly interesting since the writer became ideological. His becoming "properly" political is a welcome event for some of his watchers who have always regretted that the incandenscence of mind, word and artistic construct characteristic of the writer was not cohered by a total appreciation of society which conveyed adequately but through art, in non-physical and non-metaphysical terms how we came to this fastness in our historical journey. We watched the expense of spirit in a waste of rage against the Kongis, the Calibans, and the Oguazors who were but victims or products of a larger but undepicted drama which is political, historical and international in character.

Ogun Abibimañ is a long poem written to celebrate Mozambique's declaration of her stance of war against while-ruled Rhodesia. It is not the favored threnody but a mellow and complex panegyric... the poet riding his horses of speech at a sure canter not with the bravura of *Idanre*.

Panegyric, dramatic poem or dramatized heroic poetry? One of the businesses of the "aesthetic" school (one of which fell victim to Soyinka's fiery axe-head) is to find new terminologies for new generic categories; new names for writing which show a peculiarly African handling of modes. A piece like *Ogun Abibimañ* combines modes while it impacts the oral on the written medium. And at work throughout is an imagination essentially dramatic.

In the first section where steel usurps the forest, the lyric voice is tried and sure, as mature as in the lyric passages which accompany Elesin to his death in *Death and The King's Horseman*. The blank verse is elegant, remindful of Demoke's lines in *A Dance of the Forests*. The second part brings us to the universe of Ogun. The celebrating persona is the individual poet, not the poet of the collective will of Abibimañ, a voice he assumes at points. Ogun comes to break the illusion of Dialogue in Southern Africa and as Soyinka's rage mounts against the absurdity of that political solution, his verse-style changes into broken, talkative and word-punching lines typical of Soyinka in satiric situations. He telescopes the outrageous chain of events from Dialogue to Sanctions to Sharpeville to Dialogue as Dialogue, a dogged dog dogged the "febrile barks of Protest." Now comes Ogun, the tale that wags the dogs who all have had their day. This proverb leads into an expanded use of allegory followed by a singing in the collective voice of the new political stance, in the verbal formulations of Yoruba incantatory poetry and the images of Ijala.

The choral battle song in Yoruba crystallizes the legendary encounter. It becomes in fact a metaphor in itself for the merging of the spirit of Ogun and Shaka, a deliberate technical ploy by the writer to compact two historical and aesthetic universes. The cross-cultural effect of this work should in fact be interesting to see. For this though, the Yoruba chorus has comic and callow overtones which diffuse somewhat the essentially heroic spirit of the poem.

Enter Shaka after the choric acclaim of turmoil to speak a royal monologue in the best Shakespearean tradition. Shaka's performance is strikingly Elizabethan both in language and in the exploration of character and motivation. The merging of the Forest and savannah cultures of Ogun and Shaka provide an epic background for the god-heroes who are seemingly transformed into ancestral deities of modern Africa, rendered divine much as Ogun, Ifa, Orunmila and their fellows became gods in the mythic imagination of the Yoruba. Shaka's part-ruminative, part-delirious speech, lucid and manic in turn, is an artistic effort to objectify the contradiction in Shaka's personal history and the writer's attribution of some of Shaka's actions to a manic depression.

The third and last section of the poem is the voice of the poet, speaking as namer and ritual performer In this role, he restates the human problems which beset Southern Africa and the false ethical issues reified by some to emasculate the mode of action necessary for that violent land. From those who preach pacific love, he asks, most pertinently in these times after Soweto: can love outrace the random bullet to possess the heart of black despair?

POETICS AND THE

MYTHIC IMAGINATION

Stanley Macebuh

It would be no exaggeration to observe that Wole
Soyinka is probably the most widely-known. African
intellectual of the contemporary period. Yet the observation would seem to require considerable explanation:
for to inquire into the nature of his reputation is to
begin to understand the quite specific manner in which
the profession of 'art' can appropriately serve as the
formal demonstration of that sensibility whose truest
aspect is to be discovered more in social activity than
in a merely aesthetic posture. When one thinks, for
instance, of Achebe, one thinks of the self-effacing
author of that inimitable work of creative genius,
Things Fall Apart. But one does not usually think of
Soyinka as the author of any specific work; it is not
impossible that many of those who know him, particularly outside Africa, recognise him not simply as the
author of *Idanre* or *The Road*, or even of that endlessly
anthologised piece, 'Telephone Conversation', but
more as a man whose 'renaissance' posture deeply
impresses the twentieth century mind. In Soyinka's
own mythic terms, the difference between his reputation
and Achebe's is the difference between the mythic
impulse of Ogun and of Obatala, between the heroic
posture of 'tragic dare' and of 'harmonious resolution.'
We shall return to the crucial significance of this distinction later. Here it is sufficient to suggest that it
would probably be too limiting to see Soyinka merely
in terms of a talented playwright of the theatre. He
has, of course, experimented with just about every
major literary form—with drama, with poetry and fiction, with the essay and the diary, and, we might as well
add, with radio. One can hardly deny that his preference
has been for drama and for the dramatic in poetry,
yet it is a preference that would seem to be significant
less for his interest in theatre (some of his plays are
simply unstageable) than for his belief that it is through
drama that he can most adequately convey his thematic
preoccupations. And Soyinka's abiding concern has
been with myth, with its significance for contemporary

life in Africa. For him, 'history' has been not so much a record of human action as a demonstration of the manner in which social behaviour so often symbolises a sometimes voluntary, sometimes unwilling obedience to the subliminal impulse of the ancestral memory. If it is true, as Eliot once suggested, that there can be no culture without religion, we may be equally certain that there can be no history without myth. And to the extent that myth and history are complementary, it may be suggested that Soyinka's persistent meditation on myth is an attempt to reveal the primal foundations of African culture, and therefore of history. To say, then, that Soyinka is a dramatist is to say that he has chosen as his medium that literary form most appropriate for the communication of the hardly tangible anatomy of the ancestral memory. Soyinka is, first and foremost, a mythopoiest; his imagination is, in a quite fundamental sense, a mythic imagination.

To recognise this basic interest in myth is to begin to discover the source of Soyinka's creative strengths, and of his weaknesses. Apart from his quite astringent social criticism, he has been particularly impressive on those occasions when he has sought to reveal the primeval psychic dilemmas of African man. What has sometimes seemed the cynical pessimism of his circular vision of history, in *A Dance of the Forests*, for instance, is, in fact, an index of his belief that it is impossible to divorce culture from its mythic origins. Yet what redeems this vision from total pessimism would seem to be the consideration that though Soyinka is not exactly enthusiastic over the possibility that human history is the history of 'progress' and perfection, he appears nevertheless certain that ineluctable though mythic compulsions are, man yet still does have a measure of choice, and therefore of responsibility for the state of things in his world. Unlike the Christian world, Soyinka's world is one in which one can hardly speak meaningfully of any doctrine of grace; it is a world in which absolution is never even remotely *a priori*, never dependent on any power outside the realm of a broad concept of culture. It is this fundamental relation between myth and social behaviour that those who object to the quaintness of Soyinka's ritual dramas have failed to recognise, and it is this, too, that often elevates his works beyond the limits of merely temporary ideological agitation.

But if the advantage of Soyinka's mythic imagination is this transcendent quality, it may yet be suggested that his particular nemesis has been the problem of language. Soyinka is, without doubt, a difficult, sometimes infuriating writer. The particular ambience of myth, we may be reasonably certain, is dignified simplicity; it tends to appeal to immediate recognition, to be clear, untortured, serene. In a writer so persistently concerned with the mythic, one might therefore expect to find a certain measure of melodious ease. Because of its appeal to a 'universal' consciousness in man, myth, we are told, is eminently translatable from one language to the other; and Soyinka's own interest in Greek mythology, his recognition of certain analogies between Greek and Yoruba legend would seem to confirm this. If, then, we find in spite of this a condition of linguistic stress in Soyinka's attempts to communicate the mythic heritage of African man, the question must be asked why this is the case; and it is at this point that we begin to realise that the problem of language in Soyinka is a two-fold problem, the one deriving from Soyinka's sense of his relation to his colonial burden, the other, more internal, relating to the very nature of the body of myth with which he is preoccupied.

The fundamental intention behind Soyinka's interest in Yoruba myth has little to do with popularising the archaic; his concern would appear rather to be that of discovering in mythic history certain principles upon which contemporary behaviour might be based and by which it might legitimately be judged. Indeed, there is a profound sense in which it might be said that the chaotic nature of social behaviour in our time is the single most important justification for Soyinka's meditations on myth. His preoccupation with the tragic exactions of the god Ogun is by now well-known enough —in *A Dance of the Forests*, in *The Road*, in *Idanre;* but it needs to be reiterated that his is not a merely antiquarian interest, that the legend of the gods provides for him a means for illuminating the complexities of contemporary life in Africa. According to him, the Yoruba, for instance, are a people perpetually bound to the parallel (and sometimes complementary) impulses of two gods, Ogun and Obatala, and to understand the personality attributed to these gods by the Yoruba is to understand the origins of what might otherwise be deemed a merely neurotic condition in their contemporary behaviour. Obatala is the god of 'spiritual complacency', Ogun the god of 'tragic' dare.' "The overt optimistic nature of the total culture," Soyinka observes in his examination of this problem, evident "in the quality attributed to the Yoruba himself . . . . has in fact begun to affect his accommodativeness towards the modern world, a spiritual complacency with which he encounters threats to his humane and unique validation" ([1]). It is a condition of mind traceable to the mythic influence of Obatala, but it is equally part of Soyinka's point here that this spiritual complacency is not entirely inevitable, that the impulse of Ogun is always there, imperiously demanding that his radical will be done([2]).

In a situation, then, in which social commentary is embodied in mythic interpretation, language, if it is alien, might be expected to be problematical. And in the case of the African writer, this is so because, thanks to his colonial inheritance, to seek to understand the essence of African myth is to do so at a time when the African mind is burdened with the encumbrances of Western culture. That is to say that in a quite fundamental sense, one of the consequences of colonial history is that the once-colonised are so often obliged to view the world from a *comparative* point of view. When Keats meditates on Apollo, he never evinces any obligation to bear Gilgamesh in mind, and one does not really expect him to. Writing though he is in the English language, it is possible for him to assume a direct link between the conceptual assumptions of his language and the conceptual framework from which he derives his myths. The once-colonised, on the other hand, when they write in English or French, are almost inevitably driven to comparison, in the case of Soyinka between Ogun and Dionysos-Apollo-Prometheus, and certainly not out of a mere desire for ostentation. Indeed, that Soyinka should appear to feel obliged to suggest an analogy between Ogun and *three* Greek deities is an indication of the seriousness of the problem. For to explain the African world, when one is writing in a European language, is to assume the responsibility not merely of articulating African concepts but of making them intelligible also to those whose world view has been conditioned by the vision implicit in European languages; and, it need hardly be remarked, there are many Africans in this latter group. We shall suggest in a moment why this responsibility becomes even more uniquely vexatious in the case of Soyinka; here we may suggest that those who object to the difficulty of his language might do well to bear this general problem in mind. Part, at least, of our impression of the harsh inscrutableness of Soyinka's language may be seen as an exact equivalent in words of that unease of the mind that is the lot of all those who have suffered a modification of vision through colonialism. When they seek to penetrate this barrier and to reach towards the primal sources of their being, they are not unlikely to be as tortured in their languages as Soyinka sometimes is ([3]). For the contemporary African concerned to delve deeply enough into his ancestral past, to articulate the past is to expose oneself to the obtrusiveness of Western culture. And language, more often than not, is the vehicle of this obtrusion.

Language in Soyinka is difficult, harsh, sometimes tortured; his syntax is often archaic, his verbal structures

sometimes impenetrable. It would be pointless to seek
to overlook this condition in his works. And bearing
in mind his basic preoccupation with myth, it might
on the face of it appear an insupportable contradiction
that he should thus seem to overlook the consideration
that the language of myth is usually 'simple.' There is,
nevertheless, the possibility that a good many of Soyinka's critics have, in identifying this difficulty, yet failed
to pay sufficient attention to the internal, that is, ethnocentric compulsions in his poetic dramas that render
this condition nearly inevitable. We will in a moment
suggest reasons why the criticism of Soyinka's works
appears to us so often to exist in a vacuum. Here it is
necessary first to summarise the objections against him.

In the Fall of 1972 a group of three young Nigerian
poets resident in the United States prepared an essay
in which they attempted to identify the failures of Nigerian poetry of the contemporary period (4). We draw
attention to this essay because it embodies an almost
exhaustive list of the usual objections against Soyinka
in particular, and against the poetry of the Ibadan-
Nsukka School in general. The essay was prepared as
an angry response to the suspicion shared by many that
Nigerian poetry was by way of being taken over by
jaded European mannerisms. It came at a time also
when, particularly in the United States, the burgeoning
black consciousness had begun to lead to a feverish
search for sources and origins, for ancestral justifications.
To the extent that it sought to re-establish the need for
an authentically African vision in art, it was a welcome
venture, yet it may nevertheless be argued that, its general indictment apart, its ethnocentric rigour was deeply
tainted both by youthful rashness and by insufficient
or perhaps too elliptical an understanding of that very
tradition upon which its indictment was based.

Briefly stated, the essay began with the thesis, un-
arguable enough, that all contemporary poetry in
Africa must derive its legitimate inspiration from the
oral tradition; the exigences of our colonial inheritance
are such, however, that a good many of our poets
have allowed themselves to suffer "a divorce from
African oral tradition, tempered only by lifeless attempts
at revivalism." Incapable of accommodating a dynamic
sense of the African past in their psyche, they become
the unconvincing and inept vectors of European impulses. Their works consequently display "glaring
faults", "old-fashioned, craggy, unmusical language;
obscure and inaccessible diction; a plethora of imported
imagery." Not only is the form of their works objection-
able; they suffer also from a failure of sensibility; their
thoughts are either confused, or their "simple" ideas
are "clothed in esoteric idiom." Latinisms and Shakes-
peareanisms abound; they do not even know how to

curse properly enough in their own tongue. Okigbo
and Echeruo come in for the most vitriolic contempt;
J. P. Clark is dismissed out of hand as suffering from
"blameless blandless"; Wole Soyinka is indicted for
betraying his fertile, Yoruba inheritance.

It is not, of course, that these young poets do not have
a clear standard upon which they base their evaluations.
It may reasonably be said that implicit in their objections
is the assumption that tradition in Africa is not dead;
that all authenticity must be founded in history; that
all borrowings from elsewhere must be rigorously
judicious. As their example of authentic Africanness
in poetry, they cite, Soyinka's 'Telephone Conversation',
Okigbo's 'Path of Thunder', Okot p'Btek's *Songs*. If we
insist, as we do, that their criticism yet exists in a vacuum,
it is therefore not because they fail to propose a standard
both of creative action and critical response, but because
their standards are ultimately externally derived, because
'tradition' appears in their opinion to be good only in
so far as it is old, and because we do not see in their
essay that level of immersion in the complex impulses of
African culture that might have rendered their indict-
ments less capricious. To put it differently, there is in
this essay a 'positivist' bias, a tediously McLuhanese
interest in demotic culture. There is, to be sure, nothing
particularly wrong in supposing that there was a fun-
damentally democratic aspect to culture in Africa;
what is disturbing rather is the suspicion we have in
reading this essay that in adhering so faithfully to the
'principles' of 'practical criticism' it becomes so pre-
occupied with *means* that it hardly concerns itself with
legitimate ends. In identifying, for instance, the qualities
of the oral tradition that should be emulated in good
contemporary African poetry, it limits itself to recommen-
dations of *technique*. "One of the most telling qualities
of African oral tradition," it blandly insists, "is its
economy of means." Other qualities are "lucidity",
"normal syntax," "precise and apt imagery", "efficient
structure and logistics." All this may indeed be true
enough if one were thinking specifically of a *type* of
poetry in the oral tradition; what this essay is curiously
silent about is, what were the ends proposed? What
intrinsic value may legitimately be attached to 'simplicity'? Or, to put the question more broadly, what is
the meaning of tradition, and what essential justifications
may we find for recommending that it be emulated?

It is in this failure to grapple seriously with the fundamental question of values and ends that we begin
to suspect that this essay suffers, in its fundamental
inspiration, precisely from that same involuntary
tutelage to an alien vision for which it bitterly indicts
the objects of its anger. If 'simplicity' and 'lucidity'

are good in themselves, they must be supposed to be so
as much for African as for European poets, particularly
if it is possible to suppose that these qualities derive
from the oral traditions of Africa and Europe.   And
if that is the case, it would seem then that what is being
demanded is that African poets be *good poets*, not
good African poets—and in such a case it would be
irrational to insist on an African oral tradition as the
basis of judgment, unless this is seen as being universally identical. In any event, T. S. Eliot and I. A. Richards
become, curiously, our most reliable mentors, *not* those
examples of African oral poetry that are so copiously
cited in the essay. In a word, what is being recommended
here is not an aesthetics in which essentially *African*
values are implicated in the means employed, but one
in which a quite constricted notion of the principle of
'aesthetic pleasure' is regarded as being of foremost
significance.   Consider, for instance, the attitude taken
to the question of the writer's responsibility in society:
"If a writer wants to write poetry that says, 'destroy
the status quo , let him do so but do it well"; and if,
on the other hand, he chooses to advocate a radical
convulsion, "let him do so but do it well." We need
not go too deeply into the question of the writer's
responsibility in order to discover that this essay is
altogether un-African in its essential callousness,
particularly as it appears so willing to recommend a
concept of art so painfully devoid of ultimate value.

On a much deeper level, it may be said that while the
authors of this essay might be legitimately congratulated
for their suspicion that something is terribly wrong with
poetry in Africa—and something *is* wrong—they must
nevertheless be charged with a response to tradition
that is altogether cavalier.   One may sympathise with
the thrust of their indictment, and yet feel that they
themselves have not meditated deeply enough on the
nature and essential values of traditional African culture.
They would have us believe that it is a virtue to be true
to one's tradition, but they fail to show us precisely
wherein lies the virtue, or what the essential, not merely
formal qualities of this tradition are.   At the risk of
mounting the commonplace, it may be surmised that
any theory of art that insists on form at the expense
of content, on means to the exclusion of ends, can hardly
be judged African.   It is not enough merely to argue,
as our authors do, that the value of simplicity lies in
its capacity to enhance communication.   Communication is important, not as an end, but as a means of
transmitting and sharing ideas and ideals that have
some authentic appeal.   The language of a specific type
of traditional oral poetry may have been a 'public language', but it would be obviously facetious to suppose
that the publicness of language was invested with any-

thing close to a final cause. If Okot p'Bitek's poetry
appeals to us in so fundamental a way, it is not merely
because its language is 'simple', certainly not because
he transliterates the name Melchisedec into the more
vernacular 'Melikisedeki', but ultimately because the
sensibility that informs his poetry rigorously divests
itself of its colonial encumberance and attests to a
vision of the world that may be judged authentically
African. By the same token, if one regrets the somewhat
pretentious Latinisms in Echeruo and the classicisms
in the early Okigbo, it is finally not merely because they
might just as well have invoked the gods of Africa, but
because the borrowings of allusion and imagery are so
extreme as to suggest the possibility that they are an
exact equivalent in language of a tragic corruption of
vision. We object to some of their poetry not merely
on account of style, but because style is often in their
poems the vehicle for a modified sensibility. But it
would be purely sophistical to insist on such objections
unless we were certain that that which has been cor-
rupted is not merely language, not merely the means
of expression, but a more authentic African vision.
And this objection immediately places upon the critic
the terrible responsibility of articulating an authentically
African vision in art, an articulation that must necessarily go quite beyond the matter of 'simplicity', 'lucidity'
and 'economy of means.' It is this that the authors of
this essay have failed to do, partly out of a preoccupation, dangerously veering on dilettantism, with an
aesthetics of value-starved form, and partly also out of
the apparent fear that to articulate a traditional African
vision is to delve into those intangible realms of metaphysical reality that constitute the positivist philosopher's
nightmare.

In any event, to object to Soyinka's poetry on much
the same grounds that they object to Echeruo and Okigbo
is to evince a near-abysmal misconception of the relationship between language and vision in Soyinka's
Idanre, for instance. If there is anyone who has been
persistently exercised, and painfully so, by the problem
of language in contemporary African writing, it surely
must be Wole Soyinka. But he has not been preoccupied
with language merely as the index of style, but rather
with language as a vehicle of mythic meaning. No one
could reasonably charge him with being unduly Latinate
in his poetry; and the fact that his English sources
appear to be located in the Anglo-Saxon rigour of Donne
rather than in the Romantic surfeit of a Keats, Byron
or Yeats should suggest a certain antecedent positioning
of the poetic self with regard to the English language.
Language in Donne is, of course, more visceral, less
'musical', rather closer to the roots of the English
language than it is in Keats or Yeats. The African

writer who recognises the burden of having to express
himself in the English language must therefore decide
for himself the *type* of English he must use—whether
the harsh dissonances of a Donne or the tender melli-
fluousness of a Keats or Yeats. But such a decision
would presumably depend on an earlier choice, whether
the African poet discovers an appeal in the 'democratic'
or the 'cultic', masonic impulse in the oral tradition.
For it is clearly wrong-headed to suppose that the
democratic impulse is the only impulse evident in the
oral tradition of Africa. In any case, if the poet believes,
as Soyinka clearly does, that the way to reconciling the
contemporary poetic self to traditional impulses is
through myth, through a recapturing of the ancestral
memory as recorded in cultic ritual, the type of English
he chooses is likely to reflect this concern, to reflect the
search for roots. There is a sense, then, in which it
might be said that archaisms are the linguistic equivalent
of Soyinka's preoccupation with cultic myth.

> "*In cult funerals, the circle of initiate mourners, an
> ageless swaying grove of dark pines, raise a chant
> around a mortar of fire, and words are taken back to
> their roots, to their original poetic sources when fusion
> was total and the movement of words is the very passage
> of music and dance of images . . . Language still is the
> embryo of thought and music where myth is daily
> companion*".[5]

The roots of Soyinka's English are uncompromisingly
Anglo-Saxon rather than Hellenic or Latinate because
they represent for him the closest proximation to the
primal roots of Yoruba cultic diction. But the virtue
of 'originality' lies not merely in its freshness or quaintness but indeed in its vitality, in its ability to evoke in
the mind a memory of the dynamism of the original
Yoruba. For Soyinka, particularly in those poems in
which legend, tradition and ancestral custom constitute
the internal structure of his poetry, is in fact a *translator*.
That is to say, that to anyone who even vaguely understands the tonalities of the Yoruba language (and
curious as it may sound, none of the three young poets
we have mentioned here speaks or understands the
language), the structure and fertile ambience of Soyinka's
English derives, in fact, more from the Yoruba than
from the English. And if it is true, as we have suggested,
that Soyinka is a 'translator', we may then raise the
question whether effective translation is a matter of
equating that which is to be translated as closely as
possible to the verbose sensibility of contemporary
times, or of seeking to convey the vast ambience of
meaning implicit in the original. To compare Pope's
Homer with recent translations is to discover the pro-
blematic nature of the issue we raise here, Pope's Homer

is summative, its syntax relatively complex, but it has the redeeming virtue at least of eschewing, in Soyinka's own words, "the sterile limits of particularisation." It seeks to convey total meaning, whereas recent translations of Homer are tediously prosaic, more impressive for their clinical, literal veracity than for the sublimity or totality of the impression created. Soyinka's approach to Yoruba myth and language is comparable to Pope's approach to Homer. For him, myth is not to be understood merely in its literal particularisations; its power is not to be captured through analysis. Rather, when the senses are exposed to the language of myth, they

"do not at such moments interpret myth in their particular concretions, rather are we left only with the emotional and spiritual values and experience of those truths (which are symbolically not rationally triggered off in memory and shared as a communal experience)." [6]

To capture the fundamental dynamic of Soyinka's poetic language then, one does not look, as our essayists have done, for surface lucidity and simplicity; one does not look for that kind of 'music' that is "all clear tone and winnowed lyric, of order and harmony, stately and saintly." [7] One looks rather, for that music in language which has "undergone transformation through myth into a secret masonic correspondence with the symbolism of tragedy, a symbolic language . . . whence springs the weird disruptive melodies." [8] And the melody of Soyinka's poetry is preternaturally 'disruptive.'

The language of Soyinka's poetry is archaic, cacophonous, disruptive, precisely because it is a contemporary equivalent of Yoruba mythic language; but the ancestral myths that he works with are not those deriving from the god Obatala, whose motif is white "for transparency of heart and mind", in whose drama there is a rejection of "mystery and terror", an affirmation of calm, of "harmony." Soyinka's titular god is not Obatala but Ogun, and the particular abode of this terrible, contradictory god is in the language of disjuncture, stress, rupture and "demonic energy." If one were obliged to be charitable to the authors of the essay in review, we would presumably have to concede that in their insistence on lucidity, simplicity, clarity and harmony, they are devotees, if unconscious ones, of the god Obatala, and may therefore be allowed their preference. What is more disturbing, however, is the suspicion we have that their god is neither Obatala nor Ogun, indeed not an African god at all, that their awareness of the power and nature of myth is painfully minimal, that the justification for their position is ultimately not founded in African myth or ethos, but in fact in a vague universalist axiom which insists that

simplicity is all.   Certainly, their understanding of
Soyinka's "Dawn" veers awfully close to the pathetic.
For them,

> "not only does it not make immediate sense (you have
> to puzzle it out), but it is not even easy or pleasurable
> to read. On the contrary it is heavy, tongue-twisting,
> difficult to articulate, and it cannot keep the reader's
> attention. *And poetry is an auditory medium*" [9]
> (emphasis theirs).

It is not necessary to offer a synopsis of the poem[10]
here in order to discover that our authors are
limited by their desire that poetry be unmysterious.
It is nonsensical to seek to derive from this poem a
literal, line-by-line meaning.   Soyinka's poetry does
not work that way. The "meaning" of the poem is,
in fact, not "concrete", but a cluster of emotions and
impulses culminating in an incantatory celebration of
dawn, of life, of the creative impulse in the world. That
it comes at the very beginning of Soyinka's book of
poems should alert the reader to the possibility that it
is the equivalent, but the intensely African equivalent,
of those invocations of the epic Muse in Virgil, Homer,
Milton and others that are, curiously enough, so much
more readily recognisable to the 'educated' African
reader.   For Ogun is Soyinka's Muse and patron god,
and his thyrsus is the stave made from the palm-wine
tree.   It symbolises both the heroic labours of Ogun
and the ecstatic, wine-inspired headiness of his exactions
in the world. He is Soyinka's Muse because he is the
creative impulse, yet a creative impulse that, according
to Yoruba myth, was somewhat compromised by indis-
criminate blood-letting. The palm-fronds in the poem,
the "blood-drops" in the air, the "lone" intrusion into
"the chaste hide of the sky", the god, "night-spread in
tatters . . . aflame with kernels", all these would seem
to point to an attempt on Soyinka's part to summarize
Ogun's mythic history, to evoke and appropriate his
"willful, ecstatic being."   To those who are ignorant
of Soyinka's poetic saturation in African myth, "Dawn"
would be inevitably difficult and 'meaningless'; yet to
recognise such a spurious difficulty is not to identify
a problem inherent in the poem itself, but indeed to
confess to ignorance of the dynamic relevance of that
very 'oral tradition' that is touted as the adequate
foundation for all contemporary African   poetry.

Take, again, the translation by the authors of the
essay under review of Soyinka's "Malediction."[11]
Nothing could be more profane than their supposition
that to convey the force and impatient tartness of the
traditional curse all one need do is translate it into
readable English prose.   And particularly since they are
poets, the three of them, one might have thought they

would be the first to be outraged by so crudely lifeless
a transliteration as this:

Soyinka	Their Version
Giggles fill the water hole	May you give birth to
Offsprings by you aban- doned,	monstrosities in the streets.
And afterbirth, at cross- roads.	

Their transliteration robs Soyinka's poem of its air of
metaphysical, not merely secular or physiological monstrosity; they divest the curse of its terror, of its mystery,
of its evocation, of a vision of eternal, apocalyptic damnation. It argues not simply an ineptitude of translation
but a failure, indeed, of sensitivity. And, it would appear,
their limitation is not simply that they do not understand the Yoruba language; their rendering even of
Igbo curses is equally effeminate, equally ludicrous.
They convert the terrible into the merely ironic: "May
you go mad at the height of your prosperity." They
would presumably also translate the fearsome Igbo
curse—'Chineke kpo gi oku'—merely in the manner
of the elliptical pidgin—'God punish you' (actually, a
literal translation of the latter would probably read—
"May God burn you with fire"—though one would
expect poets to do much better than this).

To conclude. The authors of "Toward the Decolonization of African Literature" have allowed themselves
to be carried away by a 'positivist' impulse that stands
altogether in contradiction to some of the fundamental
impulses of tradition in Africa. They have sought to
convert an instinctive suspicion that contemporary
African poetry is often wrong-headed and externally
derivative into a rigid theory of art based upon a questionable understanding of the nature of the oral tradition in Africa. More specifically, when they object to the
alien imagery in Echeruo and Okigbo, they identify a
problem that requires much more rigorous examination
than they have been willing to or are capable of providing.
There is a difference, and a fundamental one, between
the sensibility implicit in Okigbo's Christian imagery
and in Soyinka's masonic diction. The imagination
that spawns such superfluous allusions as 'lumen mundi',
'nobis quoque pecatoribus' and 'lacrimae Christi' is
hardly the same as the intelligence that works through
such ancestral symbols as Ogun's stave, or the white
cockerel that is impaled on the windscreen of a car
as a sacrifice to the famished god who might otherwise
demand human blood. At best, the former achieves an
implausible wedding of the ancestral and the borrowed,
and at worst, it attests to a tragic separation of the
contemporary African psyche from its primal roots.

Soyinka's imagery, on the other hand, is persistently African, and often uncompromisingly so. He achieves in poetry much the same result that Achebe achieves in prose, though through a different route. Both of them amaze us with their near-miraculous ability to evoke a vision of our past, to recapture in these distracting times a view of the world that we recognise, through reflection, to be so authentically African. Achebe's language is just as uncompromising as Soyinka's. Poet and novelist rely so heavily on the Anglo-Saxon roots of the English language because they are determined to get to the roots of the African psyche. Soyinka's language is, however, more difficult; it creates a greater impression of tension and disjuncture because his poetic model is the poetry of the cultic worshippers of Ogun. not the 'transparent', 'simple', and 'lucid' poetry of Obatala. The authors of "Toward the Decolonization of African Literature" succeed in so far as they give voice to a general summons to African writers and critics to begin to look a little deeper into themselves. It is a call that, though hardly unprecedented, comes not too soon indeed. Yet it must nevertheless be observed that their understanding of 'tradition' appears to be a painfully limited one; and it is, finally, a limited understanding that traps them into postulating a theory of poetry that, in its exclusive insistence on the surface attributes of poetry, negates what must be judged a crucial principle of traditional art, that style and form possess value only in so far as they are a means of conveying appropriate vision.

Notes

Editor's Note: This article was originally published without a key to the footnotes and I have attempted to reconstruct it.

[1] Wole Soyinka, "The Fourth Stage," in *The Morality of Art*, ed. D. W. Jefferson (London: Routledge and Kegan Paul, 1969), p. 130.

[2] *ibid.*, pp. 126-27.

[3] The complexity of some of Soyinka's prose and verse has been repeatedly noted. In *Myth, Literature and the African World* (Cambridge: Cambridge University Press, 1976), Soyinka observes with relation to "The Fourth Stage": "I have tried now to reduce what a student of mine complained of as 'elliptical' obstacles to its comprehension." (p. ix)

[4] Chinweizu, Onwuchekwa Jemie and Ihechukwu Madubuike, "Towards the Decolonialization of African Literature," *Transition,* 48 (1975), 29-37, 54, 56-57. The article originally appeared in *Okike,* 6 (1974), 11-28.

[5] Soyinka, "The Fourth Stage," p. 124.

[6] *ibid.*, p. 125.

[7] *ibid.*, p. 128.

[8] *ibid.*, pp. 124-25.

[9] Chinweizu *et al.*, p. 30.

[10] "Dawn" appears in *Idanre and Other Poems* (London: Methuen, 1967), p. 9.

[11] Chinweizu *et al.*, pp. 31-32.

Wole Soyinka: Obscurity, Romanticism and Dylan Thomas

Robin Graham

Scholars of Wole Soyinka are indebted to Stanley Macebuh for his suggestive definition of the poet's "Mythic Imagination."[1] Used in partial defence of Soyinka'a "obscurity," the concepts myth and imagination ought to define the unique way his poetry reaches its significance. Myth expresses man's obscure, yet defiant, attempt to create order out of chaos, belief out of despair: for myths are, in a narrative form, accounts of the creation of life, the inevitability of death, and the wish for a sacrificial redemption. Creating from such darkness, how could the poet be anything but arcane, if not obscure? As for the Imagination; that faculty of "High" Romanticism expresses the mystery of the world and the vagaries of the human heart. The highest claims of art have always relied on the sanctity of the imagination as if to discount the paltriness of mere simplicity or understanding. Are we, then, to judge Soyinka's verse by the same terms as we understand, if that is the word, "The Ancient Mariner," The Lucy Poems of Wordsworth, "Prometheus Unbound," and especially, as I want to suggest, the Arch-Romantic, surviving from a previous age, Dylan Thomas? Yet Macebuh gives the hint without following through the argument, for reasons which are crucial both for the study of Soyinka, and for the study of African literature in general.

Macebuh misses the implications of his term "Imagination" and fails to place Soyinka in the right tradition through a misconception about the nature of Romantic verse. He too readily defines the language of the Romantics as "tender melliflousness;" the language of the Lucy poems, the first lines of "Lamia," ought to discount such a generalization. As a result of this confusion he rather places Soyinka in the tradition of intellectual and metaphysical poets like Donne and Eliot. According to Macebuh, just as Donne and Eliot went back to the purity of Anglo-Saxon from the decadence of Keatsian Latinisms, so Soyinka goes to the Yoruba language: for sound effects, syntax and other potentialities of expression. Language being what someone once called, "a universal whore," it is inevitably less than virginal and pure. So immediately when a critic begins to talk about purity of diction, or the virtues of Anglo-Saxon, we should be aware that his motives are less or more than literary. The English language is the language of Donne and Keats, Eliot and Soyinka. If we want to exclude Latinisms, or Keatsianisms, then it is for ethical not aesthetic reasons. And such is the case of Macebuh.

The essential point about Soyinka's obscurity, according to the critic, is a sociological one: "Soyinka's harsh inscrutableness . . . may be seen as an exact equivalent in words of that unease of mind that is the lot of those who have suffered a modification of vision through colonialism." This is the essence of the ethical defense of the "African-ness" of African literature in revealing to us the poet's responsibility to his indigenous culture, rather than the medium of his colonizing oppressor. As one critic puts it: "Taking the white man's language, dislocating his syntax, recharging his words with new strength and sometimes with new meaning before hurling them back in his teeth, while upsetting his self-righteous complacency and cliches, our poets rehabilitate such terms as Africa and blackness, beauty and peace."[2] Statements unobjectionable enough in this case, but when has it been the case that poets have *not* thrown language back in the

teeth of his audience? Certainly not since what is called the Romantic Revolution.
The sentiments could have come straight from Wordsworth's "Preface" to *Lyrical
Ballads*.[3] The poet is unique among artists in having to use the commonplace
medium of their audience, and to make it new; to make it what Dylan Thomas
called "young English" in reference to Tutuola, he has to dislocate and recharge
language to his own individual purposes. To make poetry or language serve a
sociological purpose is to appoint a mediate end which subverts the ultimate,
aesthetic end which cannot be prescribed to. Romantic art has always been
anarchic. Macebuh's judgement that Soyinka possesses a "sensibility whose truest
aspect is to be discovered more in social activity than in a merely aesthetic
posture," is, so far as our concern with art is for it *as* art, a mediate view. True,
the political, social pressures on Soyinka the man, are immense as *The Man Died*
insists, but how much are they the concern of the poet? The poet is motivated by a
Mythic Imagination which is not, as Macebuh, the critic of ethics, would like it to
be, dependent upon "social activity." Only a sociological imagination (if there is
such a thing - one might think of Camus or Sartre) can express man's relationship
with man. The Mythic Imagination searches out man's relationship with God.

In purely literary terms, the obscurity of Soyinka reveals different motives and
allegiances. Macebuh would place him in the tradition of intellectual and
obscurantist poets like Donne or Eliot. At first glance this seems to some degree
appropriate. But Soyinka does not truly belong to the tradition of dissident
intellectualism. In his recent *Myth, Literature and the African World,* he
disengaged himself from the "universal-humanoid abstraction" of the West.[4]
Soyinka would exorcise the ghost of Western abstraction with a concrete,
mythological expression "You are one-who-thinks, white-creature-in-pith-helmet-
in-African-jungle-who-thinks and, finally, white-man-who-has-problems-believ-
ing-in-his-own-existence."[5] Back to the problem of language. The poet can only
avoid insidious abstraction through the darker unity of myth: man's expression of
fear and wonder at a universe which defies his hubristic intellectual attempt to
explain or explain away the mystery.

The modernist writer's use of mythology (that is, the work of Eliot, Yeats or
Joyce), merely serves to camouflage the difference between a writer who is
inspired by myth and a writer who takes an ironic attitude towards myth, and the
absence of belief in the modern world. If these writers search for a unity of being
it is because they are hag-ridden by Manichean/Cartesian dualism, and intimidated
by a world from which it cannot simulate order. *The Waste Land* is essentially
anti-mythological: the regenerative ritual is lacking, there exists merely an Ixion-
like wheel of torture and debased repetition. "I want to die," says the Sybil who is
blessed with eternal life and cosmic prescience. Yeats's mythological poems are no
more than the expression of a sentimental nostalgia for a lost golden-age: for
Greece, or quatrocento Italy, or a utopian Irish Renaissance. And the obscurity of
such poetry is the result of mythology refracted through a conceptualizing mind.
The ironic attitude towards the mythological experience reveals an ennervating
self-consciousness. Joseph Conrad's dictum is relevant: "The habit of profound
reflection is the most pernicious of all the habits formed by the civilized man."[6]
This is not the way of Soyinka: if he is ambiguous it is not the refraction of the
mind which makes him so, but the peculiarity of myth in its ordering of
experience.

Out of the phantasmagoria of fleeting impressions, the mythical poet creates a cosmology of inherent significance. He believes in the instinctive importance of every event. Nothing goes by without being placed, through comparison and conjunction, into a cosmic pattern. He does not exist as a separate creature as "one-who-thinks," floating upon silence like Yeats's "long-legged fly." He believes in what the history of Romanticism has variously called "Pantheism," the "Pathetic Fallacy" or a variety of "Animism": the expression of a sympathy between the perceiving mind and the external world. Hence the poet can celebrate, through metaphor, all kinds of identity:

> Roots, be an anchor at my keel
> Shore my limbs against the wayward gale
>
> Reach in earth for deep sustaining draughts
> Potencies against my endless thirsts
>
> Your surface runnels end in blinds, your courses
> Choke on silt, stagnate in human curses
>
> Feet of pilgrims pause by chartered pools
> Balm seeking.[7]

The ambiguity here, of Soyinka's poem, is one of metaphor attempting to invoke a symbolic identity which resists the commonplace. The metaphors though various transmutations are progressively linked by the poet's emotional needs: "anchor" - "keel" - "shore" - "wayward gale". Later the poet calls for a cosmic energy to keep him inviolate:

> Thread
> My hands to spring-rites, to green hands of the dead.[8]

The "green hands of the dead" is not ironically obscure, but an expression of cosmic inevitability. We live to die, and we die to be reborn. Dylan Thomas reiterates the same image obsessively: "Time held me green and dying." The linguistic potentialities which allow such effects are authorized by mythology's own repetitive sympathies which equate life and death as in this famous poem by Thomas:

> The force that through the green fuse drives the flower
> Drives my green age; that blasts the roots of trees
> Is my destroyer.
> And I am dumb to tell the crooked rose
> My youth is bent by the same wintry fever.[9]

The same progression through imaginative metaphors is present here as in Soyinka: "force" - "fuse" - "drives" - "blasts". An experience is held up, felt, shaped and twisted to reveal its significance. Far from being ambiguous, these effects are a direct expression of the cosmic behaviorism which the Romantic imagination continuously reveals.

This process may be explained in reference to Soyinka's "Dawn," a poem the author uses as a kind of dedication to his first volume of poems, and one which is celebrated for its ambiguity.[10]

Breaking earth upon
A spring-haired elbow, lone
A palm beyond head-grains, spikes
A guard of prim fronds, piercing
High hairs of the wind
As one who bore the pollen highest
Blood-drops in the air, above
The even belt of tassels, above
Coarse leaf teasing on the waist, steals
The lone intruder, tearing wide
The chaste hide of the sky
O celebration of the rites of dawn
Night-spread in tatters and a god
Received, aflame with kernels.[11]

If instead of attempting to translate the poem word by word to find some prose
meaning or Yoruba folklore source, we apprehend it whole, as we do a Romantic
poem, then instead of obscurity we get intimations and revelations. The essential
emotions are generated by metaphors which identify "Dawn" with sexual
congress: "the prim fronds", a "belt of tassels", "teasing on the waist", are all
suggestive of coy, feminine sexuality, even virginity; while the great palm
"piercing high hairs of the wind", "tearing wide/The chaste hide of the sky" are
patently phallic. Along with this scenario goes the rising of the sun: "Blood-drops
in the air", "Night-spread in tatters", which suggest another sexual confrontation,
this time not with a palm "Breaking earth", but with the sun, universally a
masculine deity, ravaging the feminine symbol of night. The poem ends with a
final apotheosis which links the sun with the palm in an almost homosexual union:

                               a god
Received, aflame with kernels.

"Pollen" and "kernels" are both suggestive of regeneration, and therefore pick
up the sexual motif and link it with a god who is also a sacrifice, and an action
which is also a rite. So the poet ends: "O celebration of the rites of dawn."

There is nothing in the poem which would be impenetrable to Keats, Blake,
Dylan Thomas, or to any poet in the tradition of Romanticism. There is no
linguistic deviation in the conflicting and consorting of images not sanctioned by
the potentialities of English. And above all, there is nothing in the mythology
alien to Western thought.

Thomas's own poem, "On the Marriage Of A Virgin," celebrates the same
mysterious fascination of dawn in sexual terms, only he switches vehicle and tenor,
making sex the literal level of significance and dawn the figurative:

Waking alone in the multitude of loves when morning's light
Surprised in the opening of her nightlong eyes
His golden yesterday asleep upon the iris
And this days's sun leapt up the sky out of her thighs
Was miraculous virginity old as loaves and fishes,
Though the moment of a miracle is unending lightening
And the shipyards of Galilee's footprints hid a navy of doves.

No longer will the vibrations of the sun desire on
Her deepsea pillow where once she married alone,
Her heart all ears and eyes, lips catching the avalanche
Of the golden ghost who ringed with his streams her mercury bone
Who under the lids of her windows hoisted his golden luggage,
For a man sleeps where fire leapt down and she learns through his arm
That other sun, the jealous coursing of the unrivalled blood.

A poem no less "obscure" than "Dawn," yet potentially illuminated by the same compulsive need to ascertain a mythical view of life, and using two related experiences: virginity lost, and dawn, as identities of this. "Man," "golden ghost," and "sun" are all connected as the spouse; the "virgin" seems connected with darkness, "nightlong eyes;" and the sea "deepsea pillow," but also with the Virgin Mary: "Was miraculous virginity old as loaves and fishes." And is there not a reference to Eve, Adam, and the Incarnation in the final lines? We seem to imagine the sleeping Adam, and Eve now bereft of her virginity learning of "That other sun," perhaps God's other archetypal Creation, The Son. "Fire" suggests, as always in Thomas, the fire of creation which formed the stars. His imagination is moved profoundly by the Book of Genesis: the original dawn of the poem, a local and descriptive one, searches out its own inevitable archetype, God's creation of light upon the waters. It follows through a series of dawns: "the shipyards of Galilee's footprints hide a navy of doves,' seems to be a reference to the building of Noah's ark, and the dove which left in search of land at dawn. Mythology relies on periodicity and repetition and each beginning summons up every other. In turn this is associated with the beginning symbolized by marriage, whose archetype seems to be the "marriage" of Mary: the miracle which brought "unending lightening." The light of dawn is also the light of knowledge. Along with repetition goes the identity between macrocosm and microcosm:"her thighs" and "his arm" are the bride and the groom as well as the world and the light. Which still leaves difficulties: are "her windows" the "windows of heaven"; the "mercury bone," is it "bone of my bones"? But these are not ambiguous in the sense that we do not know to what they relate. The total implication of the poem is clearly an identity between dawn and marriage using the archetypes of Genesis, the Garden of Eden, the Flood, The Incarnation and the cosmic marriage of darkness and light, the sea and the sun. Our difficulty is in how much we want to bring into the poem; how much is it Thomas's poem and how much each individual reader's. But so far as the Mythic Imagination goes, this is a pseudo-problem. Life is simultaneous and eternal.

If we were to attempt to define the "obscurities" of the Mythic Imagination we would have to pay attention to its proliferation of associative metaphor: how the palm gathers the insistence of sexual energy about it; or how Thomas can equate genesis with the marriage of a virgin. These "obscurities" belong to the processes of mythology rather than to the arbitary potentialities of language. Myth is a faculty which flourishes on sudden and unexpected analogies and recurrences. This in itself makes the products of the Mythic Imagination impenetrable to the anatomizing, analytical mind. But Macebuh, for one, would not recognize this: "The particular ambience of myth, we may be reasonably certain, is dignified simplicity; it tends to appeal to immediate recognition, to be clear, untortured, serene."[13] One wonders of whom he is thinking: not Homer, Shelley, Jung,

Frazer, Okigbo, and certainly not the Soyinka of *Idanre*. Serenity and dignity express only part of the mythologist's emotion. Nature is also alien and forboding; myth expresses a quality of attraction and repulsion, threat and promise:

> The element of participation and sympathy, of kinship between society and nature, is not the whole story. It is complemented by a lurking sense of nature's otherness, strangeness, and lurking hostility. The typically primitive attitude toward nature is largely a tension between familiarity and watchfulness.[14]

Myth almost always determines a paradoxical and circular response to experience with its observance of a cosmic behaviorism which continually undermines itself.

For the poet, this authorizes a particular density of metaphor and counter-metaphor which matches the pulse of the Mythic Imagination. Nobody has expressed the creative act under this dispensation better than Dylan Thomas when he denied that he could "make a poem out of a single motivating experience," rather insisting: "That the *life* in any poem of mine cannot move concentrically round a central image; the life must come out of the centre; an image must be born and die in another; and any sequence of my images must be a sequence of creations, recreations, destructions, contradictions." [15] This method of creation I suggest explains the poetry of Soyinka; and in its turn explains the creative methods of the Mythic Imagination. Inevitably African Literature will have to lose its epithet; and will have to seriously question any anterior sociological claims for its function; and will have to accept that it is written in the language of Shakespeare, Keats, The Romantic Poets, and Dylan Thomas. As Echeruo once said, Soyinka "operates completely within the English tradition."[16] It is one task of the critic to establish which tradition.

FOOTNOTES

1. "Poetics and the Mythic Imagination," *Transition Ch'indaba*, 50/1 (December, 1975), 79-84.
2. Mercer Cook, quoted in "Cultural Norms and Modes of Perception in Achebe's Fiction," Lloyd W. Brown, *Research in African Literatures*, 3 (1972), 22.
3. "They who have been accustomed to the gaudiness and inane phraseology of many modern writers, if they persist in reading this book to its conclusion, will, no doubt, frequently have to struggle with feelings of strangeness and awkwardness: they will look round for poetry, and will be induced to inquire by what species of courtesy these attempts can be permitted to assume that title." *Preface to Lyrical Ballads* (1802).
4. *Myth, Literature and the African World* (London, 1976), p. 14.
5. Ibid., p. 17.
6. *Victory* (London, 1923), p. 58.
7. *A Shuttle in the Crypt* (London, 1972), p. 1.
8. Ibid., p. 4.
9. *Collected Poems 1934-1952* (London, 1971), p. 8.
10. See *Journal of Commonwealth Literature*, 8, 1 (1973), 69-80.
11. *Idanre and Other Poems*, (London, 1967), p. 9.
12. Thomas, 1971, p.119.
13. Macebuh, p.80.
14. Philip Wheelwright, "Notes on Mythopoeia," in *Myth and Literature*, ed. John B. Vickery (Lincoln, 1966), p. 63.
15. *Selected Letters of Dylan Thomas*, ed. Constantine Fitzgibbon (London, 1966), p. 191.
16. M.J.C. Echeruo, "Traditional and Borrowed Elements in Nigerian Poetry," *Nigeria Magazine*, 89 142-55.

THE INTERPRETERS - A FORM OF CRITICISM

Mark Kinkead-Weekes

Soyinka's first novel has turned out to be one of those books that are widely admired, and yet have never received the kind of attention they deserve - or so it seems to me. It is labelled "difficult", and certainly on a first reading it does present problems of structure and style. The manipulation of chronology, the seeming absence of plot, the variation of style, the co-presence of very different kinds of imagination, the unequal development of characters, and the sudden concentration on new characters in Part Two, have led commentators, in the act of praising the book's power, to voice imperfectly concealed doubts about its coherence. It is true that Soyinka has never been afraid to take risks and make demands of his audience; that he has never been satisfied with "unrelieved competence,"[1] and that he has a tendency to overload his vehicles and drive with a certain extravagance. What is disturbing, however, is that so few questions have been asked about the nature and purpose of his novel's form. If we have had to learn one lesson from twentieth century fiction, it is surely that there can be no valid judgment of structure and style whatsoever, until we know what they are *for*, what kind of in-forming vision they serve. Indeed, we cannot even be sure what a novel is "about" until we discover the peculiar nature of its "shaping spirit of imagination" and its particular "maker's rage to order words."[2] So many novels turn out to be about something quite different from what one had thought, as soon as one allows one's focus to be aligned by their form. A failure to realize form becomes, only too easily, a mistaking of subject. This in turn produces difficulties with the techniques, that may come from no more than looking in the wrong direction, or adhering obstinately to assumptions and conventions the author is trying to subvert.

There is another impression that Soyinka's book is essentially socio-political satire, mediated by the interpreters on behalf of the author. To this one might retort that the novel begins in a language, Sagoe's, in which nothing serious can be said; and ends with another, Egbo's, in which nothing can be resolved. I do not think we can make sense of the book until we see that the challenge of the form involves challenging the characters as well as the reader, and results in an interpretation of life and consciousness in a "language" the interpreters cannot command. The socio-political satire, as in all Soyinka's best work, is a station one passes through in order to arrive at more significant destinations.

One needs to start then, by asking questions about the form, and about the kind of imagination it serves. At the very beginning there is a difficulty (or a challenge) in an arresting switch of chronology. After a page of edgy conversation in the nightclub, we are plunged without warning into Egbo's past. A critic writes: "His relative inexperience in the art of fiction is revealed in the manner of Soyinka's opening, which requires the reader to assess and relate a number of widely differing personalities who are all introduced, without history, in the first few pages."[3] Yet no character in a novel can have a history until he is given one, and the difficulty would seem to lie precisely in Soyinka's extreme haste to do so for Egbo. More significant however is what looks like a concealed assumption: that in "the" art of fiction, it is the clear function of "history" to explain and relate "personalities." The emphasis is on character, understood in terms of the cause-and-effect development of the present out of the past. One might illustrate this by a fine African novel published several years later, Ngugi's *A Grain of Wheat,* since it has a comparable use of flashback and a comparable exploration of a group of characters rather than a single hero. Ngugi clearly has an explanatory view of history in terms of cause and effect. Hence his form is precisely concerned to delay judgment, to prevent a reader from coming to conclusions about any of the characters until he is in possession of the whole past, which explains each of them, and their relationships, and their communal guilt. He aims at the kind of compassion that results from such full understanding. He is careful to lead his readers tactfully, in a complex circling movement from one character to another, filling in each a little more, and a little more, so that we rapidly understand what his form is after, and willingly accept delay in the knowledge that we will understand completely at the end. Now if that is what Soyinka is trying to do, his failure would seem elementary, crass, and in an absolutely crucial position, so that the readers our critic describes as giving up "after the first fifty pages or so" are entirely justified and might well have done so sooner. But is there such a thing as *the* art of fiction?

Surely what is most arresting about Soyinka's opening is its buoyant confidence and deliberate challenge — neither of which is uncharacteristic of the man or the writer. What happens if, instead of assuming he is attempting something fairly orthodox and failing, we clear our minds of assumption and ask what purpose such an opening might serve, through the effect it makes? In that case the shock of the switch is itself the point. By plunging without warning from the "present" to the "past" we become aware of a dramatic contrast. This is the dramatist's art of juxtaposition rather than the historical novelist's art of explanation; and the effect is to make one *question* the relation of the present and the past. It is this question, rather than the personalities of the interpreters or even the character of Egbo, that seems Soyinka's prime concern. If his technique creates a totally different effect from Ngugi's, it is because he wishes to think, and to make us think, about what Ngugi takes for granted as the cornerstone of his form. This is confirmed when we discover why Egbo has been chosen for the first focus: because he is obsessed with this question himself. Moreover it is his permanent failure to solve it, rather than his character or what has happened to him in the past, that makes him what he is. The focus is held steady rather on his dilemma than his development, rather on his attitude to time and to choice than his personality. Moveover, to complete this brief comparison with Ngugi, there is no question of using historical explanation to delay judgment and create compassion. There is a judgment of Egbo; it is clearly established in the first chapter; and it will not change, though its implications will deepen. The novel's final words "only like a choice of drowning" - could serve as a summary of this flashback; however, by the end, our sense of all that they mean will have deepened into another dimension.

The explanation of Soyinka's "failure" to create and relate his characters in the nightclub would then be that he is not interested in doing so, at least not yet. He is interested in establishing a contrast between present and past. A page is enough to provide a sharply etched impression of brittleness, boredom, disgust, and an edginess that vibrates to the external storm. That is the "present" which is thrown into dramatic contrast with the journey to Osa and the past. The brittleness vanishes; the writing suddenly becomes evocative and sensitive. There is a stong sense of the "dark vitality" of Osa, (p.12) a brooding power and potential meaning - but also of its pastness. It implies a verdict on the vapid and corrupt present, but it also seems "an interlude from reality," (p.10) isolated, apparently irrelevant. Behind the familiar theme of ancestral past and urban present, however, Soyinka is clearly interested in the question of time itself. What does it mean, to live in time? What are the implications of forging, or of denying, continuity bwtween past and present? Egbo is powerfully drawn to the past. Nobody in the novel feels as he does the tug of roots, the sense of power in the past which could be tapped to make the present more meaningful. Yet he is equally repelled, because to accept his heritage is to be determined, and that is a kind of death. Yet to choose freedom is also be determined by the consequence of that choice, the death of part of the self. Egbo who lay as a child by the dark water of Oshun now denounces the past's claims on the present; Egbo who lay as a child by the unfettered waters of the "suspension" bridge cannot choose freedom either, for in choice itself lies determinism, compulsion, which the "stronga head" (p.16) will not accept. So the man who is drawn to, and fears, both kinds of being-in-time, makes no choice, drifts with the tide. Yet that too is horrible. "Don't you ever feel that you whole life might be sheer creek-surface...a mere passage, a mere reflecting medium...controlled by ferments beyond you?" (p.13). He will later gloss "mere passage" to the girl by Ogun Bridge as living from experience to experience, and we will discover how destructive that can be. Already, however, Kola has a word for it, "apostasy" (p.13),perhaps the novel's key word . At the moment it means "absolute neutrality" (p.13) "objectivity strained to its negative limits" (p.14). Soon it will mean more.

The judgment of Egbo would seem clear in outline. Yet he is a powerful and fascinating figure who thinks deeply, and registers disturbingly the pressures he feels. He is sensitive to dimensions and problems which others do not see; and he has a sense of the numinous. It is indeed by registering his great potential that we register its waste. Yet the questions he poses are real ones which seem to bother his creator. Soyinka, too, neither despises nor sentimentalizes the past; admits historical determinism but rebels against it; treasures freedom and is a passionate individualist, but recognizes the opposite need for continuity and community, with a full sense of the limiting consequences of all choice. So Egbo's first function in the novel is to realize, and force a reader to experience, the paradoxes involved in the relationship of past and present, or the denial of such relationship.

But "T-t-to make such d-d-distinctions disrupts the d-d-dome of c-c-continuity, which is wwwhat life is ...The b-b-bridge is the d-d-dome of rreligion and b-b-bridges d-d-don't jjjust g-g-go from hhhere to ththere; a bridge also faces backwards" (p.9). Sekoni holds views that are positive to Egbo's negative; and the second flashback[4] is concerned with him. It is no less abrupt a juxtaposition of two time-schemes, but the terms are different. Now we plunge without warning from the idealistic engineer, dreaming on the boat home of unleashing the transforming power of technology on an undeveloped landscape, to the pointless frustration of his desk job; and then to the way he is trapped by a corrupt system into a public disgrace which makes money for his Chief and lands Sekoni in a mental hospital. Once again the contrast is between a past whose potential was rich but has been wasted, and a present of frustration. Now however the fault lies in a corrupt society and the novel becomes bitterly satirical. Or is it as simple as that? For if we really look at Sekoni's dream (p.26) are there not several worrying features? The godlike power is to be exercised by the individual will with suspicious ease, and in a world in which human beings are conspicuously absent. The language is dreamy and indulgent in that it never tests itself against any sense of the difficulty of transformation, natural, or human. Sekoni is surely remarkably naive, in his inability to see what needs to be done before anything can be done? May it be significant that the idealism is couched in sub-Shelleyan language, abstract and out of touch with concrete reality, often absurdly inflated? Is it an accident that Soyinka makes him short-sighted, eventually fatally so? Does his stuttering not suggest an inability to think his thoughts through and communicate them coherently? Yet Sekoni struggles intensely to express something important, "insists on a purpose" (p.10), and refuses to do dirt on life itself because of human corruption. He constantly criticizes the cynicism and nihilism of his companions. Once again we are made aware both of a great potential, and of a question-mark.[5] I think that Soyinka, too, is sometimes inclined to spurts of idealism imperfectly related to concrete difficulty and complexity; but here the tendency is recreated, and placed, in both its attractiveness and its weakness. The contrast between the potential of the past and its waste in the present is, then, the product of Sekoni's inadequacy as well as the corruption of his society; to read merely satirically is not enough. Where the first flashback raises the paradoxes of relating present and past, the second raises the problem of relating the ideal and the real. One sees what the interpreters see, but does one not also question the quality of their vision?

Meanwhile, introducing and connecting these flashbacks, there is the scene in the nightclub, the "present" of Chapter 1. The opening chapter of a novel, if both are any good, will always tell us how to read. One is now perhaps in a position to see how the opening chapter is a miniature of Part One of the novel as a whole. The form involves a regular interaction between a surface of "present time" narrative and a series of contrastive plunges into the past. Their main function is not to explain the past historically, though they may do this in part as well. Rather it is to use the past to focus the inadequacies of the present, now in one way, now in another. I will risk the analogy of a talking-drum. What we hear from the surface skin depends on resonance from below; but that resonance is altered in pitch and quality by the particular ways in which the strings are tugged and relaxed, so that *different* tensions are set up between skin and sound-box. The abrupt sliding from one pitch to another is an essential part of the music. It may look like a common European form, but it is quite different and original. This is what causes the difficulty, but we may not assume that it could have been done otherwise without becoming another thing. On the other hand, once one aligns oneself, the difficulties begin to disappear.

In Chapter 1 then, we focus the group in the nightclub through the two different lenses provided by the flashbacks. The result is a sense of waste; of how a past rich in creative potential has turned into a present of "five drunken sots" (p.18). They are reacting to a corrupt and banal society, yet that does not seem the author's only concern. They seem potentially superior to the banality which surrounds them; there is still some response to the numinous and to hints of bygone meanings, as we watch them react to the *apala* music and the solitary dancer; but we are invited to see them in the light of their failure to connect past and present, ideal and real, in meaningful choice and positive energy. There is a question-mark against Sagoe's "sensitivity" which expresses itself in drunkenness and obsession with his intestines and drink-lobes. There is a question-mark against Kola's "art" which, also obsessively, issues in caricature and nihilism. There is a question-mark against Bandele's heavy-lidded withdrawal. They have not yet come into focus as "characters;" indeed, one of them never will; but the flashbacks interrogate them too, and probe the connection between their sensitivity and satiric humor, and their personal inadequacy. We already know how Egbo's disgust and aggression, the satirist in him, are related to his apostasy. Now his responses to "Owolebi," the "Black Immanent," (p.24) adds a further paradox. His sense of the numinous in the woman contrasts sharply with the profane reactions of Kola and Sagoe. But the "religious" sense issues in an anti-religious stance, an eroticism to escape consciousness and defy God. The stronga-head will no more kneel to the Almighty than to man, time, or choice. On the other hand Sekoni's stuttering pleas for unity, love, faith, beauty, goodness, reverence, continue to falter in vagueness, and their lack of foundation in anything concrete and practical. It is significant that when the storm rips the roof off a nearby slum property, we should be as aware of the similarity of Egbo and Sekoni as of their difference. Egbo comments satirically, "The sky-line has lost a tooth from its long-rotted gums." (p.16) Sekoni worries about the homeless: perhaps one should offer help? But neither stirs. The focus challenges us to interpret the different interpreters in their common lethargy and disconnection.

The form of the first chapter reveals the structure of Part One as a whole. The contrastive pattern of present and past, but with a new focus from each flashback, continues, though it is more spread-out. The design seems constructed with some care and symmetry and there should be no difficulty with the time-schemes.[6] Chapters 2 and 3 develop the "present" story; shifting between Lagos and Ibadan, and centering now on Sagoe and Kola. Chapter 4 in sharp contrast is wholly flashback, to Egbo and Simi. Chapters 5 and 6 are like Chapter 1, taking up the "present" of Sagoe from Chapter 3, but then plunging into contrastive flashbacks concerned with Sagoe, and the end of the Sekoni affair. Chapters 7 and 8 are again like chapters 2 and 3, the "present" story, as Sagoe attends the funeral and, a fortnight later, watches the albino rescue the thief from the Lagos mob. Chapter 9 is a slight variant: it does contain a crucial flashback, the second instalment of Egbo and Simi, but this is framed in the "present" story, the meeting with Bandele's student, and then the expedition to the Ogun river. In both Lagos and Ibadan it is now a fortnight since the gathering in the nightclub. Chapter 10 then concludes Part One in Ibadan by gathering most of the interpreters at Professor Oguazor's. Enough time has passed after Chapter 9 for Egbo's girl to have discovered she is pregnant and to have consulted the gynecologist who gossips about her at the party. The mood is satirical, the mode is farce, the interpreters leap into action - of a sort. Only, how is one to respond to this "climax" in the context of the whole?

The main purpose of the contrasts in Chapters 2-9 seems to be the measuring of two pairs of interpreters against each other. For some time the "present" story centers on the "profane"existence of Sagoe and Kola, and the novel's satire on society gathers pace and bite accordingly. The flashbacks, however, are used to question these two, partly in human terms but more significantly in terms we may call for the moment "religious;" while at the same time we get further critical perspectives on Egbo and Sekoni.

Sagoe's drunkenness and fantasy are partly escapist; partly an inhibition of his relationship with Dehinwa which they place on the footing of mother and child (a theme I shall touch on later); and partly, as he moves into delirium and memory, a reminder of perspectives he has tried to evade. His fantasies about his drink-lobes and his intestines are the devices of a professional cynic who cannot bear his life, and who tries to escape its pressures in terms which flatter his sensitivity and sophistication, while they help him to evade his problems. The cultivation of his drink-lobes mutes disgust, and opens an otherworld in a parody of religion. "Everyone is born with them, but you have to find them, you see. You get to know them when you become professional. There it gives a delicate trill and you know you're there. The first time, it is like confirmation ... a truly religious mement." (p.35) But where drinking takes him is into delirium. The hallucination of the dead Sir Derinola in the wardrobe is a *memento mori,* an exemplum of the final comment of death on a Judge who sold himself to a corrupt system; and a reminder that in the end nothing matters but truth. "You made your choice" cried Sagoe, (p.66) but what choice has he himself made? Memory now revives the time of his appointment to the "Independent Viewpoint," one of the satirical set-pieces of Part One. The corruption that is exposed requires no gloss, and commentators have hastened to praise the novel's power here. But what kind of power is it? One needs perhaps to observe how the satire works through an art of caricature and farce, which intensifies sardonic amusement to disgust through an imagination that creates types, sharply observed from a limited angle - the tradition of Ben Jonson and Swift, Smollett and Dickens. What then seems most significant about the young Sagoe in the lobby of the hotel is the *change* from that kind of vision. As he watches the incipient humiliation of Chief Winsala and the prophetic horror of Sir Derinola, the types suddenly become complex human beings, and the response of disgust, the enjoyment of exposure and punishment, is no longer possible. The judgment of the two Elders is not muted, but to have seen the man behind the type is to break satiric detachment. The young Sagoe acts, with horror, with pity, with a sense that something must be done to preserve a minimal human dignity even for the corrupt. But what we then watch is the transformation of that Sagoe into the Sagoe of the nightclub. His humanity ironically got him his job in a system of corruption and blackmail, but the same system blocks the publication of his article on Sekoni. He takes refuge from his fear of the madness which overtook his friend by remaining within the system, going with the tide, but sustaining himself with a bottle and the ritual readings from his gospel of Voidancy. This defines the central reality of life as excremental; [7] the response of the sensitive to obscene reality as diarrhoea or constipation; and the civilized remedy as the conversion of shitting into Voidancy ... tasteful, cultured and deodorized. The world is shit and shitting; the only rebellion against the revolting is to ritualize and fantasticate what cannot be helped, in a parody of religion and philosophy. Sagoe's satiric humor seems clearly placed in its escapism. So if, after initial amusement, one becomes bored and irritated by this immaturity, the irritation has a point, becomes part of the novel's meaning and not simply a "flaw" in the style. Another side of Soyinka himself is brought into play, but also examined, and judged.

But the *memento mori* in the wardrobe now takes him in a confused gesture to Sir Derinola's funeral. "I despised him when he was alive," (p.20) but contempt is not enough in the face of death - especially since Sagoe too is a judge who has joined the system and acquiesced in the suppression of truth. Faced also with the contrast between the ostentatious cortege and the ignobility of the poor man's funeral, he places Sir Derinola's wreaths on the unknown grave. There is still much humanity in Sagoe. He responds to the realities of death, poverty, and grief - but only in gestures whose meaning is doubtful. And as he watches the mob and the thief, the murderous violence released when a little thief becomes the scapegoat for tensions created in society by big ones, the question-marks are firmly replaced. Voyeur as well as voidante, he makes the satiric points in detachment. He plays with images of Christ and Barabbas, he thinks briefly of doing something, but it is the albino who acts. Before we reach the satiric climax, then, we should have serious doubts about the prime actor and satirist. In his satiric humor he holds our interest and directs barbed response to the evils he sees; but to note his more deeply human potential is to mark once again a sense of waste, and of evasion.

The involvement of Kola with the Faseyis now brings him into focus, though Soyinka seems more interested in him as artist than as character. He is therefore developed much less than Sagoe and we learn nothing of his past. In Chapter 1 he appeared as a caricaturist, a "godless dauber," (p.24) perhaps even a nihilist afraid of goodness and beauty (p.22); but also as the gentle protector of Sekoni. Confronted now with the social pretensions of Ayo Faseyi, Kola's immediate impulse is the caricaturist's urge to inflate and intensify the absurdity. But he is brought up short against the simple integrity and directness of Monica. Again there is the challenge to a detached and sharply angled satiric vision, from a sense of human complexity. Kola is made aware of a difficult human relationship; and of a woman who sees what he does, but nevertheless remains aware of human bonds and responsibilities, and preserves her integrity without contempt of those who fail to match it. Kola's mischief is revealed as immature, even cheap. Moreover, first in his response to the albino girl Usaye and then unmistakeably in his response to Monica herself, one detects Kola's fear of involvement. He attempts to excuse his impulse of sympathy and concern for Usaye: "I suffer from fluffy emotions" (p.49). Monica's mute wonder points the necessary question: what kind of humanity is implied by the need to offer such an apology? Still more clearly, the birth of love for Monica, "a great yearning," seems to Kola "to weaken the laws of his own creation" (p.50), and he flees - but not before his human response to Usaye has been subsumed into the artist's tendency to use people for his own purposes.

Before exploring the paradox of the godless artist who is painting the Yoruba Pantheon, we must however bring into play the flashback on Sekoni, which is positioned to act as a focus on both Sagoe and Kola. In contrast with both, Sekoni after his breakdown searches for true religion. He goes to Old Jerusalem, the meeting ground of religions, in search of the One, the Bridge. He stands "wholly awed, *beyond all concrete grasp*" (my italics) before "disturbing intimations, suddenly meaningful affinities" (p.99). Soyinka's language is ambiguous, fusing tart comment with Sekoni's sense of an immanent mystery and reverence. But when Sekoni returns he suddenly begins to find himself as an artist. Where Sagoe parodies religion as part of the technique of evasion, Sekoni's search for religion leads him to an image of man as "The Wrestler." And Kola is forced to recognize that the work has an integrity and power that are the real thing, as his own art is not, even at its most serious. We begin to see why, as we watch him painting Joe Golder as *Erinle*. Sekoni, a religious man struggling to find a religion, begins from the spirit of man in an attitude of stress and effort, but also in pilgrim's robes. Kola feels able to paint the Gods, but the only idea he has of them is of his human acquaintances "translated" (p.102). Though the conception is grandiose, the godlessness is revealed by Kola's dependence on the physical detail of Golder's peeling face, reaching a climax when an actual piece of peeled skin gets pinned into the paint as "an outgrowth from Erinle's ear" (p.103). He has no numinous awareness of the God; he makes up an idea of him out of a sense of the human that we already know is skin-deep. On the other hand Sekoni's statue, though more humble in beginning from man struggling with something he has not mastered, also becomes a "deliberate evasion" (p.100) when it gives an expression of the human spirit the particular face of Bandele. Neither attempt to connect the human with the divine is wholly valid, but Sekoni's has much the greater integrity. Yet it is Kola himself who makes us see this, and the perception and self-criticism may hold the seeds of change.

We now have to add to the problems focussed by the previous flashbacks - how to strike a balance between past and present, determinism and choice, freedom and responsibility, the ideal and the real, judgment and compassion - the problem of relating the human and the divine. The two remaining flashbacks concentrate on this, in the past of Egbo. They are positioned to make the maximum contrast with the unreligious Sagoe and Kola. But the splitting of a continuous "story" into two flashbacks separated by sixty pages is no less functional, for they embody opposite reactions. The first reveals a deeply religious sensibility unlike Sagoe and Kola, and more powerfully concrete than Sekoni. The second shows him characteristically rebelling against it, and defying God. Chapter 1 had already given us Egbo as a Janus-figure facing two ways, a religious sense producing an anti-religious stance.

"A woman is the D-d-dome of Love, sh-she is the D-d-dome of Religion" (p.26). The young Egbo sees in Simi an immanence more concrete and powerful than such abstract vaguenesses. We begin from a sex-symbol overstrained and immature, and indeed the whole episode is marked by its adolescence, which is yet treated with tenderness as well as mockery. So when the boy meets Simi's preterhuman eye there is adolescent sexuality and romanticism, but also something deeper, more dangerous, and also potentially more creative. "The creek man has found his MammyWatta" (p.52), but the jibe turns serious. After his anchorite's preparation, as Egbo absurdly tries to pull Simi from her table, he has a genuinely reverent intimation of the divinity within the courtesan's human form. "Ayaba Osa, Omo Yemoja" (p.57)[8]...she mediates a cosmic force which can drown (as we shall discover it nearly drowned Egbo on the shore as well as in the creek) but can also give riches in abundance. The boy's motives are confused. He wants sexual initiation, he wants to be a chivalrous knight and rescue from her life, but most of all he is driven to dare the space he had discovered as a child in the aeroplane, "where God lives" (p.55). The Christian evangelist's son fears sin and damnation. Yet he dares to experience, through sex, the forces of the cosmos ...wind, water, darkness ...to be "gelled" (p.123) - a vile phrase - "to the earth and heavens" (p.123). He experiences a kind of agony and death, but one in which he finds a Lawrencian rebirth and fulfilment. The "cry" (p.60) at the end is exultant as well as agonised.

Yet this exultance, which casts critical crosslights on the wordlines of Sagoe and Kola and on the abstract idealism of Sekoni, remains questionable - and the questions begin to be posed sixty pages later. Soyinka clearly believes, like Lawrence, that sex can be an avenue to communion with cosmic force, a gateway to religious experience. But he courteously rebuked a critic who went on to conflate sex and mysticism on his behalf. "I distinguish between the mystical and the sexual in religious experience, though I do recognise where the two merge"[9]. For it is one thing to see sex as a "way" in which human beings may contact cosmic force and be transformed; it is quite another to imagine that sexuality is itself religious, or mysticism sexual. In a scene both funny and terrible, Simi the courtesan disentangles herself from Olokun and separates sex from mysticism as she forces the incredulous boy to sleep with her again. Afterwards Egbo feels "like the quarry at Abeokuta when all the granite had been blown apart" (p.125). Hollow and dazed, he leaves the Lagos train and falls into an exhausted sleep under the railway bridge across the Ogun. He wakes in pitch darkness beside water the color of *adire* dye, "dripping like blood in the *oriki* of Ogun" (p.126). He feels himself in the presence of the God whose head is at Olumo rock and whose feet are in the river ...and is terrified. His sense of having sinned and blasphemed makes him fear punishment, even death. But the Egboness of Egbo, if one may put it so, immediately reacts in defiance. If there is to be vengeance, let it come. In the morning he feels reborn again through having defied. "He left with a gift that he could not define upon his body, for what traveller beards the gods in their den and departs without a divine boon. Knowledge he called it, a power for beauty often, an awareness that led him dangerously towards a rocksalt psyche, a predator on Nature. And he made it his preserve, a place of pilgrimage" (p.127). After the separation of sexuality from religion the sexual man proceeds to defy the Gods, and it is in the daring rather than the contact or communion that he now places the rebirth, redefining the earlier experience. It is clear how Egbo will use Simi, or Simi-substitutes like "Owolebi" afterwards. But if there is a boon from bearding the Gods, as many myths suggest, what kind of boon is it? Egbo accepts it "without seeking to interpret" (p.133), but can we? The language is dubious. Nothing grows from rocksalt, a predator is dangerous and destructive. The place becomes *his* preserve the pilgrimage is to an enshrining of his own defiance.

The logical urge is, then, to carry the "sacrilege"further (p.130), breaking the residual sanctity by communicating it to an unknown girl. As she reveals herself to him, however, there is the possibility of human relationship. She is refreshingly honest, courageous, self-reliant, a person he can respect. But their conversation means mutual self-revelation and commitment, and from this Egbo shies as sharply as Kola, abetted by the girl's own independence. He sleeps with her *instead*, afterwards washing her maiden blood from the rock in the river. There could be a human relationship through sex, but the prognosis is not hopeful since it begins as an evasion of relationship and ends with the words "You must not try to see me again" (p.134). The signs are that it is sex not for relationship, nor as an avenue of contact with cosmic force, nor for sexuality's sake, nor even, now, to defy the gods, though the blood drops on Ogun's toes. If the blood on the rock suggests sacrifice, it is to Egbo himself, to the momentary impulse, self-protecting, of this man who lives from moment to moment refusing choice, commitment, responsibility. "A predator on Nature"...the words echo, disturbingly.

I feel sure then, as the interpreters gather in the last chapter of Part One, that Soyinka has challenged us to see them critically, though no critic has done so. They are far more talented, sensitive and promising than those who will surround

them at Professor Oguazor's. Insofar as each of them embodies a side of their
creator they all have something of his vitality and power. Yet with the exception
of Sekoni their promise has been wasted. Even now, in the "present" story, we can
see possibilities of development and change, but the question marks remain. They
have failed, and continue to fail, to come to terms with the problems brought out
by the different ways in which they have been focussed. Hence their lives remain
pointless and evasive, where not actually destructive. Only Sekoni has wrestled,
though even he has not achieved clarity, fulfilment, the complete mastery of his
art. And Sekoni, pointedly, is absent from the party.

Soyinka gives rein now to his satiric impulse apparently. He is a good hater, and
in the creation of the compound expatriate Peter he puts together intense dislikes.
As the action moves to the Oguazors' the tone modulates into comedy, and then
into farce. The targets are wholly clear; social climbing; bitchy gossip; poor taste
hoping to be recognized as European, but exposing itself as bogus, and revealing,
along with Oguazor's phony accent and his wife's phony gentility, that they have
lost their own culture and acquired only plastic fruit and artificial flowers. Finally,
as the gossip turns to the unknown girl whom *we* know, we detect callousness and
hypocrisy. Oguazor never connects "moral turpitude" (p.148) with his own
illegitimate child, and none of the laughers see the girl as a human being. Here
again the commentators feel on terms. But as Monica's refusal to be anything but
herself, or to do what has no meaning, galvanises the interpreter into action, we
may well question the value of what they do... and of the satiric art which renders
the action.

Fortunately it does not exist in a vacuum but in the whole context of Part One.
If Soyinka "lets himself go," it is not before he has prepared us to question what
we see. As with Sagoe before, the caricature and farce tend to dehumanize. The
portrait of "Perrer," as an extreme instance, is so exaggerated, so much a
conflation of dislikes and so little an imagined person, that the intensity tends to
misfire in incredulity. The point of such art in Jonson, Swift or Dickens is that the
specialization of the focus, the freedom from complexity, the detachment
produced by farce and fable, throw the emphasis not on character and realism but
on the analysis of value. That is where the humanity of such art resides. But what
values are at work here? The first point that strikes me is the relative triviality of
the targets, so largely concerned with taste and manners. I am reminded of Sagoe
going on and on about Dehinwa's wardrobe while unable to respond to the real
problems of their relationship. There is of course the deeper question of hypocrisy
and lack of human concern. But do the interpreters not share Oguazor's inability
to connect his judgments with himself? There has been insistent questioning of
their lack of value and responsibility, their failure in human relationship, their
substitution of the urge to denigrate for a more complex human response. The
point applies, as it has applied before, to the satiric impulse itself; to detachment,
dehumanization and fantastication on an inadequate basis of value and commitment. Are the interpreters not, like the Lagos mob, releasing their tensions on the
surface symptoms while the real disease, the atrophy of value, meaningful choice,
and relationship, remains as it was? Is the protest not an evasion, the episode a
false climax, the satiric frenzy with the high-life and the plastic fruit both negative
and self-indulgent? For me the real significance of Chapter 10, in its formal
context of systematic questioning, is the challenge to have done with facile

response to the surface symptoms of malaise. It is the function of Part Two to explore the causes, in an altogether deeper dimension.

Soyinka indeed has a habit in his plays of using a two-part structure to transform our view of what we have been watching: a first part predominantly satiric, comic, and done in human terms; a second part tragic, mythic, and aware of forces and perspectives beyond the human. In *The Interpreters* the two-part structure is also the pivotal example of the whole technique of contrastive juxtapositon characteristic of the form. We have done now with satiric Fable and we have also done with History; except insofar as Soyinka can use the past, on occasion, fused into the texture of present consciousness, secure that we know enough to understand. *What we get in Part Two is an exact repetition of the "present story" of Part One.* Again we begin in the nightclub, we attend a "second funeral," we eat with the Faseyis, we watch the young man run, we see Kola painting, there is another "sacrifice," and at the end the interpreters confront the Oguazor clique once more. Only this time we begin by confirming Part One's criticism of the interpreters, and learn to recast it in deeper and darker terms. Instead of the flashbacks, we are provided with lenses of a different kind of "focal length." Part Two moves beyond Fable and History into Myth.[10]

How does Chapter 11 re-orchestrate Chapter 1? "The rains of May become in July slit arteries of the sacrificial bull ...hidden in convulsive cloud humps" (p.155). The status of this style is uncertain yet, but the opening promotes an uneasy sense of forces and perspectives beyond the human. In darkness and storm Sekoni is killed on the road; the most promising interpreter is cut off just as he had begun to grow. The grief of the others is real, but their reactions show them fixed in their former postures. Egbo by Ogun river sheds "bitter angry tears" (p.155); Sagoe is "locked in beer and vomit for a week" until Dehinwa reads the bible of Voidancy to him, and never has it seemed more adolescent, futile and escapist. Kola's brush on his canvas of the Gods "faltered and worked blindly in spasms of grief and unbelieving" (p.156). Death in Part One spoke only in hallucination its *memento mori* and its call to judgement: ought the "sacrifice" of Sekoni not to make a "difference to his friends? It does .. but only to Bandele. His human concern for the family shows up the self-enclosure of the others; he is the only one to attend the funeral. Afterwards Egbo finds him "seated rock-like in the dark" (p.156); he seems to acquire a mysterious brooding power. If one has hardly mentioned Bandele so far, it is because in Part One he remains so shadowy. One might be forgiven for thinking that Soyinka gave him his extraordinary physique in order to stop him vanishing altogether. It is not really so. Sekoni sensed something in him, and on re-reading it is remarkable how firmly, though unobtrusively, he is there as a moral questioner as well as an enigma. Soyinka has not been interested in his character or his past; yet to review the little he says in Part One is to be struck by the quality of moral challenge and human concern. He can judge as well as another too. His is that pungent remark on the social sensitivity of the Oguazors's dogs, that if you drive a big enough car "they lie on the road and let you kill them" (p.139). Yet he remains on terms with those he judges. Is it because, as his reputation suggests, he is lazy, that he does not make a stand? He begins to, now, though we cannot see just how in the darkness. Then, as the interpreters gather again in the nightclub, there begins to be a new language in which to judge the old postures. There is a bogus "African" floor-show this time, as against the Oguazors "European' one, and Egbo is ready with his jibe; "The nightclub salesman of Sango has defected to more watery deities" (p.158). Now however the judgment is immediately and explicitly retorted on them. "Sekoni's death had left them all wet, bedraggled, the paint running down their acceptance of life where they thought the image was set, running down in ugly patches. They felt caught flat-footed, and Kola thought, not a bit like the finished work tonight, more like five figures from my Pantheon risen from a trough of turpentine" (p.158). They have no right to their sense of superiority, and even Lasunwon, the butt of Part One, is allowed to say so. He is terribly tactless in his anger, but he is right, and the verdict can include Sekoni despite of grief. Yet it is no longer on a purely human scale. If they are unfinished and patchy as men, they look even more so if we think of them as god-like. Finally, where Part One would have had a flashback, there is the first of the new lenses; a man who claims to have been resurrected from the dead. He may be a charlatan, he is physically repulsive "as if he had no natural blood" (p.160), but his presence is compelling and his verdict incisive. He will not talk seriously to the Interpreters in their old haunt "where life looks cheap" (p.161). Can they be "resurrected" to new life in any sense?

The opening chapter of Part Two, then, challenges us to come to terms with a cosmos, with a new seriousness and judgment in the face of death, and with a new language for measuring the vaunted superiority of the interpreters. Yet only Bandele seems to be changing, though Kola sees something through his tears. Above all we have in Lazarus a new kind of focus on death and life, on man and God.

As they listen to Lazarus in his church he looks sicker than ever, but his account of his experience carries at least personal conviction. Something happened, as Bandele recognizes, and transformed the man; gave him new life, a new name, a new coloration, a new sense of purpose and vocation. What he preaches is an African version of the Christian mystery, that all men must die to their old corruption and be resurrected in Christ. He seems to have transformed the young thief into an apostle to replace the dead one; and as the cross is carried in ecstasy round the church, as the young apostle washes feet, as the woman thrashes on the floor in prophecy, the wind of the Spirit seems to be producing a new human harvest. But what does this mean? How is one to interpret? The interpreters, predictably, are cynical. Sagoe suspects a publicity stunt; but welcomes a "story," a goldmine, a whole series to fill empty space. The journalist should perhaps verify the facts but the truth is not important. Egbo refuses to believe in the transformation of the boy and is repelled by the possessed woman. Noah is an "apostate" (p.177), merely reflecting the fanatic zeal of Lazarus, but not truly transformed - like Judas. And the prophet's violation of her body offends the sexual man. He could respond to the tranquillity of "serene joys and sublimated passions" in the worshippers of *Ela* and *Orisha-nla,* but not to these "throes of a scotched boa" (p.176). The two reactions are linked by the common reference to the rainbow; both the boy and the woman purport to have become links between earth and heaven, at the cost of an extreme evacuation (not merely sublimation) of their own personality, and this is true of Lazarus also. The stubborn individualist, and the anti-religious defier of what is beyond him, rejects both sides of the proposition. What does strike him, though, is the suggestion in Lazarus's power, that he should not have rejected his throne in Osa; that one should not be afraid of power if one wishes to transform. But he is clearly thinking about transforming others, not himself. Kola's cynical atheism goes even further. He sees Noah as an image of apostasy that goes back to Christ himself, whom Kola regards as a "technicolour purity" offering an "ambiguous covenant" (p.178), an emptiness making promises in the language of duplicity. But the boy could be useful for the Pantheon, not "on the Cross or any such waste of time," but to give a hint of *Esumare*. The separation of Bandele becomes unmistakeable now. It is not that he "believes" what Lazarus preaches, but he has come looking for a meaning in Sekoni's death, and in that seriousness he sees how self-centered the others are, how ready to use people, how cheaply cynical. Sagoe has his story, Kola something for his picture, Egbo new food for his obsession. What Bandele is getting is "knowledge of the new generation of interpreters" (p.178), and he expresses it in sharply critical terms. Put Lazarus at the most bizarre, dreaming of assisting at the Second Coming, nevertheless "this man did go through some critical experience. If he has chosen to interpret it in a way that would bring some kind of meaning into people's lives, who are you to scoff at it....None of you minds much what suffering you cause" (p.179). The irresponsibility of both scoffing and seeking to use is also clear to him. "Just be careful. When you create your own myth don't carelessly promote another's, and perhaps a more harmful one" (p.178) Lazarus is not to be simply believed or disbelieved; but the inner truth of his myth, behind the facts of whether he did actually die black and live again as an albino, is to be questioned seriously and responsibly, not absorbed into their endless egotism and carelessness. But the critics do not care to be criticized. "you sound so fuckin' superior" (p.178), "You have become so insufferably critical and interfering" (p.179). Bandele retreats, but he has made his points.

In the next chapter, the second of the new lenses is dramatically juxtaposed with Lazarus: Joe Golder, another "unnatural" white black man, also powerfully rendered and puzzling to those who assume that the novel is essentially a character study of the five Nigerian intellectuals, and a satire on their society through them.[11] Why should Soyinka devote an entire chapter at this late stage to yet another "minor character" in Part One, who in this case isn't even a Nigerian? I hope we shall find the answer, again, in the dramatic contrast implied by the formal juxtaposition. What makes Golder such an arresting figure is his embodiment of unresolved oppositions, which crackle dangerously in everything he is and says. He looks white but is partly black; he wants desperately to be black, but he can never escape his "white" thoughts and education. He has a powerfully male body, but he is a homosexual, and once more he cannot help being what with part of himself he loathes. He continually offers kindness, he needs contact, he wants communication; but he is at the same time aggressive, egotistic, spiteful, misanthropic. To listen to him is to experience a dizzying see-saw from moment to moment. "We were great friends. I liked him a lot and I hated his guts. God I hated his guts" (p.192). He is dangerous. He is also pathetically vulnerable. How are we to interpret such a condition? Sagoe, though he can register the puzzlement and irritation anyone might feel, is not the man to give us any deeper understanding or response. He is, as always, anxious to retreat into his own lethargy; and he is all the quicker to resent Golder's complex demands on him. When he does discover Golder's homosexuality his attitude is an accurate index to his response as a whole. He has learnt to ignore any language which in "hints and searching questions" challenges complex response and risks misunderstanding. But when the language becomes plain, "he simply pulled down a cast-iron shutter and developed a judo chop" (199). This is exactly how he interprets Golder. But what *is* "the matter" with the man? The first clue, I think, is to be found in the picture on his wall. "It showed white streaks on a fully black background. It could have been forked lightning on a black sky but he knew it wasn't. The tongues which dated from the main gash were wet, dripping. No power or violence but a deliberate viscosity, the trapped dreg of milk pushing through wrinkled film and trickling uncertainly" (p.193). Sagoe finds it "sick" and "sickening," but he doesn't care to diagnose the illness. "It *could* have been forked lightning on a black sky..." Again D. H. Lawrence, or for that matter Blake, may help one to understand Soyinka, though this is in no sense to suggest dependence. For surely the implication is like theirs, that the human psyche is a conflict between opposed forces which can, if they marry and explode into one another, transform the human being and become the source of creative power and fulfillment. "Without contraries is no progression."[12] Conversely, however, where the conflict is not accepted, where human beings seek to ignore or suppress part of themselves, or see-saw between partialities, there is the merely "mixed-up": sick, self-hating, destructive. Sagoe's impression that he himself is healthy is obtuse with a familiar obtuseness. What he might have seen in the picture is not just the sickness of another but a challenge to heal himself. There is however another clue to Joe Golder. We have had it for some while, though it is still implicit. Nevertheless, perhaps it is time now to try to get beneath the surface of Kola's skin-deep relation of the sick homosexual and Yoruba God? - for this may help us to see the point of the juxtaposition with Lazarus. I think Lazarus and Golder are opposite ways of focussing the question of how man can be transformed into something more god-like. Lazarus sees man as destroyed and remade by a power from without, answering his desperate cry "O God deliver me" (p.169), and becoming "flooded" with "the sense of a miracle," "For the Lord giveth and the Lord taken away" (p.170). Golder is a man apparently caught in hopeless opposition, but to measure him against *Erinle* is to reinforce the sense of what he could be, transformed in the crucible of clashing forces from within. For *Erinle* is bisexual and contradictory. He is both fierce predator and beneficent river, a god both of violence and healing. They seem opposites, but as Golder had said to Kola, the Yoruba Gods are not hermaphrodite, neither one thing nor the other. For Soyinka, it is intrinsic to the Yoruba sense of deity that there is a vital connection between opposites: there is, for example, healing in violence and violence in healing. To fix on one aspect to the exclusion of the opposite is to distort the nature, and inhibit the potential, of the god-like power that is in man, and can transform him. To *be* both fully is to explode contraries into power and progression; to tap the divine forces in the universe, and to become more godlike.

It is now clear how the new focus of Part Two is functioning. Part One, even when it explored the problem of connecting the human and the divine, was concerned with human attitudes, choices, and commitments or non-commitments. It was drawn to a human scale. The new dimension of Part Two seeks to interpret the human being in a language which continually suggests that he is only truly seen when he is seen as the location of universal forces, which will destroy or transform according to whether man works with or against them. To these forces men give the names of God in the myths by which they try to understand their operation in the world. The vision of Part Two is therefore deeply religious - but it is not credal or dogmatic. Soyinka preaches no theology, Christian or Yoruba. He does however use myth to show how the inadequacies of the interpreters are to be interpreted on a deeper level and in a more mysterious language than before, subsuming the criticisms of Part One. Lazarus and Golder become two different ways of focussing on how the interpreters fail to activate or come to terms with the forces that could transform them. The angles are opposite, one beginning from God and the other from man, but they both give a new definition to apostasy.

The next movement of the fiction develops these perspectives in two contrasted kinds of "ordeal by fire." The phrase is used humorously in Chapter 14 as Kola is lambasted by old Mrs. Faseyi for his lies and his flight (p.210); yet Kola *is* put to a test, which Sagoe has already failed. We are asked to apply what we have just learned, on the human scale first. We watch Kola also refusing to come to terms, either with Faseyi and Monica, or with the contradictions in his own feelings. There must be an "opposite" side to Faseyi that would explain how someone with Monica's perception and integrity could fall in love with him, and why someone like Bandele should remain his friend. (We shall glimpse it at the end.) But Kola sees him with "no generosity" (p.214), and persists indeed in feeding a one-sided view of him, to Bandele's mounting criticism of his interference. And as he does so, he succumbs to a sick travesty of his own feelings for Monica. Childishly, he wants to take Monica away from the man in fair fight, but the more he feeds his simplification of Faseyi, the more he finds "in his mouth, a slow sick taste which soon involved Monica, until he found he was despising her" - for marrying such a man (p.213). The more he contributes to the disease of one-sidedness, the sicker he feels, and the more liable he is to destroy his love. He leaves the house "defeated," resenting "this contamination of Monica," but also sensing that he has "betrayed" her (p.214). It is true. The contamination comes from failure to acknowledge and respond to the contradictions in others and in himself. Then Joe Golder arrives at the studio with his disease, that Kola is sure he understands, and is "in no mood to deal with" (p.215). But our attitude to Golder's tragedy, and to his danger, ought to have been transformed by the previous chapter. To measure Kola in that light, is to measure far more sharply than in Part One his failure either to understand, or to respond. Even on the human scale, the criticism of sickness has intensified.

The contrasting ordeal by fire is perhaps the most extraordinary single chapter in the novel. Kola, pursuing his plans to use "Noah" for his picture, and Egbo, pursuing his instinct that Lazarus may have something to teach him about using power on others, find themselves in a flooded landscape, looking for the church. And Egbo, remembering his own encounter with *Olokun* as a child, discovers Lazarus trying to make Noah go through an ordeal both by water and by fire. What is he doing? Bandele had suspected that Lazarus might be hoping to transform the boy into *more* than "Noah" (the just man saved from the flood to bear witness to the Covenant). Can Lazarus be trying to create a miracle; to turn the boy into the Master of Water and Fire—into Christ, Shango, Olokun, God? Or does the explanation lie in his own terror of fire, and his fear of the deluge as the wrath of God? Is he creating a rite of expiation and purgation, whereby God might be appeased as He has obviously not been by the mere conversion of Noah - and the rains would cease? One cannot be sure but it is certain that, one way or the other, Lazarus is trying to make Noah transform himself still further, into a vehicle of great power. The suspense mounts. The flames scorch the white sleeves, the boat begins to crack at the seams and settle, the water gleams with its "feeler eyes of *Olokun;* would the canoe remain beyond endurance, burnt offering at midnight for the God?" (p.223) But Noah breaks and runs again, in panic; and Lazarus is left "alone with the enormous burden of his defeat" (p.224). It would appear, as in *The Road*, that the attempt to force transformation is blasphemous and doomed. And yet as Egbo, unpitying walks "back in the direction Noah had taken," is it not also the road of apostasy that is the "secret" of defeat?

At the start of Chapter 16, Soyinka brings the whole Myth of the Yoruba Gods to the surface in a single page of summary, in densely suggestive and allusive prose. This is the one place in the novel where there is radical obscurity for a non-Yoruba reader - yet I am not sure whether Soyinka is to blame for not spelling it out. For the passage allows one to concentrate on the structure of the myth rather than its details. The story begins with creation, but becomes the story of fragmentation, when the "first apostate" shattered the One into the Many and their oppositions. But out of fragmentation, opposition, can come both destruction and disease; and fertility and growth.[13] What was implicit in the treatment of Golder's picture has become explicit in the background of Kola's. And "Kola said, 'It requires only the bridge, or the ladder between heaven and earth...the link, that is all'" (P.225). He is talking about the painting, but he alerts us also to what Soyinka wishes to do with the mythic lens, as the human story moves to its climax. We are being prepared to look at the painting, to follow the tragedy, to watch the sacrifice ...and to judge in terms which insist on the link between the human and the divine. All that is "required" is the link, but is the requirement met? Part One asked us to judge whether the interpreters could "bridge" certain human problems. Part Two subsumes these into a more radical and darker question.

In completing his picture, Kola at last leaves his nihilism behind. The failure to paint Noah as *Esumare* has revealed to him both Noah's apostasy and his own "overdose of cynicism" (p.227). He concludes that he is "not really an artist," that his intimations are too fragmentary and disjointed. Monica tells him what we already know: that his disbelief comes from failure to believe in himself; that he is afraid of compassion and tenderness as if they might weaken him; that he misunderstands his own nature and that of others; that "Bandele also thinks you all live callous, indifferent lives" (p.228). Yet the human relationship grows, and Kola begins to commit himself to it. Moreover he now sees Lazarus more truly and paints him as *Esumare*. For Lazarus has not been deceived by Noah. He knows, and has proved with the other "apostles," that "there must be something to convert ...the more evil a man has known ...the more strength I have got from him"(p.229). The murderer and the saint are nearer each other than either is to the nonentity. Opposites bifurcate from the same forces and can turn into one another. Now Kola puts on canvas what Lazarus has given him: the idea of "an arched figure rising not from a dry grave, but from a primordial chaos of gaseous whorls and flood waters He is wreathed in nothing but light, a pure rainbow translucence" (p.232). Kola has telescoped Hebrew, Christian, and Yoruba, and made the rainbow-god-man into a symbol of continuous resurrection from chaos into light and form - no longer an ambiguous covenant, but the sign of a meeting of the human with divine force always available, bridging chaotic past and resolved present, arching between the heavens and the elements. The godless dauber has become an optimist, a builder of bridges - at least in paint. Egbo of course cannot accept "an optimist's delusion of continuity" (p.233).

And yet what Kola has put into the picture with new eyes, throws into high relief the human application of the idea in the rest of the painting and in the life outside the studio. For in painting Egbo as *Ogun* and Golder as *Erinle* Kola has only seen one aspect of both the God and the man. And to miss out the artist in *Ogun* or the healer in *Erinle* is to do worse than simplify: it is to make the God purely negative and destructive, denying him even the meaning of his violence. To turn the point round and apply it to man is a sombre warning. For if man is created in the image of God and has it in him to grow more godlike, his lapse into one-sidedness will produce the same purely destructive violence, unable to create or heal. Egbo quarrels angrily with the "selectiveness" (p.233), but as usual fails to turn his point upon himself - and this poses yet again the question of whether any of the interpreters can come to terms with themselves, or with others, or with relationship and responsibility. And this includes Kola too. For it is one thing to paint a visionary idea of transformation, linking man with divine power, and forging radiant form out of chaotic opposition. But what the completion of the painting leads to is a human death. Having brought Noah to Ibadan, Kola forgets all about him. Egbo sees that it is unfair to paint him as *Atowoda* because his apostasy is not the wilful kind, but absolute vacuity. Yet no human being is a vacuum, and Egbo, too, is so interested in his idea that he forgets all about the boy, and leaves him in the studio with Golder. Only Lazarus feels responsible. But before Noah is found he has run once too often from the attempts of others to use him ... off the edge of Golder's balcony. It is Bandele - again as usual - who has to pick up the pieces, break the news to Lazarus, and take care of the shattered wreck of Golder. But Egbo sees neither his own responsibility for the tragedy, nor any link whasoever with the hysterical man in the car. To be told he is a homosexual is not to see a man of opposites become destructive, but a "noxious insect" who makes his flesh "crawl in disgust" (p.236), so that he wipes his hand in the grass to remove any claim to common humanity, any trace of human contact.

The penultimate chapter of Part One ended with the sacrifice of a girl's virginity; the penultimate chapter of Part Two ends with the sacrifice of a boy's life. The final stage in both is a call to judgment - but now it must unquestionably be a judgment on the interpreters. Egbo had brought a ram, but "Bandele had said 'What do you need the ram for? Haven't you had your sacrifice?' " (p.243). We have a judge, asking the right questions.

Bandele's rising anger at his friends articulates a final critical "placing" in human terms, but their failure to see what is "eating" him, what is wrong with Sagoe's voidancy and Golder's concert *now*, is an inability to speak or understand the language of guilt and expiation, the call of the death to change. Sagoe and Kola will marry better women than themselves, and live better lives to that extent, but that is the limit of their language, and their vision. And Bandele will not tell Egbo the girl's name, nor allow him to vent anger and turn responsibility on the "fuckin' quack" (p.242). He adds emphatically, "When *you*" (my italics) "are sure what *you* want to do, you are to tell me and I will pass it on." It seems to his former friends that he is "increasingly inscrutable" (p.244), "as if he had neither pity nor indulgence," as if he is (in the "theatre" or at the "exhibition") "like a timeless image, brooding over lesser beings."[14] Yet this is the final failure in their language, and in their image of man. For they simply do not understand what they have done, or are doing. Joe Golder singing "Sometimes I feel like a motherless child" (p.246); Kola feeling that "what was lacking ..was the power to shake out events one by one" (p.244); Egbo failing to see any connection between himself and the "castrated bull"bellowing his "cleavage from the world of understanding" (p.246); can none of them command a fully human language. They have among them sacrificed a life, to nothing, for nothing. It has no meaning for them.

So, when they are juxtaposed again with Oguazor and his cronies, there is no mistaking where the emphasis falls. The moral hypocrisy and lack of human concern in the medical men is clear enough still, but the judgment cannot be made now without applying *a fortiori* to those who presume to condemn, and wish to punish. For Egbo to spit on Lumoye is a greater hypocrisy than Oguazor's, and a greater irresponsibility than Lumoye's, for neither has seduced the girl nor had a share in the death of the boy. Faseyi's hesitant humanity for someone unknown to him is more than any of the interpreters has managed for Noah. Bandele does not fail to judge the "medical" men, but his judgment implacably includes those who have destroyed without healing or creativity. "He was looking at them with pity, only this pity was more terrible than his hardness, inexorable..."(p.250). "'I hope you all live to bury your daughters'" (p.251). They listen "unbelieving," "in confusion," while Egbo crystallizes in the closing words their essential paralysis.

But Part Two has sought to subsume the purely human judgment into deeper terms; and if we can say that the human failure of the interpreters is all the worse because of the superior potential they have squandered, the verdict is intensified since we have learnt to see that potential as god-like. Egbo had complained of Kola's picture, that he had fixed on a "single" aspect of *Ogun*, "frozen at the height of carnage" (p.233). "Even the moment of Ogun's belated awareness would have been ...at least that does contain poetic possibilities ...and then there is Ogun of the forge ...but he leaves all that to record me as this bestial gore-blinded thug." But as Egbo advances on Lumoye with "eyes outheld on black cuspids, embers on the end of a blacksmith's tongs" (p.249) he *is* that travesty of the God. Not only has he failed to activate the "opposite," but the atrophy translates the creativity into violence and makes the violence meaningless. The failure to be god-like, we have learnt, is the commitment to destruction and disease. (That is why the theatre bell is like "a leper's peal" (p.251).) And " only like a choice of drowning" means more now than the failure to choose, to connect past and present, to be responsible. It is the confirmation that, for Egbo, the commitment to anything beyond himself means *only* self-extinction. The creek, the surf, Oshun, the unfettered waters under the suspension bridge, the river Ogun, have all been subsumed into the nauseous blackness of the "dye"-pit, reduced to "that which means *I* must drown, horribly " Yet these waters all bear the names of Gods who contain something violent and potentially destructive, but who can give new life in abundance. (Just as a sacrifice kills, but can expiate, purge, contact the godhead, and transform). Egbo has chosen, but not Simi, not the girl. He has chosen to drown both his humanity and his godliness; the full definition of apostasy.

Bandele's judgment is not merely human either. The images insist: Bandele "unyeilding, like the staff of Ogboni" (p.244), "Bandele, old and immutable as the Royal mothers of Benin throne, old and cruel as the *Ogboni* is conclave pronouncing the Word" (p.250). Do the *Ogboni* not judge sins against the earth, and share with the Queen Mothers of Benin the function of a court of appeal, against the failures of the Oba who links man with the Pantheon of the sky? There is that curious substratum which sees the god-like interpreters as also motherless children; both drawn to "matriarch symbols" (p.122) like Sagoe and Egbo; and also rebelling against the mother like Golder, "unable to be flung clear" (p.245);

and like Kola, wishing "if only we were" motherless (p.244). Also there seems to be an association between "mother" and water and earth, which we see in Egbo's termite-statue by the river, and in the immanence of "Owolebi" - but which culminates in the rejection of the nauseous. This is the significance of that powerful passage (p.246) in which Egbo's subsonscious tells him something he does not grasp: the connection between Golder and himself he so insistently denies. For the "stress of consciousness" not only fuses past and present, but also himself in the surf, Golder, and the child walking by the rims of the enormous dye-pits which are buried in black sand soggy with piss, and falling into the foul depths. There is a deep link between Golder's rejection of women and Egbo's horror of drowning. The novel records not only the failure of men to rise to the potential of Those who ascended to the Sky, but also the blasphemy against the Mother, earth and water, the sources of fertility which they can only see as drowning. So "I hope you all live to bury your daughters" is not only a human verdict. but a prophecy of what it means to blaspheme against the source of fertility and continuity.

Of course the book is "difficult." I have however tried to show that it is neither incoherent nor obscure, and that it tells one how to "interpret" - if one will only listen.[15] The difficulty is inherent in the challenge: to pierce through a superficial language and superficial judgments in dealing with a sick society; and to criticize the facile critics who see the symptoms outside themselves, but cannot diagnose the disease that includes them, along with those they presume to criticize. Yet if one tries to align one's self with the form and respond to the challenge of the juxtapositions one does learn a language and find that one can interpret. I suspect I have sounded more confident than I feel about my results. It is never comfortable to differ from all accounts one has read, and I am well aware of the dangers of an expatriate account of a very Yoruba book. But interpretation must precede criticism; one must at least try to learn the language, before what one says can mean anything.

I respect *The Interpreters* on this side of idolatry too. There are several criticisms one might have made. But I should like to conclude with what I most admire about it: the courage of its self-exploration. I have tried to argue that the book is not, above all not, a mere satire on the sort of "corruption" represented by obvious targets like Sir Derinola, Winsala, the Managing Director, or the Oguazor clique. Soyinka takes us *through* that, to the sources of his quarrel with its too-facile judges. But if the book is the start of his challenge to his own sort- the Nigerian "intellectuals," it does not become so without springing from a quarrel with himself. All the interpreters share Soyinka's ebullient vitality and intelligence, but that is particularly because each of them, I think, is a facet of himself thrown into action, but scrutinized to uncommon depth and with unusual honesty. And that is not an "easy" thing....

FOOTNOTE

Page references are to the edition in the "African Writers Series," with Introduction and Notes by Eldred Jones, (London: Heinemann, 1970).

1. Soyinka's "friendly"criticism of Chinua Achebe; *cf.* Achebe's Preface to *Girls at War and Other Stories* (London: Heinemann, 1972).
2. I borrow phrases from Coleridge's "Dejection" and Wallace Stevens's "The Idea of Order at Key West."

3. Gerald Moore, *Wole Soyinka* (London: Evans, 1971), p.79.
4. I assimilate the brief flashback on pp. 16-17 to the bigger one on Egbo.
5. I differ somewhat in emphasis here from Eldred Jones, see his note, p.253; and his treatment of Sekoni in "Progress and Civilisations in the Work of Wole Soyinka" in *Perspectives on African Literature*, ed. Christopher Heywood (London: Heinemann, 1971), pp. 134-35.
6. Soyinka may seem to trip himself up on p.122, when Egbo seems to suggest that the incident with "Owolebi" happened before "the event of the visit home." I think, however, he only means that his memory of the expedition has just made him forget "Owolebi," a moment ago.
7. The analogy with Ayi Kwei Armah seems too close for accident, especially if, as I have been told, the name "Sagoe" suggest a Ghanaian origin. Did Soyinka know of the writing of *The Beautyful Ones Are Not Yet Born* at the time?
8. "Queen of the sea, Daughter of Yemoja," according to Professor Jones, p.260; thus, presumably, Olukun, and by extension also the other water deities born of Yemoja.
9. Quoted by Moore, p.82.
10. I enlarge on "Fable", "History" and "Myth" as different kinds of imagination, involving different kinds of characterization, procedure, and style, in the final Chapter of *William Golding, A Critical Study* (London: Faber, 1965).
11. *E.g.*, Margaret Laurence on Lazarus in *Long Drums and Cannons* (London: Macmillan, 1968), p.73; Eldred Jones on Lazarus and Golder in his "Introduction", p.4.
12. From the "Argument" of Blake's *The Marriage of Heaven and Hell.*
13. See also the treatment of Ogun, and of Atowoda in Soyinka's long poem "Idanre."
14. Moore complains (p.84) of how "the others have to act with heedless unconcern" in order to highlight the moral passion of "Bandele," and calls this a "distortion." The contrast is well taken, but I have tried to show the consistency throughout.
15. *E.g.*, Charles Larson, *The Emergence of African Fiction* (Bloomington: Indiana Univiserty Press, 1972), p.246: "There is no real beginning or ending to Soyinka's story...little, if anything, has been resolved by the end of the novel, and one has the impression that the arrangement of the scenes within the book itself could have been considerably different than it is without noticeably altering the impact or the meaning of the work itself."

The Man Died

Peter Enahoro

Shortly after the war of Biafran secession, Nigeria's Head of State, General Yakubu Gowon, passed a message to Wole Soyinka, the playwright and novelist. "Tell him", Gowon told a friend of Soyinka's, "I said, Bygones is bygones. Right? Use my exact words—bygones is bygones." Soyinka's reply to Gowon's offer of truce is a full-blooded four letter word: "My a—e!" It is the answer of searing rage—and Soyinka's book simply bristles with fury.

He was detained for eighteen months during the Nigerian civil war. He spent fifteen of those months in solitary confinement. He was never formally charged, but he understood that he had been detained allegedly for trying to purchase an aircraft for the Biafran leader, which Soyinka indignantly denies. (To him Ojukwu was "that ceremonial fop in the East.") Soyinka admits that he went to Biafra but only to argue an alternative to war. On his return the Federal authorities accorded him a welcome a shade less violent than the Gestapo would have wished to give Rudolf Hess had that gentleman returned safely to Nazi Germany from his one-man mission to the British enemy. Soyinka was put in chains—literally; interrogated, kept incommunicado, while every subterfuge, from cajoling to direct threats, was used to try to incriminate him.

The Man Died is essentially about Soyinka's experiences in captivity, but it encompasses other times and places outside the prison walls. We meet the intellectual well before his arrest disdaining the cosy campus ivory towers into which so many Nigerian intellectuals hastily retreat, in a land where academicians measure their success by the length of the car they drive. When we next meet the author he is a nagging petitioner on behalf of the young majors whose abortive coup toppled the civilian regime in January 1966. In the south they are heroes; in the north they are dastardly criminals—and Soyinka is in the north on a mission of political education, trying to set up the ground work for a congress of enlightened youths, when the May riots—the dress-rehearsals for the horrid massacres which preceded the civil war—are unleashed.

Soyinka lays down his political thoughts in the manner of an enraged man pounding a table with his fist, which is fair enough for a writer in a continent where too many are only too willing to compromise and keep their political thoughts well hidden, even sometimes, one suspects, from themselves. ("The man dies in all who keep silent in the face of tyranny," Soyinka says.) The thundering political snippets are engaging, but the real attention must focus on Soyinka in jail: a man in captivity. He says that his book is not a textbook for survival, "but the private record of one survival." Yet he succeeds in creating an empathy in the reader and one is compellingly drawn to jail with him living every moment of it— sharing his towering indignation as one self-important official after another struts about the place bullying, shouting, corrupting, threatening, scrounging from the prisoners. Fearful cries echo in the dead of night...a man goes berserk...an execution squad marches the condemned to the gallows...a warder returns from a hanging to resume guard duty...two bragging self-confessed murdering soldiers are freed from detention...It is enough to make a man lose his mind.

Soyinka had two beliefs which he held on to with a conviction bordering on religious fanaticism. He believed that those who put him in jail hated him, and he was convinced that there was a conspiracy to destroy his mind, if not liquidate him

239

altogether. The evidence he supplies for this is thin; and one feels sometimes that he is stretching the argument a bit. He questions, for example, the motive of the Nigerian Government in withholding denial of his death although rumors of this had been circulating abroad for two months. He does not make allowance for the xenophobia which gripped Nigeria during the civil war and which caused all inquiries concerning sensitive matters to be answered in hostile silence.

Soyinka does not appear to have been wounded as much by the injustices of his detention as he was by a feeling of personal affront—yet it was probably this which saved his mind. The man we discover behind bars is not whimpering in self-pity; he is loftily outraged. He sustains himself with a deep contempt for the powers which imprisoned him, and by his defiance of his gaolers. This was his secret weapon: hatred he could take, kindness would have killed him. "I wanted eyes of hate and fear around me to keep me constantly alert," he writes.

If there was a plot to drive him insane the conspirators certainly came close to achieving it. He was denied reading material, pen, mail. To keep his mind working he devised little games of his own. One of them was weaving fantasies around the objects about him—a lizard, a praying mantis, a gecko. On recapturing these and other such moments Soyinka has produced a work of such excellent poetic prose that doubts are sure to arise whether this really was total recall or whether the inventiveness of the dramatist had taken the better of him, for truthfully some of it is suspiciously too good to be true: too polished. Because we do find Soyinka saying "At some point the games which I played with mathematics must have gone too far. I moved into greater and greater absurdities and plunged at some point over the brink of rational principles into clearly unhealthy regions. My recollections of this phase remain hazy and a little frightening," which seems more like it.

Soyinka wrote his book long after he was released from jail, but time obviously did not cool his exasperation. Perhaps he should have tarried a while longer? For transparently just though his anger is, and although he tells us that at least a dozen times, the format, title, and concept of the book were changed because he could not decide "what to include, what suspend, and what totally to erase." Soyinka's very agreeable irreverence is sometimes perverted by his still smouldering wrath. One feels occasionally that the author is determined to show that the pen is mightier than the sword—and succeeds mercilessly but calculatedly. He will be accused of not having resisted the temptation to get his own back.

This book is a welcome departure from the cold statistics, the sick "objective" political analyses, and the dull economic ramblings around which the two sides to the Nigerian civil war have been argued. Until now it has seemed as though those thousands and thousands who died in the riots, in the massacres and subsequently in the civil war were not human beings but just numbers. Soyinka has put a human face on those casualty figures.

There are no faceless Ibos in his book; they are Agu Noris, the well-known musician; Samuel Ikoku, the unyielding Leftist, and others with familiar names and faces. And of course there is Wole Soyinka himself, through whom we relive a side of the Nigerian tragedy about which so little has been written. Until now.

The Man Died

A.R. Crewe

As an African student in England it gives me a sense of great satisfaction to point out to English acquaintances the superiority of *Africa Magazine,* in terms of balanced reporting and credibility, over its Western counterparts such as *Time* and *Newsweek.* It is this sense of confidence I have in the magazine which made a serious lapse in your January number doubly disturbing for me.

I am thinking of Peter Enahoro's review of *The Man Died,* by Wole Soyinka. I sincerely hope I am wrong, and that Mr. Enahoro has merely misread the book; but the article struck me as deliberately ambiguous in the worst traditions of *Time* style double-talk. What is in the end most ironical about it—does Mr. Enahoro see the irony, I wonder?—is that it turns out to be a walking parody of the very attitudes Soyinka identifies as currently crippling Nigerian morale: timidity, moral indignation of the "Oh dear, what can be done?" variety, and uneasy hostility to those who actually do—who say too much too loud and too clear.

The article is spotted with tell-tale indications of the reviewer's real attitude, for all the apparent approbation with which he showers the book. It creates the impression of being a highly-conscious exercise in the technique of damning with faint praise.

Technique 1: *Put Your Man on the Defensive:*

According to Mr. Enahoro, Soyinka "indignantly denies" the charge of collaboration with Ojukwu made against him by Nigerian Security; he "admits" that he went to Biafra, "but only" to argue an alternative to the war. So, although it looks like straight reporting of Soyinka's account, the spurious impression is created that Soyinka was both rattled and on the defensive in the face of his accusers; whereas nothing is clearer than the fact that he felt no need to deny, justify or admit anything— he simply doesn't feel answerable to framed accusations.

Technique 2: *Disarm Your Man with a Patronizing Smile of Indulgence:*

Taking into account the credit which Mr. Enahoro does give Soyinka for his record of outspoken concern and active involvement in Nigerian social and political life— and which could hardly be withheld—we note nevertheless that Soyinka is referred to as "the intellectual" (i.e. no doubt lacking in that great modern virtue "pragmatism"). The main moral thrust of the book is simply shrugged off, attention directed towards windy atmospherics about Soyinka's style, as some kind of fascinating esoteric curiosity: "The thundering political *snippets are engaging* (my emphasis), but the real attention must focus on Soyinka in jail." Leaving aside the cheek of the word "engaging," Soyinka is not offering "snippets." The book rests on a single, unified purpose—to challenge the Nigerian conscience out of a state of increasingly self-corrupting apathy. Soyinka's own case is merely that central consciousness around which events take shape; he is one of those selected by circumstances to bear witness in the flesh to the collective moral failure of the nation. His responses as an innocent victim of the circular pattern of power-lust, guilt and self-protective cruelty are a conscious incarnation-in-action of that deep resolve not to surrender which he enjoins on his fellow-countrymen. But these responses are an organic part of the political "analysis," "Message" or whatever you like to call it, of the book—and inseparable from it.

Technique 3: *Cast doubt on Motivation and Factual Accuracy:*

Mr. Enahoro says that "Soyinka does not seem to have been wounded as much by the injustice of his detention as he was by a feeling of personal affront." Obviously, again, the two things are inseparable. To be the victim of the unlimited power of offended mediocrity is an affront not to be borne by any man. And Soyinka's response is both his own and (hopefully) that of every Nigerian.

The reviewer is also sceptical about Soyinka's recapture of some of his prison experiences. He finds them "too polished," and "suspiciously too good to be true." But it seems hardly fair to hold it against Soyinka that he was not incoherent where the rest of us would have been. Every word of the book provides evidence of the fact that it was his relentless struggle to control his experiences and continually re-define his humanity that saved him. It is this success that Mr. Enahoro finds too polished.

Why this undercurrent of resentment, which prompts Mr. Enahoro to complain that Soyinka seems "determined to show that the pen is mightier than the sword," and that "he succeeds mercilessly but calculatedly?" But the reviewer finally gives himself away when he concludes of Soyinka that "he will be accused of not having resisted the temptation to get his own back." Mr. Enahoro might just as well have echoed General Gowon's own message to Soyinka after his release: "Tell him I say bygones is bygones." The man died, a dog died, the matter is dead.

Soyinka's Black Orpheus

Dan Izevbaye

> Olóhùn-iyò tuned up and began to sing and as
> he sang flames burst out and smoke engulfed
> us where we stood; as it was for us, so also for
> the king of birds and even the sand elves,
> everyone forgot about the fight and began to
> dance.

Forest of a Thousand Daemons

The term "Black Orpheus" was Sartre's description of the *négritude* poets in
Senghor's anthology, who had attempted to shake off their alienation from
spiritual roots by returning to their native land.[1] This was some time after
Fagunwa the Yoruba novelist had adapted the idea in his novel about a quest by a
group of Yoruba hunters.[2] Sartre saw a resemblance to the Orpheus myth in the
lyrical "descent of the Negro into himself" (p. 21) and interpreted it as a quest for
inner harmony by an exiled black soul fleeing through the death corridors of a
white culture in order to recover his vital self. Harmony and unity play an
important part in Sartre's definition of Black Orpheus. The progress of the black
poet begins as a flight from European mineralization of his humanity towards a
recovery of his animal or vegetal nature. (p. 48)

But *négritude* poetry which Sartre described in 1948 as "the sole great
revolutionary poetry" in our times (p. 11) is described by Soyinka writing twenty
years later as the "literature of self-worship." Unlike Sartre who saw a union of
two selves as the goal of the Black Orpheus, Soyinka saw a turning into one self
and the danger that Black Orpheus might turn narcissist.[3] As many writers have
pointed out, Soyinka was rejecting not the main argument of *négritude* but the
display.[4] It is easy to find support for the *négritude* quality described by Sartre as
the "profound unity of vegetal and sexual symbols in original Negro poetry" by
pointing to the primacy of vegetal and sexual imagery in Soyinka's work. Even his
famous quip, with its witty "tiger/tigritude," "duiker/duikeritude" pun, refers us
to an African vernacular style which depends largely on puns and on references to
animal life. The witticism can be used as a gloss on a Fagunwa tale in which the
leopard displays his beauty and announces that "if we exempt worthies like the
antelope and the duiker, few animals surpass me in beauty."[5]

Sartre and Soyinka also differ in their views of the social status of the black
poet. For Sartre the racial issue is at the fore, rather than the place of the poet
within his black community. So he uses the idea of an African collective mind to
argue that when the black poet expresses himself most lyrically he "attains most
surely to great group poetry" and "speaks for all Negroes." (p. 21) Soyinka's
intrepretation of the Orpheus myth begins from a more dynamic Yoruba
conception of the status of the individual in his community. The story of the
separation of the gods which we find in Yoruba creation myths appears to be the
exemplar for the Yoruba conception of individualism. The myth suggests that
separation is an evolutionary stage after original unity and is a necessary stage
before meaningful community. The theme of separation or fragmentation appears

to be such a fundamental one that the myth contains al least two or three such motifs as variations or as complementary versions.[6] It is from this myth that Soyinka derives the principle of separation in that part of "Idanre" in which he calls for a refusal to become a mere "spoonful of protoplasmic broth" in "one omni-sentient cauldron" and recommends instead that we "celebrate the stray electron."

Some forms of Yoruba literature celebrate both individualism and the value of the individualist to his society. Folktales with human heroes often celebrate the hunter as an outstanding individual. He can be a benefactor of his community only after fulfilling himself as an individual. It is this two-part principle—the need for individual fulfillment as a condition for community service—which provides the form that is adapted by writers like Fagunwa, Tutuola and Soyinka. In the first part of the story the hero, usually a hunter, wanders into an uncharted forest in quest of fulfillment. The hazards become the test of his manhood, and his achievements in the forest become the criterion for letting him lead a mission on behalf of his community.[7]

The second part of the story is more serious in intent, and deals more or less with the social mission undertaken by the hero. This is the two-part form of *The Forest of a Thousand Daemons* as well as Soyinka's *The Interpreters*. Different as the two works are in other respects, we can relate them by reference to the principle of the two-part "form of criticism" which a discerning critic has introduced into the criticism of *The Interpreters*.[8] In the two novels the first part gives the hero the opportunity to fulfill himself, while in the second part there is an evaluation of the use that has been made of this opportunity. Terror and fear provide both the literary thrill and the spiritual measure in these *rites de passage*. Multiple beads of fearful incidents are strung around the hero's courage in *The Forest of a Thousand Daemons* as a test of his manhood.

In *The Interpreters* fear also becomes a spiritual gateway. Its importance is brought out by the frequency with which it is used to mark the moments of achievement or failure in the characters' opportunity for fulfillment. Chapter nine is full of such moments of fear—Egbo's meeting with Simi and with the girl undergraduate and under Olokemeji bridge; it also occurs elsewhere—Noah at the fire passage, Lazarus's vision of death, and Kola's recognition of his failure as an artist because "he dared not, truly, be fulfilled." (p. 218) The meaning of fear comes through in one of those rare moments when Egbo perceives the meaning of fulfillment. He wakes under the bridge "feeling night a womb of the gods and a passage for travellers" and "left with a gift"—"for which traveller beards the gods in their den and departs without a divine boon." (p. 127) The hunter who ventures into the Forest of a Thousand Daemons also acknowledges the occupational hazards which accompany heroic fulfillment: "The aggressive man dies the death of war, the swimmer dies the death of water, the vainglorious dies the death of women." (p. 36) It is after the hero has fulfilled himself and found fame in the first part of the work that he is chosen in the second part to lead other hunters on a mission for his community in the manner of the Argonauts.

The Forest of a Thousand Daemons relates to the Black Orpheus tradition in two respects. First, there is an occasional revaluation of black cultures and a direct appeal for unity among black communities. Then Orpheus's contest with the sirens is reinterpreted as an allegory of the poet's role in leading the resistance against European cultural assimilation. On their way to their national missions

Fagunwa's hunters are lured by a "singing in heaven" so melodious they have never heard the like: "The voices were many and they sang as one." (p.96). They lose a companion who "plunged into the dome of heaven." Some said that "he was transformed into a ghommid" while others "claimed that the gatekeepers of heaven took pity on him, cloaked him in the garb of immortality and admitted him into heaven." (pp. 95-96) As for the others, it was only the singing of Olóhùn-iyó that saved them by recalling them to their mission. Soyinka's artistes can match this social function. The àpàlà drummers in *The Interpreters* "taught style to the new *oyinbos*" (p. 21), working within the same artistic form as the hunter in *The Forest of a Thousand Daemons* who won royal favors by tempting the king to dance:

> When I had truly excelled myself, the king himself rose from the throne and plunged into the dance. I was now thoroughly aroused and I dug the crook into the drum skin, darted into the fray and crowded the king with music. (p. 44)[9]

If these artistes win patronage from the great by offering them cultured entertainment, they can retain their professional independence. Soyinka's àpàlà drummers "gauged the mood, like true professionals, speaking to each other, not to their audience, who would, if they chose, not *know* this language." (p. 21)

The service of the poet is not to the great alone. It is useful to recall at this stage that in nearly all versions of the Orpheus myth the most important social function performed by the poet comes from his power to tame wild beasts—that is, the power of his music to soothe the savage breast. The universality of this motif clearly testifies to traditional medical faith in the beneficent effect of the poet's art. Yoruba incantations by which men gain control over the forces of evil are not merely magical charms but a distinct poetic genre. Similarly there is a close link between the poetic names of herbs and their healing properties. This has often been used to support the theory that the poetic phrases in incantations are not merely puns but were originally verbal definitions of the curative properties in the herbs used.[10] If tranquilizers used in the treatment of madmen are associated with images and puns in poetry, it is not difficult to see how the practice of healing makes possible the myth about the power of poetry to humanize the man of violence.

This function of poetry explains how the subject of madness and violence relates to the imagery of healing in *Madmen and Specialists,* and it explains the revelation in *Season of Anomy*[11] where a doctor tells the poet-hero how he "gave up this whole business of words" and suddenly "switched over to medicine." (p. 228) Soyinka's interest in the social role of the poet as healer dates from *Idanre and other poems* (1967),[12] a collection which marks the eruption of violence in Nigeria. In "Civilian and Soldier," one of the poems in this collection, a civilian promises to tempt a soldier away from the "lead festival" of the soldier's friends and initiate him into the "trade of living" by shooting him "clean and fair/With meat and bread." (p. 53) The 1966 poems in *Idanre* thus mark the beginning of the poet-as-Orpheus theme. However, this theme is developed mainly in his prose works rather than the poems.

In *The Interpreters*, the work which immediately precedes *Idanre*, Soyinka develops his main characters as Prometheans, and not, as he was later to do, as types of Orpheus. The difference between *The Interpreters* and the later writing can be explained mainly by reference to the main events in Nigeria at the time of publication. *The Interpreters* came out when Nigeria was not yet the area of violence presented in *Idanre*. In contrast to *The Man Died* where Soyinka shifts emphasis from social to individual responsibility by arguing that "Violence and death are personal things" (p. 161),[13] *The Interpreters* presents us with Sagoe's vision of a society in which, "next to death . . . shit is the most vernacular atmosphere of our beloved country." (p. 108) The problem in the later works is seen as one of violence and Soyinka brings an Orpheus to the scene. In *The Interpreters* the problem is that of social development. Sagoe presents that unflattering definition of a developing capital: "Every loud city has its slums, and Isàlè-Èkó symbolised the victory of the modern African capital over European nations in this one aspect of civilisation." (p. 72) To this society Soyinka brings two potential Prometheans. Egbo, invited by his people to be an "enlightened ruler" (p. 12), is fashioned after Ogún, the god of iron and war. Sékoní the electrical engineer is modelled after Sangó, the god who in tradition possesses the Promethean gift of fire but uses it only as the sign of his wrath. Sékoni starts off with a more earthbound purpose. On his voyage home he has a Promethean dream of using his power over electricity for industrial development on earth:

> He sat on a tall water spout high above the tallest trees and beyond low clouds . . . he opened his palm to the gurgle of power from the charging prisoner, shafts of power nudged the monolith along the fissures, little gasps of organic ecstasy and paths were opened . . . (p. 26)

The god Ogún, after whom Egbo is fashioned, is similarly a pathfinder and human benefactor. He taught men the creative art of metallurgy. But he is also a god of violence and destruction. Egbo is as closely identified with Ogún as Sékoni is with Sàngó, but only the negative side of Ogún is developed in him, especially the thirst for blood. Apart from his love for sacrificing others to himself, even his pronouncements and deeds are direct allusions to Ogún: the dye drops dripping at the dye pits which he frequented in his youth become Ogún's praise name: the onomatopoetic sound of blood drops becomes a pun on the usual Yoruba salute to royalty: "the indigo streams from *àdíré* hung up to dry, dripping like blood in the *oriki* of Ogun, *tó tó tó tó tó*."[14] (p. 126) At the display of "The Pantheon" the blood link between Ogún and Egbo is again established through Egbo's words: "The moment that you say *tó*, my knife will go in the neck of this ram. *Tó*, and a fountain of blood will strike the ceiling of this studio." (p. 225) The reference here is to bloodshed only; there is nothing of the awesome majesty of blood sacrifice associated with Ogún.

A similar ambivalence exists in Egbo's relation to water. Òshún the sacred river which he frequented in his youth was the legendary secondary wife of Sàngó. Egbo is discovered at her side at midnight. His later failure as an adult is persistently described as "a choice of drowning" (pp. 120, 251), and when he gazes into the water now, what he sees is "a sleepy coil of python . . . voluptuous mermaid arms . . . infinitely coy and maternal." (p. 14) Egbo is unable to leave his adolescence behind, and a regression even occurs during a sexual encounter when he asks to be allowed to lie in darkness and cry. (p. 60) Just as Sagoe, with his "traumatic centre of castor oil" (p. 84), thinks only of voidance, so Egbo relates his life to the drowning of his mother by picking maternal lovers and showing a self-destructive love for water. Egbo's problem is commented on through the fire-eater in the night-club who falls into a small puddle. Egbo's comment, "The night-club salesman of Sango has defected to more watery deities" (p. 158), is an ironical comment on Egbo himself, since he has been described earlier as one unable to avoid "the fate of a burnt-out fire-eater." (p. 12)

If Egbo's failure is wholly a personal one, Sékoní's defeat has a mainly social cause. This Promethean figure "sought the hand of kindred spirits for the flare of static electricity, but it slipped with grease and pointed to his desk . . . " (p. 27) The greased palm is the social corruption that defeated the idealist engineer. These two different kinds of hero may be described as "failed Protheans," a term borrowed from *The Man Died* (p. 88), Soyinka's personal account of his detention and the main source of material for the second novel. The social cause of Sékoní's frustration provides one explanation why a Promethean should fail. But the story of Sékoní is not merely a story of social frustrations; the portrait of Sékoní betrays a rejection of the Promethean motive because of its implicit questioning of Promethean ambition. Soyinka is only partially sympathetic to Sékoní whom he presents as "short-sighted" (p. 155), presumably for thinking that "the logic of nature's growth" can be "bettered by the cabalistic equations of the sprouting derrick." (p. 27) He nevertheless insists on the social flaw, especially in the tribute to Okigbo in *A Shuttle in the Crypt* where he expresses doubt about the value of Promethean sacrifice.[15] This doubt prepares the way for the final, violent suppression of the Promethean idea whenever it suggests itself in *The Man Died*. It does suggest itself at least once: "My liver is mended. I await the vultures for there are no eagles here." (p. 187) But although the writer's egotism is never conquered in the work, the idea of a Promethean is resolutely suppressed: "History is too full of failed Protheans bathing their wounded spirits in the tragic stream./Destroy the tragic lure!" (p. 88)

The egotism which comes through so strongly in *The Man Died* is offered as the precondition for survival. It becomes clear that theories of the African artist as a group representative never included the possibility of a state of anomie in Africa. The egotism emerges from the writer's presentation of a state of himself as a model for lesser beings: "If *he* could break and break so abjectly then anyone can break." (p. 79) The mind that recognizes a threat to its humanity must become a nay-sayer: "The man dies in all who keep silent in the face of tyranny." (p. 13) Inevitably, attention is turned to the prisoners' need to preserve "a spark of human essence" and on "the animality of the gaolers." (p. 98) Humanity can be preserved or recovered through the art of song, as when "the brutalized humanity beneath us" sang, and "involved us all, strangers to their homes, in one common humanity." (p. 110)

The gaolers on the other hand are presented, rather uncharitably, through animal imagery. In accordance with the aesthetic scheme they are depicted as creatures of brute flesh and warm blood lacking in song. First, Polyphemus, "eight feet tall, a thickly cicatriced tower of menace . . . I know Polyphemus will be the priest of the rites of submission." (pp. 125-26) Then comes Hogroth "in the midst of his marshland wanderings . . . *Hraagrh hraagrh hraagrh* . . . *ptuh—splat!*/ Pig! . . . Do you belong to the same species as lay claims to souls, to sensing and thinking?" (p. 133) But the encounter between brute and poet is easy for the poet who, like Adam, conjures by the magic word: "His naming was easy—Hogroth.

Slowly the stomach settles back and ceases to heave." (p. 132) In the imagined encounter Wole Beowulf triumphs, as a matter of course: "Hogroth dead. New glow in the universe. I hear the prison celebrating." (p. 133) Inevitably too, we encounter Caliban (not the colonial creature), but his musical ear is not even accepted as an index of his humanity because his creator's malice is far too strong. Caliban sings a "mystery dirge first into himself and then in a reckless challenge to the heavens . . . Caliban never sleeps. Nor do I when Caliban patrols the night." (pp. 134-35 *passim*)

After peopling his world with such creatures Soyinka is now fully prepared to assume the role of Orpheus, the figure who has now displaced Prometheus as his idea of a culture hero. Soyinka shows this new direction to the reader during the account of his nostalgic memory of Cocteau's *Orphée Negre* [sic] which precedes the birth of a child in the prison. The prison becomes "their nether world," and the crying baby is therefore a "full-throated freak." (p. 198) He names her Persephone. But the child has been incorrectly identified. If the child is a freak born in the wrong season, she cannot be Persephone (who, in the winter months, is Queen of the Underworld) unless there is a conflation of the two figures here. She can only be Eurydice. The renaming is done in *Season of Anomy* where the heroine, Irìyísé (litterally "dew on the feet") is abducted and kept in a prison (described in *The Man Died* as "their nether world"). The hero, Ofeyi (literally either "he loves this one" or more probably "this love") searches for his lost Irìyísé, passing through a wasteland, a territory governed by Anubis, the jackal-headed one who brings "the plague of rabid dogs" (p. 159), then through "the formal doorway to the territory of hell." (p. 192) Ofeyi's descent into the mortuary begins on a hopeful note because Soyinka conflates the myths of the Nativity and the *Katabasis* (a technique he attempted with the less success in *The Man Died*, p. 198): "There is no more room in the mortuary." (p. 220) It is certain that Irìyísé would not be found in this mortuary, but "the ritual had to be undergone.' (p. 226) So Ofeyi moves with his companions through the hall of death while their "living bodies felt clammy hands about them sucking their vitality into a universal deathness." (p. 222)

It will be seen from this summary of plot that the outlines of the Orpheus myth are strongly pronounced in *Season of Anomy*, and that Soyinka abondons the veiled allusiveness of *The Interpreters* for an explicitness which ensures that no reader will miss the deliberate focus on the social significance of the myth. There is not much use in retelling a well-known story that is readily available elsewhere if the teller cannot add some new meaning or introduce a new manner in the telling of it. Soyinka offers us both in *Season of Anomy*.

The most important deviation from the usual versions of the myth is the vindication of Ofeyi's conviction that Irìyísé could not be in the morgue. Soyinka's interpretation does not differ much from the others. Irìyísé like the dying goddesses before her, and especially like Persephone, is the spirit of spring whose departure marks the descent of winter on the landscape. The induction ceremony of the first chapter marks her out as the goddess of earth, therefore she cannot now be among the dead: "her living essence could not be summed up in one of these wax parodies of the human condition." (p. 226) At this stage Soyinka has stepped beyond the usual meaning of the myth to place his antiscientific definition of man before us. The passage in which he achieves this comes just before Ofeyi's "eternal alarm at human recognition." As poet, Ofeyi is only a popularizer and

merely witty. But he is intense enough to elicit some of the book's finest writing
from Soyinka as he stands in the mortuary scene before essential organs of human
life laid out in a glass chamber. The effectiveness of the passage comes from the
functioning of the images. Factual description, compassion, the tragedy of
thwarted human aspiration and the futility of monuments are caught in a single set
of images:

> The brain was a fallen meteor: craters, ridges, a network of irrigation channels
> formed a microcosm of the world from which it had fallen. A heart sat in glazed
> aloneness on the top of a glass case, a funerary ornament above a body lying
> piecemeal, not in state. (p. 223)

To match such writing in *The Man Died* we have to turn to the imaginatively
evoked primeval world of reptiles in the counterpointed twin chapters, XXXVI
and XXXVII, in which the comic world of lizards is placed against the heroic
world of geckos. The physical beauty of the reptile's world is a thin veil drawn
across the essential violence of the landscape, and the comedy of the lizard
chapter is a very thin mask over Soyinka's disapproval of lizards. Lizards
"copulate incessantly," cannot keep their minds on the immediate business at
hand, are "undignified in hunt, lacking even the failed majesty of the pirate." On
the other hand, the more aggressive gecko is presented as a more fascinating
creature. Its eyes are "massive Ancient Mariner eyes. One by one the flies come
to him unresisting." Since the lizard and the gecko are half-brothers, what is there
about the lizard, one may ask, that Soyinka finds so contemptable? What is that
"ancestral trauma" needing to be "exorcised some day at some great lizard
meet"? The only answer offered is that the lizard "constantly nods his head" in
that harsh landscape. To Soyinka the nay-sayer, this is the antithesis of
manhood—the man has died in the lizard world, and this robs the male lizard of
"a place among the higher predators." (pp. 265-67 *passim)* In other word's,
Soyinka constantly emphasizes the importance of the aggressive instinct in the
everyday world. This theme has a long history in Soyinka and is not reducible to a
clear-cut conflict between violent methods and peaceful ones. It began when
Soyinka first became the protégé of Ogún, who is both warrior and artist. Since
then the pen and the sword have often been placed in trembling balance rather
than in direct opposition—the warrior in Soyinka is not always a villain, but shares
honors with the artist: Mulieru with Demoke in *A Dance of the Forests,* Fajuyi
with Okigbo in the poems. What is stressed, therefore, is not violence *per se,* but
the toughness required to cope with an uncongenial environment. In *Kongi's
Harvest* Segi, who dissuades her lover from his vengeful path by urging him to
preach life ("only life is worth preaching, my prince"), is contradicted by the
realism of a situation in which the political conflict outlasts the formal limits of the
play.

Soyinka revives the tension between the claims of counter-violence and peaceful
resistance in the prison diary and the second novel. *The Man Died* reveals how
Soyinka personally experienced the dilemma: the suffering spirit who claims he has
learnt to starve his violence into calm too quickly turns into a malevolent *anjonnu*
straining at the leash of patience as he emerges from the man-made "pit of
anguish." Soyinka seeks a less ambiguous resolution in *Season of Anomy* by
presenting the problem in the more clearly polarized form of two angels fighting

for Ofeyi's soul. Ofeyi's relative quiescence in the midst of all the violence in this work is apparently influenced by a dream which brings him the realization that to meet violence with violence is to trade one's humanity for the bestiality of the aggressor. Attacked by jackals in the dream, Ofeyi involuntarily turns jackal to save himself. This nightmare makes him learn the secret of mob violence: "even innocents donned a mask of the jackal to ensure safety from the hunting pack." (p. 160) Throughout the novel the dentist treats Ofeyi as a naive person for putting off the mask of the jackal. But even the man of violence admits at one point that the naive and simple man may be ennobled by a single heroic effort, like the arduous trek which Ofeyi undertakes for the love of Irìyísé. The actual historical parallels of the trek are inferior to its archetypal significance as an elixir which writers like Faulkner have found useful for injecting into the rustic veins of their simple characters.

It should be conceded that Ofeyi gets caught up in the general preparation for confrontation at the end of the novel—he goes with the Dentist, the man of violence, and parts with that woman of peace, Taiila. But it is also important to remember that he does not sell out to the dentist. He remains "naive" and even takes his role as Orpheus so seriously that he attempts to charm the warder Suberu—who is the watchdog Cerberus—by mere incantation. But although Suberu's face "retained the same mask of blankness" after the verbal persuasion, the attempt actually succeeds. It is made to work because it is partly flattery and partly the self-mockery of an artist reciting his credo before a potential convert. Ofeyi tries to show Suberu, that "dark horse of images," that the artist is more than equal to the warrior: "You grasp a situation of chaos and—bang bang—you impose your order on it. Rather like those men of uniform who thereby claim to control other lives in perpetuity." (p. 315) In spite of the Dentist's cynicism, therefore, Ofeyi's magic words penetrate the mind of Suberu, so that the two men do not need the strength of a Heracles to drag Suberu with them out of Temoko.

At various points in *Season of Anomy* social problems blend with spiritual meanings, and allegory with symbolism. Irìyísé is made to represent the claims of life. She is the silent arbiter in the struggle for Ofeyi's allegiance carried on by his two "angels," the Dentist, an extractor and agent of violence, and Taiila, an exotic character with other-worldly ideals whose name, I am told, is Sanskrit for oil. Just as the Dentist is concerned with healing by extraction to prevent the spread of infection, so Taiila stands for the soothing power of restorative oil. What she suggests is much more than I can hope to discuss here, but it is not all spiritual. A touch of the mundane occurs in the scene where Ofeyi, exactly like Egbo before him, launches out in a boat to make his choice. Like Osa in *The Interpreters,* this pool "stank of history. Slaves, gold, oil." In one historical vision that reaches back to the slave past, oil is endowed with ambivalent associations: Ofeyi remembers that "the oil trade flowed into a smell of death, disruption and desolation, flowed in turn into tankers for the new oil." But he can also think of "rotted earth-flesh reborn into life-giving oil." (pp. 90-91)

The "rotted earth-flesh" here is the industrial equivalent of the buried corn of mythology which provides the titles of the five sections of the novel; Soyinka is working his country's economic history into his story through the motif of rebirth. It is the importance of this motif as a structuring device which causes Soyinka to make another adaptation of the Orpheus myth by extending Ofeyi's quest beyond the halls of death and into the prison yard. Irìyísé is now discovered in the yard of lunatics beyond the cell of lepers. This extension adds social allegory to the symbolism already implicit in the myth. An allegorical intention has earlier been hinted at in the punning first sentence which suggests contradictory ideas of social order and good government: "A quaint anomaly, had long governed and policed itself, was so singly-knit that it obtained a tax assessment for the whole populace . . . " (p. 2) The social paradox suggested by the opposition between "anomaly" and "governed and policed itself," locates the areas of order and of anomie for the reader. Throughout the book the novelist suggests, through his manipulation of language, that words can give an accurate indication of social health. The Custodian of the Grain insists that his pastoral community Aiyéró (which stands in opposition to the wise, fallen world of Aiyetomo),[16] should be pronounced as Aiyéró, not Aiyéro (i.e. "the world is upright" not "the world is bitter"): "If you find the world bitter don't foist your despair on us. *Aiye ti wa ró...* It works, it is upright and balanced because we have made it so." The old man rejects Ofeyi's quarrel with the fuss about "a little tonal deflection":

> it tells a lot you see. It isn't only that you change the meaning to what it isn't, to the opposite of what it is, but it tells a lot of your state of mind. You've been defeated by life and it shows in your tone.(p. 8)

The figures of lepers and lunatics in the last chapter perform a similar function as language in the first sentence. They are created as the symptoms of the state of social health. The prison yard lepers, "viperous and chastened, predatory and hunted" (p. 295) and fighting over pieces of meat, alienate Ofeyi on his way to recovering Irìyísé . Next come the lunatics, parodying justice. One sat "with a blanket round his shoulders and a headgeur, clearly improvised to resemble a turban or wig." Another "held his audience in rapt attention, full of urbane gestures and flourishes." (p. 311) The allegorical hints thrown out by these human figures can be approached only obliquely, not pinned to specific issues.

Referring to the more explicit references and allusions in *The Man Died*, a reviewer criticized Soyinka for his heavy reliance on non-African thinkers.[17] With reference to *Season of Anomy*, may our writers borrow myths from "white" cultures? It is true that the use to which Soyinka puts the Orpheus myth shows his alienation. But the problem takes us back to early attempts to reduce all world cultures to mere variations of Greek and Roman culture. And Frobenius found Prester John at Ife; Nadel discovered another Byzantium in Bida; Fraz er's dying god also died in Benin; and Robert Graves can locate Yoruba evidence that the lost Atlantis is no myth. Africans too have collaborated by tracing cultural sources to Egypt and the Middle East, using similarities of names and structural features as proofs of cultural diffusion and even racial descent.[18]

Perhaps *Season of Anomy* provides one answer to the problem. Soyinka's method distinguishes the vital revival of Orpheus and Eurydice from the merely inert transplant of St. George who "sat symbolical on his leaden steed." (p. 45) It is a moral distinction too, exposing the merely pretentious, the "Florentine moment in the heart of a festering continent." (p. 44) And he shows through word play that a myth can be made indigenous by the right manipulation of language, form and social experience. Ofeyi and Irìyísé are meaningful names in Yoruba. They may be unusual, but they are not improbable names. And yet they sound like Yoruba descendants of Greek Orpheus and Eurydice.

Notes

[1] Sartre's introduction to Senghor's *Anthologie de la nouvelle poésie nègre et malgache de langue française* (Paris, 1948), is available in an English translation by S. W. Allen, entitled *Black Orpheus* (Paris, 1963). Quotations and page numbers refer to the translation.

[2] The novel *Ogboju Ode Ninu Igbo Irunmale,* was first published in 1938.

[3] Wole Soyinka, "And After the Narcissist?" *African Forum,* 1, 4 (1966), p. 56.

[4] See, for example, Janheinz Jahn, *A History of Neo-African Literature,* (London, 1968), pp. 265-66.

[5] Wole Soyinka and D. O. Fagunwa, *Forest of a Thousand Daemons,* (London, 1968), p. 119.

[6] The myth sometimes includes the following incidents: Ogún quarrels with his peers and goes into seclusion: Atowódá the slave rolls a stone on his master, shattering the original godhead into 1001 deities; the aetiological motif of the tortoise shell pieced around divine breath and used as the vessel for creating matter out of the void.

[7] In the Tutuola chapter of *Seven African Writers* (London, 1962), Gerald Moore describes the first part of Tutuola's tales as dealing with Initiation.

[8] Mark Kinkead-Weekes, *"The Interpreters*—A Form of Criticism." See elsewhere in this collection (Abiola Irele, ed). All quotations from *The Interpreters* are taken from the 1965 edition published in London.

[9] Hunters have their own poetic genre in *Ijálá* and are expected to know a lot of incantations (ófò). The hunter is thus not only explorer, provider of meat and defender of the town, he is often also drummer, poet and teller of fantastic adventure tales.

[10] For example, Pierre Verger, "Tranquillizers and Stimulants in Yoruba Herbal Treatment," in *The Traditional Background to Medical Practice in Nigeria* (Ibadan, 1971), pp. 50-55.

[11] *Season of Anomy* (London, 1973). All quotations are from this edition.

[12] *Idanre and Other Poems* (London, 1967). All quotations are from this edition.

[13] *The Man Died* (London, 1972). All quotations are from this edition.

[14] "Tó tóo" means "Hail!"

[15] *Shuttle in the Crypt* (London, 1972), p. 59.

[16] Aiyero is also the fictitious setting of a Yoruba novel *Kékeré Ekún,* by A. Olabimtan (Lagos, 1967). Compare Soyinka's opening sentence in *Season of Anomy* with a Nigerian journalist's description of the Yoruba commune of Aiyétòró (the word means "our world is as peaceful and undisturbed as springwater"), the real town from which the fictional town derived its name:

> There is a community town in the Western State [of Nigeria] that goes by the name Aiyetoro which has a [long] tradition of isolation . . Apart from the tax which the community pays to the Western State Government they have nothing to do with the outside world. For example, every financial year the community counts all the adults who are eligible to pay tax and the bulk sum is paid to tax authorities at the other end, no policeman, no law enforcing agencies at Aiyetoro. (Candido, "Nigeria's Weird and Mythical 'Republics,' " *New Nigeria,* 4 December 1974, 5.

[17] Adamu Ciroma in the *New Nigerian,* 5 April 1973, p. 2.

[18] For example, J. Olumide Lucas, *The Religion of the Yorubas* (Lagos, 1948) and, more recently, Modupe Oduyoye, *The Vocabulary of Yoruba Religious Discourse* (Ibadan, 1971), and Kemi Morgan, *The Myth of Yoruba Ancestry,* (Ibadan, 1974?).

Wole Soyinka: A Selected Bibliography

Primary Sources
- A. Poetry
- B. Plays
- C. Novels
- D. Actualities
- E. Translations
- F. Short Stories
- G. Essays
- H. Interviews
- I. Editorial Responsibilities

Secondary Sources
- Biographical Studies
- Reviews of Publications
- Reviews of Productions
- Literary Criticism

Primary Sources

A. Poetry

(a) Collections

Idanre and Other Poems. London: Methuen, 1967; New York: Hill and Wang, 1968.

Poems from Prison. London: Rex Collings, 1969.

A Shuttle in the Crypt. London: Collings/Eyre Methuen, 1971; New York: Hill and Wang. 1972; New York: Farrar, Straus and Giroux, 1972.

Ogun Abibiman. London: Rex Collings, 1976.

(b) Outside Collections. I have listed only poems, or selections which include poems, which are not in Soyinka's collections listed above. I have omitted "Telephone Conversation" which has been authologized at least 13 times and is easily available.

"An African Proverb"; "Conversational Fragment"; "Telephone Conversation"; "The Artist and the Clochard"; "Queue"; "My Next Door Neighbour"; "Audience to Author"; "To a Lady who Meant Well"; "Epitaph"; "Poisoners of the World Unite"; "Nursery Tail-piece"; "Castration Blues"; "The Blacksmith's Song"; "The Myths"; "Stage"; "Deserted Markets"; "Half Caste"; "Kenny's Blues"; "Alagemo." Program presented at the Royal Court, November 1959. Mimeographed, available at the Royal Court.

"Abiku"; "Death in the Dawn;" "Requiem;" *West African Verse*. Ed. Donatus Ibe Nwoga. London: Longman, 1967, pp. 62-67. Also published Atlantic Heights, New Jersey: Humanities, 1967.

"Abiku"; "The Immigrant"; *You'd Better Believe It: Black Verse in English*. Ed. Paul Breman, Harmondsworth: Penguin, 1973, pp. 316-17.

"Archetype," *New York Times*, 8 June 1969.

"Apollodorus on the Niger," *Ibadan*, 30 (July 1975), 37.

"Audience to Performer," *Horn* (Ibadan), 4, 1(1960), 4.

"The Dancer," *Nigeria Magazine,* Independence Issue (October 1960), 222.

"Emergency Sketches," satirical verses, appeared in the Nigerian Press during 1962.

"Committee Man," *Horn* (Ibadan), 4, 3(1961), 10-11.

"Epitaph for Say Tokyo Kid," *Horn* (Ibadan), 4, 5(1962), 10-11.

"For Now the Sun Moves"; "Lament for the Rains"; "Oriki Emu"; "Praise of Palm Wine"; "Egun"/"Maledictions"; "Alimotu Adengbe"/"Alimotu of the Golden Gourd," *Proceedings of the First Rite of the Harmattan Solstice.* Mimegraphed, Lagos: 1966. (Source: Eldred D. Jones.)

"For Three Children," *Ibadan,* 12 (June 1961), 28.

"The Gallant's Prayer," *The Eagle* (University of Ibadan), 3, 3(13 April 1954), 6. (See B. Lindfors, "Popular Literature for an African Elite.")

"General Franco's Condition," *Transition/Ch'Indaba* (Accra), 50/1 (December 1975), 9.

"The Ghoul Flushed"; "The Meetings is Called . . ."; "Sixteen Places"; *Anvil* (Ibadan), 1, 1(21 February - 6 March 1970), 3.

"Immigrant Poems," *Negro Verse,* Ed. Anselm Hollo, London: Vista Books, 1964.

"Insulation," *Ibadan,* 5(February 1959), 24.

"Poisoners of the World Unite," "Proverb: Okonjo de Hunter," *Horn* (Ibadan), 3, 3(1960), 4-7 and 9.

"Requiem," *African Writing To-Day.* Ed. Ezekiel Mphahlele, Harmondsworth: Penguin, 1967, pp. 43-45.

"Stage," *Horn* (Ibadan), 4, 1(1960), 1.

"Telephone Conversation"; "Death in the Dawn"; "Requiem"; "Prisoner"; "I Think it Rains"; "Season"; "Night"; "Abiku"; *Modern Poetry from Africa.* Ed. Gerald Moore and Ulli Beier. Harmondsworth: Penguin, 1963, pp. 111-19.

"Three Poems"; "The Immigrant"; "The Other Immigrant"; "My Next Door Neighbour;" *Black Orpheus,* 5 (May 1959), 9-11.

"Thunder to Storm," *The University Voice* (Ibadan), 2 (January 1953),   21. (See: B. Lindfors, "The Early Writings of Wole Soyinka.")

"Two in London"; "The Immigrant"; "The Other Immigrant"; *An African Treasury.* Ed. Langston Hughes, New York: Pyramid Books, 1960, and London: Gollancz, 1961, pp. 194-99.

B. *Plays*

(a) *Major Collections in Print*

Collected Plays I: A Dance of the Forests: The Swamp Dwellers; The Strong Breed; The Road; The Bacchae of Euripides. London: Oxford University Press, 1973.

Collected Plays II: The Lion and the Jewel; Kongi's Harvest; The Trials of Brother Jero; Jero's Metamorphosis; Madmen and Specialists. London: Oxford University Press, 1974.

(b) *Other published plays, radio plays and revue sketches*
Before the Blackout. Ibadan: Orisun Acting Editions, n.d. (Note "Wole Soyinka with Orisun Theatre.")

Before the Blackout ànd *Camwood on the Leaves.* New York: Third Press, 1974.

Camwood on the Leaves. London: Methuen Playscripts, 1974.

Death and the King's Horseman. London: Eyre Methuen, 1975; New York: Norton, 1976.

The Detainee. BBC, Mimeographed, 1965. *

The Invention. Royal Court, Mimeographed, 1959. *

The House of Banigeji, Act 2 in *Reflections.* Ed. Frances Ademola. Lagos: African Universities Press, 1962, pp. 88-93. "Blacksmith's Song" from the play which was in the Royal Court Programme, 1959.

* These are not exactly "published," but they are accessible at Bush House and the Royal Court respectively.

C. *Novels*

The Interpreters. London: Andre Deutsch, 1965; London: Heinemann and Deutsch, 1970; New York: Collier, 1970; London: Holmes and Meier, 1972; London: Fontana, 1973.

Season of Anomy. London: Rex Collings, 1973; New York: Third Press, 1974.

D. *Actualities*

The Man Died. London: Rex Collings, 1972: New York: Harper Row 1973; Harmondsworth: Penguin, 1976,

E. *Translations*

The Forest of a Thousand Daemons. London: Nelson, 1968; Atlantic Heights, New Jersey: Humanities, 1969. (A translation of *Ogboju Ode Ninu Igbo Irunmale* by D. O. Fagunwa.)

F. *Short Stories*

"Egbe's Sworn Enemy," *Geste* (University of Leeds) 5, 8(21 April 1960), 22-26. (See B. Lindfors: "Egbe's Sworn Enemy - Soyinka's Popular Sport.")

"Keffi's Birthday Treat," *Nigerian Radio Times* (Lagos), July 1954, 15-16.   (See B. Lindfors: "The Early Writings of Wole Soyinka.")

"Madame Etienne's Establishment," *Gryphon*   (University of Leeds),   March 1957, 11-22.

"A Tale of Two Cities," *Gryphon* (University of Leeds), Autumn 1957, pp. 16-22.

"A Tale of Two   *New Nigerian Forum* (London), 2 (May 1958), pp. 26-30.

G. *Essays, Articles, Published Papers, etc.*

(a) Collection

Myth, Literature and the African World. London: Cambridge University Press, 1976.

(b) Outside Collections

"Aesthetic Illusions:Prescriptions for the Suicide of Poetry," *Third Press Review* (New York), 1, 1(1975), 30-31, 65-68. (See "Neo-Tanzanism" below.)

"African Personality," *Radio Times* (Lagos), 22 January 1961, 6-7.

"African Writers - A New Union," *Africa Currents* (London), 2 (Summer 1975), 19-22.

"Amos Tutuola on Stage," *Ibadan*, 16(June 1963), 23-24.

"And After the Narcissist," *African Forum*, 1, 4(Spring 1966), 53-64.

Autobiographical Statement. *World Authors 1950-1970: A Companion Volume to Twentieth Century Authors* Ed. John Wakeman. New York: H. H. Wilson Co., 1975, pp. 1356-57.

"A Change of Heart is Needed for People Who Make Films Like This," *Drum* (Lagos), August 1961, 36-37.

"The Choice and Use of Language," *Cultural Events in Africa*, 75 (1971), 3-6.

"Cor Teach," *Ibadan*, 7 (November 1959), 26-27.

"Declaration of African Writers, January 1975," *Issue* (Brandeis), 4, 4(Winter 1974), 8; *Research in African Literatures*, 6(Spring 1975), 58-59. (Signed by Soyinka and Dennis Brutus.)

"Drama and the Revolutionary Ideal," *In Person: Achebe, Awoonor and Soyinka.* Ed. Karen L. Morell. Seattle, Washington: Inst. for Comparative Foreign Area Studies, 1975, pp. 61-88.

"The Fourth Stage: Through the Mysteries of Ogun to the Origin of Yoruba Tragedy," *The Morality of Art.* Ed. D. W. Jefferson. London: Routledge and Kegan Paul, 1969, pp. 119-34. (Also the Appendix to *Myth, Literature and the African World,* above.)

"From a Common Back Cloth: A Reassessment of the African Literary Image," *American Scholar*, 32, (1963), 387-97. Also in *AMSAC Newsletter* (New York), 6, 6(February 1964), 4-6.

"The Future of African Writing," *The Horn* (Ibadan), 4, 1(June 1960), 10-16.

"Gbohun-Gbohun - The Nigerian Playwright Wole Soyinka on his Dealings with the BBC," *The Listener* (London), 2 November 1972, pp. 581-83.

"Guiné-Bissau: An African Revolution," *Transition* (Accra), 45 (1974), 9-11.

"Let's Think Again About the Aftermath of This War," *Nigerian Daily Sketch* (Lagos), 4 August 1967, 8.

"A Maverick in America," *Ibadan*, 22 (1966), 59-61. (Review of *America, Their America* by J. P. Clark.)

"Neo-Tarzanism: The Poetics of Pseudo-Tradition." *Transition* (Accra), 48 (1975), 38-44.

"The Nigerian Stage: A Study in Tyranny, and Individual Survival," *Colloquium on Negro Art.* Paris: Presence Africaine, 1968, pp.538-49. (Or 1966, pp. 495-504.)

"Nigeria's International Film Festival," *Nigeria Magazine,* 79 (1963), 307-10.

"Of Power and Change," *African Statesman* (Lagos), 1, 3(July-September 1966), 17-19.

"Oga Look Properly," *Radio Times* (Lagos), 18 September 1960, 7.

"The Old Boys' Dinner," *Radio Times* (Lagos), 11 September 1960, 7.

"On this Adaptation." Programme Note for the National Theatre, London, production of *The Bacchae of Euripides.*

"Paris: Wole Soyinka," *Radio Times* (Lagos), 6 November 1960.

"Salutations to the Gut," *Reflections.* Ed. Frances Ademola. Lagos: African Universities Press, 1962, pp.109-15. Also in *Africa in Prose.* Ed. O. R. Dathorne and Willfried Feuser. Harmondsworth: Penguin, 1969, pp.355-64.

"Theatre in Nigeria." *Cultural Events in Africa,* 5(1965), i.

"Towards a True Theatre," *Nigeria Magazine,* 75 (December 1962), 58-60. Also in *Transition/Chi'Indaba* (Accra), 50/1 (December 1975), 63-64.

"The Writer in a Modern African State," *The Writer in Modern Africa.* Ed. Per Wästberg. Uppsala: The Scandinavian Institute of African Studies; New York: Africana, 1968; pp.14-21. Also in *L'Afrique Actuelle* (Paris), 19 (June 1967), pp.5-7; *Transition* (Accra), 31 (June-July 1967), 11-13; *The African Reader.* Ed. Wilfred Cartey and Martin Kilson. New York: Vintage, 1970, pp.135-42, with the title and opening altered; *Atlas* (New York), 15 (January 1968), pp.36-39, (also altered slightly.)

H. Interviews

Agetua, John, Ed. *Interviews with Six Nigerian Writers.* Benin City: Bendel Newspaper Corporation, 1973.
—————. *When the Man Died.* Benin City: John Agetua, 1975, pp.31-46.

Akarogun, Alan. "Wole Soyinka," *Spear Magazine* (Lagos), May 1966, 16-19 and 42.

Assensoh. "Interview with Prof. Wole Soyinka," *Afriscope* (Lagos), 6, 7 (July 1976), 39-40. Also in *Africa Currents* (London), 7 (Autumn 1976 - Winter 1977), 26-29.

Duerden, Dennis and Cosmo Pieterse, eds. *African Writers Talking.* London: Heinemann, pp.169-80; New York: Africana, 1972.

Gates, Louis. "An Interview with Wole Soyinka," *Black World,* 24, 10 (1975), 30-48.

"History and African Conscience," *Africa* (London), 58 (June 1976), 109-10.

Jeyifous, Biodun. "A *Transition* Interview," *Transition* (Accra), 42 (1973), 62-64.

"Militant Interview," *The Militant* (University of Ibadan), 2, 1(December 1972), 3-7.

"Televised Discussion," "Penthouse Theatre," "Class Discussion," *In Person: Achebe, Awoonor and Soyinka.* Ed. Karen L. Morell, Seattle, Washington: Inst. of Comparative and Foreign Area Studies, 1975, pp. 89-130.

Wilmer, Valerie. "Wole Soyinka Talks to *Flamingo,*" *Flamingo* (London), March 1966, 14, 15 and 17.

1. Editorial Responsibilities in chronological order

Editor, *The Eagle* (University College, Ibadan) 3, 2 and 3, 3(1953-54).

Co-Editor, with Mphahlele and Beier, *BO,* 7-13 (1960-63).

Editorial Committee, *Okike* (Enugu, Nigeria), April 1971 until, at least, December 1971, with Achebe *et al.*

Editor, *Transition* (Accra), 45-50 and, its successor, *Ch 'Indaba,* 1 *et. seq.*

Editor, *Poems of Black Africa,* London: Secker and Warburg, 1975: New York: Hill and Wang, 1975.

Biographical Studies

Anon. "National Dramatist," *West Africa,* 19 December 1964, p.1417.

Anon. "Our Authors and Performing Artists - 1," *Nigeria Magazine,* 88 (March 1966), 57-64.

Gibbs, James. "Bio-Bibliography: Wole Soyinka," *Africana Library Journal,* 3, (1972), 15-22.

_____   "Date-line on Soyinka," *New Theatre Magazine,* 12, 2 **(1972), 12-14.**

Herdeck, Donald. *African Authors: A Companion to Black African Writing, Volume I: 1300-1973.* Washington, D.C.: Black Orpheus Press, 1973.

Idapo, Coz. "The Ways of a Rebel," *Drum,* July 1963, 36-37.

Jahn, Janheinz, Ulla Schild and Almut Nordmann, *Who's Who in African Literature: Biographies, Works, Commentaries.* Tubingen: Horst Erdmann, 1972.

Jones, Eldred. *Contemporary Poets.* Ed. Rosalie Murphy, London: St. James Press; New York: St. Martin's, 1970, pp.1032-34.

Thompson, P. "Soyinka," *The Penguin Companion to Literature IV.* Ed. D. R. Dudley and D. M. Young, Baltimore: Penguin, 1969.

Wakeman, John, ed., *World Authors 1950-1970: A Companion volume to Twentieth Century Authors,* New York: H. H. Wilson Co., 1975, pp.1356-58.

Zell, Hans M. and Helene Silver, eds. *A Reader's Guide to African Literature,* London: Heinemenn, 1972; New York: Africana, 1971.

Reviews of Soyinka's Publications

A Dance of the Forests, 1963

Beier, Ulli. *Black Orpheus,* 8 (1960), 57-58.

Watson, Ian. *Transition,* 27 (1966), 24-26.

Five Plays, 1963

Esslin, Martin, *Black Orpheus,* 19 (March 1966), 33-39. Also *Introduction to African Literature.* Ed. Ulli Beier, London: Longman and Evanston: Northwestern, 1967.

Jones, D.A.N. *New Statesman* (London), 29 January 1965, p.164.

Wright, Edgar. *East Africa Journal,* 2, 7 (November 1965), 35-38.

Yankowitz, Susan. *African Forum,* 1, 4 (Spring 1966), 129-33.

The Interpreters, 1965

Aniebo, I.N.C. *Nigeria Magazine,* 86 (1965), 218-21.

Jones, Eldred. *Bulletin for the Association of African Literature in English* (Fourah Bay), 4 (1966), 13-18.

King, Bruce, *Black Orpheus,* 19 (March 1966), 55.

Moore, Gerald, *New African,* 4, 7 (September 1965), 156.

Thompson, John. *African Forum* (New York) 1, 2 (Fall 1965), 108-09.

'Idanre' and Other Poems, 1967

Aidoo, Ama Ata. *West Africa,* 13 January 1968, 40-41.

Anon., *Times* (London), 18 November 1967, 22e.

Ayagere, Solomon. *Nigeria Magazine, 96 (March-May 1968), 52.*

Kongi's Harvest, 1967

Arden, John. *New Theatre Magazine,* 12, 2 (1972), 25-26.

Banham, Martin. *Books Abroad,* 42, 1 (1968), 170.

Larson, Charles. *Africa Report,* 13, 5 (May 1968), 55-57.

The Forest of a Thousand Daemons, 1968

Afolayan, Adebisi. *Journal of Nigerian English Studies Association* (Ibadan), 3, 1 (1969), 133-39.

The Man Died, 1972

Calder, Angus. *New Stateman* (London), 8 December 1972, 866.
Ciroma, Adamu. *New Nigerian* (Kaduna), 5 April 1973, 2.

Crewe, A. R. *Africa,* 20 (April 1973), 64 and 66.

Enahoro, Peter. *Africa,* 17 (January 1973), 42-43.

Larson, Charles. *The Nation* (New York), 5 November 1973, 472.

O'Brien, Conor Cruise. *World* 13 February 1973, 46,48.

Povey, John F. *Conch Review of Books,* 2, 1-2 (March-June 1971), 152-56.

A Shuttle in the Crypt, 1972

Jones, Eldred Durosimi. *African Literature Today,* 6 (1973), 174-75.

Priebe, Richard. *Books Abroad,* 47 (1973), 407.

Madmen and Specialists, 1973

        Banham, Martin. *Journal of Commonwealth Literature,* 8, 1(June 1973), 124-26.

        Calder, Angus. *New Statesman,* (London), 28 April 1972, 564-65.

Season of Anomy, 1974

        Ackroyd, Peter. *The Spectator,*(London), 15 December 1973, 787.

        Anon, *Times Literary Supplement,* **14 December 1973, 1529.**

        Davis, Russell. *The Observer,* **9 December 1973, 36.**

        Larson, Charles, *Books Abroad,* 48 (1974), 522.

        Schmidt, Nancy J. *Conch Review of Books,* 3, 1 (1975), 269-71.

        Shrapnel, Norman. *The Guardian* **(London), 5 January 1974, 25.**

        Tarrow-Mordi, Dita. *Africa, International Business Economics and Political Monthly,* 32 (April 1974), 62-63

        Wright, Edgar. *African Literature Today,* 8 (1976), 115-120

The Bacchae of Euripides, 1974

        Kerr, Susan. *Books Abroad,* 49, (1975), 175-76

        Masters, Anthony. *Times Educational Supplement,* 9 August 1974.

The Jero Plays, 1974

        Anon.*Times Literary Supplement,* 8 February 1974.

Reviews of Productions of Soyinka's Plays

The Lion and The Jewel and *The Swamp Dwellers* produced by Geoffrey Axworthy and Ken Post, Ibadan, Feb 1959.

        Maclean, Una, Molly Mahood and Phebean Ogundipe. "Three Views of *The Swamp Dwellers," Ibadan,* 6 (June 1959), 27-30

An Evening of Poetry, Songs and Drama by Soyinka, at the Royal Court, November 1959.

        Brien, Alan. "Where Spades are Trumps,"*The Spectator,* (London), 203 (6 November 1959), 629-30.

The Trials of Brother Jero produced at Ibadan.

        Banham, Martin and Abiola Irele. "The Wandering Plays," *The Horn* (Ibadan), 4, 1 (1960), 17-22.

A Dance of the Forests produced by Soyinka at Ibadan, October 1960

        Bare. "Forests," *African Horizon* (Zaria), 2 (January 1961), 8-11.

        Cockshutt, Una. *Ibadan,* 10 (November 1960), 30-32.

Before the Blackout, produced by Soyinka at Lagos and Ibadan, March 1965.

        McDermott, John. *The Sunday Times* (Lagos), 21 March 1965.

Kongi's Harvest produced by Soyinka at Lagos, August 1975, Ibadan and, later, Dakar.

        Berry, Boyd. M. *Ibadan,* 23 (October 1966), 53-55.

Nagenda, John. *"Kongi's Harvest* in Tails," *New African,* 5, 5 (1966), 101-2.

The Road, presented by Stage Sixty at Stratford East, September 1965.

Brien, Alan. "Nigeria's Dramatised Ritual," *The Sunday Telegraph* (London), 19 September 1965.

Gilliatt, Penelope. "A Nigerian Original," *The Observer,* (London), 19 September 1965.

Pieterse, Cosmo. "Dramatic Riches," *Journal of Commonwealth Literature,* 2 (December 1966), 168-71.

Serumaga, Robert. "Reaction of the Critics to *The Road,*" *Cultural Events in Africa,* 11 (October 1965), i-ii.

The Trials of Brother Jero at the Hampstead Theatre Club, June 1966.

Anon. "Harsh Comedy on a Lagos Beach," *The Times* (London), 29 June 1966, 7d.

Bryden, Ronald. "The Voice of Africa," *The Observer,* (London), 3 June 1966.

Jones, D.A.N. "Soyinka," *New Statesman* (London), 8 July 1966, 63-66.

The Lion and the Jewel at the Royal Court, London, December 1966.

Anon. *The Lion and the Jewel. Cultural Events in Africa,* 25 (December 1966), 2-3. (Summary of reviews.)

Anon. "Sheer Ingenuity of Soyinka's Plot," *The Times* (London), 13 December 1966, 6.

Bryden, Ronald. *The Observer* (London), 18 December 1966, 20.

Peter, Lewis. "As the Bard himself might have put it," *The Daily Mail* (London), 13 December 1966.

The Lion and the Jewel produced by G.A. Wilson and A.M. Opoku, Accra, September 1967, revived 1968.

Senanu, K.E. "Thoughts on Creating the Popular Theatre 1 and 2," *Legon Observer* (Legon), 2, 21 (29 September 1967), 25-27; 22 (13 October 1967), 22-23.

The Strong Breed and *The Trials of Brother Jero* presented at the Greenwich Mews Theatre, New York, November 1967.

Anon. "Infectious Humanity," *Times* (New York), 17 November 1967, 48 and 50.

Clurman, Harold. *The Nation* (New York), 4 December 1967, 606.

Smith, Michael. *The Village Voice* (New York), 23 November 1967.

Kongi's Harvest presented by the Negro Ensemble Company at St. Mark's New York, April 1968.

Clurman, Harold. *The Nation* (New York), 26 April 1968, 581.

Kerr, Walter. "Tantalizing But Blurred," *New York Times,* 21 April 1968, II, 5: 3.

Oliver, Edith. "The Play at St. Mark's," *The New Yorker* (New York), 27 April 1968, 86, and 91.

Kongi's Harvest, Second Nigerian production by Soyinka at Ife, 1969.

Dedenuola, Jibola. "Soyinka Rocks Ibadan with *Kongi's Harvest*," *Ibadan Literary Review* (Ibadan), 1 (December 1969), 1-3.

Oke, Ole. "Tragedy Beautifully Rendered," *Nigeria Magazine*, 102 (September - November 1969), 525-27.

Kongi's Harvest produced by G.A. Wilson, Accra, April 1970.

Senanu, K.E. *Legon Observer* (Legon), 8 May 1970, 21-22.

Madmen and Specialists produced by Soyinka at New Haven, Conn., and in Harlem, August 1970.

Berry, Boyd. "On Looking at *Madmen and Specialists*," *Pan-African Journal*, 5 (1972), 461-71.

La danse de la fôret, extracts from *A Dance of the Forests* produced by Soyinka in Paris, July 1972.

Osofisan, Femi. "Soyinka in Paris," *West Africa*, 21 July 1972, 25.

The Bacchae of Euripides produced by R. Joffe at the National Theatre, London, August 1973.

Darlington, W.A. "A Case of Believe it or Not," *The Daily Telegraph* (London), 3 September 1973.

Hobson, Harold. "Agony and Ecstasy," *The Sunday Times* (London), 5 August 1973.

Hunt, Albert. "Amateurs in Horror," *New Society* (London), 9 August 1973, 342-43.

Ítzen, Catherine. *The Tribune* (London) 17 August 1973.

Shulman, Milton. "Review," *Evening Standard* (London), 3 August 1973.

Stephen Gilbert, W. "Directors Bearing Gifts," *Plays and Players* (London), September 1973, 22-25.

Wardle, Irving. "Mangled Re-Write of *The Bacchae*," *The Times* (London), 3 August 1973.

Death and the King's Horseman produced by Soyinka at Ife, December 1976.

Moore, Gerald. "Soyinka's New Play," *West Africa*, 10 January 1977, 60-61.

Opera: Wonyosi produced by Soyinka at Ife, December 1977.

Relich, Mano. "Soyinka's *Beggars' Opera*," *West Africa*, 30 January 1978, 188-89.

Literary Criticism

Adedeji, Joel A. "Oral Tradition and the Contemporary Theatre in Nigeria," *Research in African Literatures*, 2, (1971), 134-49.

Adegbiji, Segun. "The Dilemma of the Satirist," *Spear* (Lagos), July 1972, pp. 29-30.

Adelugba, Dapo. "Nigeria - Theatre Survey," *New Theatre Magazine*, 12, 2(1972), 15-16.

Adetugbo, Abiodun. "Form and Style," *Introduction to Nigerian Literature*. Ed. Bruce King. London: Longman, 1971, pp. 173-192.

Agetua, John, ed. *When The Man Died: Views, Reviews and Interviews on Soyinka's Controversial Book*. Benin City: John Agetua, 1975.

Allen, Samuel W. "Two African Writers: Soyinka and Senghor," *Negro Digest* (Chicago), June 1967, pp. 54-64.

Amankulor, James Nduke, "Dramatic Technique and Meaning in *The Road,*" *Ba Shiru* (University of Wisc.), 7, 1 (1976), 53-59.

Anozie, Sunday O. "Language and the Modern Experience of Tragedy," *Conch* (Austin, Texas), 1, 2(September 1969), 37-44.

Ansah, Paul. "The Situation in African Literature Since 1960," *Presence Africaine,* Special Number 1970, pp. 244-71.

Asalache, Khadambi. "The Making of a Poet: Wole Soyinka." *Presence Africaine,* 67(1968), 172-74.

Awoonor, Kofi. (Previously "George Awoonor Williams.") *The Breast of the Earth: A Survey of the History, Culture and Literature of Africa South of the Sahara.* New York: Anchor, 1975.

Axworthy, Geoffrey. "The Arts Theatre and the School of Drama," *Ibadan,* 18 (February 1964), 62-64.

Bamikunle, Aderemi. "What is '*As*'? Why '*As*'? A Thematic Exigesis of Wole Soyinka's *Madmen and Specialists,*" *Work in Progress* (Department of English, Ahmadu Bello University, Zaria), 2 (1973), 126-49.

Banham, Martin. "Drama in the Commonwealth: Nigeria," *New Theatre Magazine,* 1, 4 (July 1960), 18-21.

—— · "Nigerian Dramatists in English and the Traditional Nigerian Theatre," *Journal of Commonwealth Literature,* 3 (July 1967), 97-102. Also published in *Insight* (Lagos), 20 (April 1968), 29-30, and in *Readings in Commonwealth Literature,* ed. William Walsh, London: Oxford University Press, 1973, pp. 135-41.

—— · "Note on Nigerian Theatre: 1966," *Bulletin of the Association for African Literature in English* (Freetown), 4 (March 1966), 31-36.

—— · "A Piece that we may fairly call our own," *Ibadan,* 12 (January 1961), 15-18.

—— · "Playwright/Producer/Actor/Academic: Soyinka in the Nigerian Theatre," *New Theatre Magazine,* 12, 2 (1972), 10-11.

Bischofberger, Otto. *Tradition und Wandel aus der Sicht der Romanschriftsteller Kameruns und Nigerias.* Einsiedeln, Switzerland: Etzel Druck, n.d.

Bodunrin, A. "Wole Soyinka: Poet, Satirist and Political Neophyte," *African Statesman* (Lagos), 2, 3 (November 1967), 19, 21, 23 and 27.

Brambilla, C. "Wole Soyinka, l'Anti Senghor," *Nigrizia* (Verona), 86 (1969), 19-24.

Brown, Nigel, *Notes on Wole Soyinka's Kongi's Harvest* London: Heineman, 1973.

Cartey, Wilfred. *Whispers from a Continent: The Literature of Contemporary Black Africa.* New York: Random House, 1969: London. Heinemann, 1971.

Chinweizu, with Onwuchekwa Jemie and Ihechukwu Madubuike. "Towards the Decolonization of African Literature," *Okike* (Enugu/Amherst), 6 December 1974), 11-28. Also published in *Transition* (Accra), 48 (1975), 29-37, 54, 56-57.

Clark, J.P. *The Example of Shakespeare*. London: Longman, Evanston: Northwestern, 1970.

Collings, Rex. "Wole Soyinka: A Personal View," *New Statesman* (London), 76 (20 December 1968), p. 879. Also published in *African Arts*, 2, 3 (Spring 1969), 82-84.

A Correspondent. "Why Did Wole Quit?" *Afriscope* (Yaba, Nigeria), May 1972, pp. 13-15.

Cuche, F.X. "L'Utilization des techniques du théâtre traditionnel dan le théâtre negro-africain moderne," *Le Théâtre Negro-africaine*. Paris: Presence Africaine, 1971, 137-42.

Cvjeticanin, Biserka. "Soyinkin Simbolicki Svijet," ("Soyinka's Symbolic World,") *Knjiz-vena Smotra* (Zagreb), 20 (1975), 17-29.

Dameron, Charles F, Jnr. "An Assault on Tyranny: Soyinka's Recent Writings," *Africa Today*, 23, 2 (April - June 1976) 65-67.

Dathorne, O.R. "African Literature IV: Ritual and Ceremony in Okigbo's Poetry," *Journal of Commonwealth Literature*, 5 (1968), 79-91.

———.   "The Beginnings of the West African Novel," *Nigeria Magazine*, 93 (June 1967), 168-70

———.   *The Black Mind: A History of African Literature*. Minneapolis: University of Minnesota Press, 1974.

Davis, Ann. "Dramatic Theory of Wole Soyinka," *Ba Shiru* (U. of Wisc.), 7, 1 (1976), 1-12.

Duerden, Dennis. "African Sharpshooter, *New Society* (London), 8 December 1966, p. 879.

———.   "A Triumph for Wole Soyinka," *New Society* (London), 28 April 1966, pp. 21-22.

Echeruo, M.J.C. "Traditional and Borrowed Elements in Nigerian Poetry," *Nigeria Magazine*, 89 (June 1966), 142-55.

Ekom, Ernest. "The Development of Theatre in Nigeria 1960-1967," *Journal of the New African Literature and the Arts*, 11/12 (1971), 36-49.

Emenyonu, N. "Post-war Writing in Nigeria," *Issue: A Quarterly Journal of Africanist Opinion* (Brandeis U.) 3, 2 (Summer 1973), 49-54. Also in *Ufahamu* (Los Angeles), 4, 1 (1973), 77-92

Erapu, Laban. *Notes on Wole Soyinka's The Lion and the Jewel*. Nairobi: Heinemann, 1975.

Esslin, Martin. "A Major Poetic Dramatist—Wole Soyinka," *New Theatre Magazine*, 12, 2 (1972), pp. 9-10.

Ferguson, John. "Nigerian Drama in English," *Modern Drama*, 11, 1 (May 1968), 10-26.

Fiebach, J. "On the Social Function of Modern African Drama and Brecht," *Darlite* (Dar es Salaam), 4, 2 (March 1970), pp. 5-19.

Gibbs, James. "Interpreting and Interpreter," *Joliso, East African Journal of Literature and Society* (Nairobi), 1, 2 (1973), pp. 110-25.

———.   "The Origins of *A Dance of the Forests*," *African Literature Today*, 8 (1976), 66-71.

———.   "Soyinka and Ghana," *Legon Observer* (Legon), 6, 5 (19 July 1971), pp. 22 and 24.

—— ·   *Study Aid to 'Kongi's Harvest'*. London: Rex Collings, 1972.

—— ·   "Wole Soyinka and Radio," *Legon Observer* (Legon), 8, 21 (19-
1 October-November 1973), pp. 508-10.

Gleason, Judith. "Out of the Irony of Words," *Transition*, 18 (1965), pp. 34-38.

—— ·   *This Africa: Novels by Africans in English and French*. Evanston:
Northwestern University Press, 1965.

Gordimer, Nadine. *The Black Interpreters*. Johannesburg: Spro-Cas/Raven, 1973.

—— ·   "Interpreters: Some Themes and Directions in African Literature," *Kenyan Review*, 32, 1 (1971), 9-26.

Graham-White, Anthony. "African Drama, a Renaissance," *Ba Shiru* (University of Wisc.)
5, 1 (1973), pp. 78-83.

—— ·   *The Drama of Black Africa*. New York: French, 1974.

Gurr, Andrew. "Aesthetics versus Evolution: Three Points for African Criticism," *Joliso,
East African Journal of Literature and Society* (Nairobi), 1, 1 (1973), pp. 5-8.

—— ·   "Third World Drama: Soyinka and Tragedy," *Joliso*, 2, 2 (1974),
pp. 13-20. Also, in a revised form, in *JCL*, 10, 3 (April 1976), pp. 45-52.

Heywood, Annemarie. "The Fox's Dance: The Staging of Soyinka's Plays," *African Literature
Today*, 8 (1976), 42-51.

Irele, Abiola. "Tradition and the Yoruba Writer: D.O. Fagunwa, Amos Tutuola and Wole
Soyinka," *Odu*, New Series 11 (January 1975), pp. 75-100.

—— ,   and Oyin Ogunba. *Black African Theatre*. Ibadan: Ibadan
University Press, 1978.

Izevbaye, Dan. "African Literature Defined: The Record of a Controversy," *Ibadan Studies in
English*, 1, 1 (May—June 1969), 56-69.

—— ·   "Criticism and Literature in Africa," *Perspectives on African
Literature*. Ed. Christopher Heywood, New York: Africana, and London:
Heinemann, 1971.

—— ·   "Language and Meaning in *The Road*," *African Literature
Today*, 8 (1976), 52-65.

—— ·   "Politics in Nigerian Poetry," *Presence Africaine*, 78 (1971), 143-
67.

—— ·   "Soyinka's Black Orpheus," *Neo-African Literature and Culture*.
Ed. Bernth Lindfors and Ulla Schild. Wiesbaden: B. Heymann, 1976, pp. 147-58.
58.

Jabbi, Bu-Buakei. "The Form of Discovery in *Brother Jero*," *Obsidian* (Fredonia, New
York), 2, 3 (1976), 26-33.

Jahn, Janheinz. *A History of Neo-African Literature*. London: Faber, 1968.

—— ·   "Le théâtralite du théâtre nigérian modern", *Le Théâtre negro-
africain*. Paris: Presence Africaine, 1971, pp. 167-74.

Johnson, Chris. "Performance and Role-playing in Soyinka's *Madmen and Specialists*,"
Journal of Commonwealth Literature, 10, 3 (April 1976), 27-33.

Jones, Eldred Durosimi. "The Decolonization of African Literature," *The Writer in Modern Africa.* Ed. Per Wästberg, Uppsala: Scandinavian Inst. for African Studies; New York: Africana, 1968, pp. 71-78.

———.   "The Essential Soyinka," *Introduction to Nigerian Literature.* Ed. Bruce King. Lagos and London: University of Lagos and Evans, 1971, pp. 113-34; New York: Africana, 1972.

———.   "*The Interpreters,* Wole Soyinka: Reading Notes," *African Literature Today,* 2 (1969), 42-50.

———.   "Jungle Drums and Wailing Piano: West African Fiction and Poetry in English," *African Forum,* 1, 4 (1966), 93-106.

———.   "Naked into Harvest-Tide: The Harvest Image in Soyinka's 'Idanre'," *African Literature Today,* 6 (1973), 145-51.

———.   "Nationalism and the Writer," *Commonwealth Literature.* Ed. John Press, London: Heinemann, 1965, pp. 151-56.

———.   "A Note on Editing *The Interpreters,* a novel by Wole Soyinka," *Editing Twentieth Century Texts.* Ed. Francess G. Halpenny. Toronto: University of Toronto Press, 1972, pp. 93-101.

———.   "Progress and Civilization in the Work of Wole Soyinka," in *Perspectives on African Literature.* Ed. Christopher Heywood. London: Heinemann; New York: Africana, pp. 129-37.

———.   "Wole Soyinka: Critical Approaches," *The Critical Evaluation of African Literature.* Ed. Edgar Wright. London: Heinemann, 1973, pp. 51-72.

———.   *The Writing of Wole Soyinka* . London: Heinemann, 1973. As *Wole Soyinka,* New York: Twayne, 1973. Reviewed by Dapo Adelugba, *Research in African Literatures,* 5, (1974), 254-59; Martin Banham, *African Literature Today,* 7 (1975), 153-4; Lloyd Brown, *Conch Review of Books,* 2, 1-2 (March-June 1974), 152-56; Hugh Dinwiddy, *African Affairs* (London), 74, 295 (April 1975), 242-3; Richard Priebe, *Books Abroad,* 48 (1974), 833-34.

Katamba, Francis, "Death and Man in the Earlier work of Wole Soyinka," *Journal of Commonwealth Literature,* 9, 3 (April 1975), 63-71.

Khaznadar, Cherif. Efficacité de Wole Soyinka," *Jeune Afrique,* 25 March 1972, p. 48.

Kiiru, Muchugu. "Elitism in Soyinka's *The Interpreters,*" *Busara* (Nairobi), 6, 1 (1974), 12-16.

King, Bruce. *Introduction to Nigerian Literature.* Lagos and London: University of Lagos and Evans, 1971, "Introduction."

———.   "Two Nigerian Writers: Tutuola and Soyinka," *Southern Review,* 6, 3 (Summer 1970), 843-52.

Klima, Vladimir. *Modern Nigerian Novels.* Prague: Oriental Institute, 1969.

Knight, G. Wilson. *Neglected Powers.* London: Phoenix House, 1971.

Knipp, T. "Black African Literature and the New African States," *Books Abroad,* 44 (1970), 373-79.

Kolade, Christopher. "Looking at Drama in Nigeria," *African Forum*, 1, 3 (Winter 1966), 77-79.

Kronenfeld, J.Z. "The 'Communalistic' African and the 'Individualistic' European: Some Comments on Misleading Generalizations in Western Criticism of Soyinka and Achebe," *Research in African Literatures*, 6, (1975), 199-225.

Laburthe-Tolra, Philippe. "Soyinka, ou la tigritude," *Abbia* (Yaounde), 19 (March 1968), 55-67.

Larson, Charles R. *The Emergence of African Fiction*. Bloomington, Indiana and London: Indiana University Press, 1971.

——— .   "Soyinka's First Play," *Africa Today*, 18, 4 (October 1971), 80-83.

——— .   "Wole Soyinka: Nigeria's Leading Social Critic," *New York Times Book Review*, 12 December 1972, pp. 6-7 and 10.

Laurence, Margaret. *Long Drums and Cannons*. London: Macmillian, 1969.

Leslie, Omolara Ogundipe. "African Aesthetics and Literature," *Ufahamu* (Los Angeles), 4, 1 (1973), 4-7. Also in *Okike* (Amherst), 4 (December 1973), 81-89.

——— .   "Ogun Abibimañ," *Opon Ifa* (Ibadan), 1, 3 (June 1976), Supplement i-iv.

Lindfors, Bernth. "Characteristics of Yoruba and Igbo Prose Styles in English, *Common Wealth*.Ed. Anna Rutherford. Aarhus: Akademisk Boghandel, 1972, pp. 47-61.

——— .   "The Early Writings of Wole Soyinka," *Journal of African Studies* (Los Angeles), 2, 1 (1975), 64-86.

——— .   *Folklore in Nigerian Literature*. New York: Africana, 1974. Includes "Wole Soyinka and the Horses of Speech," originally in *Essays on African Literature*, ed. W.L. Ballard, Spectrum Monograph Series in the Arts and Sciences, 3. Atlanta: School of Arts and Sciences, Georgia State University, 1973.

——— .   "Nigerian Novels of 1965," *Africa Report*, June 1966, 68 69.

——— .   "Popular Literature for a Nigerian Elite," *Journal of Modern African Studies* (London), 12 (1974), 471-86.

——— .   "Wole Soyinka Talking Through his Hat," *Commonwealth Literature and the Modern World*. Ed. Hena Maes-Jelinek. Brussels: Didier, 1975, pp. 115-25.

Luvai, Arthur. "The Poetry of Wole Soyinka and Christopher Okigbo," *Standpoints on African Literature*. Ed. Chris Wanjala. Nairobi: East African Literature Bureau, 1974, pp. 284-301.

Macebuh, Stanley. "Poetics and the Mythic Imagination," *Transition/Ch'Indaba* (Accra), 50/1 (December 1975), 75-84.

Maclean, Una. "Soyinka's International Drama," *Black Orpheus*, 15 (August 1964), 46-51.

Mahood, M.M. "Drama in New Born States," *Presence Africaine*, English ed. 60 (1966), 23-29.

—— .   "West African Writers in the World of Frantz Fanon," *English Department Workpapers: Burning Issues in African Literature* (Cape Coast), 1 (March 1971), 43-44.

McCartney, Barney C. "Tradition and Satire in Wole Soyinka's *Madmen and Specialists,"* *World Literature Written in English,* 14 (1975), 506-13.

McNeive, Kay. *African Theatre Bibliography.* Lawrence, Kansas: University of Kansas, 1966.

Maximin, Daniel. "Le théâtre de Wole Soyinka," *Presence Africaine,* 79 (1971), 103-117.

Melamu, Moteane. "A Possible Reading of Wole Soyinka's *The Interpreters,"* *Marang* (Gaborone), 1 (Winter 1977), no pagination.

M.J.A. "Clark and Soyinka at the Commonwealth Arts Festival," *New African,* 4, 8 (October 1965), 195.

Moore, Gerald. Ed. *African Literature and the Universities.* Ibadan: Ibadan University Press, 1965.

—— .   *The Chosen Tongue.* Longman: London, 1969.

—— .   "The Debate on Existence in African Literature," *Presence Africaine,* 81 (1972), 18-48.

—— .   "The Imagery of Death in African Poetry," *Africa,* 38 (1968), pp. 57-70.

—— .   "Modern African Literature and Tradition," *African Affairs* (London), 66 (1967), 246-47.

—— .   "The Negro Poet and his Landscape," *Introduction to African Literature.* Ed. Ulli Beier. London: Longman; Evanston: Northwestern University Press, 1967, pp. 151-64.

—— .   "Poetry and the Nigerian Crisis," *Black Orpheus,* 2, 3 (1969), 10-13.

—— .   *Wole Soyinka.* London: Evans; New York: Africana, 1971. Reviewed by Dapo Adelugba, *Research in African Literatures,* 5 (1974), 254-59; Anon, "African Exports," *Times Literary Supplement,* 27 July 1973; Anon., *West Africa,* 30 June 1972, p. 822; Martin Banham, *Africana Library Journal* 7 (1975), pp. 153-4; Richard F. Bauerle, *Books Abroad,* 46 (1972), 729-30; Lloyd Brown, *Conch Review of Books,* 2, 1-2 (March-June 1974), 152-56; Angus Calder, *New Statesman* (London), 28 April 1972, pp. 564-65; James Gibbs, *Legon Observer* (Legon), 7, 10 (19 May - 1 June 1972), 244-45; J. Ramsaran, *New Theatre Magazine,* 12, 2 (1972), 26-27; C.L. Rowe, *A Current Bibliography of African Affairs* (Washington, D.C.), 5, 5-6 (1972), 526-7.

Mootry, Maria K. "Soyinka and Yoruba Mythology," *Ba Shiru* (U. of Wisc.), 7, 1 (1976), 23-34.

Moyo, S. Phaniso. "*The Road:* A Slice of the Yoruba Pantheon," *Ba Shiru* (U. of Wisc.), 2, 1/2 (Fall 1970-Spring 1971), 89-93.

Mphahlele, Ezekiel. *The African Image.* London: Faber, 1974.

—— ·   "The New Mood in African Literature," *Africa Today*, 19, 4 (1972), 54-70.

Mutiso, Gabriel. "A Note on Soyinka," *Joe* (Nairobi), September 1973, pp. 25-26.

—— ·   "Perceptions on Social and Political Actions and Processes in Literature," *Journal of the New African Literature and the Arts*, 9-10 (1971), 12-43.

—— ·   "Women in African Literature," *East Africa Journal*, 8, 3 (1971), 4-13.

Nagenda, John. "Notes on Two African Playwrights," *New African*, September 1965, p. 171.

Nazareth, Peter. *Literature and Society in Modern Africa*, Nairobi: East African Literature Bureau, 1972. Also published as *An African View on Literature*, Evanston: Northwestern University Press, 1974.

—— ·   "Wole Soyinka: Dramatist," *Student Theatre* (Leeds), October 1964.

Ngugi wa Thiong'o (formerly James Ngugi). "Satire in Nigeria," *Protest and Conflict in African Literature*. Ed. Cosmo Pieterse and Donald Munro, London: Heinemann, 1969, pp. 56-59. Also published as "Wole Soyinka, T.M. Aluko and the Satiric Voice," in *Homecoming*. London: Heinemann, 1972, pp. 55-56.

Nkosi, Lewis, "African Literature: Part 2, English Speaking West Africa," *Africa Report*, 7, 11 (December 1962), 15-17, 31.

—— ·   "African Writers of Today," *The Classic* (Johannesburg), 1, 4 (1965), 58-78.

—— ·   *Home and Exile*. London: Longman, 1965.

—— ·   "Nigerian Writers," *New African*, 1, 11 (November 1962), 10-11.

Nwoga, Donatus I. "Obscurity and Commitment in Modern African Literature," *African Literature Today*, 6 (1973), 26-45.

—— ·   "Shadows of Christian Civilization," *Presence Africaine*, 79 (1971), 35-50.

Nwoko, Demas. "Search for a New African Theatre," *Presence Africaine*, 72 (1969), 49-75.

Obiechina, E.N. *Culture, Tradition and Society in the West African Novel*. London: Cambridge University Press, 1975.

Obumselu, Ben. "The Background of Modern African Literature," *Ibadan*, 22 (June 1966), 46-59.

Ogunba, Oyin. "Language in an Age of Transition: Shakespeare and Soyinka," *Journal of the Nigerian English Studies Association* (Ibadan), 6, 1 (1974), 109-20.

—— ·   "Modern Drama in West Africa," *Perspectives on African Literature*. Ed. Christopher Heywood. London: Heineman, 1971; New York: Africana, 1972.

—— ·   *The Movement of Transition: A Study of the Plays of Wole Soyinka*. Ibadan: Ibadan University Press, 1975.

——— ·   "The Traditional Content of the Plays of Wole Soyinka, 1 and 2"
     African Literature Today, 4 (1970), 2-18; 5 (1971), 106-15.

Okpaku, Joseph. "The Writer in Politics - Christopher Okigbo, Wole Soyinka and the
     Nigerian Crisis," *Journal of the New African Literature and the Arts,* 4 (Fall
     1967), 1-13.

Olafioye, Toye, "Cultural Conventions in Soyinka's Art," *Ba Shiru* (U. of Wisc.) 7, 1
     (1976), 67-70.

Olney, James. *Tell Me Africa: An Approach to African Literature.* Princeton: Princeton
     University Press, 1973.

O'Malley, Patrick (Padraig O'Maille). *Dudhuchas.* Baile Atha Cliath: Saisrseal Agus Dill,
     1972,

——— ·   "A Pillow of the Clouds," *Feasta* (Baile Atha Cliath), September
     1970, pp. 14-17.

Omotoso, Kole. "The Exiles, Beti and Soyinka," *Afriscope* (Yaba), 4, 3 (February 1974),
     55-56.

——— ·   "More Mirrors of Annihilation," *Afriscope* (Yaba), 4, 7 (July
     1974), 42-43.

——— ·   "Politics, Propaganda and Prostitution," *Afriscope* (Yaba), 4, 11
     (November 1974), 45,47,49.

——— ·   "Wole Soyinka: What is He to Us?" *Afriscope* (Yaba), 4, 5 (May
     1974), 58-60.

O'Neal, John: "Theatre in Yorubaland: An American's Impression," *Black World,* 19 (July
     1970), 39-48.

Osofisan, Femi. "Anubis Resurgent: Chaos and Political Vision in Recent Fiction," *Le
     Français au Nigéria,* 10, 2 (1975), 13-23.

——— :   "Comment," *Opon Ifa* (Ibadan), 1, 3 (June 1976), 75-77.

Peters, Jonathan. *The Dance of the Masks: Senghor, Achebe and Soyinka.* Washington,
     D.C.: Three Continents Press, 1978.

Povey, John. "Bartered Birthright: A Comment on the Attitude to the Past in West African
     Writing," *National Identity.* Ed. K.L. Goodwin, London: Heinemann, 1970,
     pp. 38-50.

——— ·   "Changing Themes in the Nigerian Novel," *Journal of the New
     African Literature and the Arts,* 1 (1966), 3-11.

——— ·   "Contemporary West African Writing in English," *Books
     Abroad,* 40 (1966), 253-60.

——— ·   "The Nigerian War: The Writer's Eye," *Journal of African
     Studies* (Los Angeles), 1, 3 (Fall 1974), 345-60.

——— ·   "West African Drama in English," *Comparative Drama,* 1, 2
     (1967), 110-22.

——— ·   "Wole Soyinka and the Nigerian Drama," *Tri-Quarterly,* 5
     (Spring 1966), 129-35.

——— ·   "Wole Soyinka. Two Nigerian Comedies," *Comparative Drama,*

3, 2 (1969), pp. 120-32.

Priebe, Richard. "Soyinka's Brother Jero: Prophet, Politician and Trickster," *Pan-African Journal*, 4, 4 (1971), 431-39.

Ramsaran, J.A. "African Potential," *Books Abroad*, 41 (1967) 39-40.

———. "African Twilight: Folktale and Myths in Nigerian Literature," *Ibadan*, 15 (March 1963), 17-19.

Ravenscroft, Arthur. "African Literature V: Novels of Disillusion," *Journal of Commonwealth Literature*, 6 (1969), 12-37. Also published in *Readings in Commonwealth Literature*. Ed. W. Walsh, London: Oxford University Press, 1973, pp. 186-205.

———. "The Nigerian Civil War in Nigerian Literature," *Commonwealth Literature in the Modern World*. Ed. H. Maes-Jelinek. Brussels: Didier, 1975, pp. 105-13.

Reckord, Barry. "Notes on Two Nigerian Playwrights," *New African*, 4, 7 (September 1965), 171.

Ricard, Alain. "Les paradoxes de Wole Soyinka," *Presence Africaine*, 72 (1969), 202-11.

———. *Théâtre et nationalisme: Wole Soyinka et LeRoi Jones*. Paris: Presence Africaine, 1972.

Richard, René. "Le peinture sociale comme nouvre d'inspiration dans *le Lion et la Perle* de Wole Soyinka," *Le Théâtre négro-africaine*. Paris: Presence Africaine, 1971, pp. 105-12.

Rønning, H. "Wole Soyinka: mot et nytt afrikansk formsprak," *Stemmer fra den tredje verden*. Ed. Y. Ostvedt, Oslo: Gyldendal Norsk Forlag, 1970.

Roscoe, Adrian A. *Mother is Gold: A Study in West African Literature*, Cambridge: Cambridge University Press, 1971.

Rutimirwa, Alex. "Exultation in Art: Interpreting Soyinka's *The Interpreters* (An Introduction)," *Dhana* 5, 1 (1975), 24-28.

Salt, M.J. "Mr. Wilson's Interpretation of a Soyinka Poem," *Journal of Commonwealth Literature*, 9, 3 (1975), 76-78.

Schmidt, Nancy J. "Nigerian Fiction and the African Oral Tradition," *Journal of the New African Literature and the Arts*, 5-6 (Fall 1968), 10-19.

Scott, C. "Some Aspects of the Structural Unity of 'Idanre'," *World Literature Written in English*, 20 (1971), 11-14.

Scott-Kennedy, J. *In Search of African Theatre*, New York: Scribner, 1973.

Senghor, Leopold. "De la Negritude: si Wole Soyinka et Ezekiel Mphahlele etaient francophones," *L'Afrique Actuelle* (Paris), 37 (1969), 22-30.

Ssensalo, B.M. "The Conflict between Traditional and Modern Africa in Soyinka's Drama and Prose," *Penpoint* (Makerere), 25 (1970) 14-18.

Staudt, Kathleen. "The Characterization of Women by Soyinka and Armah," *Afras Review* (Sussex) 1, 1 (1975), 40-43.

Stewart, James. "Return to his Native Village," *Busara* (Nairobi), 1, 1 (1968), 37-39.

Stevenson, W.H. *"The Horn:* What it Was and What it Did," *Research in African Literatures,* 6 (1975), 5-31.

Stuart, D. "African Literature III: The Modern Writer in his Context," *Journal of Commonwealth Literature,* 4 (December 1967), 113-29.

Taiwo, Oladele. *An Introduction to West African Literature.* London: Nelson, 1967.

Tibble, Anne. *African/English Literature.*London: Peter Owen, 1965.

Tighe, C. "In Detentio Preventione in Aeternum: Soyinka's *A Shuttle in the Crypt,"* *Journal of Commonwealth Literature,* 10, 3 (April 1977), 9-22.

Tucker, Martin. *Africa in Modern Literature.* New York: Frederick Ungar, 1967.

———. "West African Literature: The Second Decade," *Africa Today,* (May 1966) 7-9; 13, 6 (June 1966), 7-8.

Udoeyop, Nyong J. *Three Nigerian Poets: A Critical Study of the Poetry of Soyinka, Clark and Okigbo.* Ibadan: Ibadan University Press, 1973.

Vincent, Theo. "The Modern Inheritance: Studies in J.P. Clark's *The Raft* and Wole Soyinka's *The Road,"* *Oduma,* 2, 1 (August 1974), 38-41, 44-49.

Wali, O. "The Dead-end of African Literature," *Transition,* 10 (1963), 13-15.

———. "The New African Novelists," *Freedomways* (New York), 6, 2 (1966), 163-71.

Walker, Bill. "Mime in *The Lion and The Jewel,"* *World Literature Written in English,* 12, 1 (1973), 37-44.

W[hitman], K[aye]. "Soyinka Before and After," *West Africa,* 2 June 1971, pp. 692-93.

Wilkinson, Nick. "Demoke's Choice in Soyinka's *A Dance of the Forests,"* *Journal of Commonwealth Literature,* 10, 3 (April 1976), 22-27.

Wilson, Roderick. "Complexity and Confusion in Soyinka's Shorter Poems," *Journal of Commonwealth Literature,* 8, 1 (June 1973), 69-80.

Young, Peter. "Mechanism to Medium: The Language of West African Literature in English," *Common Wealth.* Ed. Anna Rutherford, Aarhus: Akademisk Boghandel, 1972, pp. 35-46.

Notes on Contributors

The contributors to this volume represent a wide cross-section of those concerned with Soyinka's work.

There are Nigerian academics such as Abiola Irele, Professor of Modern Languages at the University of Ibadan, D. S. Izevbaye, Acting Head of the Department of English at the University of Ibadan and Donatus Nwogu, Professor of English at the University of Nigeria, Nsukka. There is a Ghanaian, K. E. Senanu, Professor of English at the University of Ghana, Legon. There are a number of British and American teachers who have spent some time in Africa. The established ones include Andrew Gurr, now Professor at Reading but previously in Nairobi, Mark Kinkead-Weekes, currently Provost at Rutherford College, the University of Kent, but previously at Ibadan, Bernth Lindfors of the University of Texas who has done research in both East and West Africa, and Gerald Moore of Makerere, Sussex and now Port Harcourt. There are also younger men, such as Mario Relich who was a lecturer at Ife from 1976 to 1978 and who is now an Arts tutor with the Open University and based in Edinburgh, and Nick Wilkinson who did a Ph.D. at Sussex and has been a lecturer at the University of Nigeria.

Students, both African and non-African are represented. A. R. Crewe wrote on *The Man Died* from a British University and Ann B. Davies published her paper on Soyinka's dramatic theory while a graduate student at the University of Wisconsin at Madison.

The London productions of Soyinka's plays are reviewed by well-known British theatre critics, Penelope Gilliatt and Ronald Bryden. The latter has, incidentally, followed Soyinka's career since 1959 and was among those who used the press to bring pressure to bear on the Nigerian Government while Soyinka was in detention. Albert Hunt is a creative as well as a critical presence in the British theatre and he too has followed Soyinka's career with interest.

Among other contributors, it is particularly pleasant to be able to include some of the most vigorous Nigerian writers and thinkers. Men and women who are often at the center of controversy, or contribute cogent arguments to current debates. These are Molara Ogundipe-Leslie, now emerging as a poet as well as a critic and commentator; Stanley Macebuh, best known in Nigeria for his pieces in the *Daily Times,* and Peter Enahoro, senior Nigerian columnist. It is particularly significant to see Soyinka, the writer-activist, in a context provided by these three, a context in which literature and life are intermeshed.

I would like to take this opportunity to thank all those who have contributed to this volume, particularly those who have guided me on the editorial side. Donald E. Herdeck and Bernth Lindfors have been patient and understanding with a novice editor, they have done all in their power to remove the flaws from this volume. For those that remain I take full responsibility.

I would like to say one final word of thanks to Bernth Lindfors for sending a succession of articles about Soyinka from the States to a series of addresses in Malawi, the U. K. and Nigeria. Without those articles my knowledge of work on Soyinka would be much more limited.

James Gibbs